Helmut Philipps

DUB – The Sound of Surprise

Reunion, 13 years after our interview for this book. Errol Brown, now 74 years old, is a live and studio engineer, and a legendary dub mixer for artists such as Bob Marley, Ziggy Marley, Marcia Griffiths, Culture, Busy Signal, Rebelution, Buju Banton, Steel Pulse, and many others. Germany 2024.

Helmut Philipps

DUB

The Sound of Surprise

Translated by Ursula “Munchy” Münch

EDITION OLMS ZÜRICH

First English Language Edition

EDITION OLMS AG
Rosengartenstr. 13B
CH-8608 Bubikon/Zürich

Mail: info@edition-olms.com
Web: www.edition-olms.com

ISBN 978-3-283-01326-4

Bibliographic information from the Deutsche Nationalbibliothek
The Deutsche Nationalbibliothek lists this publication in the Deutsche Nationalbibliografie; detailed bibliographic data are available on the Internet at http://dnb.d-nb.de.

Translated from the German by Ursula "Munchy" Münch
Editorial and proof reading by Eugene Edwards

Design front cover: Maja Bernard
Design back cover: Caspar Frei
Layout and typesetting for the content: Michael Schmitz

Printed in the Netherlands

Table of Contents

Brother Sound, France + Blackwood Sound System, Germany.

Channel One Sound System, UK

About this book

> "I want to study the musicians before me. But I want to study what they thought, what they felt, and why they did what they did – not the notes they played."
>
> (Makaya McCraven[1])

In the early 1970s, something began in Jamaica's recording studios that would wield significant influence over the handling of music recordings. The catalyst was purely pragmatic, and the outcome was a fusion of technology and music. Jamaica's invention conquered the world. It has revolutionized international charts and club music, influenced contemporary music in all its facets, even classical. 50 years later, the innovation is established as a global genre under the name "dub". However, the actual meaning, purpose and origin seem to have been lost along the way.

"Dub is drum and bass," said Pat Kelly. "No," countered Lloyd James, dub was more than that. "Dub music is a creation of an engineer." To this Sylvan Morris added "dub has a cultural significance." Those expressing themselves here are among the initiators. As sound engineers, they were significantly involved in the genesis of a style that emerged in Kingston as a reggae derivative and was to develop independently under the name "dub". Today, a broad majority of people believe that dub means echo.

This book chronicles the history of Jamaican dub. It questions the myths and legends that surround the genre, shows how it came about, and what it has become. It also clarifies how, of all people, an elderly, white reggae lover and sound engineer from Germany took on the role of the dub-wise with a few imported records many years ago. The albums *Super Ape* and *Heart Of The Congos* suggested to me that there was another, unimagined level in music between the sounds and instruments, to which a then little-known individual named Lee Perry opened wide the door. Over the years, several hundred Upsetter records have accumulated on my shelves. They were joined by recordings by a youth named Scientist, who revealed the new and expressive possibilities of a mixing console with his works.

Ever since I heard the first dub albums, this Jamaican style has fascinated me. Later I mixed dubs myself at concerts and in the studio[2], and was always of the opinion that dub belongs to reggae like Blue Mountain coffee to Jamaica. I wanted to ascertain whether this still holds true.

1 In: Universal Being Documentary, International Anthem 2020. Translated quote from „Organische Musik" ("Organic music"), German newspaper FAZ.net August 19, 2020 (last accessed February 12, 2024)

2 Under the name H.P. Setter

About this book

Inspired by the custom that has been practiced since the 70s, when a music producer met a studio engineer for a dub session, to call the resulting albums a "dub conference"[3], I set out to be the "producer" of a book, to confer with the fathers, thought leaders, and inventors of dub technology. Straight from the lion's mouth I wanted to hear what motivated them to break reggae down into its individual parts in order to reassemble them with reverb, echo and deeper bass. I wanted to learn the origins of the process, including where it happened, and spoke to its veterans and pioneers. Among them are some who are scarcely recognized today, despite their decisive influence on development. Others would also have fitted well into this context but were not available for discussion for various reasons. There is also a sad list of legends who have passed away, such as Sid Bucknor, Ruddy Thomas, Osbourne Ruddock, Errol Thompson, Ossie Hibbert and Philip Smart, for whom contemporary witnesses and companions tried to fill the gap.

Dub – The Sound of Surprise is the extended version of my book *Dub Conference. 50 years Dub from Jamaica*[4], published in Germany in 2022. The readers of the German reggae magazine Riddim voted it the best book of the year twice in a row, and it served as the basis for a month-long exhibition on "50 Years of Dub from Jamaica". The expanded English version has been updated to include more facts, more interviews, more sources, more dub, additional chapters and 350 illustrations.

Dub – The Sound of Surprise preserves the memory of a bygone era of Jamaican music culture whose firsthand witnesses are fading away. Since it was first published, other dub pioneers have died, including Pat Kelly, Lee Perry, Bunny Lee, Style Scott, Soljie Hamilton, and Sylvan Morris. The English version is dedicated to their memory. The descriptions of the individuals focus on their relationship to dub and do not provide complete biographies, which would have exceeded the thematic framework and scope of the book.

Historical reflections on reggae can easily be compared to reaching into a lottery drum. Even in Jamaica, today's memories are often quite different by tomorrow. Oscillating between self-centered and vague, they are full of contradictions and relative when it comes to information about time and people. Artists in particular often get confused about their own biographies. "Memory is not a reliable quantity in life." says the Norwegian writer Karl-Ove Knausgård, because it "doesn't prioritize the truth."[5] The reggae documentary maker David Katz also admits "every book ever written about reggae has caveats (including those I wrote

3 For example *Harry Mudie meets King Tubby in Dub Conference Vol. 1–3* (Jamaica 1976), *Winston Edwards & Blackbeard – Dub Conference At 10 Downing Street* (UK 1980) or *The Simeons – Dub Conference in London* (1978).

4 Original title: *Dub Konferenz. 50 Jahre Dub aus Jamaika* Strzelecki Books Cologne.

5 Karl-Ove Knausgård: *My Struggle: Book 3 – Boyhood Island*, novel 2014. Quoted from "Abschied von den Eltern" ("Farewell to Parents"), Swiss newspaper *Neue Zürcher Zeitung* July 22, 2014.

myself)"[6] and this horribile dictu must also apply to some of the data in this book. Despite my best efforts, 100% accuracy is not guaranteed.

Helmut Philipps, spring 2024

Author's notes

The book contains quotations from people who speak in a Jamaican language known as Patwa. The author has retained the use of Patwa expressions and phrases to convey their statements authentically.

Album and book titles as well as names of journals or magazines are italicized, and individual songs, titles, essays, and quotations are in "quotation marks". Quotations without attribution come from conversations or correspondence between the author and those quoted.

Additions in (round) brackets act as explanations, additions in [square] brackets are by the author and complete half-sentences.

Details about record releases can be found in the footnotes.

Since the history of dub music goes hand in hand with the development of studio technology, excursions into the field of electrical engineering are unavoidable. However, they are limited to what is necessary; without them, the progression of events would not be understandable.

Kokoteni HiFi, Germany.

6 David Katz: Book review *Reggae Going International 1967–1976: The Bunny 'Striker' Lee Story*, in German reggae print magazine RIDDIM 03/2012.

Streetdance in Kingston, ca. 2000.

Prologue: Counteraction, Dub-Wise

"See dem a dubwise
and dem no dub wise

see dem a dub school
and dem a dub fool

see dem a dub club
and dem a dub scrub.

Dem need fi do the history check
weh it a come from."

(France Nooks & Prince Alla[1])

"Counteraction!" they call it in Jamaica. The term comes from the sound system culture of a country in which competing for the audience's favour is one of the nation's preferred pastimes. You slam this word in the face of your opponent, shout it at them or use it to smugly announce impending devastation. It happens when sound systems – or just "sounds" – compete against each other in a so-called "clash". Their weapons are records, so it's about sophistication in musical selection and brilliance in presentation. A sound presents a music track; the competitor has to react. When he's confident, he replies with a counteraction. He might use a recording that relates to the previous hit or even top it, and use a text specifically aimed at the opponent, or a counterstatement called "speech" in sound system slang. The competition lasts several rounds; the audience decides the winner. It's an all-night event and in the end the winner takes home a trophy in the form of a cup. The British radio DJ and clash veteran David Rodigan calls the procedure "the musical equivalent of a chess game"[2] and a great pleasure.

The clash is a special form of reggae entertainment. Its energy is fueled by the fascination for musical exclusivity and the fun of competition; its roots lie in the mobile open-air discotheques that emerged in downtown Kingston in the 1950s as an alternative to the leisure activities of uptown society. According to U-Roy, the pioneer of Jamaican toasting, "the poor people's enjoyment in Jamaica, because we nah have a whole heap a money to go up inna big club. The ghetto people enjoy themselves by coming to the dance and have a lot of fun."[3] It started with small speaker systems and record players at street corners and in open spaces. As technology advanced, the systems grew and became "huge like 20, 30 something inches steel horns and we sometimes have two or three of those in the tree top. So people from miles away could hear the sound system."[4] Each sound is eager to have something others cannot offer. Be it the greater range, the more sophisticated sound, the more virtuoso disc jockeys (called "selector" in Jamaica), or the most dazzling entertainers (called "MCs" or master of ceremonies). But above all it's the choice of music. It has to stand out from the others and, if possible, include recordings no one else possesses.

The craving for exclusivity dates back from the time before ska and reggae. In the early days, sounds operated with imported records from the United States, and scraped off the labels so rival spies couldn't identify which tracks the audience enjoyed. In 1949, Ken Khouri (1917–2003), son of a Lebanese immigrant father and Cuban mother born in Jamaica, bought a disc recording machine for wedding or birthday greetings in Miami for $350 and brought it to the island. It was the start of Jamaica's own music and recording production. Khouri began recording mento music with it and started to organize the sale of his own records in his home and a club in St. Andrew, west of Kingston.[5] Two years later, Kingston businessman Stanley Motta (1915–1993) purchased a similar device that he could connect a microphone to and adjust the volume of, enough to record mento bands in a back room of a lumber mill on Hanover Street. Even though both equipment and location were still far from what would later be understood as a proper audio studio, this was the first recording facility in Jamaica. The medium on which recordings were stored were so-called acetates, thin metal discs coated with a lay-

1 "Dubwise", album *Havana Meets Kingston*, Baco Records 2017.
2 David Rodigan: "My name was adopted by a Kingston gangster. He's dead now" in: *The Guardian* February 23, 2017.
3 DVD Documentary "Return Of The Rub-A-Dub Style", Walking Road Films USA 2009.
4 Scientist ibid.
5 In 1961, in the start-up boom of the impending independence, Khouri set up the company "Federal Records Ltd." in Kingston at No. 220 Foreshore Drive, later Marcus Garvey Drive, with the help of Australian engineer Graeme Goodall (also spelled Graham in some publications); an all-inclusive empire with recording and mastering studio, record pressing plant and distribution. In 1981, the studio and pressing plant were sold to the Tuff Gong company, which still owns them today.

er of lacquer into which recordings were scratched. These discs could be played on a gramophone immediately, but because of their soft surface they did not last very long, as the needle made the groove deeper with each use. The fact that the acetates were playable set the foundation for reggae's passion for dubplates. From the very beginning, Khouri also cut recordings for sound systems on his machine that were colloquially known as "soft wax". Normally, however, Khouri and Motta shipped their discs to London, where the Decca company used an electroplating process to create a stamp from them and then press 10-inch shellac 78s. They were delivered to Jamaica and mostly bought by tourists or the Jamaican upper class, while the sound systems downtown had already turned to rhythm & blues and jazz, and viewed mento as the music of the colonial era coming to an end. This was not without good reason, because mento, often declared as the origin of Jamaican music, came from the desire of European slave masters for entertainment, right down to its instrumentation. In the early stages, it was rather common for singers to become crowd pullers through soft wax recordings without their records being available for the public to buy. When mono became stereo and the multi-track recording process found its way into Jamaica's post-independence studios at the end of the 1960s, the sounds changed their exclusivity policy. They now preferred to invest in special versions of successful hit singles, which had not been possible before technically. They changed the lyrics of the songs to include the name of their sound and requested an alternative mix. Soon people were talking about "dubplates" or "specials".

At the same time, interest in instrumental versions of well-known songs increased, because sounds were no longer just playing records. Their entertainment programme now also included performances by musicians and singers. They needed playbacks, which usually came from proper hits. Through the possibilities of multi-track technology, these originally pure instrumental versions developed into idiosyncratic rhythm reductions, characterized by naked beats of bass and drums, enriched with reverb or echo effects, infused with vocals fading in, or shreds of melody. Created by the studios' sound engineers, these special, exclusive mixes were called "dub". Originally and by definition, dub is a version of an existing music track that has been broken down into its individual components exclusively for the use of sound systems. These versions "were required to give the mic men the space to express themselves.[6]"

Dub became the live platform for deejays and singers in the Jamaican dancehall.

Around 1970/71, due to great demand, the first dub mixes were pressed onto the B-sides of new singles, and in 1973 an independent art form emerged in LP format. The appearance of occasional deejay tracks on various early dub LPs showed the dominance of deejay culture. In the development of this special Jamaican song interpretation, it increasingly determined the scene. Big Youth was involved in Prince Buster's *The Message Dubwise* as early as 1973, and again in 1978 together with I-Roy on Sylvan Morris' *Cultural Dub*[7]. In between, long-playing records appeared that presented deejays on one side and matching dubs on the other, such as:

- **U-Roy – Dread In A Africa** (Hit 1976) produced in 1975 with dubs by Errol Thompson, released a year later as a pre-release with a neutral cover, was not released regularly until 2022 on Jamaican Art Records, NL
- **U-Roy – African Roots** (Celluloid 1976), identical with **The Best Of U-Roy** (Live and Love 1976), with dubs from Tubby's studio
- **Rasta Have Ambition** (Live and Love 1976) with the deejays Dillinger, Shortie The President, Prince Jazzbo, Dr Alimentado and Jah Stitch plus King Tubby dubs from **King Tubby presents Dub From The Roots** released one year before
- **Dread Locks In Jamaica** (Live and Love 1976) with the deejays Jah Stitch, U Brown, Little Joe (= Ranking Joe), Tapper Zukie and Dillinger plus dubs from Tubby's studio
- **Strictly Rockers In A Dread Land** (Live and Love 1976) with the deejays Jah Youth, U Brown, Dillinger, Jah Woosh, Jah Stitch, Prince Jazzbo plus dubs from Tubby's studio
- **Straight To Babylon Chest** (Live and Love 1976) with the deejays I-Roy, Prince Jazzbo, Dr Alimentado and Jah Stitch
- **I-Roy – Can't Conquer Rasta** (Justice 1976) with dubs mixed by Prince Jammy at Tubby's studio
- **Lone Ranger – On The Other Side Of Dub** (Studio One 1977)

6 Booklet *Duke Reid International Disco Series* Doctor Bird UK 2021.

7 Harry J, USA.

On The Other Side Of Dub was produced by Coxson Dodd. The owner of the Studio One label with his studio attached explained years later in an interview: "The dub LP was one of the things that (was) responsible for breaking new deejays and artist. Because they had the rhythm now to rehearse on, you know. They could deejay until they got perfect."[8]

With the dub long-playing records, global expansion began, abstracting the local dub phenomenon into an international production innovation. Initially they were only intended for sound systems, that's why Coxson printed in 1974 their intended purpose "Sounds & System" on the covers of the first pressings of his *Mellow Dub* und *Ital Dub* LPs; however, the albums soon became export hits for an entirely different group of buyers. Jamaica's music producers, always looking for additional income, recognized their potential and sold dub in LP format to the UK. Often – and frequently without the knowledge of the engineers involved – in the form of master tapes, which were assembled there and pressed onto vinyl. In Kingston's record stores those products could hardly be found since they mainly sold singles. In its homeland, dub did not take place as a solitary event and, apart from its integration into the sound system culture, remained a stranger in its own country. The best place to find what you were looking for was in a souvenir shop by the Jamaica Tourist Board at Kingston airport, which sold dub LPs in addition to t-shirts and other memorabilia.

8 *Studio One Story*, Soul Jazz DVD 2002.

Dub conquered a market outside Jamaica. There it lost its roots, served as a blueprint for the remix of pop music and developed a life of its own. In 2010, Christopher Partridge meticulously researched and analyzed the (sub-)cultural reinterpretation of the dub technique, which had started in England. For his book *DUB in Babylon*[9], Partridge, Professor of Religious Studies at the University of Lancaster, combed through essays and studies on immigrant sociology, liner notes of recordings and the mass of interviews and articles in the British music press, which had been discussing the topic since 1974. The journalists' interest was caught when Lee Perry's then life and business partner Pauline Morrison came to London with the original version of the *Blackboard Jungle Dub* LP – which was initially called *Upsetters 14 Dub Blackboard Jungle* – but had no cover. She told Perry biographer David Katz in retrospect: "I pressed 300 in Jamaica, brought 100 with me to England and went around to record shops. I remember Chris Lane (the later owner of Fashion Records) put in the magazine (*Blues and Soul*): This dub album will go down in history."[10] Lane would be proved right. In 1975, Keith Hudson's *Pick A Dub* became the first dub LP in the UK to be officially licensed on the Atra label[11], in a recolored cover, after it had previously come to London as a black and white packaged pre-release on Hudson's Mamba label. As early as 1976, the leading Rock magazine *Melody Maker* described the dub technique as "the supreme sound of surprise" and spoke of "the most interesting new abstract concept since Ornette Coleman undermined the dictatorship of Western harmony".[12]

In the UK, too, dub was spreading primarily through the sound systems. However, unlike in Jamaica, it was a cultural refuge for the un-

9 Christopher Partridge: *DUB in Babylon. Understanding the Evolution and Significance of DUB REGGAE in Jamaica and Britain from King Tubby to Post-punk*, London 2010.

10 From a mail correspondence with David Katz in October 2011.

11 The owner is Brent Clarke from Trinidad, brother of Sebastian Clarke, who presented the first description of Reggae history in book form with *Jah Music* in 1980.

12 Richard Williams: "The Sound Of Surprise", Melody Maker August 21, 1976 page 21. To understand the magnitude of this comparison: The art and music worlds have been buzzing about Ornette Coloman ever since he had "designed" Free Jazz fifteen years

derground in exile. In this environment, dub became a militant, sacred statement against a repressive, racist society. Bass and dub acted as spiritual transmitters in these places. The subversively celebrated mixture of underground and rebellion exuded an enormous fascination for British youth. Middle-class kids from the hippie-cannabis-LSD environment understood dub as the soundscape of their trips into mind-expansion. Jamaica's reverb and echo orgies fulfilled the promises made by psychedelic rock. When Sex Pistols singer Johnny Rotten/John Lydon played his favorite music on John Peel's radio show and presented almost exclusively dub and reggae[13], the underdog punks of the British working class discovered a revolutionary attitude in the Jamaican remix that corresponded to their own political anger. In addition, dub technique helped to overcome the limits of the own musical craftsmanship. It didn't take long for the new admirers to amputate dub from its original environment. The style created for reggae sound systems became romanticized and misused.

At the end of his analysis, Partridge stated that "dub, since the post-punk period and certainly in later rave and club context – which tend to be predominantly white – lacks 'reggae culture'."[14] As final proof, he cited a British study from 2006, which said that most of those who use dub today are "white and in full-time education or full-time employment. This is quite different from the cultures within which dub had its genesis."[15]

Dub is a concept that started out as a single B-side, became bolder and innovative and changed the world as an LP. In this process dub changed colour; a black functional product became an art form from which a white genre developed, using the same name. As with every intellectual mind game, it has moved further away from its origins.

Five decades after its incarnation, a degenerated dub cacophony is raging worldwide, in which dub is no longer recognizable for what it is, let alone for what it wanted to be. There is rock dub, punk dub, folk dub, jazz dub, classical dub, disco dub, techno dub, ambient dub, the list is endless. Nowadays, every musical minimalism and every echo used as a style runs the risk of being interpreted as dub. Dub seems watered down in the "holy seriousness"[16] of random terminology, is digitally located in "Cyber Zion"[17], squeezed in as sensationalism over subsonic deep bass, placed in abstract spaces of intellectual deconstruction. Dub became an easy target for absurd mind games. "Garvey's Ghost" und "Heidegger's Geist"[18] are the inspiration for a feature section that is constantly doing dub a disservice through speculative interpretation. In 2023, the perception was heading towards the "religious hypnotic charging"[19] and in 2011 "spiritually and stonedly happy blank places of dub"[20] were being

earlier. When Coleman was booked for New York's Five Spot Club in 1959, two planned weeks turned into ten and all of the city's cultural celebrities showed up, including Leonhard Bernstein, Miles Davis, James Baldwin, Norman Mailer and the painter Robert Rauschenberg.

13 After the Sex Pistols ended, Johnny Lydon even worked as a talent scout for Richard Branson's record company Virgin in Jamaica.

14 Christopher Partridge ibid p. 249.

15 Gordon Lynch & Emily Badger: The Mainstream Post-Rave Club Scene as a Secondary Institution: A British Perspective, in: Culture and Religion 7, 2006 p. 32.

16 Klaus Walter in: "Punky Reggae Party mit House" ("Punky Reggae Party with House"), German newspaper TAZ September 17, 2012.

17 Steve Goodman in: *Sonic Warfare – Sound, Affect and the Ecology of Fear*, p. 160, Cambridge 2010.

18 Ian Penman: „Klang!" Garvey's Ghost meets Heidegger's Geist. In: Experiencing The Soundtrack, Sidney 2001.

19 Swiss newspaper *Neue Zürcher Zeitung* on Simon Reynold's book *Futuromania*, October 17, 2023.

20 Diedrich Diederichsen in: „Karg, scharf, grau und genau. Zum neuen Album der stilbildenden britischen Post-Punk-Band Gang Of Four" ("Bare, sharp, gray and precise.

invoked. Spiritual, stoned and blank spaces – none of which dub ever wanted to be. Such attributes were only later persistently assigned to it by its primarily European reception, a perspective to which Jamaican self-presentation in combination with the reggae profit industry has contributed its share. The international perception of dub went hand in hand with the rise of roots and Rastafari reggae, and was therefore subject to the same stoned dreadlock clichés. In 1975, producer Pat Francis aka Jah Lloyd described his LP *Herb Dub* in the liner notes on the back cover as a "tribute to the herb" that "will take you far, far away"[21]; in 1979, on the front of the album *Rock A Dub*[22], released on the British label Jamaica Sound (and repressed by the German Bellaphon), the following was written under the image of Rasta smoking like a dragon: "Strictly Rockers Dubbing And Rootsy Smoking 'Cos Babylon Must Fall". In a conversation with King Jammy, we will learn that British documentary filmmakers in the 80s cemented this image forever by deliberately staging the stoner atmosphere that was popular in Europe for their films in the Kingston studios. Although dub has been floating around mixers and music magazines for half a century now, there has been little research into its cultural calibration. Even Partridge has admitted that a general study of dub history is long overdue.[23] The first person to approach the topic from a scientific perspective was the American author and lecturer Michael Veal in 2007, with a study that had the apt subtitle: *Soundscapes & Shattered Songs in Jamaican Reggae*[24]. The book David Rodigan later described as "very heavy reading" has nevertheless made a great contribution by its general approach, despite various errata in technical descriptions or personnel.[25]

However, some of Veal's interpretations are controversial. He also followed the common practice of Afrocentric interpretation, which in America and the Caribbean assumes African roots per se in every form of musical expression of the successive generations of slaves. This compliant automatism in research into the origins of black music has long since been disproved in detail by the Austrian musicologist Maximilian Hendler.[26] Veal's classification of dub as "reflecting the ruination of an idealized African past"[27] or as "electronic music of African exiles several generations removed"[28] is contradicted not only by dub veterans such as Soljie Hamilton and Scientist. Dub is a product of the (electrical) technical evolution in sound recording and therefore can hardly be seen as a continuum from a time when there was no electricity. Also, dub, at least in its Jamaican form, was never as complex as it was posthumously made out to be, also by Veal. It was a simple day-to-day business in which the studios' mixing boards turned into play stations, and dub became the playground in which the engineers were supposed to

About the new album by the style-defining British post-punk band Gang of Four") German newspaper *Süddeutsche Zeitung* feature section from January 29/30, 2011.

21 Sleeve Notes LP *Herb Dub* 1975 on Micron and on Teem Records. Was released in the same year as *Kaya Dub* on Kaya Records in the US, with identical mixes but in a different track order and with different song titles.

22 Produced by Page One, a pseudonym of Jamaican producer Winston Holness aka Niney The Observer.

23 Christopher Partridge ibid, introduction.

24 Michael E. Veal: *DUB Soundscapes & Shattered Songs in Jamaican Reggae*, Wesleyan University Press 2007.

25 For example, Errol Brown's uncle was not the Treasure Isle engineer Byron Smith, but the owner Duke Reid. *Catch A Fire* by the Wailers was recorded at Harry J on 8 and not on 16 tracks (both p. 105). Lee Perry did not destroy his studio in 1979 (p. 13), but only closed it. It was destroyed by fire in 1983. Above all, no Jamaican engineer understood dub as "low-fi production" (p. 257), on the contrary. People like King Tubby, Scientist and Ernest Hoo Kim were focused on high-end sound results.

26 See the analysis by Maximilian Hendler *Vorgeschichte des Jazz* (Prehistory of Jazz), Graz 2008. Hendler refutes the common assumption that music played by Afro-Americans must have its roots in Africa, because African-American musicians also come from Africa. A point of view that is also widespread in reggae research.

27 Michael E. Veal ibid p. 218.

28 Ibid p. 255.

go nuts on behalf of sound operators and producers. While the Jamaican audience celebrated these technical gadgets as playbacks at sound system dances, long-playing records were sold outside the country in respectable numbers to a clientele for whom the cultural context was foreign, even irrelevant. For these customers, dub was given the status of "music of the sound engineers", although the original motivation for its creation came from the Jamaican sound systems.

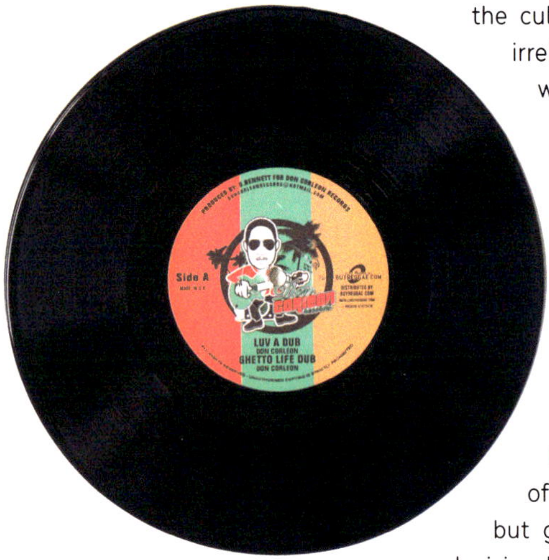

When Jamaica, like the rest of the world, let machines make music towards the end of the 1980s, this led to the extinction of the native dub, but gave the genre a decisive boost in Europe. From the DNA of the remains, clones such as neo dub, digi dub, steppers dub, hyperdub and the apparently related evolutions such as jungle and drum'n'bass emerged in digital laboratories. In the haze of this dancefloor subbass culture, the dubstep that prevailed in clubs at the beginning of the millennium seemed to be the last link in a long chain of misunderstandings. This was something the British engineer Mad Professor also agreed with, even though he released a dub album entitled *The Roots Of Dubstep* in 2011.

There was no discussion along the lines as to whether dub is an (analogue) improvisational art or whether it can be programmed (digitally). The standing of computers seemed clear, with the Jamaican studios no longer making any significant contribution, and the hype from England taking all the attention.

Then, in 2010, came the unexpected turnaround. Accidentally, the then 33-year-old Donovan "Don Corleon" Bennett, a successful producer from Kingston and shadow man behind artists like Protoje, Gentleman and Rihanna, came across the old tradition of his homeland. His cousin Protoje had a Scientist LP in the car that made him curious. Don Corleon studied the technology via YouTube videos, consulted with Mad Professor and began dubbing as it had been done in the analogue years. His album *HD In Dub*[29] appeared at a time of recollection in Jamaican music, to which the Busy Signal album *Reggae Music Again* released in 2012, also contributed. It said "it's been a long long time, we nah have no vibes like this". Parallel to the Busy Signal album, a vinyl LP with dub versions was released, something Jamaica hadn't seen in two decades.[30] Bands and artists like Dubtonic Kru or Protoje started to describe their performances as dub. Jamaica's young generation of musicians now rocked with the flavor of the 70s and a desire to improvise.

Even though the term "dub" did not catch on for concerts, a set of events emerged at around the same time, including "Inner City Dub" in the community of Tivoli Gardens, "Dub School" in Vineyard Town, "Vinyl Thursdays" that originated in Papine, and "Dubwise", a series that started out around 2013/14 at the Driftwood Bar on Mannings Hill Road, eventually turning into a global brand with events from Miami to Trinidad and its own location, the Dubwise Café in New Kingston. In the hills above the city, the "Kingston Dub Club", founded in 2012, has established itself with a sound system and live music. In 2013, Tarrus Riley shot the video for his song "Gimme Likkle One Drop" there. Many millions of YouTube clicks later, the location remains an internationally known hot spot of the roots, dub and reggae renaissance, frequented by musicians, Rastas, uptown residents and reggae tourists. Suns Of Dub including melodica player Addis Pablo are common guests at the "Dub Club". He revived the tradition of his father Augustus Pablo (1954–1999), whose instrumental music played a distinctive role in the emergence of dub culture. The son says: "Most people start from the past and then take it to the future. But we start from the future and take it to the past."[31]

Rory Gilligan also regularly plays at the "Kingston Dub Club". The veteran selector of the "Stone Love" sound system wants to go back to the "revolutionary roots" of the 70s. In 2007 and 2010 he produced the al-

29 Released only digitally, individual tracks released as limited 10-inch vinyls were available via buyreggae.com.
30 *Busy Signal – Reggae Dubb'N Again*, VP Records 2012.
31 „Addis Pablo. Suns Of Dub. Bridging The Gap" German Reggae print magazine *RIDDIM* 03/2014.

bums *Movement*[32] and *Gravity*[33] with the band Rootz Underground, not only setting a high standard of sound technology, but also anticipating everything that would later be interpreted by Protoje's Indiggnation band or Raging Fyah as a musical expression of a nu roots movement. From realpolitik and Rasta topics in the lyrics to guitar solos and collective improvisations that shake up the rigid song and sound structures of reggae, Gilligan built up artists like Samory I and Jah9, and initiated a label by the appropriate name "Black Dub Music". He focused specifically on female voices such as Kristine Alicia (*Songs From Zion* 2017), Keida ("Ganja Tea"), Nadine Sutherland ("Karma"), Indrani ("Journey") and Nelly Stharre ("Find Your Roots"). With dubs, remixes and exclusive dubplates, as well as several new interpretations of the soul classic "Is It Because I'm Black"[34] which was repeatedly covered in Jamaica, he was looking for a way back to "more spiritual sound, frequencies and voices".[35]

Following the concept of "preserving for the generation now and the generation to come to know where this t'ing a come from"[36] producer Gussie Clarke published a lavishly stocked box-set in 2018.[37] Besides three CDs with the LPs he produced, *Black Foundation Dub*[38], *Dread At The Controls Dub*[39] and *The Mighty Diamonds – Dubwise*[40] it also included a DVD with a one-hour group discussion called "Dub Talk!", in which Clarke met a 16-person panel of key players. The large round comprised of sound system operators Mikey Faith from "Emperor Faith HiFi", Papa Jaro from "Killamanjaro" and Finger Man aka "Tippertone", besides the selectors Danny Dreadlocks and Jah Screw, as well as the studio engineers Sylvan Morris and Soljie Hamilton, and also Carolyn Cooper, professor of Literature and Cultural Studies at the University of the West Indies in Kingston. The discussion was led by Mutabaruka. Clarke put forward the thesis that Jamaica did not recognize that the creativity of its engineers had created an independent music format with dub. The debate turned into a fiasco. Unsuccessfully, Mutabaruka and Clarke tried to have the group focus on the topic of "dub as a form of musical expression" while the sound operators and selectors only saw dub as specials and dubplates with just one important aspect i.e. that the sound's name was mentioned in them. Danny Dreadlocks asked what all the talk about dub as music was about. "Dub nah go work unless you have a couple of deejays fe talk pon di riddim!"[41] In her following analysis of the conversation, Cooper suggested that the foundation's representatives needed to be brought into conversation with today's young generation: "We can't go back. But it's important for the youths to understand the foundation of the music."

When looking for the youth of the next dub generation, Carolyn Cooper might have a hard time finding anything in Jamaica. At least she would come across dancehall producer and Grammy winner Romaine Arnett aka Teflon Zincfence[42]. In 2018 he surprised everybody with *Dub Policy*, a promising sound-creative statement album. The set consist-

32 Riverstone Records 2007.
33 Riverstone Records 2010.
34 Syl Johnson 1969.
35 „Die fantastische Metamorphose des Rory Stone Love" ("The fantastic metamorphosis of Rory Stone Love") by Ursula "Munchy" Munch in German Reggae print magazine *RIDDIM* 06/2014.
36 Gussie Clarke – *Dub Anthology* Music Works Records 2018
37 Music Works Records.
38 Burning Sounds UK 1977.
39 Hawkeye UK 1978.
40 Music Works Records JA 1981
41 Scientist also repeatedly called out to the audience during a live dub set in Berlin's Café Zapata in 2010: "Someone must deejay!"
42 Romaine "Teflon" Arnett aka Zincfence from Spanish Town participated in the Chronixx EPs *Hooked On Chronixx* 2011 and *Dread & Terrible* 2014. For the production "Blazin'" with Koffee he received a Grammy in 2020.

ed of six programmed, bass-heavy tracks that are full of reminiscences of the golden era of dub. Zincfence incorporated vocal samples by U-Roy, Prince Far I and Prince Francis from Studio One, and used original samples and new overdubs to construct an impressive dub remake of the over 40-year-old Bunny Lee production "No Wicked Shall Enter The Kingdom Of Zion" aka "Fittest Of The Fittest" by Barry Brown. In memory of a monumental King Tubby mix, he called his adaptation "A Ruffer Version". This title lead to some confusion, since Tubby's "Ruffer Version"[43] is actually Johnny Clarke's song "Don't Trouble Trouble". *Dub Policy* remained a singular action and appeared only as an mp3-file.

Three years later Dubtonic Kru guitarist Omar "Jallanzo" Johnson dropped *Dubbin' It & Lovin' It*, a gently mixed collection of less brutal riddims compared to Zincfence. Only two of them had vocal versions at the time of publication; the playbacks served primarily as templates for live dubbing. He was not alone in this. King Jammy, Mad Professor, Scientist, Laurent "Tippy I-Grade" Alfred from the US Virgin Islands, the Germans Jah Schulz and Captain Yossarian, as well as international neo dub sound systems have been dubbing live with laptop and small mixing consoles in front of real or streamed audiences. In these moments, dub becomes a temporary event. Jallanzo continues live what he had already practiced in the studio with the band Dubtonic Kru. "Back in those days when they were mixing there was a vibe [in the studio]", said the keyboard player Luke Dixon, "same thing with us. It is brought on stage, right in front of your eyes." Jubba White, the drummer added: "The base is being roots, rock [and] Jamaican rub'a'dub style." But Jallanzo had moved away from rub'a'dub. His steppers' beats are influenced by the neo dub style from the UK.

A dub newcomer like Collin Bulby York, who mixed *Use Your Loaf Dub* for the US Record Store Day in 2017, is no longer a youth; he has been known as a producer and engineer since the late 1980s.[44] His dub LP, recorded by A-class musicians such as drummer Kirk Bennett, was analogue mixed at Mixing Lab studio in Kingston, and released in an edition of 750 copies, distributed by Lion Vibes. The title "Use your Loaf" is a proverb that encourages you to think before doing anything. However, Bulby's unleashed echoes were not designed to show Jamaica the way in search of the lost dub. On the other hand, his album was the only one that was released physically. Jallanzo's *Dubbin' It & Lovin' It*, Zincfence' *Dub Policy* and Don Corleon's *HD In Dub* appeared only digitally. Which is also an indication of the interest in real albums.

Anyone who pressed new dub onto vinyl at that time complained about stacks of records in the warehouse that no one wanted. By contrast, reissues of historical dub albums sold out rapidly. It was these old LPs, rather than B-sides, maxi or showcase mixes, that spread the word of Jamaica's dub outside the traditional scene. For these reasons, the number of albums that have come and are still coming from Jamaica are a significant indicator of the influence of the Jamaican original. In the twelve years from the first LPs in 1973 to their sudden death due to digitalization in 1985, an estimated 600 dub LPs came from Jamaica, although an exact number cannot be determined. Lists like Smokey Room's[45] "Dub LP Archive", which has not been updated for a long while and lists 358 albums, allow approximate estimates. Gaps have got to be filled with the individual knowledge of collectors. Even though reissue labels such as Pressure Sounds in the UK, or Dub Store in Japan, have recently reissued sought-after rarities from that time, you shouldn't be fooled. Since the turn of the millennium, no more than 20 new dub albums have come from Jamaica, including periodic releases by King Jammy and albums by the "immigrant worker" Alborosie.

In 2015, singer Protoje called his third long player *Ancient Future*, and referred to the symbiosis of tradition and innovation, which the author Dutty Bookman associated with the controversial marketing term "Reggae Revival" back in 2011. "What we see happening in the local creative industries is that the conscious, Afrocentric, often Rastafari reggae aesthetic is making a powerful comeback in various art forms and cultural expressions. Music unsurprisingly leads the way, with a new crop of singers and musicians who are emerging to give expression to this awakening."[46] Bookman recognized a roots historicism that was returning to its origins. Also, the future of dub lies in its own past, but very little happens in this sector. Jamaica's producers and engineers no longer seem to be interested in the international competition for their own creation. 50 years after its initial spark, the desire for counteraction can hardly be heard anymore.

43 Not to be mixed up with "A Rougher Version", which is based on Jackie Edwards' version of Burning Spears "Invasion".

44 Bulby has worked for artists such as Shabba Ranks, Super Cat, Sean Paul, Beres Hammond, Rihanna, Britney Spears and Sinehead O'Connor, among others.

45 http://dubwise.smokeyroom.net/.

46 http://www.jamaicansmusic.com/news/Culture/Reggae_Revival_Online_Movement. (last accessed October 31, 2022) The quote originally appeared on the website www.reggae-revival.com, which is no longer accessible.

Overture of a New Genre

"If it nuh go so, it go near so."

(Jamaican proverb)

One of the oldest stories of dub folklore tells of Rudolph "Ruddy" Redwood. With his "Supreme Ruler of Sound" system, Redwood ruled Spanish Town, the former capital in the southeast of Jamaica. It was 1968 and Redwood headed to Kingston, just a few miles away. As always, when the weekend came up, he checked the city's recording studios to get the latest dubplates for the Saturday dance. His route took him to Treasure Isle studio on Bond Street, where a serious mishap occurred. Byron "Smitty" Smith, the in-house engineer forgot to turn on the vocal track while cutting the song on the acetate of the dubplate machine. Nobody can remember exactly whose song was being played – it was probably The Paragons' – but they do remember that only the music could be heard. Smitty wanted to stop the process, but Ruddy said let it stay, I'll take it as it is. No sooner said than done! At the next dance, Redwood first put on the song at prime time, then played the dubplate instrumental. The audience went crazy. He had to play it over and over again, and the legends vary from six times in a row to more than twenty! On Monday, Ruddy brought back the random mistake to Treasure Isle, saying press it as it is on the back of the single. It's the beginning of instrumental versions.

Until that day, Jamaican singles had one song on each side. After the mighty buzz Spanish Town's "Supreme Ruler" had created with his instrumental playback, producers started to press the instrumental versions of their songs onto singles' B-sides. The instrumental reduced the cost of production, doubled the profits and was loved by the fans. Clearly, Jamaica still had a great passion for instrumental music, actually a legacy of the ska period and which would play a crucial role again a few years later when Augustus Pablo's "Java" was voted "Instrumental Of The Year" in 1972. Again this led to the first ever dub LP record.

This random coincidence at Treasure Isle studio is generally seen as the beginning of dub. A man named Osbourne Ruddock, better known as King Tubby, witnessed the incident as he was in the studio waiting for new dubplates with producer Bunny Lee. Tubby was an electronics specialist who built amplifiers for sound systems. Besides that, he ran his own "King Tubby's Home Town Hi Fi" sound, whose legendary high-fidelity sound resonates into today's historiography. This fact Tubby's friend Bunny Lee put into perspective when he said that amplifiers by Seymour Williams, operator of "King Stereo", the second big sound system in Spanish Town, sounded much better, especially in the bass.

Inspired by Ruddy Redwood's experiences, Tubby began to play with the vocal track on his dubplates. He even took it one step further by not entirely eliminating the vocals but fading them in and out. The result left listeners both amazed and ecstatic, because they could not understand what was happening technically. They believed Tubby had developed a mysterious amplifier that allowed him to turn the voice of a record on and off. He aided his attempts by the purchase of a record cutting machine which he used to set up his own dubplate studio in his home on Dromilly Avenue, in the Waterhouse community, initially equipped only with a 2-track tape recorder and a home-built mini mixer.

This phase, among other things, established Tubby's reputation as the inventor of dub. Actually, it is still too early to talk about dub at this point. It was still the time of soft wax acetates. Since the early 1960s, two tracks had been used in production, one for the music, the other for the vocals, but after recording, the individual elements within the music were no longer accessible, something essential for a creative understanding of dub. With two tracks, you could not separate anything apart from the vocals. However, since Jamaican studios also used the common process of "bouncing", intermediate stages of production were still feasable.

Bouncing was a process of submixing that originated out of the limited technical facilities then available, and was common in studios around the world. To enable it, two tape machines were linked in order to combine recordings from the two tracks of one device into one track of the other. This resulted in a free track on the second tape machine which could be used to record again. This sub mix was then combined again with the next recording onto a track from the first device in order to get another free track. This process could be repeated as often as desired, although the decreasing signal-to-noise ratio limited its application. According to David Katz, Linford Anderson, the former in-house engineer at WIRL or Dynamic Sounds studio[1], reported that in some cases, they bounced up to four times: "We did the band on two tracks. Drum and bass on one track and the rest of the instruments on the other track. Then we bounce it onto one track of another two track (machine) and put horns (on the second track). Then bounce again (onto the first machine) and go for the vocals. If we need to do another (overdub) we have to dub back again to the other machine."[2]

The technique provided variability in studio work, and also helped to create requested sounds much easier. Sylvan Morris, who only experienced Studio One operation with 2-track technology, remembers: "The sound men came and wanted just a rhythm. So you had to improvise. You had to give some bass and drum, (but) everyone would want a different version. This is how the drum and bass thing came about."[3] The initial idea came from the sound systems, as they used it to bring on their deejays, who have been an integral part of the music scene since U-Roy emerged at the end of the 1960s. The hysteria created at these dances, combined with special instrumental versions of well-known hits, was the fertile soil for an emerging musical-technical innovation that would later be called "dub". All it took was one step more: recording devices would have to be able to tape more than on just two tracks.

Until then, bouncing had occasionally been used to create a new piece from a completed production. One of the first was Clement Seymore Dodd (1932–2004), known as "Coxson"[4], owner of "Studio One", short for his company "Recording & Publishing Studios Ltd" located on Brentford Road at "The End", a former jazz club. In 1966, Coxson took the backing track of the Wailers' song "Jailhouse", and turned it into the instrumental track "Green Collie", with harmonica player Roy Richards. In 1968, in another studio, Lee Perry reversed the vocals for the B-side of his Burt Walters production "Honey Love", a Drifters cover, and the result, "Evol Yenoh", aptly spelt the original moniker backwards. A year later, Perry covered the Coasters' hit "Yakety Yak" with Dave Barker; for "The Tackro", the B-side, he went back to the first recording step of bass and drums, and overdubbed it with organ and vocal gimmicks. Such frolics could only be achieved with two tape machines, and would not have been possible without bouncing.

Perry's proto-dub experiments took place at Dynamic studio, where he found a congenial partner in the engineer Linford Anderson. Anderson (1941–2020), born in Clarendon, came to Kingston in 1959, first working as an accountant before he got a job at the radio station RJR. It turned out he had a talent for sound engineering, which led him to join Edward Seaga's WIRL[5] in 1963, where he was trained by Graeme Goodall.

The Australian Goodall (1932–2014) came to Jamaica via London in 1957 to help set up the "Radio Jamaica Rediffusion" RJR, the radio station run by the British. Six months after completing his three-year task, the Jamaican government hired him to support the establishment of

1 The studio was originally called West Indies Records Ltd. (WIRL) and was built 1958 by the later Prime Minister Edward Seaga. In 1964 he sold the business to George Benson and Clifford "Bunny" Rae, who brought in Ronnie Nasralla and band leader Byron Lee (1935–2008) well-known for his appearance in "James Bond – Dr. No". Lee's wife Sheila, a niece of Ken Khouri, became the business manager. On May 1, 1969, the company was re-named Dynamic Sounds Recording Company Ltd., and subsequently expanded into one of the best-equipped studios in the Caribbean with two recording rooms. The smaller one was converted from originally 2 to 4 to 8 tracks and was mainly booked by local customers. The large room had 8/16/24 tracks and was designed for international productions. Besides Byron Lee and his Dragonaires, the Rolling Stones, Eric Clapton, Paul Simon, Roberta Flack, Joe Cocker, Elton John, Cat Stevens and Stevie Wonder all recorded here, among others.

2 From an email correspondence with David Katz in October 2011.

3 *Sylvan Morris. Tales Of Brentford Road* by Tero Kaski, in: More Axe 7, Finland 1989.

4 Clement Dodd's nickname was "Coxson", the widely known spelling "Coxsone" is the name of one of his record labels.

5 Edward Seaga, Jamaica's Prime Minister from 1980 to '89, came to Jamaica shortly after his birth in 1930 as a child of Scottish/Lebanese immigrants, was baptized there, studied anthropology at Harvard, returned to Jamaica and became one of the country's first music entrepreneurs. In the 1950s he recorded records of Jamaican folk music and founded the West Indies Records Limited company WIRL. At the beginning of his political career, he sold the business to Byron Lee.

the country's own broadcaster "Jamaica Broadcasting Corporation" JBC. Before his arrival on the island, the British colony had no trained sound engineers. Goodall became an instructor, planned the Federal recording studio on behalf of Ken Khouri in 1961, which later became Bob Marley's Tuff Gong studio, and got Coxson's stuttering Studio One operation up and running. In the early days of the Jamaican music industry, Goodall participated in almost all recordings until the mid-1960s. In 1962 he was involved in the founding of Island Records, sold his share to Chris Blackwell after three years, and used the proceeds to found the labels Doctor Bird and Pyramid in the UK. On the latter label, Desmond Dekker's international hit "The Israelites", was released in 1968.

When Anderson met Goodall, he was right in the process of converting the West Indies Records Limited studio WIRL into Dynamic Sounds studio for Byron Lee. Anderson was promoted to lead recording engineer in the new company, and put in charge of mastering, the final step from a recording becoming a record. As such, he met Lee Perry when the latter brought recordings from Studio One to press on behalf of Coxson. The two became friends and in 1967, when Perry was no longer working for Coxson, they founded the Upset label together with Dynamic trainer Barrington Lambert. "People Funny Boy" was one of their releases, and became the first international success for Perry, after licensing it to Doctor Bird. The B-side was a version of Bob Dylan's "Blowing In The Wind" sung by Burt Walters, infused with howling sounds of the wind. In 1969, Linford scored a terrific hit under the name Andy Capp, with the single "Pop A Top", which was based on the bass figure of an old sound system-proof mambo instrumental[6], from which he created 13 different versions by bouncing and adding additionally recorded tracks.[7]

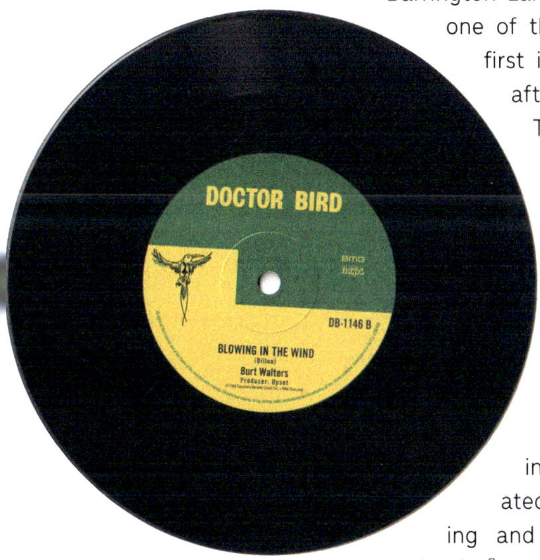

Although Anderson and Perry complemented each other perfectly, their creations were more experiments in creating new pieces of music than making dubs suitable for sound systems. One thing, however, was clearly noticeable, and was that these attempts were signposts, or pointers to the future. Dub was in the air.

"Real dub music started on 4-track", said King Jammy. In 1969, Byron Lee purchased an adequate tape recorder for Dynamic Sounds studio, located on Bell Road in Kingston 11, halfway between Brentford Road and Dromilly Avenue. He bought it in Miami, along with a used, custom-made mixing board. These items made bouncing no longer necessary. The individual elements of a recording were now next to one another, with drums and bass on the first track, organ, piano and guitars on the second, the brass section on the third and the vocals on the fourth. Each track could be put together, accessed, and edited individually. In the very same year, on this multitrack wonder machine, Clancy Eccles produced the single "Herb Man", with deejay King Stitt. It ushered in a new era. Immediately afterwards, he had Linford Anderson mix a version of the track in which individual instruments were faded in and out. Eccles called the mix "Phantom" and released it as an instrumental single in 1970 under The Dynamites[8], the name of his favourite session band. It was one of the first, if not the first ever, vinyl dub release taken from a 4-track tape machine, and had been created with the help of an extraordinary mixing board that King Tubby would later really take full advantage of.

6 Bop-A-Loos – "South Parkway Mambo", Mercury 1955.
7 including a Derrick Morgan remake of "Fat Man" and the Val Bennett instrumental "South Park Rock".

8 The Dynamites or Clancy Eccles All Stars were a group of more than 20 musicians with whom Clancy Eccles worked in a variety of combinations at the end of the 1960s. They included Winston Grennan, Ernest Ranglin, Gladdy Anderson, Winston Wright, Deadly Hedley, Val Bennett, Bobby Ellis, Johnny 'Dizzy' Moore, Uziah 'Sticky' Thompson and others.

STUDIO ONE
ITAL
DUB
By: DUB SPECIALIST
ALL SONGS ARE PUBLISHED BY JAMREC MUSIC
PRODUCED BY C. S. DODD.

STUDIO ONE
Mello DUB
By DUB SPECIALIST
ALL SONGS ARE PUBLISHED BY JAMREC MUSIC
PRODUCED BY C. S. DODD.

ROOTS
DUB

ZODIAC
SOUNDS

Sylvan Morris: Dub has Cultural Significance

> "The drum and bass started when the sound men come and bought the dubplate. They were the ones who instigated this thing!"
>
> (Sylvan Morris[1])

An elderly lady in the waiting area of a bank in Kingston listened to me talking about meeting Sylvan Morris and remarked that "Jamaicans don't save." Unlike the majority of the country, she didn't blame the government, as for her it was a matter of attitude. "A retirement plan" she said, "is not part of our way of life."

Sylvan Morris was one of the studio pioneers who responded to the sound men's demands for special dubplate mixes early on. As studio engineer, he shaped Jamaica's sound for more than four decades and has long been considered one of reggae's most experienced engineers. About him it is said that "he could hear the finished product before it was mixed". All that remains today is a shadow, as only the veterans of the early days still recall him. I found Sylvan Morris in a house once owned by Byron Lee in Richmond Park, a fairly decent area of Kingston. This was where he lived, and the place seemed to be the only thing that was still decent in his life. A rotting wreck that was once his car served as a handrail in front of his porch. Morris was blind, a long-term consequence of diabetes, which had left him unemployed and lonely. The final act of his existence had all the characteristics typical of the tragedies of his country, in which there is no consideration given to a retirement plan.

Sylvan Morris was born on August 13, 1946 in Trenchtown. Electrical devices were the boy's favourite toys; he took them apart and built them back together again. As a twelve-year-old, the neighborhood would come and have him fix its irons and radios. In the early 1960s, Morris followed Graeme Goodall's call, and joined Dynamic Sounds studio as an assistant.

In 1967, Morris went to Duke Reid's Treasure Isle studio for six months. He worked there with Byron "Smitty" Smith, who came from Federal Records and was also trained by Goodall. Smith was to have the mis-

hap with the vocal track for Ruddy Redwood the following year.[2] After this short interlude, Morris moved on to Reid's arch-rival Coxson Dodd, where he was given free rein and, with his technical measures, created the foundation for the legendary Studio One sound, which remained unchanged for decades. Then in-house producer and Heptones singer Leroy Sibbles, who, as the resident bass player at Coxson's studio, created one immortal bass line after another, wrote the text for the Heptones song "Hypocrite"[3] after having left Coxson at Joe Gibbs' studio. The

1 Interview Babylon Falling 2008.

2 See chapter "Overture of a New Genre"

3 Released in 1971 as single on JOGIBS Record Globe and on the Trojan album *The Heptones & Their Friends meet The Now Generation* in 1972, which was re-released by 17 North Parade/VP Records in 2009. See the interview "Leroy's Gonna Fight" by Peter I on reggae-vibes.com p. 3.

lyrics addressed to Morris contained the lines "You're just being used. When they're through, you will be refused... You will get hurt somehow, I know that time will tell on you." Sibbles later explained the meaning. "He (Morris) put in more than just engineering. He put his life in it. That guy put everything he had in it and got nothing out of it."[4]

In 1972 Sylvan Morris moved on to Harry Johnson (1945–2013). Johnson had just invested a lot of money in a new studio on Roosevelt Avenue, after selling the intro of his instrumental "The Liquidator", successful in the UK, to the American gospel and soul band The Staple Singers for their hit "I'll Take You There". For years to come, Harry J's studio was state of the art, with the best acoustics Kingston's recording scene had to offer. Morris himself became resident engineer and, with Bob Marley, recorded *Natty Dread* in 1974, and two years later, *Rastaman Vibration*, among others. In the following years, he was the engineer for countless dub albums created inside Harry J's studio, including epic works such as Keith Hudson's *Pick A Dub* or Big Youth's *Reggae Gi Dem Dub*. Under his own name, in 1975, the LP *Morris On Dub*[5] with its notorious Nipplegate cover, was released, as well as the visually entirely different *Cultural Dub*[6] in 1978, both on his employer's labels. Another album entitled *Reggae Workshop*[7] did not have his name in the title, and instead Sylvan Morris was credited as arranger on the label. On the back cover, pictures showed him working at Harry J's studio equipment and he was listed as the engineer and responsible for the "sound effects". This was apparently a reference to King Tubby, who at the same time – *Reggae Workshop* was released in 1975 – caused a sensation with his studio's high

4 Leroy Sibbles in: Jim Dooley – *Interviews From The Culture Reggae Archive* London 2013 p. 38

5 On Jaywax, was also released in the same year by the English Trojan label as *Leslie Butler – Ja-Gan* including two additional tracks.

6 Excerpts from these two LPs were released in 2012 on the Dutch label Dr. Buster Dynamite in a vinyl edition limited to 500 copies as *Harry J The Producer, Joe White The Artist, Sylvan Morris The Engineer – Roosevelt Ave Dub 1975–1978*. It also included three tracks from the record *Joe White – Jah Jah Dub*, also mixed by Sylvan Morris and released on Roosevelt in 1975, with the 16 minutes title track filling the entire B-side.

7 B & M Records, Jamaica 1975

pass filter. Here, and also in later mixes like Bunny Wailers *Dubd'sco Vol. 1*[8], Morris managed to achieve almost identical effects by making changes on the equalizer during the mix.

In 1986, Sylvan Morris returned to Dynamic Sounds and stayed there into the new millennium. During that time, he also installed and repaired the vinyl cutting machines at Gussie Clarke's Music Works studio, at Black Scorpio and at Tuff Gong. The consequences of untreated diabetes increasingly limited him; and in the end he could only copy cassettes. His worsening blindness forced him to stop working all together. At the time of the following interview, he was 65.

Tell me about your training in electronics.

Sylvan Morris: The early training was done at an electronic establishment by the name of COMTECH at the top of Eastwood Park Road, that's a little bit above Half Way Tree. COMTECH used to work on communication equipment, by that time it was VHF, very high frequency equipment. The taxi cabs, we used to have yellow cabs and checkered cabs in those days. People would call the stations and they would call the taxis. So, we used to fix those equipments, both the main station and the mobile in the vehicles. I worked on these equipments at the age of, like 15. I eventually went to Technical High School, and did a course in radio and TV and audio equipment. That was around 1962. I left there and came directly to Dynamic Sounds, that time it was WIRL,

Sylvan Morris at Harry J Studio

West Indies Recordings Limited. It was just changing over from the gentleman Eddie Seaga.

The later Prime Minister of the JLP, who was active in the music business before becoming a politician...[9]

Yes. Byron Lee bought it from him. I came in just at that time. Somehow, they heard about me. I went to Dynamic Sounds, and there was a man named Graeme Goodall. He put me under his wing, and the two of us we wired up a three-track [tape machine]

8 Solomonic JA 1979

9 Edward Seaga, born 1930, was leader of the conservative JLP from 1974 to 2005 and head of government from 1980 to 1989.

in those days. Then I went by Coxson; this is where the whole thing started.

Before that you were briefly at Treasure Isle.

Well, I am going to tell you the truth, I didn't do much work at Duke Reid. They had Smitty there and Duke Reid. Matter of fact, that was one of the reasons I left there so quick.

At Studio One you changed the entire recording process.

I rebuilt the studio my way because after I recorded a few things I realised that there was a sound that I wanted. The mics at Studio One, they were not in perfect working order. They dropped them, some of them were bent and they have been straightened out and them things. There was even an RCA mic that they called the ribbon mic...

At that time, they were considered the ultimate recording technology.

...the ribbon was broken. These two-track tapes had a little piece of silver in them so I formulated the piece like an accordion thing and then put it within the mic so it started picking up the sound. [But] it didn't pick up much high frequencies so we used that for bass. I noticed from early there is a deep sound that comes out of the back of the speaker box. Behind the speaker, within the box, there is an acoustic sound of the box itself that is deep. So, I put the mic right at the back.

Hence the unmistakable bass sound from Studio One that no one could copy. A fixed ribbon microphone and the back of the speaker.

Yeah. The next part now was the piano. Because of the fact that the microphones were not that good the sound coming through the console was lacking frequency.

What type of mixing console was that?

It was a Lang, a Japanese board. There was two equalizers that we had by the name of Pultec. I used the Pultec to bring in the middles and whatever [frequency] was missing. I had to use all two of them 'cause in those days you didn't have the fantastic ones you have nowadays where you can go in between the different frequencies. So that is how the main sound was created. [You also] hear a kind of echo sound. You hear it, but it was more felt. When I'm voicing the vocals go into the tape-recorder, I feedbacked the playback head, cut off the extreme bass end and feed it back into the voices. I had to work it out, listen it. This is what made the voices sound so sweet.

Through the doubling...

Yes. If you listen, most of the Heptones tunes, Alton Ellis, Bob Marley, the whole of those tunes in those time had the sweet voice. It was a total different sound than before I came to Studio One. There was a uniqueness with it in them times. It wasn't predominant. The echo time was so good, you just feel it.

How did you set the echo time?

I didn't have to. In those days we used 7 ½ IPS to get more tunes on the tape, sometimes 15 IPS, but hardly. When Coxson saw me doing this return delay from the playback head, he went to the States and bought this piece of equipment by the name of Sound Dimension[10]...

...the name your in-house band chose in 1967...

... it had a continued looper, about two feet[11], and it had three heads: recording, erasing and the playback head. In those days them never reach the stage of integrated circuits and all that. They had to use mechanical. The playback head now it was at a lever so you could move it a little and get a different timing. That's how come we get a lot of these effects.

You also had a reverb device, a spring reverb.

Space Expander was the name of it.

How many machines did you work with?

Sometimes we use three, sometimes two.

And that's what you used for the bounce? How did that work?

We do the drum and bass on one track, the rest of the riddim on another track. When we finished, we mix it together to [one track of] another tape recorder, replay it back now and do the voices.

After the mixing, how did you create the dubplates? Did you go back to the original recording before the bounce?

10 Other sources such as the info of the Soul Jazz album *Sound Dimension – Jamaica Soul Shake Vol. 1* (2006) state that Coxson brought the device from the UK after a tour with Jackie Mittoo & The Soul Vendors.

11 2 feet = approx. 61 cm.

Well, I had different methods. What we do depends on how the tune sound. Sometimes the tune sounds so powerful we had to do everything live and run two tapes at the same time. There are some occasions where we had to do everything live, both voice and everything. We take the whole thing, have the voice on one [track] and everything else on the next one. But because of the fact that we want to have a dub now, we press two tape, one here, one there. This one have drum, bass, riddim track on one, voices on the other track, and that one have the drum and bass on one and riddims (meaning: offbeat) on a separate track. I had to have two tapes. So I can get the drum and bass now for the dubplate. Them time had [sounds] like Prince Patrick, Black Arrows, Jah Love, and we used to cater for them.

And how did it feel to take the music apart and use only fragments?

Yeah, water it down to a certain degree. But as you know, how a lot of things, sometimes when you look back you look at it different. This is another thing that I would have to give the sound men a lot of credit for. They hear something in it that you don't hear. In terms of excitability. When they go into the dancehall they observe the people and see how excited they are in relation to certain things. So they come to you and say "take out that" or "cut down that". Sometimes you don't like the idea but eventually you go back and hear it and realise the marketability of that thing. I wasn't really that keen until I realised that the sound men got something going.

Did you go to the dances yourself to see how people react?

Yes. I was not really a great dance lover but sometimes they used to invite me and I go and listen and see what's happening.

And has that changed your opinion?

Yes, definitely. Without a doubt.

You said it was sound men who gave you the idea. Because everyone wanted their version to be special, you had to come up with more and more tricks to make the dubplates sound different. Sometimes through echo, sometimes with unexpected reverb or through equalizers that spiced up the drums.[12] It sounds like you think it wasn't the studio engineers but sound men who invented dub.

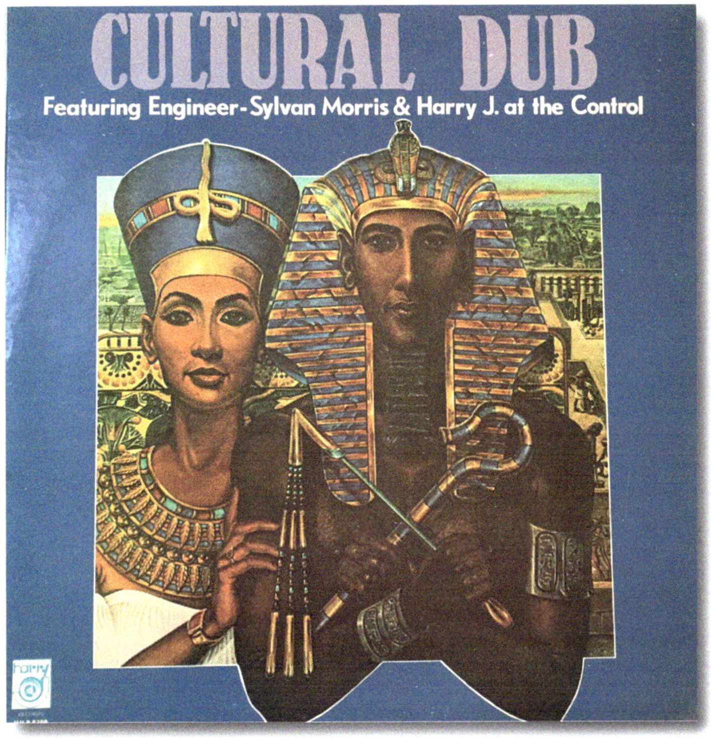

Yes, in the true sense. To be totally frank to you: we do the electronical things but the person who brought about the full idea is the sound man.

Is there a particular person, whose name you'd put first?

(Hesitates to answer) It would still have to be me, you know. I am going to tell you why I say that. In other words, you would have to say the sound men told you what they wanted. The drum and bass thing in the true sense of say. As I said I didn't actually like it. But I still had to do it, cause nobody else was there to do it. Sometimes three, four different sound men come and want a different sound on the same tune. So, me had to separate this... drop in that, drop out that...

And all of that with two tracks.

12 Studio One Story, Soul Jazz DVD 2002

On the 2-track. So, I use my engineerity (i.e. know-how), use the Pultec, equalize each track differently. Someday I take out a little of the bass, some of them never had the drum and bass. I have to work all different kind of things. Cause it's four different men come in here I have to find four different sound of the whole song.

But all that was only for the dubplates. When the first dub albums came out of Studio One in 1974, you were already at Harry J, where two albums were released under your name in 1975 and 1978: *Morris On Dub* and *Cultural Dub*. Plus, countless more dub LPs that list you as mixing engineer on the back.

It was Harry J do these things. Most time when we were mixing music, we usually mix the A-side and the version, or the dub version as the case might be. Sometimes you have both versions, B-side instrumental version and dub version. But it was not done like "Okay, we make a dub album". They just compile them.

That means the two albums under your name were only single dub tracks that were compiled?

No, Morris On Dub and Cultural Dub definitely were done as a dub mix.

And who came up with the idea of the naked woman on the cover of *Morris On Dub*? Rather unusual artwork for a dub LP.

[That was] Harry J and him madness. When I say mad, I mean mad musically, which sometimes is very good.

***Cultural Dub* was a lot more serious.**

Cause dub had a cultural significance.

Do you know how many LPs of your mixes were pressed back then?

No idea. Harry J told me that he gave it to somebody like... I'm not certain.

You probably never saw any money for these releases either?

You better believe it.

Is that why you complain that you haven't been treated well anywhere?

What really happen to me, I work as if I'm doing something for my own self and for my spiritual life. I love the music so much that when I work I just work. Whatever I'm doing, I do it as if it's mine.

What was the technical equipment like at Harry J during your time there?

When I just went there, there was a board with 16 channel, I don't remember the name, and an 8-track machine. They didn't have 16-track yet. But shortly after we got the Helios, that was one of the high-class boards. I think Chris Blackwell was the one who got it for Harry J. It was a reasonably good board, you know.

Is that what you used to record the next Marley records after *Catch A Fire*?

Yeah.

But even before the Helios Harry J's studio had a higher sound quality than Studio One.

Yeah man, without a doubt. You must remember, at that time we had started going into the full transistorized, integrated and Darlington circuits. Not fully, some of the amplifiers would [still] be vacuum tubes. We now getting solid state sound, which is much better. Even on the tape recorders.

Also, the room acoustics at Harry J were more sophisticated.

Yes, it was a bigger studio. We had a lot of sound partitions and a drum booth. Studio One didn't have a drum booth until later on. In Harry J's studio we could separate the drum set and didn´t have as much leakage.

How long did you stay at Harry J?

I think it's about 15 years.

It is said that during your time at Studio One you trained the young Errol Thompson, who later became an influential engineer at Randy's and Joe Gibbs'.

Errol Thompson was really an engineer within himself, I think he had some training in electronics. I didn't do much training where he is concerned. We sit down and reason and he would ask me certain questions. So, I gave him a lot of insights and hints and thing, but to be frankly I didn't give him direct full training.

Our conversation fades out with a long excursus on the spiritual myths of life, music in general and reggae in particular. Sylvan Morris, who has experienced hundreds of artists in his active professional life, mixed thousands of dubs, and recorded thousands upon thousands of songs, raves about extraordinary moments and the connection between composition, interpretation and situation: "Because the people suffered, both in the Apartheid regime and the suffering of the poorer classes, they call out in their prayers, in their songs and in their hopes for a higher power to give them help. It's out of this yearning for a betterment of suffering they create tunes and music. Even within the music of an instrument you can hear the feeling of the spirit of the man who is playing. I can feel that. There is a certain spirit, even without lyrics. There are certain artists, whenever they start to sing their tune to the musicians, it's a total different thing than when the ordinary individual sing. People like Burning Spear. When the man come in and start sing it's like the whole studio transform. The musicians them get a different feeling, when they start playing, they feel it. Bob Marley, Toots and the Maytals, you understand? It's like when them start to sing you feel the music, the musicians change, the whole spiritual outlook changes. There's a lot of tunes that were written, not even by just them alone, the majority of these tunes were done at Coxson. And when them start to play I danced to see if I can feel it. I always keep that, they used to call me 'the dancing engineer'. Most of the tunes you hear, it's my spirit. When I say my spirit I'm not trying to be egoistic or anything, but when it sounds right to me the spirit lick me, and I say 'Yes, that's it!' So, it's that time I start to move."

On June 17, 2023, Sylvan Morris was found dead in his home in St. Andrew. He was 74 years old.

Unknown Sound System, Kingston ca. 2000.

Blackwood Sound System, Germany.

Errol Thompson, Joe Gibbs and the first Dub LPs

"Them times man used to 'ave sound system as hooliganism business but now it can even nationalize. Because is that them use fe help win election y'know. Sound system come in such a demand that every weekend if a man naw go to no party or no session is like some part o' him life gone. Man not going ah club again, no even want hear no juke box again."

(King Tubby[1])

"Real dub music started on 4-track", so said King Jammy. Soon after a 4-track tape recorder appeared in Kingston's Dynamic studio and the "Phantom" single, produced by Clancy Eccles, heralded a turning point in the evolution of dub[2], a second groundbreaking multi-track tape machine emerged downtown. Vincent Chin (1937–2003), son of a Chinese carpenter who came to Kingston in 1920, purchased it for his company.

Vincent started out in the mid-1950s as a jukebox service technician for the Syrian Jamaican Isaac Issa. On his behalf, he travelled across the island to maintain the jukeboxes set up in bars all over the country. He exchanged singles and collected the coins. Since Issa's company didn't have any use for the old records, Vincent got to buy them for a small fee and stored them in his garage. When this was full, he rented a small shop on Kingston's East and Tower Street in 1958, and opened the first Randy's Record Shop. The name was inspired by a US record store in Nashville that produced a radio show which could be heard in Jamaica on shortwave when the weather was clear. The program played exactly the R'n'B that could also be heard on the sound systems, and to which the country gravitated more and more after mento began fading.

In 1962 Jamaica became independent, and an energetic phase of change began. Inspired by a pioneer spirit of "we can become something", companies and businesses were set up, especially in the cities and mostly by the middle class. Also, the local music industry benefitted enormously, a process in which the merchant Vincent Chin would play an important role. His second-hand record store, opened before independence, was doing well, and soon the premises became too small. In 1962, Randy's Records Shop moved to a former ice cream parlour in downtown, at 17 North Parade. Vincent Chin was now called "Randy" and was recommended as the country's first professional record dealer and distributor. "You name it, we have it" was his slogan, displayed above the entrance. Here you could find what Jamaica was craving, i.e. imported US records and products by the young Jamaican labels. Usually on Fridays, new singles arrived and both sounds and private clients lined up to stock up for house parties and dances on the weekend. Patricia, Randy's wife, was the heart of the store. She had a nose for hits, controlled the stocks, and supported both artists and producers. Patricia ran the store while Vincent was still on the move every day. In the meantime, however, he was traveling around, buying the latest tunes by Federal, Studio One, Treasure Isle, Beverley's, and all the other production companies that emerged in the boom of the early years. Additionally, Vincent started producing singles himself. Given the Chins' strong business sense, it was only logical that they too would soon think about setting up their own studio. In 1968, after one year of construction, Randy's recording studio opened on the floor above the record shop. In reference to the address, it was officially called "Studio 17", but was generally simply called "Randy's". It consisted of a control room equipped with high-quality technology and a spacious, wooden recording room that provided excellent acoustics. Besides this, there was a dub cutting room (in which only mono editing was possible, done by Dennis Thompson until 1974[3]), a lounge, and later a drum booth. At the beginning, the recording was done on a 3-track tape machine.

Clive Chin took over the management. He was Vincent's eldest son, born on May 14, 1954, and the child of a premarital liaison with school sweetheart Yvonne Fay Lauder.[4] Clive coordinated the processes, was responsible for the wiring and set up the microphones. His school mate Errol Thompson became the resident engineer. The first in-house band was Soul Syndicate with Earl 'Chinna' Smith, Fully Fullwood and Santa Davis, followed by Skin, Flesh & Bones including Sly Dunbar, Lloyd Parks and Ansel Collins. Errol Thompson, born December 29, 1948, gained his first

1 In: "Marcus Garvey Meets The Rockers Uptown" *Black Music* February 1976 p. 34.
2 See chapter "Overture of a New Genre".

3 Dennis Thompson became tour engineer for Bob Marley, worked after his death for Steel Pulse, Burning Spear, Maxi Priest, Sizzla, Capleton and others, eventually moved to the US and was responsible there for the live sound of P Diddy, Missy Elliot, Busta Rhymes, 50 Cent, Marcus Miller and Alicia Keys among others.
4 When Clive was born, his father was 17, his mother 16 years old.

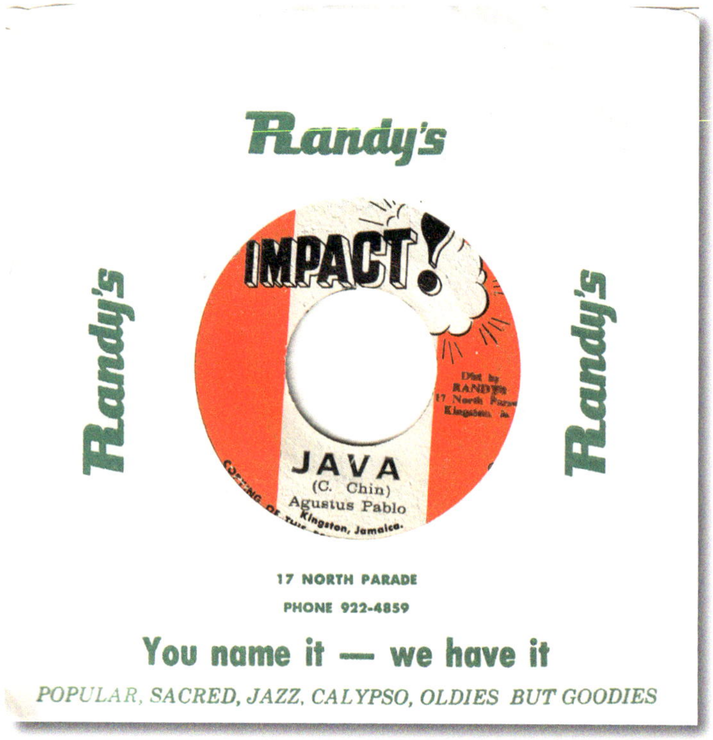

experience at Studio One. At the age of 22, he took over the executive chair inside Randy's studio with a five-year younger boss Clive Chin. It was 1970, and the two were about to create history.

"Randy's had the sound that the people wanted, which you can call the ghetto sound. It was the real roots sound", said singer Pat Kelly[5], who occasionally filled in as an engineer at North Parade. Just one year after its opening, the studio, located in the heart of downtown, was already in full swing. Hits flowed like water, primarily for the local market, plus attracting respectable international successes. The South African Hugh Masakela rented a room, as did French singer and actor Serge Gainsbourg. Lee Perry produced *Soul Rebel* with the Wailers here, Burning Spear recorded the *Marcus Garvey* album shortly before the studio closed in 1975, as did Peter Tosh the singles "Legalize It" and "Equal Rights".

When Randy's founded the IMPACT! label in 1971 for its own releases, Clive became the in-house producer. He and Errol began to experiment. Ever since Vincent had installed a 4-track tape machine in their studio, the two Jamaican youths enjoyed it as their toy. Errol knew what the sounds wanted. His uncle ran the "El Gong" sound system in Harbour View, where he took care of the setup and wiring. In the studio, Errol was the inventive head, and Clive gave him the space he needed. The two developed into a groundbreaking creative duo. According to the principle of "more tracks, more possibilities", they separated the instruments into individual tracks to add more variability to the mix. They recorded sounds like breaking glass or flushing toilets and mixed them into the music. They did whatever came into their minds and was technically possible. There were no limits to what was allowed, the duo knew no inhibitions. Errol manipulated the frequencies during the mix and created sound effects that Tubby would later become famous for, using his high pass filter. Any of their shenanigans were preserved on 2-track master tapes. "Myself and Errol started experimenting dub, long before even Tubby's followed doing dub" Clive insisted. "Perry was using the studio, so obviously he got a bit of what we were doing, and also Herman Chin-Loy from Aquarius got a bit of it."[6]

Herman Chin-Loy (unrelated to the Chins), and a young musician named Horace Swaby played significant supporting roles in the events that followed. Both born in 1954, Swaby had been close friends with Clive since their high school days together at Kingston College. Already as teenagers, "Chinno" and "Swabo", as they liked to call one another, were eager and excited about music. When one later supported the fortunes of the studio for the Chin dynasty, he gladly booked the other to play keyboards. When Herman Chin-Loy recorded at Randy's for his Aquarius label, he preferred to have Swaby on instrumental pieces, which he usually released under the fantasy name "Augustus Pablo". "Good afternoon, here is the news. Great Booga Booga from Aruba, mama you dada jaffa center, my kill a brombrom locka to me snacka ugga T, while I present this iggy iggy. Here it comes!"[7] was the nonsense opener of his 1971 single "Iggy Iggy". Here, Swaby played the melodica for the first time, calling himself Augstus Pablo from then on. It was a time when Jamaica was obsessed with instrumental music, including crazy spoken intros, and the floating minor chords from a kids' instrument, made in Germany by Hohner, were putting the country and its people into raptures.

5 DVD documentary "Randy's 50th Anniversary" VP Records 2008.

6 ibid.

7 Quoted from the Jamaican Observer on January 30, 2011 "Roasting and toasting" by James Moss Solomon

This sound was all the rage, and the hype of the year. After a failed attempt to produce a love song with his old friend Dennis Wright, and after the Chosen Few had given up recording on the playback that had already been finished the previous year, Clive got his friend Pablo to overdub the riddim with one of his naive melodica melodies, at least as a dubplate for his "Black Moses" sound system. At the beginning, Clive and Errol put an echo-filled spaghetti western intro, spoken by Scotty and Bunny Brown (member of the Chosen Few): "From the East of the Rio Cobre to the West of the Rio Cobre, here's the hottest, Java!" The result was cut on dubplate and immediately presented in Randy's shop downstairs. No one expected the tune to trigger such humongous hype! Jukebox operators, sound system owners and private people ordered "Java" in such numbers that three Jamaican pressing plants could barely keep up. Marking the birth of the Far East Sound, "Java" became the instrumental hit of the year and the starting point of the first dub album.

Errol and Clive were not the only ones who recognized dub as marketable. Back in 1969, Alvin Ranglin and his Gloria's Allstars had already released "Jumping Dick", an instrumental, on British Pama Records.[8] Its mix switched between full instrumentation and drum and bass parts. As previously mentioned, Lee Perry and Linford Anderson played with multitracking at Dynamic studio. Ken Khouri also recognized the sign of the times. He owned an Ampex 3-track tape machine and an EMT plate reverb from Germany. Even before "Java", Lloyd Daley aka The Matador had produced vocal trio The Victors' single "Me A Tell Yuh" using this equipment, and engineer Louis "Buddy" Davidson had mixed a dubplate of it for "Prince Jackie's Hi-Fi" sound. He took off the vocals, soaked the picking guitar in extreme reverb and called the result "More Echo". In 1971, on his Syndicate label, Daley released the tune, and the dubplate of it as the B-side.[9]

In 1972, Khouri himself released *Unlimited,* the fifth LP by the highly successful singer Ken Boothe on his in-house Federal label, on which every song was followed by the dub version, announced on the cover as "rub-a-dub it to the very last drop". Produced by singer and producer Lloyd Charmers (1938–2012), this was the first combination of vocal and dubs in LP format, an idea which later, in dub's heyday, would become highly popular as "Showcase LP".

8 LP *Reggae For Days*, 1970 as 7-inch on the Pama sub label Camel.

9 The Victors had previously recorded as The Bassies for Studio One and Sonia Pottinger. Their single was released in the UK on PAMA's Escort label.

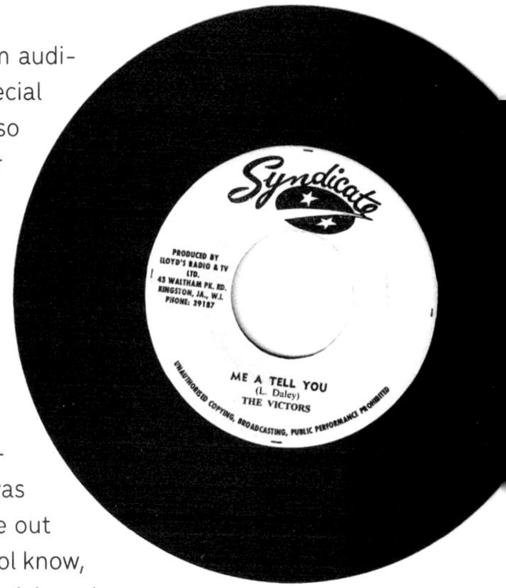

No one could ignore the sound system audience's steadily growing interest in special mixes of well-known tunes. "Java" also triggered an enormous demand for dubplates. Motivated by the commercial success of the title, Randy's decided to produce the first IMPACT! LP. Previously, only singles had been released on the in-house label. They were even willing to take on the financial risk of releasing only dub(plate) mixes, which was unprecedented. Clive remembered "There was a big thing in the 70s about who came out with the first dub. Well, I know, and Errol know, that we did the first dub and it was called *Java Java Java Java Dub*."[10] In fact, the word "dub" did not appear on the title of this debut. It only said "Java" four times on the cover, solely due to the design, so that it could be read both diagonally and sideways. Even though mixes of other hits also appeared on the album, the title was reminiscent of the hype surrounding the previous year's instrumental giant. *Java Java Java Java* was first published in 1973 with an edition of 200 copies. Since then, it has been re-released on a regular basis[11], while copies of the first edition were swapping hands in collectors' circles for crazy money.[12]

Java Java Java Java brought dub to the LP stock exchange, with Errol Thompson being the first pioneering broker. After the predecessors of bouncing and acetate/soft wax/dubplate/special mix, Errol's engineering skills planted a seed inside

10 DVD documentary "Randy's 50th Anniversary" VP Records 2008.

11 The song titles of the first edition were changed later for unknown reasons.

12 Additional confusion was caused by Clive, who referred to the album in several interviews as "Java Java Dub", probably because that was easier than repeating "Java" four times. This expression was mistakenly adopted by some publications. *Java Java Dub*, however, was an album released in 1989 by the British REBEL sub label, featuring vocal, deejay and instrumental tracks, including some "Java" versions, and looking like an original IMPACT! release.

Randy's studio that rapidly blossomed, spreading dub as an LP genre with Usain Bolt gold speed around the studios and labels in Kingston. In 1973, four more albums were released, year zero in the history of the dub LP. Errol, referred to as "ET" or "Errol T", was directly or indirectly involved in all of them. Besides *Java Java Java Java* he also mixed the LP *Dub Serial – More Dub* at Joe Gibbs' studio, without anyone at Randy's knowing about it. In the previous months, like industrial spies, Herman Chin-Loy and Lee Perry had observed him drawing inspiration for their own albums *Aquarius Dub* and *Upsetters 14 Dub Blackboard Jungle,* some of the former even recorded at Randy's. Later on, the latter would be called just *Blackboard Jungle Dub*, and was primarily mixed by King Tubby, but completed with Perry mixes from his own Black Ark studio, which was finished around Christmas time. Errol had also installed the wiring there. And even *The Message,* Prince Buster's LP, released on a British label, came with a cover version of "Java". Given the focus on one person, the conclusion is obvious, and is that Errol Thompson was the most influential dubbist in the early days.

However, is *Java Java Java Java* really the first ever dub LP in history? It is certain that Joe Gibbs was offering the *Dub Serial* LP mixed by Errol as a pre-release under the name *Dub Sequeldo* via mail order already in December 1972, and for the bold price of 50 US dollars, while a normal LP cost less than a tenth of that. Be that as it may, since this was not yet a regular release, two other people were fighting to be first offender, an ultimately insignificant award, as the LP format played no role in the creation and development of dub. The decisive course was set previously on dubplates and single B-sides. However, the LP became the distinctive medium for the international distribution of dub. With it, dub took the crucial step of exposure to the public outside the reggae world. Herman Chin-Loy claimed to have been the initiator, and never got tired of insisting that his *Aquarius Dub* was the first LP of the genre. "I was selling records in the shop and people would come in asking for dub records. Sound systems were playing them on soft wax and I asked myself how I can get the same sort of music to sell. I did what I had to do and put it on record. I mixed it with the help of the engineer and the musicians. I instructed them to get the sound I wanted. Then Coxson put

out *Dub Store Special*. It was underground for the roots people. Then it went commercial and Randy's put out *Java Java Java Java*, Joe Gibbs *Dub Serial* und *African Dub Chapter One*, Rupie Edwards, Federal and then Scratch with *Blackboard Jungle*. Every dub album came after."[13] Clive Chin countered that he had delivery notes from Federal to prove that no comparable album was pressed before *Java Java Java Java*. However, no one has seen the evidence yet.

Obviously, Chin-Loy had mixed up the chronology of the first albums, and Coxson also followed the trend a year later, although he also later tried

13 Quoted from the booklet of the 4 CD box *Evolution Of Dub Volume 1. The Origin Of The Species*, Greensleeves Records 2009.

in interviews to position himself as the first.[14] However, his memories remained "always very vague".[15] According to school friend and then UK importer George Price "Peckings", he came out with *Dub Store Special* in 1974[16]. According to the re-release[17], *African Dub All-Mighty* (aka *Chapter One*) by Joe Gibbs & Errol Thompson appeared in 1975, as did Rupie Edwards' *Dub Basket*, at least according to the label. Meanwhile, Chin-Loy wrote on the cover of the *Aquarius Dub* re-releases: "Jamaica's first dub album. Originally released 1971". The intention to rewrite history is obvious, especially as the label on the first pressing still read 1973. Also, the claim that he mixed it himself was eventually corrected by the publisher: "I just get [bassist] Val Douglas, [drummer] Michael Richards and [guitarist] Mikey Chung, and about half an hour it take to do that in Dynamic's second studio. Carlton Lee mixed that album, that's half an hour, too."[18]

Aquarius Dub was unmistakably a hasty move. Raw and minimalistic, without effects, and except for the dub of Dennis Brown's "It's Too Late" (not created in that session), it was devoid of any vocal fade ins. For the interaction of drums, bass and offbeat, Chin-Loy relied on the power of certain songs from his catalogue, such as Alton Ellis' "My Little Daughter", Dennis Brown's "Song My Mother Used To Sing" as well as Augustus Pablo's "Cassava Piece", which later became a hit single in the UK when adapted by King Tubby as "King Tubby Meets Rockers Uptown". In terms of dubbing, the production provides little. *Java Java Java Java*, on the other hand, is of a completely different caliber. Errol Thompson and Clive Chin also presented Dennis Brown twice ("Cheater", "Meet Me At The Corner"), copied two established riddims from Studio One with "Guiding Star" and "Swing Easy", and included big names such as Max Romeo or The Heptones, and of course Pablo's "Java" in the line-up.

14 See David Katz 2013 "In Search of the First Dub LP", www.redbullmusicacademy.com/magazine/.
15 From a mail correspondence with Steve Barrow in June 2014.
16 ibid.
17 Carter Van Pelt in the booklet of the 4 CD box *African Dub Chapters 1,2,3&4 All-Mighty*, VP Music Group / 17 North Parade 2007.
18 Quoted from David Katz "In Search of the First Dub LP" ibid.

Their playbacks were more sophisticated because they were not based on replayed riddims like Chin-Loy's but came from the carefully arranged original singles; also, their mixes were bolder and sounded better. As a special gimmick, they staged a little audio play on the playback of Lloyd Parks' "Ordinary Man", with Errol playing the role of a musician looking for a job.

The question of who copied who remains. Who was the first? Both Chin-Loy of Aquarius and Clive Chin representing Randy's were clever business people, both competing in the recording market. Quite reasonably, both producers had similar ideas for the selection of the riddims, and partly relied on the same artists. *Java Java Java Java,* however, did show a deeper and more creative approach than *Aquarius Dub,* which was produced in haste and was clearly still in the tradition of the dubplate mixes for sound systems. Ultimately, none of these competitors succeeded in claiming the title for the first dub album. The question also remained as to the significance of the *Dub Sequeldo* LP. Chin-Loy undermined his argument by maneuvering around facts and juggling dates, so that eventually Clive Chin seemed to have the more convincing case. However, regardless of who it was, it is a fact that none of the people here spearheaded dub. They shared the fate of many innovators who created something that only later attracted attention and became a phenomenon. Just like Elvis didn't invent rock'n'roll and the Sex Pistols did not invent punk, Thompson, Chin and Chin-Loy only played minor roles, if any, in dub's international reception. Here two others are celebrated as the first, namely Perry and Tubby, but neither were entirely responsible, as we shall see. Perhaps history should not concern itself with this question but smile at the Solomonic-Jamaican verdict of Prince Buster, who describes his LP *The Message*, also mixed by Carlton Lee at Dynamics and released in the same year, not as the first, but "the first good dub LP".[19]

In 1975, Errol Thompson caused the demise of Randy's studio by moving on to Joe Gibbs. His new employer was born Joel Gibson on the North coast of Jamaica in 1945[20]. He grew up in Montego Bay, studied electronics via a correspondence course in the USA, and was temporarily employed by a Canadian company that was overseeing the standardization of broadcast frequencies in Jamaica. In 1962, Gibbs moved to Kingston and, four years later, opened an electrical shop for radio and TV equipment. Situated directly across from Leslie Kong's "Beverly's Ice Cream Parlour & Record Shop", Gibbs was able to observe how lucrative the record business was becoming. He decided to enter the business and started with productions, initially using Lee Perry as producer, Lyn Taitt & The Jets as musicians, and Bunny Lee for promotion. In 1968, Gibbs built a small 2-track studio behind his shop, moved the studio several times and in 1971 ended up on 20 North Parade, not far from Randy's. By then, Lee Perry had set up his own business and was replaced by Niney The Observer, who recommended Errol Thompson as engineer. Gibbs and Thompson met and immediately developed a bond that would last their entire lives. After the meeting, ET initially stayed at Randy's but started working for Gibbs after hours. After officially moving to Joe Gibbs, one of his first major works at the new workplace was, at the request of Winston Rodney aka Burning Spear, mixing the *Marcus Garvey* LP[21], which was recorded at Randy's, as well as the dub counterpart *Garvey's Ghost*[22]. This was an exceptional album that impressed with a bone-dry, innovative stereo mix with barely any reverb or echo, whose contemplative character primarily came through its stoic beats and subtle shifts between left and right.

Joe Gibbs was a technology nerd and always wanted to make optimal use of all frequencies to achieve the best possible sound. In Errol Thompson he met a like-minded character who shared the same aspirations. When they planned to increase the amount of technological equipment, Thompson convinced Gibbs to buy the larger of the two consoles from Dynamic studio to expand his own to 16 tracks. It was the same Sound Techniques board like the one at Randy's, which Errol mastered perfectly. King Tubby had already purchased the smaller MCI console from Dynamic. Curiously, the two consoles on which Linford Anderson, Lee Perry and Carlton Lee made their first humble attempts at dub were now fully taken advantage of in the hands of Errol Thompson and, respectively, King Tubby and his cohort of engineers. Gibbs and ET decided to work together as business partners, henceforth calling themselves The Mighty Two. They were celebrated for their *African Dub* series, spread over five LPs released between 1975 and '84. Errol continued what he had started at Randy's. Especially in the third part, he incorporated acoustic appliques into his mixes like synthesizer sounds, explosions, sirens, running water, screaming children, bicycle and telephone bells and more besides. Wrongly, the booklet for the dub compilation *No Bones For The Dogs* attributed these "quirky noises"[23] to Joe Gibbs. "Joe Gibbs was an investor. The man who really had hands on to the session

19 Ibid.
20 While other sources state 1942 or 1943.

21 Island Records 1975.
22 Island Records 1976
23 Booklet of the compilation *Joe Gibbs & The Professionels – No Bones For The Dogs. Dubs From The Mighty Two 1974 to 1979* Pressure Sounds 2002

was Errol Thompson", remembered Joseph Hill[24], lead singer of the vocal trio Culture, who died in 2006 and whose international career had started with *Two Sevens Clash* (1977) and *International Herb* (1979) at Joe Gibbs. German reggae author Hermann Moter has confirmed this. He stayed in Kingston for several months in the autumn of 1980 and spent time at Joe Gibbs place almost every day. Moter recalled "Errol was calm and focused. As far as the controls were concerned, he had everything under control. Nobody could distract him, and he didn't have to jump around the control room like a dervish to show that was he putting his heart and soul into it. What ET did at this mixing desk wasn't nearly as spectacular as watching Lee Perry, on the contrary."[25]

All of the ideas in terms of dub creativity Errol brought to the table at Joe Gibbs had previously been applied at Randy's, if not yet in the LP format. His "Extraordinary Version" of Lloyd Parks' "Ordinary Man" for example, included bizarre tape and engine noises as early as 1972; and the 1973 dubs for Hubert Lee's "Something On Your Mind" and Charlie Ace's talkover version "Country Boy", are sprinkled with ghostly reversed voices. Nevertheless, and although Lee Perry has long been mixing outside noises into his mixes, the dubs from Joe Gibbs' studio are considered innovative. However, the glory that the Mighty Two generated with this belonged solely to engineer ET.

In the second half of the 1970s, Joe Gibbs and Errol Thompson became a successful national and international production duo as The Mighty Two, a fact that was instrumental in securing a major deal with US record company A&M for Dennis Brown. Their catalogue included Gregory Isaacs, Althea & Donna, The Mighty Diamonds, Peter Tosh, Prince Far I, Trinity, Kojak & Liza, Ranking Joe, I Roy, Luie Lepkie and many others. Besides the legendary *African Dub* series, the most popular dub albums from Gibbs' studio were the LPs *State Of Emergency* from 1976, and the *'79 Majestic Dub*. The LP *Dub I*, mixed by Errol T in 1975 in just one day on behalf of Pete Weston for Micron Music, remained undiscovered for a long time. It lacked marketing and distribution as Micron were facing ruin at the time, and had no means to promote it. As a result, only 300 copies were pressed, which have been circulating among collectors at exorbitant prices ever since.[26] *Dub I* is an impressive album, with playbacks by producer Jimmy Radway, in which Errol proved that he could create the same sound shifts that King Tubby had just caused a sensation with. His "Awn Yah!", a dub to Leroy Smart's "Mirror Mirror", sounded like it had been drawn through Tubby's high pass filter.

In the early 80s, Gibbs failed to compensate songwriter Don Devaney[27] over licenses for the global hit "Someone Loves You Honey", produced by Gibbs with June Lodge[28]. He was sued, lost the court case and subsequently had to close his studio due to insolvency. Errol remained by his side and took care of the management of his supermarket in Kingston. In 1993, the former studio was reopened at its old location, whereupon Errol became sound engineer again, but also continued to run the shop. On November 13, 2004, a few weeks before his 56th birthday, Errol Thompson died after a series of strokes. His partner Joe Gibbs survived him until February 21, 2008.

24 In an interview with BBC discjockey and host Mark Lamarr on August 31, 2004. To be found on the DoCD/DVD *Culture – Natty Dread Taking Over*, 17 North Parade/VP Records 2012.

25 From mail correspondence with German author Hermann Moter, October 2011.

26 In 2008 the album was re-released in a remastered version on the British reissue label Pressure Sounds.

27 Don Devaney wrote the title in 1978 for the US country singer Charley Pride. Although it became No. 1 on the country charts, it remained far below the international success of Gibbs' version with June Lodge.

28 The London-born singer later went by the name J.C. Lodge and had another, albeit not quite as successful, international crossover hit with "Telephone Love" in 1988.

Errol Thompson, Joe Gibbs and the first Dub LPs

Umojah Sound System Nairobi

Randy's Studio 2012: mixing board, various tape machines (2, 3, 16-track), organ, dub cutter.

Clive Chin: The Story of Java Java Java Java

"Dub is the skeleton of reggae. Stripped down [and] raw."

(Mad Professor[1])

In 1978, Randy's studio on North Parade ceased operations. After failed efforts to compensate for Errol Thompson's departure with engineers like Karl Pitterson and Pat Kelly, the studio's door remained closed. Randy's had left the game, and the precious equipment was never used again. Organ, grand piano, mixing console, tape machines, everything that was too heavy to be carried out was left behind, slowly to decay. Those devices are still there, some of them in a dilapidated condition with the hourly prices from 1974 still attached to one of them:

- 2-track recording 30 $ / 2-track mixing 25 $
- 4-track recording 35 $ / 4-track mixing 30 $
- 8-track recording 48 $ / 8-track mixing 40 $

For decades, Randy's remained a dump, a grotesque storage room full of rotting electronic equipment. It was guarded by a friendly factotum[2] who granted entry for a bottle of Red Stripe, while veterans reminisced in the anteroom. The studio was cleaned up in the mid-2010s. Plasterboard walls were installed where Jamaican music history had been written. Afterwards, Randy's was an unfinished construction site, an electronics graveyard put neatly in order, and its old price tag continued to decline.

Blaming the closure on the political conditions under the left-wing government and the brutal 1976 election campaign is only half of the story. In fact, following the re-election of Michael Manley's PNP, Vincent and Patricia Chin had already emigrated to New York as part of the wave of exodus of Jamaica's economic elite. In addition, there was no answer to Errol Thompson's departure, and Randy's was overtaken by Joe Gibbs on the left and Channel One on the right. Suddenly Randy's studio was obsolete.

For Clive Chin, the development was a catastrophe, and caught him completely off guard. Suddenly unemployed, the successful, full-time producer and father of a two-year old son, with his own apartment and

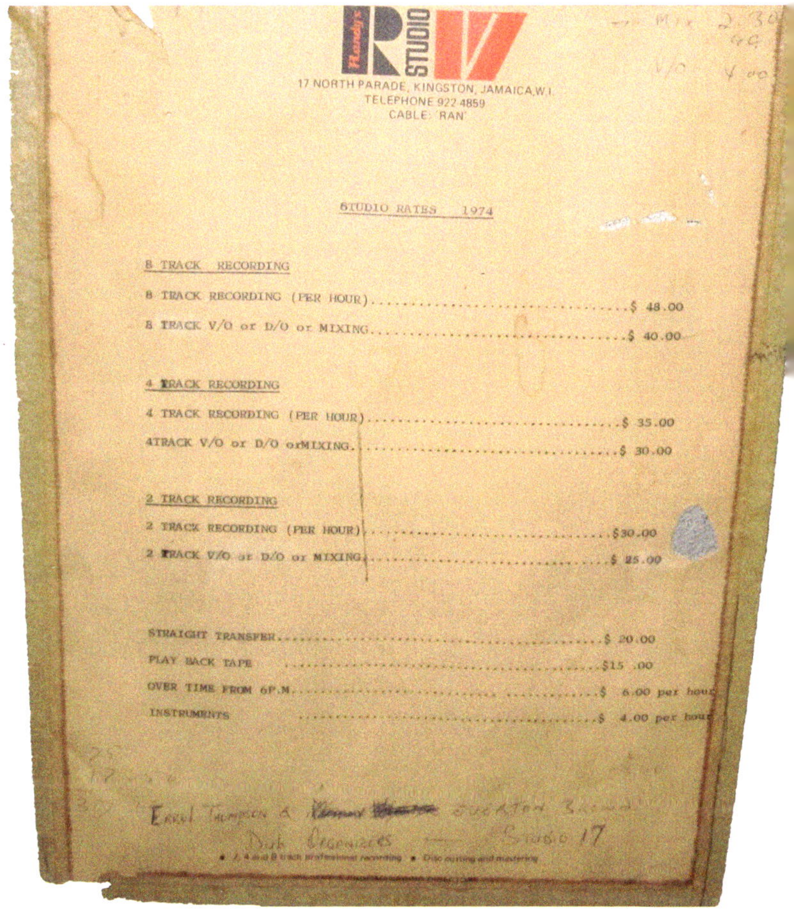
Randy's Studio
17 NORTH PARADE, KINGSTON, JAMAICA, W.I.
TELEPHONE 922 4859
CABLE: 'RAN'

STUDIO RATES 1974

8 TRACK RECORDING
8 TRACK RECORDING (PER HOUR) .... $ 48.00
8 TRACK V/O or D/O or MIXING .... $ 40.00

4 TRACK RECORDING
4 TRACK RECORDING (PER HOUR) .... $ 35.00
4TRACK V/O or D/O orMIXING. .... $ 30.00

2 TRACK RECORDING
2 TRACK RECORDING (PER HOUR) $30.00
2 TRACK V/O or D/O or MIXING .... $ 25.00

STRAIGHT TRANSFER .... $ 20.00
PLAY BACK TAPE .... $15 .00
OVER TIME FROM 6P.M .... $ 6.00 per hour
INSTRUMENTS .... $ 4.00 per hour

Randy's Studio 2012: pricelist from 1974.

new car, was left traumatized. "A lot of the business people decided to leave the island. I was totally distraught about the whole idea. It wasn't a good time for me",[3] Clive recalls with unmistakable bitterness. From now on, this was the motto of his life: "I was on the cutting edge of production when my father decided to close the studio." Clive Chin fell into a deep pit of depression, lost a great deal of weight and became skel-

1 Bassline Of A City, Museum of London 2020.
2 Carl Lauder, brother of Clive's mother.
3 In an unpublished interview by Adrian Nowak on April 8, 2013 in Cologne

eton-like or a "bony man" as he put it himself[4], and found that there was no work for him at the other studios in Kingston. So, he followed his father and stepmother to New York City. They had opened a record shop in Jamaica, Queens in 1979. It soon became apparent that "VP Records", named after their initials, would become the cornerstone for what is the world's largest label and distribution network for reggae today. Clive Chin copied the idea behind the name and opened the "J & C Kitchen" restaurant on Jamaica Avenue with wife Juliet. The various Caribbean specialties were highly popular but required an enormous effort of time and commitment. After eight years, both restaurant and marriage were over. Clive started at VP Records but missed Randy's original spirit. He didn't feel comfortable, left the company and started to go through unreleased master tapes from the days at "his" former studio in Kingston. Since then, he has presented his discoveries around the world alongside oldies, goodies, and anecdotes from the good old days as a selector. Clive Chin is great to dive into memories with, even if some of them are not free of tragedy or contradict the views expressed in other interviews. The conversation documented here took place in 2011 at the Belgian Reggae Geel festival.

Clive Chin: Stepping back in time, we're talking 'bout 69/70. We had built our studio above our record shop Randy's and bought a 4-track Ampex tape machine. All our outboard equipment was being brought in from the United States. The person who hooked that up was a man by the name of Bill Garnett. My father had commissioned him to put together all that stuff. Bill Garnett came from West Indies (WIRL) before Byron Lee bought the company. He was our technical engineer at the time. When he moved to the United States, Errol (Thompson) stepped in as a young engineer.

Errol and you knew each other from the Choir High School in Kingston.

We went to school together. He got a job working at an electronics company and from there he developed the skills as an engineer at Studio One under the leadership of Sylvan Morris. When he came for the opening of Randy's I told my dad he's the perfect person to employ.[5] So that's where the relationship between me and Errol developed. I started as an apprentice under Errol by hooking up the mics, number the jacks, tell him which jack was going into the bass...

How did you record the bass?

We used to do it two ways, middle and bottom. We took a straight line out from the Ampeg amplifier and mic the speaker box of the amplifier. We would take the drum and the bass and tie that on one track, sometime we tie the lead guitar with the bass to get that pluckin' sound. The riddim piano we tied it with the riddim guitar on a second track. The percussion instruments we would always tie in with the riddim.

What mixing board did you use for the recording?

Talking about "Java" that was all outboard equipment. About '72 went into '73 my dad bought the Sound Techniques board. It was the same board that was at Dynamics. When Dynamics was changing that board, Joe Gibbs bought it, cause Errol told him he knew everything about that board.

That means *Java Java Java Java* was mixed without a console or faders?

Yes, *Java Java Java Java* was produced by 8 in and 4 out, and it was all outboard equipment. There weren't faders, there were (rotary) knobs. We had to turn these knobs. The preamps primarily were Ampeg, the equalizer was a Soundcraft, the limiter a Pultec. We had to limit the snare and the bass drum. Very raw technique. The sound was dirty, not too clean like Federal, but that's why a lot of the producers would like the sound.

How were you able to dub with such minimal equipment?

When myself and Errol decided to do dub mixes it wasn't an intentional thing; we thought it would be sellable. It would be just finding different techniques [for dubplates]. Different elements to add to it, you know. The sound systems were looking for different mixes of the tunes. We had guys like "Emperor Faith" that will come up and say: I want this version to sound different. We never had the ability of [sampled] sound effects to play into the music,

4 ibid.

5 In the liner notes for *Impact All Stars – Forward The Bass. Dub From Randy's 1972–1975* (Blood & Fire 1998) Clive is quoted "It wasn't me who recommended Errol to my father, it was a guy name Gordon who use to tune our organ."

Dennis Thompson (left), Errol Thompson (on phone), Clive Chin and Augustus Pablo (right).

so we'd create our own. Sometime we crash bokkles (bottles) in the studio. One area in the studio would have nothing but broken bokkles. Next thing we take an RCA boom mic, the mic for the bass drum, into the toilet and flash to get that "ssssshhhh" sound.

Errol later became famous for such acoustic gimmicks at Joe Gibbs.

Errol was behind all that dub sound. Even while he was working at Randy's he would work nights for Joe Gibbs. The truth came out after Gibbo wanted to join the ranks of dub.

There are many striking parallels in dub effects from Joe Gibbs' and Randy's studio. Only that strange feedback effect of Pablo's version of Alton Ellis' "Too Late To Turn Back" cannot be found again. Although it seems like Errol tried several times to copy it on the version of Nicky Thomas' "God Bless the Children" on *Serial Dub*.

No, I made a mistake by doing that, and it pissed off Errol. He was doing the final mix of the track on the "Too Late" riddim. I just bun a nice cotton spliff, bow over the board to inject supm (something) and [accidentally] push up the fader: "dddiiiiiiiiirrr-rrrrrrrr!!!". Everybody look round pon me: Ey, you jus' f*** up the mix. And I? Kiss teeth! Cho! Special

And then you decided to keep the mishap as a gimmick?

(Laughs) Every spoil is a style, you know.

Your first dubs didn't have any echoes. They rather worked by the changes of the frequencies, were focused on drum and bass and the fading in and out of certain parts.

Yeah, the delay came a bit later. And again, the reason for that is the sound systems were looking for different mixes of the tunes. Sometimes while the tape would be playing Errol would turn it back and forth to get that "chrchrchrchrchr" (rewind sound) that

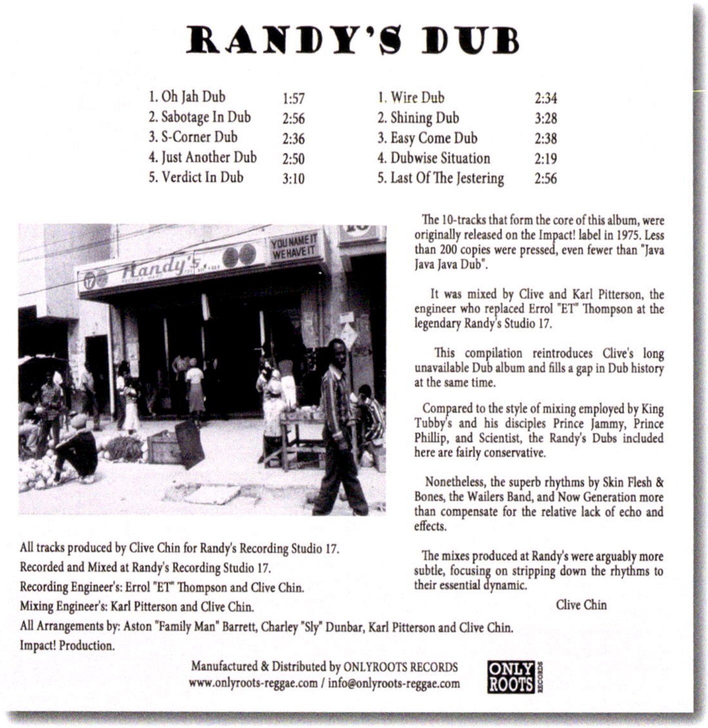

went through songs like "Westbound Train" or "Cassandra". It's just what people hear in their head; they would ask for that kind of sound. And as I said, it was all fun. Nothing was done like writing music scores for an instrumental symphony. Everything was done just messing around with the board. We wind the tapes forward, slow it down, add likkle things… Ey, I used to play maracas or shaker. When you shake it and you add delay to it, it has such an incredible sound. You must remember, the independent producers when they would come, Clancy Eccles, Niney or Scratch or Striker, they would watch the clock. We don't watch clock. We had time unlimited.

Because it was your own studio, time wasn't money for you.

Exact, we didn't have to pay. We just turn the machines down, leave the tape as where it is, go have lunch. We come back, belly full, and start again. And we wouldn't scrap a mix. Some people would say: oh no, that one wasn't so, let's do it over again. We take it, we keep it. Cause you never know if you'll ever get that sound again. We had one reel of tape with nothing but "Java" mix. Opposed to one man would say: Bwoy there's too much mix of this, let's do something different.

And did you use this reservoir for Java Java Java Java, or did you mix extra tunes for the album?

No, no. Most was done for the purpose of a B-side of a vocal song. Some of them again was more experimenting with the ordinary version. Some of our 7-inch singles come out with different versions; we did not call it "reissue" at that time. We just call it "Version 1", "Version 2", "Version 3…"

So, you had enough material in stock. Why did you decide to put together an entire album of versions or dubs?

The "Java" 7-inch sold an extra-astronomical amount, we had three pairs of stampers running. Dynamic, Federal and Record Specialist. Then it was [voted] "Instrumental Record Of The Year" and my stepmother Pat commissioned the album.

How many copies did you press for the first edition?

200. The reason is it was a new item. Everything was experimental. The cover was designed by a company that did the painting. We paid for this cover; we bought this artwork. Not like "Randy's Dub" which came after and was mixed between myself and Karl Pitterson. It didn't come out with any cover; it was done in a disco sleeve that had a hole where you see [the label].[6] *Java Java Java Java* was a testing format. You move from one stage of the business into another stage. We had no clue how far this would go.

This new product, who was it intended for?

A few went overseas, mostly into England. Nothing into America. It went primarily between sound system owners. Because we just introduced the intro of the song, like we used the first few bars of Dennis Brown's "Cheater" or Heptones' "Guiding Star" or "Meet Me At The Corner" and then we go straight into the drum and bass. So, the deejays could step in and voice over the drum and bass track.

How did you create the audio play for the version of Lloyd Parks' "Ordinary Man"?

Errol was very innovated. He would play part of the "Ordinary Version" and would talk like he's a musician wanting a job. Bingy Bunny[7] take on the role of the engineer and says: can you play bass? Errol with his baby voice answers: yeah, I can play bass but played the guitar, and Bingy: leave the studio, man! (Clive is still laughing as he tells the story.) That was something just spontaneous, nothing sit down and write up. Anything that came to our mind...

Why did you change up the song titles and the track order for the second edition of *Java Java Java Java*?

(Clive doesn't seem to remember and says:) We should have kept the original titles ...

And you added a sticker to the cover stating: "Instrumentals DUBWISE Versions".

It had to identify what *Java Java Java Java* was. Because there was really no story behind it. Our advantage was that we not just had the studio and the cutting and mastering facilities, we [also] had the distribution in our shop. That's how we could be able to do numbers, you know. Sometimes certain records come out, we press a thousand and in two seconds the thousand is gone. Once you have something out on the market that is moving and selling, other people will follow quick. They don't wait. Because you have to jump on it while the momentum is hot. You must be aware we're all into the competition.

Joe Gibbs released *Dub Serial* in that same year, also mixed by Errol.

Hmmm, could be possible. I would say: probably the same year. I know that album you're talking. It was an underground dub album.

What do you answer to those who say Tubby invented dub? And how do you view all the others who worked for him or at Channel One? Philip Smart, Scientist, Jammy's, Professor, Barnabas, Soljie...

Well, Tubby actually revolutionised it, but the whole idea of dub was between myself and Errol. Then you had guys like Lee Perry, Herman Chin-Loy, they came after. I mean, 'nuff respect to Scientist and all a dem, but dem guys to me are students under the time we were doing it.

Why did Errol move on to Joe Gibbs despite your successful collaboration?

The combination between myself and Errol was very dynamic. I am really proud that I had that opportunity to be involved at a young age, because the fresher you are the fresher are your ideas. You have to have the energy, that is one. And then you have to make it exciting, bring in fresh ideas, not the old school. The love was there, don't get me wrong. But the influential part of [Gibbo's] saying: I will not only give you a little bit more of your salary but I am going to make you a partner. That made it more interesting for him to move on.

6 *Randy's Dub* appeared in 1975 on IMPACT! with less than 200 copies und was reissued in 1998 by Blood & Fire under the title *Impact All Stars – Forward The Bass. Dub From Randy's 1972–1975*. An original copy was sold for $2,800 on Discogs in 2021. In 2015, *Randy's Dub* was released in France on Only Roots Records, with a cover showing Clive Chin at the mixing desk.

7 Eric 'Bingy Bunny' Lamont (1955–1993) was a guitarist and played with The Morwells and Roots Radics.

Were you angry when you found out that he had been secretly working for Joe Gibbs for a long while?

Yeah, yeah. (bitterly disappointed) Yeah, I found it out… Errol would work late hours, not only work five days a week but seven days. The majority of work came down on him, and then he would complain that he's not getting enough rest. We had to take a little bit of strain off him. So, I would work on the weekends and he would work the five days. I would primarily do the family's productions and he would do the engineering for the independent people. Because they feel more confident in having Errol opposed to having me.

Errol eventually left during an ongoing production…

Errol left when we were right in the middle of doing the "Marcus Garvey" album[8] for Jack Ruby. I was pissed off (kiss teeth). But anyway George Philpott[9] came in and he more or less finished the album. All the basic elements on the tracks were recorded here [at Randy's]. Then after it was voiced, it went up to Joe Gibbs and Errol mixed it up there.[10] After that short stay with Philpott, I found that Karl Pitterson would be available. He came on board after working with Bunny Wailer on the *Blackheart Man* album (with Chris Blackwell at Aquarius). But again, Karl [was] short lived, he got hired by Chris Blackwell to come to Nassau, Compass Point. Then Pat Kelly stepped in for a few months. [But

8 *Burning Spear* – Marcus Garvey, Island Records 1975.

9 George Philpott was born George Phillips in Kingston in 1942. Ken Lack, owner of the Caltone label, renamed him Phil Pratt for some unknown reason. Under this name he started as a producer, founded various labels and released several dub albums. Including *Dub In Blood* on Sun Shot 1976 (identical with *The Best Dub Album In The World* 1976 on Student and not to be mixed up with Scientist's album by the same name from 1980), *The War Is In On Dub Style* on Phil Pratt 198X, *Star Wars Dub* 1978 on Burning Sound and *Dial M For Murder In Dub Style* 1980 on Express. Although he filled in as an engineer at Randy's, Pratt never mixed his dub LPs himself.

10 The dub version *Garvey's Ghost*, Island Records 1976, was mixed in London.

now] Channel One was heavily booked, Joe Gibbs as well. That's where the vacuum came to us...

... and Randy's closed in 1978...

(with great regret) Yeah. It's a shame. But you have to look at it that everybody had a little part to play. Federal already had faded out when Randy's would take that significant role in the 70s. That was the best time [for reggae music]. I like some of the 80s, but the 90s, cho! (derogatory)...

A new generation of producers came along.

Some of them I would not even call them producers, cause a lot of them didn't have the skills of a producer. They had the finance, you know. They pay for studio time and would come to listen to the last bit of it. To me a producer has to be there from the start to the finish. For me Perry was the classical guy. He was very innovated, know what he wanted and got what he wanted. His stuff is timeless, too. Look on the equipment he got, sort of toy machines, but at the time it was very creative. The music today is more like a blueprint. There's no more creativity there's more programmetivity.

Very nice neologism. This "programmetivity" neglects an important element of the music, the sound of the room in which it is recorded. Randy's also had an unmistakable dry, wooden sound. Machines and computers don't take into consideration the reflections of the walls that make the sound of a studio unique and unmistakable.

This is a major point you just brought up.

What was it like, when Lee Perry produced at Randy's, who was at the mixing desk? (I asked Clive that same question in different contexts at each meeting. The answer was always the same.)

Errol. Perry's creativity comes by the way he performs. He was a character, you know. He come in with little flask of white rum, sprinkling the rum in the four corners of the studio, drink the rest of it and then start dance and parade around. [Other] people always saying "blessings", wanting to make sure to come out with a hit. Perry flash a likkle white rum.

Super Power Sound System, Germany.

KING TUBBYS PRESENTS
SOUNDCLASH
DUBPLATE STYLE
dis ya wan ya a go straight to a Di-Bi... Di-Bi Sound BWOY HEAD!

Dub Basket Chapter II
Rupie Edwards All Stars
A KING TUBBY'S MIX

CHANT DOWN BABYLON KINGDOM: YABBA YOUTH

BEWARE

King Tubby: Genius and Myth

"We never really get famous until around May, 1968. "

(King Tubby[1])

It is often claimed that King Tubby invented dub, supposedly by chance when he accidentally forgot to turn on the vocal track while cutting a dubplate. Actually, that was the story of Ruddy Redwood at Treasure Isle studio, the true facts of which have long since been clarified. Yet this fairy tale has persisted, rolling like a snowball through dub mythology. Not just Clive Chin has had to fight an almost hopeless battle against this false historical preconception. What is the case is that the man they called the "King" did not actually invent dub but made it spectacular. Much of what made him a legend, however, was not the work of the man himself but of his studio. Its centerpiece was a mixing console that could do something no other console could. The man behind it was an electronics specialist, a certified jazz lover who enjoyed making music sound different from anything people were used to at the time. And he was encouraged to do so by a producer who liked to eat chicken wings.

Osbourne Ruddock was born in Kingston on January 28, 1941. One of eight children, the family lived downtown, on High Holborn Street, near the harbour. Early on, he was given the name "Tubby", supposedly by a nanny. The nickname was based on his mother's maiden name, which was supposedly "Tubman", but we have no confirmation of this. In the early 1950s, the family moved to 18 Dromilly Avenue in Waterhouse, which is where the boy's interest in technology started to grow. After school, he attended the National Technical College in Kingston, and at the same time, built a small shack in the yard of the house where he fixed radios. He also collected electronic waste and built amplifiers. His repair service was in such demand that he had to hire an employee, who was Barry Williams. Barry had built the powerful Hercules units belonging to the "King Edward's Giant Sound" system, and he had the reputation of being a magician. From him, Tubby learned the secrets of amplifier construction.

In 1957, Tubby first appeared with his own speaker system when he played jazz and rhythm & blues at birthday parties and weddings in his local community. Even though this was still far from a proper sound system, he consolidated his reputation as a music connoisseur and electronics specialist. His self-built amplifiers and loudspeakers grew over time, and from 1964 he called his set-up "King Tubby's Hometown Hi Fi". It was supposed to be just a bit of fun for Waterhouse and the surrounding areas, but suddenly he was being proclaimed king of the local dances; this started at a party on Antigua Road. In one of his rare interviews[2] in 1975, as Tubby explained to Carl Gayle, of the British magazine *Black Music*: "Most people that build amplifiers, them try to copy the foreign principle. They can't get the sound I get. I make my own transformer and all the necessary little things for it. They have to buy a standardized transformer. I get special components which they can't get on the market out here to buy."[3]

A little bit of show, bling bling and secrecy were definitely among the "necessary little things" for Tubby. The cases for his amplifiers were chrome-plated, the speaker system decorated with colourful, rhythmically glowing lamps, and his funnel-shaped speakers were hung in the trees to project the sound for miles. When the island fell into a collective dancehall frenzy at the end of the 1960s, thanks to the new style of deejay U-Roy's toasting, Tubby wooed him away from "Sir George the Atomic" three miles down the road on Penn Street in Jones Town in 1968.[4] With him on the mic he presented his latest gimmick, live echo! "You're listening to King Tubby's Hi Fi" U-Roy announced and the last word seemed to repeat forever "Hi Fi... Hi Fi... Hi Fi... Hi Fi..." It sounded like magic, no one ever heard the like before. The audience went crazy and carried the King on their shoulders through the dance. It was a celebration because no one understood how he had done it. In fact, it was pretty simple. Tubby had modified a cassette recorder and hid it in an amplifier case. When the sound men lined up the next morning to order

1 In: "Marcus Garvey Meets The Rockers Uptown" *Black Music* February 1976 p. 34.

2 Only two written interviews are known from King Tubby, both of which were published in the UK. The first appeared in the February 1976 article "Marcus Garvey Meets The Rockers Uptown" in *Black Music* magazine and was written by Jamaican-born Carl Gayle. A second one was published in the summer of 1977 by Dave Hendley in *Blues and Soul* magazine.

3 "Marcus Garvey Meets The Rockers Uptown" ibid p. 34.

4 U-Roy also confirmed this when he said that he had already switched to "Sir George The Atomic" when Tubby approached him personally and poached him. See "U-Roy. Godfather Of The Deejay School" in German Reggae print magazine *RIDDIM* 01/2013.

such an amplifier, he refused to give them the echo and didn't tell them how it worked for a long time.

The performance of his sound carried Tubby's reputation across the island, and increased his clientele. In the mid-1960s, he took over the maintenance of Duke Reid's Treasure Isle studio equipment, including the dubplate cutting machine. When he told Carl Gayle about it, rumour has it that he also operated the machine. "No, no, no!" Jammy replied when asked, "Tubbys used to work for Duke Reid, built amplifiers for him, but he didn't work at Treasure Isle." However, he did cooperate with Reid. Not only did he order dubplates from him for his sound, which is why he was there when Ruddy Redwood had the mishap with the vocal track, but he also borrowed equipment from Reid for his own dub cutting studio. Towards the end of the 1960s, he put it into operation in his apartment on Dromilly Avenue, modestly equipped with a Presto disc cutter, a 2-track tape recorder and a self-built mini mixer. Bunny Lee, Lee Scratch Perry and Augustus Pablo were among the first to frequent his establishment; Tubby operated a downtown-friendly pricing policy. However, his "music room", as he called it, was not a recording studio, but simply an editing room for dubplates. Bunny Lee urged Tubby to turn it into a "real" studio that could be used to mix music, or at least record vocals. He convinced him to buy a 4-track tape machine that had been discarded from Dynamic, with the matching MCI console. Dynamic had expanded its capacities and wanted to get rid of the old technology, and so in 1972 Tubby came into possession of the very equipment with which the engineer Linford Anderson had set the dub train in motion two years earlier with the single "Phantom".[5]

Tubby designed the wiring of his new console so that its outputs could be connected either to a 2-track master tape or to the acetate cutting machine. This made him the only person on the island[6] at this point in time who could cut a mix directly onto a dubplate without having to create a master first.

The mixer that was now at his disposal was high standard for its time, and came from Music Centers Incorporated, a US company. It was designed by the American Groover C. "Jeep" Harned (1930–2003), who sold the company to Sony in 1982. One year before his death, Harned was honored with the title "Hero of Florida" by the National American Recording Academy (NARAS for short, responsible for awarding the Grammys) for

5 See chapter "Overture of a New Genre".
6 Channel One took over this type of wiring later and also connected the mixer directly to the dub cutting machine.

his contributions to the standardization of studio technology. Byron Lee, for whom only the best was good enough, had taken over the console from a studio in Miami. Besides an integrated remote control for the tape machine, it featured twelve input channels that could be linked to four outputs. Each individual channel strip was equipped with a triple sound control for treble, mid and bass frequencies, as well as a rotary knob to add reverb. The channels did not have a mute switch. To take a signal out of the mix with the MCI, the fader had to be pulled down entirely.[7] King Jammy said that he and Tubby later swapped the controls for smoother, faster-moving faders.[8] The specialty about the mixer was the big knob at the top right. Hard to identify on black and white photos, but clearly visible on the cover of the *Big Joe – At The Control* LP[9] is a red button that would allow Tubby's studio to control the dub landscape

7 The lack of a mute switch led to a technique that became the standard and has most engineers still use fader movements instead of the mute switch when dubbing.
8 Liner notes *King Tubby & Prince Jammy – Dub Gone 2 Crazy: In Fine Style 1975–1979*, Blood & Fire 1996.
9 Live And Love UK 1978

for the next few years. It was a high pass filter[10] that could be adjusted to ten levels, and could be selected from each individual channel, enabling sound effects that no other console could copy. The filter was an optional extra from the manufacturer, and was not installed by Tubby, as has sometimes been suggested,[11] a fact that photos from the pre-sale Dynamic studio prove.

It took some time until Tubby was ready to use the red knob in the mix. As a perfectionist, he initially perceived the resulting effect as a technical error. For the first time, albeit extremely subtly, the filter was used on Tommy McCook's "The Mighty Gates Of Goza"[12], an instrumental version of Slim Smith's "Everybody Needs Love". Bunny Lee said he had persuaded Tubby to do it because as a producer he was always looking for innovations and he had heard something similar from Randy's studio on the dub version "Different Fashion" of Delroy Wilson's "Have Some Mercy"[13]. For similar reasons that same year, Lee instructed Soul Syndicate drummer Carlton "Santa" Davis to play the beat more "spacey" during a recording session at Duke Reid. Lee had heard something by Sly Dunbar when the drummer had tried to imitate the current Philly sound from America in the Channel One studio for Delroy Wilson's "It's A Shame" by opening the top and bottom cymbal of the hi-hat with every accent of the offbeat. The resulting rhythmic hissing was innovative, and made the beat seem to fly forward. This was the effect Lee had had in mind; he secretly called it "flyers", which, as he admitted, was a term a bit outside the box. "It's not the right name, really."[14] As Bunny Lee used to stuff himself with tons of chicken wings during his studio sessions, the musicians joked: "Striker, when you a go fly?"[15] When Santa Davis followed Lee's request and played the "flyers" for him, the term "flying cymbals" was born.

The first song Lee produced using this technique was Earl Zero's "None Shall Escape The Judgement", and once again, the carelessness of a Treasure Isle engineer created history. When the music was bounced from eight to four tracks so that it could be mixed at King Tubby's, Sid

10 The MCI console had selectable levels at 70, 100, 150, 250, 500, 1000, 2000, 3000, 5000 and 7500 Hertz.

11 As e.g., Paul Sullivan in: *Remixology. Tracing The Dub Diaspora* London 2014 p. 31 + 46.

12 On the LP *Bunny Lee & King Tubby Present Tommy McCook And The Aggravators [sic] – Brass Rockers*, released in 1975 in Jamaica on Total Sounds and Striker Lee as well as in the UK by the name Cookin' on Horse, a sub label of Trojan.

13 Released in Jamaica in 1973 on Dee Jay, in England in 1974 on Cactus.

14 *Reggae Going International 1967–1976. The Bunny ‚Striker' Lee Story* London 2012 p. 125.

15 ibid + p. 179 et seq.

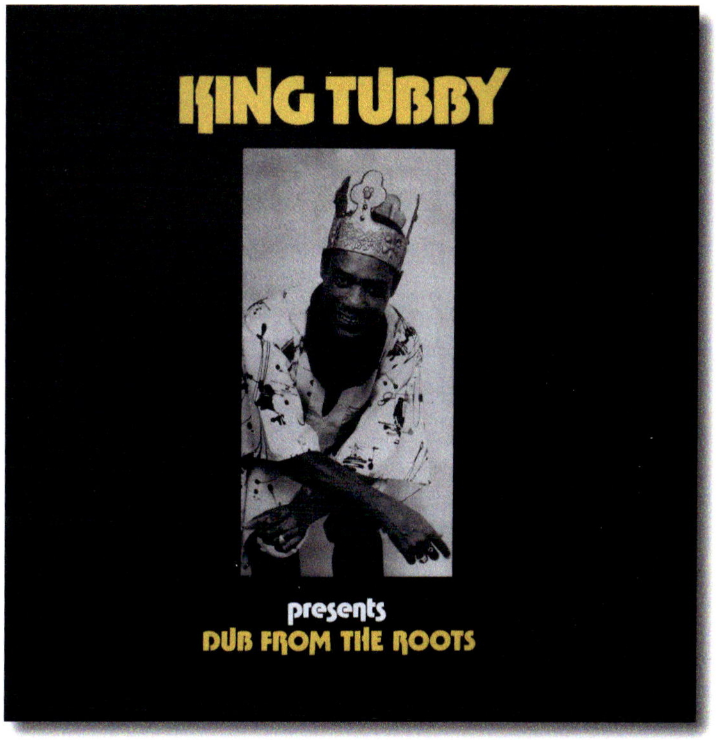

Bucknor, the engineer, forgot the vocals, something that was only noticed at Tubby's studio. Johnny Clarke, who happened to be there, said he could sing the song, too, and with just one take the recording was a wrap. As usual, dubplates were created subsequently, with Tubby using the high pass filter on the flying cymbals, adding a new effect to the new beat.[16] The dancehall audiences in Jamaica, the UK and the States were blown away when this yet unheard sound was presented to them at the appropriate volume. The course was set for success for the next two years; Johnny Clarke had his first mega hit, Striker Lee had a new beat, and King Tubby had an exclusive dub sound that was made possible only in his studio. At Dynamic they cursed the day they had given away the MCI desk!

After dub had opened up a new market for LPs in 1973, Bunny Lee also ordered an album from Tubby calling it *King Tubby The Dub Master*

16 When "None Shall Escape The Judgement" was mixed for the single release in 1974, Bunny Lee had Philip Smart mix the dub for the B-side, which upset Tubby greatly. See *Reggae Going International 1967–1976. The Bunny ‚Striker' Lee Story* ibid p. 181.

Presents Dub From The Roots. He ran his latest flying cymbal playbacks through the red button on the MCI console, since he had recognized that the most effective sound variations were achieved using treble sounds such as drum cymbals or horns. The LP was released in 1974 and showed Tubby wearing a cardboard crown, an image he would never be able to shake off. A year later, a second LP followed, identical in concept except for one word in the title, showing the King with his crown on the mixing desk called *King Tubby The Dub Master Presents The Roots Of Dub*. Both were released on Total Sound, Lee's internationally distributed label, and the latter also on Grounation, the UK label distributed by Phonogram, along with the following: "Produced and manufactured in the original mono sound. In accordance with the wishes of King Tubby and his producer Bunny Lee." The LPs were sold primarily via the UK. Dub was well on its way to establishing itself in Europe.

The final decisive push came from a Jamaican immigrant. Winston Edwards, born in Buff Bay in 1953, was friends with Lee Perry and entered the record business at the end of the 1960s, initiated by Joe Gibbs. In 1974 he moved to London, founded the Fay Music label and responded to the dub signals from the city's underground with the LP *Natty Locks Dub*. The recordings and mixes came from the studios of Joe Gibbs, Lee Perry and King Tubby, and were spiced up with brass overdubs in London's Berry Street studios. The album achieved moderate success. Edwards explained why it initially attracted only little attention by saying that "there was a lack of promotion. Black people would buy dub but the white folks didn't understand dub music because nobody was prepared to promote a dub album."[17] At this point, Jamaican music, with its semi-official pre-release imports, didn't play a role in the regular London record shops, while in the reggae stores horrendous sums were charged for dub LPs. *Natty Locks Dub* was the wrong LP at the wrong time. However, thanks to articles by Carl Gayle in *Black Music* magazine, and initial references in *Blues and Soul* and *Melody Maker*, the interest in the new sounds from Kingston gradually grew.

17 Quoted from the liner notes of the 4 CD Box *Evolution Of Dub Volume 7*, VP Records 2012

In 1975, Edwards opened the Fay Music Record Shop in south-east London and, supported by Carl Gayle, used flyers, ads and posters to announce *King Tubby Meets The Upsetter At the Grass Roots of Dub*, an album that would be a breakthrough, released in 1974. This pushed the boundaries of a previously limited market. Through clever distribution and promotion, it was available everywhere, and became the best-selling reggae album of the year. Edwards had produced it, personally supervised the recordings, claiming that King Tubby and Lee Perry each mixed one side of the LP. Later he had to admit that it could have been different.[18] The tracks were indeed created at Joe Gibbs' and Lee Perry's, but were not dubs of existing songs, being primarily instrumental tracks, with Vin Gordon's trombone as lead instrument. The final mixes, whoever they came from, certainly had a dubby feel, but could hardly have been mixed on the consoles that the back cover said were in King Tubby

18 Ibid.

and Lee Perry's studios, also because King Tubby definitely had a different desk.

Regardless of these contradictions, the success of *King Tubby Meets The Upsetter At the Grass Roots of Dub* irrevocably established the mixing console as an instrument, and dub as an innovative art form outside Jamaica. When Island Records made the dub mix "King Tubby Meets Rockers Uptown" the A-side of a single in England in 1975, relegating Jacob Miller's vocal version "Baby I Love You So"[19] to the B-side, the King with the cardboard crown became the main protagonist of the new genre. He was the first pop star who neither sang, nor danced or played an instrument, but used knobs, faders, and equalizers instead.

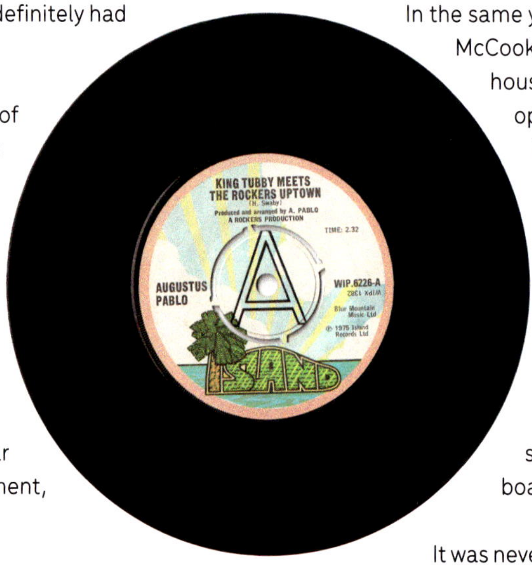

In the same year, Bunny Lee had Skatalites co-founder Tommy McCook (1927–1998), then bandleader of Treasure Isle in-house band Supersonics, improvise with his tenor saxophone on a selection of flying cymbal playbacks at Tubby's studio. The result was entitled *Bunny Lee & King Tubby present Tommy McCook and The Aggrovators – Brass Rockers* and released in 1975 on Total Sounds and Striker Lee. This was the first project to combine the technical deformations of dub with musical overdubs, the perfect playground for Tubby's passion for jazz. His mixes fused the improvisational freedom of the instrumentalist with the creative freedom of the sound engineer. Tubby improvised on the mixing board, and used it like a musical instrument virtuoso.

It was nevertheless noticeable that his interest in studio work was waning. The British magazine *Blues and Soul* diagnosed him

19 Both tracks were versions of Augustus Pablo's instrumental "Cassava Piece".

with an increasing lack of quality and a certain "fatigue"[20] creeping in over the course of 1975. When in Jamaica similar views were aired because he no longer played his sound as a regular, Tubby reacted with demonstrative power. On September 26, 1975, he performed at the National Arena in Kingston and, after the supporting program with the Wailers and other bands, played right around the clock, twelve hours non-stop, from six in the evening until six the next morning. Some of the dubs recorded especially for this night appeared shortly after on the album *King Tubby Surrounded By The Dreads At The National Arena*, first released in 1976 in England on Winston Edwards' Fay Music label. The LP was repeatedly reissued with changing artwork, including a version in white-coloured vinyl on the Belgian EMI Bestseller label. The very first issue had no cover, only an information sheet with liner notes, reprinted on the back covers of subsequent issues. There Carl Gayle wrote: "The Dreads hail the King. He continues to be the King of the Dub Rock, at his Musical Chamber".

However, even this sensational action could not hide the fact that Tubby's main interest lay in a completely different area. He was not a passionate sound engineer, but rather a passionate electronics specialist. He had been persuaded to work in the studio by Bunny Lee, who saw him as an affordable sound genius. Tubby, however, with the soldering iron in his hand, wanted to repair, improve and develop electronic devices. He was far more interested in the construction of a new mixing board than operating it. When the like-minded Scientist worked for him, the two spent every minute discussing the advantages of fader automation, long before it was actually technically available. Ultimately, it was only logical that Tubby was to increasingly withdraw from active studio work. He left the day-to-day business to an army of students and employees, and only sat down at the desk for selected customers like Mikey Dread or Yabby You. For the latter, Tubby made a rare exception in 1976 and, assisted by Pat Kelly, mixed his LP *Prophets – Walls Of Jerusalem*[21] half vocal, half dub, in stereo. In its early days, dub did not have a wide form of expression divided into left and right, as the music of the sound systems was traditionally mono. For the same reason, *Upsetters 14 Dub Blackboard Jungle,* mixed by Tubby for Lee Perry, was pressed in stereo only on the first issue; all later ones were mono, e.g., *Blackboard Jungle Dub*.

According to Bunny Lee, *The Roots Of Dub*, *Dub From The Roots* and *Brass Rockers* remained the only dub albums designed by Tubby as long players: "All of those Tubbys albums that you see out on the street, most of them are frauds, as it was only three albums that Tubby did."[22] The ultra-rare *E-E Saw Dub* mixed by Tubby, identical to the equally rare *ABC Dub* and *King Tubby Meets Jacob Miller In A Tenement Yard,* released by Motion in 2006, played no role in this context. Irrespective of the title, it was simply an experimental project by Touter Harvey, the keyboard player of the Fat Man Riddim Section, who never intended it for official release, but was merely exploring the capabilities of a new synthesizer. All other LPs bearing the name "King Tubby" were either compilations of B-sides he had mixed, or they were works from his studio, yet not with Tubby himself on the mixing board. To date, well over 100 dub albums have been released under the often abused "Tubby" trademark. So "mixed at King Tubby's" does not automatically mean "mixed by King Tubby", or in other words, not everything labeled King Tubby contains the real King Tubby.

Tubby's disinterest in the assembly-line studio processes of voicing, mixing and dubplates intensified when he too became a victim of the violent unrest that Jamaica had been suffering from since the 1972 election. The left-wing PNP under Michael Manley had replaced Hugh Shearer's conservative JLP, and both parties maintained combat troops that they had recruited and supplied with weapons – so-called "vote-getters" – but whose control had long since slipped away from them. These gangs had become a plague, dividing the city and country into districts and terrorizing political opponents. The PNP's most feared allegiance in the capital was the Spanglers Posse, while the JLP's was initially called the Tivoli Gang and, from 1980, the Shower Posse. In 1975, Jamaica was feeling the pangs of another bloody election campaign, and moved towards a state of emergency. The American CIA and the Cuban Secret Service were also involved in the deadly roulette of political interests. In the wake of this atmosphere, the local police destroyed Tubby's sound system at a dance in St Thomas, claiming "King Tubby's Hometown Hi Fi" was a badman sound from the Kingston ghetto. Although Tubby was considered one of the most approachable and friendly people in the mu-

20 Quoted from "King Tubby – Mister Dub" by Dave Hendley in *Natty Dread* No. 19, France 2003.

21 Released first without cover in 1976 in a small edition on Prophets. A year later it appeared in the UK with an apocalyptic cover design and partly different song titles as "Yabba Youth" on Nationwide entitled *Chant Down Babylon Kingdom*. Yabby You later re-pressed it on his blue Prophet label and called it *King Tubby Meet Vivian Jackson (Yabby You)*. In 2013, Pressure Sounds reissued the LP with bonus tracks as *Walls Of Jerusalem*.

22 *Reggae Going International 1967–1976. The Bunny ‚Striker' Lee Story* ibid p. 134 as well as in a conversation with the author, see chapter "Bunny Lee: the Kingmaker".

18 Dromilly Avenue, Kingston 2017.

sic business, his sound had a reputation for being a go-to for bad guys. "Pure bad man follow the sound", the deejay I-Roy later reported[23].

Tubby installed a camera on his house so he could identify the visitors outside the gate. His studio was located in a critical area, where the spheres of influence of the PNP (Waterhouse) and JLP (Tower Hill) bordered each other and political gangsters controlled access. Anyone who wanted to go to Dromilly Avenue often came across roadblocks and was only allowed to pass if they knew the password, which was "musician". Tubby's sound system did not remain untouched by this toxic atmosphere. At his place, sympathizers of the Spanglers Posse dropped by and occasionally put pressure on the music programme, as a recording of a dance from 1974 shows. That evening, U-Roy was urged to announce a song with the words "a beloved fellow asked me to play this musical disc," and put on an unreleased dub of Delroy Wilson's "Have Some Mercy".[24] Tubby called it "Spanglers' Shower", and it wasn't the only version of the tune with a Spanglers name. Over the Delroy Wilson song, Augustus Pablo also recorded an exclusive "Hometown Hi Fi" dub for Tubby called "Spangler's Clap". Devastated by the destruction, Tubby left the remains of his sound with U-Roy, who never got the system back running. It ended up as seats for the people hanging out in the studio's yard.

Henceforth Tubby focused on the construction of amplifiers, and by the mid-1970s, two thirds of Jamaica's sound systems were equipped with devices he had built. The majority of studio work was done by others. The first person to whom Tubby gave access to his console was Philip Smart. He came from Havendale, one of Kingston's middle-class communities, and was friends with Augustus Pablo. He had already observed Errol Thompson working at Randy's and hung out at Tubby every day after school. Since Bunny Lee, the main customer, seemed to get along well with the new guy, Smart received the studio key, including dub authorization. He mixed the dub on the B-side of the single "None Shall Escape The Judgement", whereupon Lee named him the prince in the king's court. He was not to remain the only prince, though. First, Lee and Smart indulged in crowned heads and sprawling LP titles, and compiled dubs by

23 Liner notes of *I-Roy – Don't Check Me With No Lightweight Stuff (1972–75)*, Blood & Fire 1997.

24 To be heard on the recording "King Tubbys 1974 Home Town Daddy U Roy".

King Tubby and Prince Philips [sic] for an album entitled *Bunny Lee The Version Master presents Creation Of Dub*[25]. A year later, Smart emigrated to the US to open the HCF studio in Brooklyn in 1982, where Shaggy's "Mr. Boombastic" was created. Tubby's old childhood friend Lloyd James now took on the role of prince, the temporary vacancy being filled by Pat Kelly. Among others, Kelly mixed for The Prophets, who comprised of Vivian Jackson aka Yabby You (1946–2010) and various harmony singers.[26] This is how *King Tubby's Prophecies Of Dub* was born, an album released in 1976 under the heading *The Prophets* on Prestige. Not to be confused with the coverless *King Tubby's Prophesy of Dub* on the British Prophets label from the same year, which was actually mixed by Tubby.[27] When Lloyd James became the new in-house engineer in 1976, Bunny Lee was so impressed by his mixing skills that he immediately proclaimed him the new "prince". The newly crowned engineer created his own sound identity through the productions with Black Uhuru, and only left when 17-year-old Hopeton Overton Brown, aka Scientist, began to shake the throne at the end of the 1970s. In addition to the resident engineers and occasional temporary workers like Gussie Clarke, Tubby – especially after Scientist had said goodbye – was constantly training young talent to take his place at the mixing desk: Phantom, Banton, Peego, Professor... The latter should not be confused with the British engineer Mad Professor[28] or with the deejay Ranking Dread, who, like Professor, was called Winston Brown in real life. Brown had learned from his brother how transformers were wound, and equippped with this knowledge he came to Tubby in 1978, ending up at the mixing desk. He oversaw countless productions, mixed hits like Johnny Osbourne's "Ice Cream Love" and, despite the LP *Scientist v The Professor – Dub Duel At King Tubby's*[29], remained a largely forgotten

25 First released on Total Sounds, then in England with changed titles on Live And Love under *Tommy McCook & The Aggrovators* as *King Tubby Meets The Agrovators At Dub Station*. In 2011 reissued by Jamaican Recordings.

26 Usually Alrick Forbes and Dada Smith, but sometimes Willi Williams with Bunny Rugs or the Gladiators.

27 Reissued in 1985 by Blood & Fire under the name Yabby You.

28 In 2011, an album that added even more confusion was released on Jamaican Recordings called *Scientist meets The Crazy Mad Professor at Channel One*, supposedly with dubs by Professor and Scientist

29 Produced by Roy Cousins, Kingdom UK 1983

View down the street from 18 Dromilly Avenue, 2017.

engineer who, although there were hardly any photos of him, ended up on the cover of *King Tubby's Lost Treasures*[30], curiously enough. In 1983, Brown told Canadian *Reggae Quarterly* magazine: "I give all the credit to Tubbs. I learn everything from him. Everything."[31] Professor was succeeded by a youth named Fatman, who is discussed later.

Tubby knew his studio and workshop were in good hands, and was devoting himself to a new passion. He was tired of only being able to focus on vocals or mixing music recorded by others on four tracks. Tubby wanted to produce himself, and dreamed of 24 tracks. He devoured specialist literature on acoustics and studio construction, immersed himself in meticulous plans, and began building a second studio behind the house on Dromilly Avenue. From the hand-picked wooden cladding to the technology, every little thing had to be tailor-made. The project became Tubby's "ultimate obsession", at least, that's how David Rodigan, British radio DJ, perceived it. He and Tubby maintained a friendly relationship during this time. He saw the new studio nearing its final completion, but cannot recall any recording or production ever taking place there. King Jammy, who had been friends with Tubby since his youth, also said that this studio never went beyond the status of test runs. Both of their accounts contradict British reggae historian Steve Barrow, who maintains the studio was put into operation in 1985, and Tubby recorded "Tempo" there, his first self-produced hit.[32] Perhaps Barrow fell for the cover of the LP *King Tubby – Majestic Dub*[33], released in the UK on the Star label in the mid-80s. It showed a painting of a studio with a 24-track tape machine and a sprawling console. At it, on a throne with a crown and scepter, sits King Tubby. However, the image by New York painter Jamaal Pete is a painted copy of a photo of Bunny Lee at the mixing desk at Dynamic studio, which became the cover of the LP *Bunny Lee & The Aggrovators Presents Super Dub Disco Style.*[34]

In that year, 1985, reggae experienced its greatest musical upheaval. Jammy, who was still going by the moniker "Prince" at the time, now had his own studio where he and musician Noel Davey produced Jamaica's first digital riddim on a cheap Casio keyboard. "Sleng Teng" was its name, after the single by Wayne Smith, and when this innovative beat was unleashed onto the dancehall its sound redefined the future. Shortly afterwards, Davey delivered a second, similar riddim to Jammy, who

30 Jamaican Recordings 2001.
31 *Reggae Quarterly* Vol.1 No. 3 by Beth Lesser p. 24.
32 Booklet of *Dub Gone Crazy. The Evolution of Dub at King Tubby's 1975–1979*, Blood & Fire 1994.
33 A Bunny Lee production with mixes by Scientist and Prince Jammy from the 1970s
34 Jamaica Sound 1979.

could not make another hit from it, though only King Tubby with singer Anthony Red Rose managed it. "Tempo" gave the new digital sound analogue warmth and, with its lyrics, caricatures the new bass as "an idiot sound, we call that low-fi". It became Tubby's greatest success as a producer.

The style break caused by the computer changed Jamaica's music landscape. One of the most prominent victims of digitalization was dub, without being immediately noticeable. The enthusiasm about the new sound led the producers pressing the bare digital riddims onto the B-sides of singles, returning to the instrumental versions from the pre-dub era. Suddenly, dub skills were obsolete. The new digi sound was spectacular enough, fulfilled its purpose in the dancehall, raw as it was and, with its modest arrangements, offered too little from which an effective dub could be created.

Tubby also moved to digital production. Over the following four years he released hundreds of singles and numerous albums on five different

labels.[35] The digital Tubby, however, could not compare to the analogue King. Despite veritable hits like Courtney Melody's "Ninja Mi Ninja" or Red Rose & King Kong's "Two Big Bull In A One Pen", it's more quantity than quality. Another reason was because Tubby was focusing on the role of financier, while the artistic side was left to his team, and the young musicians of the Firehouse Crew. He preferred to tinker with the completion of the new studio, and usually didn't go home until late at night. On one such evening, it was February 6, 1989, shortly after 1am, he had reached 85 Sherlock Crescent, his apartment, parking his car in the driveway. Suddenly a man appeared in front of him, pressed a gun to his body and pulled the trigger. A single shot is all it took, and Osbourne Ruddock, Jamaica's greatest force in sound and dub, was dead. The murderer took Tubby's valuables – money, watch, necklace, a registered weapon – and disappeared into the night. Tubby was only 48 and his murderer was never caught.

35 Firehouse, Waterhouse, Taurus, Pioneer Muzik, Kingston 11.

On the day of his passing, King Tubby became immortal. He became an icon, a myth that is only slightly in harmony with actual history. King Tubby was not the inventor of dub, even though he claimed to Carl Gayle he had been.[36] It is questionable whether any one person deserves this award. The genesis of dub was a result of the rival Jamaican entertainment industry's obsession with exclusivity, in the form of dubplates. Added to this was technical progress enabled by multi-track technology. Even before Tubby, both factors had already led Linford Anderson, Buddy Davidson, Sylvan Morris, Errol Thompson and other sound engineers to design music outside the usual song norms during the mixing process. While his predecessors sometimes indulged in bizarre experiments, it is Tubby's great achievement to have brought musicality into the dub process. On top of this came a substantial dose of electrical engineering brilliance, and the luck of having an extraordinary mixing console. From all this, Tubby created the prototype of a sonic aesthetic that led to extensive changes in contemporary popular music, particularly in the club and dance scenes. In this environment, Tubby is revered like a saint. His memory is surrounded by fictional folklore, often because many well-intentioned individuals who talk about him lack a deep understanding of studio technology. The small addition of a word like "old", intended to demonstrate Tubby's special sophistication, tells us that he knew how to use obsolete, dated equipment for his innovations, but it also changes and transfigures his history. Statements like "Tubby even made his own echo delay unit by passing a loop of tape over the heads of an old two-track machine"[37], are untrue, as they overlook the fact that, already early in the analogue era, this process was part and parcel of standard studio work worldwide. The machine referred to was actually not so old but simply a second 4-track (!) one. Tubby had three tape recorders in his studio, two half-inch 4-track machines[38], one of which the music came from, the other used as an echo generator, as well as a 2-track machine for the (master) recording of the mix. In addition, he owned a Grampian 636 Spring Reverb, later traded for a Fisher Spring Reverb, used to generate the explosive effects typical of his sound, and last but not least an AKG Echo Chamber. This had been recommended to him in Stanley Motta's electronics shop. Furthermore, Tubby had a compressor that he used for vocals and Tannoy speakers as studio monitors. The so-called "old" or "limited"[39] equipment, often associated with sub-

36 In "Marcus Garvey Meets The Rockers Uptown" ibid p. 34 Tubby told the Treasure Isle story about Ruddy Redwood, as if it was his story.
37 Booklet of *Dub Gone Crazy. The Evolution of Dub at King Tubby's 1975–1979*, Blood & Fire 1994, or also *Remixology. Tracing The Dub Diaspora*.
38 one Scully and one Ampex.
39 David Toop: *Ocean Of Sound* London 1995 p. 117.

liminal developing world romanticism, was among the best available at the time, and had also been electronically enhanced or "tuned" by him. King Tubby's technique was clearly "Hi Fi", not "Low Fi".

Much of what Tubby is credited as having invented, such as hitting spring reverb or playing extraneous noises, also happened at the same time at Studio One, Randy's, Joe Gibbs and Lee Perry's Black Ark. Given the temporal and spatial density of events, it is impossible to determine who copied who, and neither is it necessary. Even though writers of King Tubby's history should be a little more careful and copy-and-paste the inaccuracies of others less, his status as the king of dub art remains undisputed, regardless of who was first. In *Perfecting Sound Forever*[40], New York music critic Greg Milner describes how far his influence is felt. Milner sees Tubby's musical staging of the studio, and the way he disassembled and reassembled music as foreshadowing what has become commonplace in the digital world. Since computers have replaced the tape recorder as the recording medium, it has become normal to move, disassemble and rearrange recorded segments at will. Milner sums up thus "Tubby's legacy extends far beyond the musical genres most closely linked to dub. The salient point is not that he invented the remix. It's that the concept of the remix reinvented modern music."[41]

All that remains to be added here is to clarify the fate of the studio and the MCI console after Tubby's murder. The equipment, including the desk, was purchased by Byron Lee's brother Neville for Sonic Sounds, his record pressing plant, and used to edit master tapes. From there, Tappa Zukie's brother "Blackbeard" Sinclair bought it in the mid-90s, and used it to run a makeshift studio inside his house in Portmore, before selling it on to Seattle. Since then, it has remained in the local Museum of Pop Culture in that city, in desolate condition that Tubby would never have allowed, and is occasionally sent around the world as a display exhibit. The second console from the new studio stayed at Sonic Sounds.

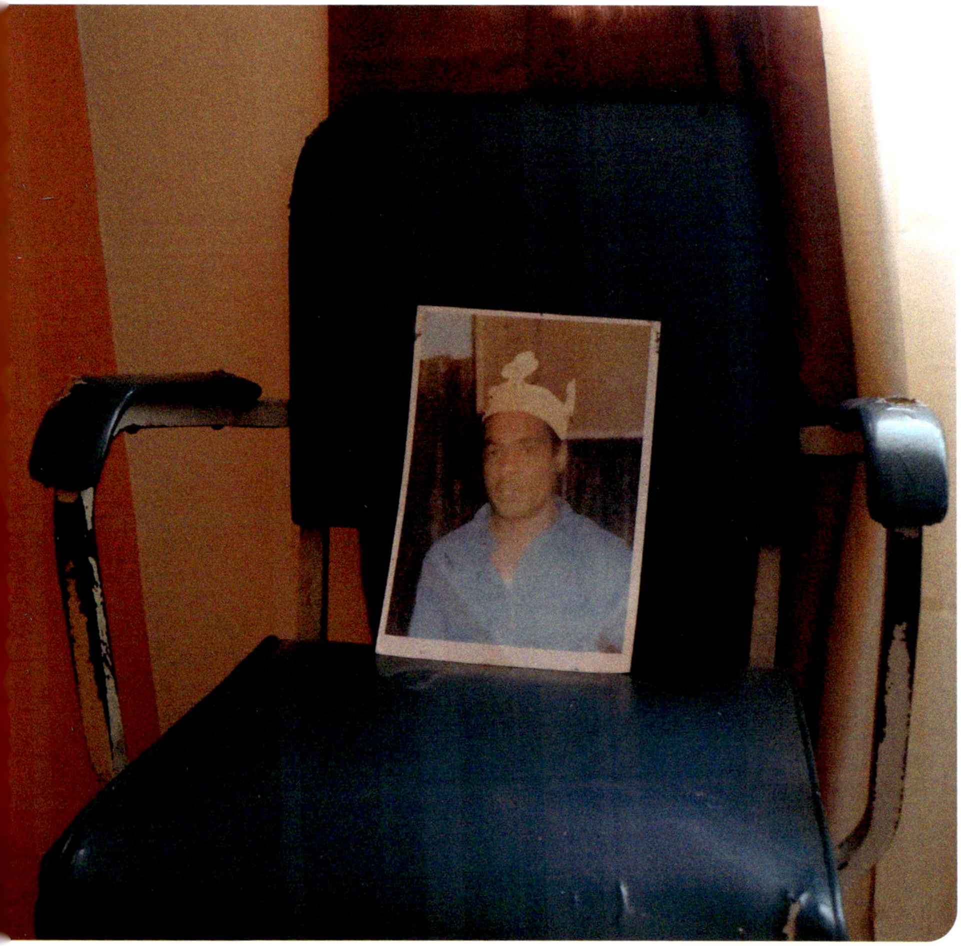

King Tubby's chair from his workshop on Dromilly Avenue, stored in a room in Bunny Lee's studio in Duhaney Park, Kingston, 2014.

40 Greg Milner: *Perfecting Sound Forever. The Story Of Recorded Music*, Granta Books UK 2009, Paperback 2010.
41 ibid p. 302.

David Rodigan: Memories of King Tubby

A man with a suitcase full of dubplates, David Rodigan travels the world as a representative of the international reggae movement for the UN. Insiders consider him one of the world's most influential disc jockeys, and even in Jamaica his reputation as a reggae ambassador follows that of Bob Marley. Rodigan was born in Germany in 1951, the child of a Scottish soldier. Aged seven, the family moved to London. Rodigan was fascinated by radio at an early age, and began collecting records as a teenager, quickly developing a love for soul and ska. Although he was trained as an actor, appeared on stage in Shakespeare plays and took on numerous roles on British television, his life was dominated by radio and reggae. Eventually, he gave up acting and became a presenter for BBC Radio London, Capital Radio and the BFBS. This was followed by a daily program on Kiss FM in 1990, which he reduced to a weekly format from 1999 until his departure in 2012. Since then, he has been on air on BBC 1Xtra. In 2005, David Rodigan was inducted into the Radio Academy Hall of Fame, and in 2012 the Queen awarded him the OBE (Order of the British Empire).

King Tubby and David Rodigan, 1985.

The man who popularised reggae on the radio and became a feared clash opponent across the globe with his dubplate collection and one-man sound system show, has since been able to refer to himself as "Sir David Rodigan". In Jamaica, Sir David receives the utmost respect both on the streets and among singers, deejays, musicians, producers, and studio owners. He has been coming to the island since the 1970s, met Osbourne Ruddock, aka King Tubby, in 1979, and regularly visited his studio hunting for new dubplates. An intensive friendship between them developed.

May I suggest that you and Tubby were close friends?

David Rodigan: I'd like to think so. I'm proud to say that we were close friends. Tubby asked me if I would have my picture taken with him. He asked me! I never forget this moment. Does he have any idea what this means to me?

Are you referring to the photo from 1985 that appeared on the back of the tribute LP *A Salut To King Tubby*[1] which was released after his murder?

You can see from what I was wearing that it's a very old photograph. When he asked me if I would pose for a photograph with him, in my head I just pfffhh... Tubby was a private person, he didn't give himself over easily to people. [Later] we would frequently talk on the phone. I spent long time with him when he built the new studio. I think it would be truthful to say that we were close friends. We had a mutual respect and admiration. Tubby fascinated me. When I first met him, he was very cool, almost standoffish. Years later he told me "When I met you, I was observing you."

Checking you out...

Yeah. He said: "Jammy told me what you were doing and why you were doing it. And that you were genuine. Jammy said 'Tubbs, this man has a real genuine passion, he's like us.' But I didn't know you, and I needed to know you." I had heard Tubby changed English pounds for the Jamaican dollars and I'd get a good rate. It was in the backroom, he picked up the *Gleaner* and found the rate in the paper. I looked at him and said: I was told I would get a better rate from you. He said "Oh no, this is the rate". That made me think that this man was very pure. It wasn't a hustle. It was like "I can do this, but this is the rate, so that's the rate". It wasn't a black-market deal, it was like "yeah, I can change the money for you". I then said: You think I could do an interview with you? "Interview? Not now." You know, [every] other engineer [would

1 Released on the Taurus label 1989

have said]: Yah man, you can interview me for BBC radio London. It was humility there. I'm convinced I was tested first.

Being tested is something that continued with your first dub-plate session.

The first time I wanted to cut a dub he put this tape on, he played this tune for me and I said "No!". He played three or four songs, and then he looked at me as if to say "You're wasting my time", and I looked back at him.

Jamaicans love this game. He played you weak songs to see how you'd react.

Yeah. [There was] a suitcase full of tapes, more than one suitcase. Artists would leave their tapes there in the hope that Tubbys could sell the dubs. The dubs promoted the artist and earn money for them. It was a process, they had to leave the tapes somewhere. So Tubby was playing me something by somebody. I didn't like it and he smiled. He took out his keys and threw the keys to this boy and pointed to this cupboard down on the floor. The boy opened the cupboard and took out a multi-track. Tubby told him to string it up, pressed play and I heard this voice. I shivered but didn't know who it was. I just said "Oh my God, please. I have to cut that!" It was Michael Prophet from the first album with Yabby You. I cut that dubplate and said "Yes!". Jammys and Tubbys smiled and looked at each other as if to say, "He's passed the test." I get the feeling that's what it was. I remember also on the original dubplate was that logo of the black and white. The sleeves had this fascinating artwork. It was in this colour, a little tan with brown and black with this zigzag. Later of course the famous four colour dubplate sleeve with Waterhouse on one side, Firehouse on the other side. It was again that attention to detail. Tubby wanted everything to be perfect.

The British sound system owner Fatman had already used this design for his dub LPs back then: For example, he took the cover with the star for *King Tubby, Prince Jammy And Scientist – First, second and third generation of Dub*[2] and his *Unleashed Dub From King Tubby's Studio*[3] was put in a blue "Waterhouse" cover[4]... Could you tell that Tubby was not satisfied with studio work alone? That he wanted more?

When I arrived in Jamaica he was already at that stage of delegating. Jammys was there as the assistant engineer because clearly Tubbys couldn't do everything on his own. There was the electronic stuff that he was doing as well. Tubbys was an electronic genius. When I went to the studio one day he was out on the road. Tubby was [often] driving around Waterhouse. When [his sound was] playing in Waterhouse he would turn up on a bicycle to tune his sound system and then leave... I said: When he's coming back? – "Oh, we'll find him." – You'll find him? – "Yeah, we'll get him on the phone." Tubby had an antenna in his back-garden so they could contact him. And that was 1979, he had a two-way antenna! "Yo Tubbs, Rodigan is here." – "I know." I stood there and just thought: Oh shit, this guy is in a league of his own.

What was Tubby like when he dubbed? Did he improvise or did he know what he wanted?

When I saw him working, he was very relaxed and concentrated. He knew exactly what he was doing. The point is that dub is the moment. It can never be reproduced. And often, as we know, they didn't make copies other than what was transferred onto the master and then cut on a disk.

That's why Michael Veal also got tangled up in his analysis[5] trying to measure dub events in bars and timing

[Veal's book] was too, what I would call post-graduate doctorate. And it was very heavy reading. Veal didn't speak easily to the man in the street. I always remember that Jackie Mittoo[6] story. He told me he was rehearsing in the studio and was playing jazz. And suddenly a hand on the shoulder and Coxson (the studio owner) leaned down and said "Jackie, remember, it's just reggae." In other words, keep it simple.

2 1981 on the British KG Imperial label.
3 1991 on the British Fatman label with mixes from the 1970s.
4 Since 2002 the design for the "Firehouse" dubplate covers is used for maxi single releases of the Pressure Sounds LP *Firehouse Revolution – King Tubby's Productions in the Digital Era 1985–89* and for single re-releases of the Japanese Dub Store label
5 Michael E. Veal: *DUB Soundscapes & Shattered Songs in Jamaican Reggae*, ibid.
6 Jackie Mittoo (1948–1990), founding member of the Skatalites, keyboard player and musical director at Studio One.

This irretrievable moment in the creation of a dub can also be found in the improvisations of jazz.

Tubby certainly had an appreciation of jazz music. As our friendship developed, I was invited into a room at the house and in that room was the biggest collection of jazz records I have ever seen. It was unbelievable. Tubby had surrounded himself with these jazz recordings and immersed himself in the original albums by the greats. And it struck a chord with me not then but afterwards, when he was dubbing, he was jazzing it up, wasn't he? Another thing I remember now is on the dubplate sometimes you'd hear "red light", and if my memory serves me correctly, that's because there wasn't a red light.

The red light that was connected to the record button on the tape?

Yeah. It's all quite small. Here's the area where the desk is, next to the desk is a cupboard [with the tapes], and a very small room with egg boxes and pieces of foam with literally room for one person, maybe two [for recording vocals]. And Tubbys would speak and you hear him say "red light" or "ready"...

...to signal to the musicians that they were actually recording...

Yeah, that's why he said "red light". On the front of "Firehouse Rock" by The Wailing Souls you hear a throat clearing. They lived with the mistakes, it's a natural evolution. That's what dub was, the engineers horsing around, having fun. I don't think they realised the significance of it. It's the beauty of innocence, isn't it? Some dubs were more kind of out there than others. "Cow Town Skank" by I-Roy[7] is [such] an example of King Tubby. In the beginning of the song there's car brakes screeching and a horn going off. Then you hear a conversation between Bunny Lee and I-Roy: "Wha' happen I-Roy, what a nice car the man have... Where the man go forward to?" – "Is Cow Town I man rest right now..." That car was Bunny Lee's car. Tubbys took a microphone on a lead, took it out of the window, run it down the side of the bungalow, into the front garden. It was all recorded live outside at Tubby's.

Perry did similar things, recording children or goats outside.

Yeah, crazy things. Big Youth and Keith Hudson bringing the motorbike inside Dynamic studios. They brought it into the studio![8] 'Cause they didn't have sound effects albums, so they had to create...

...sounds, that were omnipresent in Jamaica.

Exactly. Screeching tires, vrooom, vrooom. Just crazy. Mad. Truly inspirational. When you think of what was created, why was it so inspiring? Why does it still haunt me when I play these dubs? Why is it when I sit home on my own with no one in the house and I turn the music up full volume and say: Sorry neighbours, for ten minutes I'm going to the moon. And I play some Tubby's dubs, turn it up and get this feeling that washes over me. Why? It was the fact that anything could happen. Look at Stalag. Never mind all the dubs and songs, just listen to the original riddim, what sound they were able to create. [Tubby's studio] was that watering hall, it was that meeting place, and everything was immaculate. Tubbys was fastidious about smoking and tidiness. Everything had to be very, very tidy. The floors were shining and there was often a nice fragrance in the house. If anyone did dare to smoke when he wasn't there, they'd have a warning system: "Tubbys is coming! Tubbys is coming!" The studio had strong air conditioning and they were blowing and open the windows. I will never forget, he walked into the studio and he stood there like a school teacher and said "Who's been smoking in here?" – "Not me Mr. Tubbs, not me." It was so funny, "Who has been smoking?" In Jamaica! I laughed but he was deadly serious.

Can you recall the first recordings that you identified as dub?

The first discovery I made of dub music was on a B-side of a Joe Gibbs record, Joe Gibbs & The Destroyers, which had always crazy echo on it.[9] The A-side wasn't really good, but the B-side was crazy. I said: What is this? And I remember King Stitt and "Herbsman Shuffle" on a Clancy Eccles album, "tek a lick, tek a lick." That was the beginnings of dub.

7 First released in 1972 as the only release on I-Roy's own Royco Inc. label with the Pablo version "Fiat 125" on the back. Then on Justice, on Move & Groove and a year later on the LP *Presenting I Roy on Gussie and Trojan*.

8 1972 for the intro of the Big Youth single "S90 Skank/Ace 90 Skank", a deejay version of Hudson's "We Will Make It Up" on his Mafia label.

9 Meaning "Nevada Joe", 1969 on the blue – British – Amalgamated label; the version was entitled "Straight To The Head" and included obscure echo effects on the vocals.

The version was called "Phantom" and was still mixed very cautiously by Linford Anderson. Tubby later did it over in a more dynamic way.[10]

No one knew the word dub then. It was called a version, just version. Sound boys and sound men that I knew from that time said that the instrumental was everything. Organ instrumentals, piano instrumentals, violin...

... repeater drumming...

... anything that was different. And from that the engineers would slightly change it. Next thing was they would put a bit of echo in it and then it just happened. It wasn't somebody sitting down and saying, I found a secret.

Sylvan Morris said it was the sound men who came up with the idea, not the engineers.

I would totally agree with that. Sylvan Morris has a point. I met him several times in the late 70s. He was a gentle, beautiful mind. He mixed for me at Harry J, I have most admiration for him. Without Sylvan Morris we wouldn't have those Studio One recordings. Just a few days ago I read an interview with him in which he made a very interesting explanation. He described dub as "a development of what we were already doing by way of instrumental music." He said the sound men would drive us crazy. They always wanted something special. That made us, the engineers, try to think of something to make this different for the sound men.

Which contradicts the popular theory that Tubby invented dub. That wouldn't even work with the timing. Because when the first dub LPs appeared in 1973 after various single B-sides, Tubby had just bought the 4-track equipment from Dynamic that enabled him to dub. Until then, his studio was only equipped for cutting dubplates. At this point Linford Anderson and especially Errol Thompson had already set the course with their technical possibilities.

10 Both Anderson's and Tubby's mixes can be found on the 1976 release by Clan Disc *Sound System International Dub LP* by the Clancy Eccles All Stars, re-released in 2009 with the same title by *Pressure Sounds as King Tubby & The Clancy Eccles All Stars*.

What you're saying is correct. Tubby could not have been the creator, 'cause he wasn't in a position to create it. We're Sherlock Holmes and Dr. Watson now. The time and the procedure of elimination of facts would suggest that it was Errol Thompson. By the way my Errol Thompson story is I went to meet him one Sunday lunchtime. I was taken to his house by Gussie Clarke and I was really looking forward to meeting him. [But] Errol Thompson was not interested in meeting me, ha ha ha. He was counting the money on his coffee table that he was earning from his ice cream parlour in Kingston Downtown. He was much more interested in that.

Back to Tubby...

I remember that the Tubby's dub albums came later. The first time I saw Tubby [mixing a dub] was 1974 "Watergate Rock", which is a dub version of Larry Marshalls "I Admire You".[11]

In the very same year *King Tubby The Dub Master Presents Dub From The Roots* was released, and dub was now an international LP format.

Yeah, we have to surely agree that the idea of the dub as a dub experience was an album experience, wasn't it?

Not in Jamaica, only in Europe.

But we have to respect that it was primarily when it became an album experience. This was a very significant transition.

Through the albums, a Jamaican sound system creation became a white, European music culture.

And it moved on very quickly.

Everyone developed their own interpretation, which usually had its origins in the UK. The spiritual dub by Jah Shaka, the University of Dub with steppers dub, later drum'n'bass and dubstep.

Oh yeah, it's an evolution. One of the questions I've always asked is why is it that dub music has a particular resonance with young teenagers. The biggest audience for it is always young teenagers and early twenties. Strange. I think young people have a similar obsession that we had when we first heard this music. These

11 Released on Black & White, produced by Carlton Patterson.

young people are younger versions of you and me with this discovering something which is really exciting. But they want to create their own. Dubstep is their interpretation.

That has nothing to do with reggae anymore.

No, no, no. NO! It's not what you and I know it to be. But when I do shows (in techno clubs like Fabric in London) and I play my King Tubby dubs, they go crazy. Because of the energy and the bass.

It's true, dubstep brings the same physical experience through the bass waves. But what gets overlooked is the original, the human factor and the cultural context. Dub is based on real instruments, is analogue and arises from improvisation and not programming.

Of course dub is an analogue experience.

Which at some point Tubby did not seem to be interested anymore. He had found a new passion.

His passion was the multitrack, 16- or 24-track studios, that was the obsession. He bought books and he studied how to build a studio. He went down to Kingston wharf, and he handpicked every single plank of wood that was in that studio. He studied how he should build and shape it to get the best acoustic. This was, I believe, his ultimate obsession. To create his own unique multitrack recording studio. He had done so, he had finished, and he built it with his own hands, in the back garden. When he finished building it, he took me in. The door alone was hand carved in Jamaican mahogany wood. It was that rose dark mahogany, Jamaican dark brown redwood. Rich embellished, beautifully lacquered. It said "King Tubby's Studio". We went in and I said "This is amazing". It was massive. I did sit in the new studio with Tubby and he described how he built it almost one wooden plank at a time.

There are people who say that Tubby's digital productions like "Tempo"[12] were created in the new studio in the back house. But to me "Tempo" sounds like the MCI console.

"Tempo" was created and recorded much earlier by the Firehouse Crew[13] in his original studio. The 24-track studio had been more or less completed, but I am not sure if he had actually recorded anything there.

Door of Tubby's new studio building at the back of 18 Dromilly Avenue, 2017.

Interim author's remark: after Tubby's death, the new studio, which was never used, was cleared and the equipment sold, only the mahogany door remaining. No one was interested in it for 30 years. When the French reggae historian Thibault Ehrengardt published a biography of King Tubby[14] in 2020, he addressed rumors such as the Japanese had stolen the door, or it would be in Herbie Miller's Jamaica Music Museum. King Tubby's family would express interest in the door. The fact is, neither the Jamaica Music Museum nor King Tubby's descendants did anything to save the door from decay. Ehrengardt mentioned Leroy Fatman Thompson, who told him, he "went there with some German journalist the other day"[15], and the door was still where it always was. That "German journalist" is the author of this book. Together with Leroy Fatman I went there in 2017 and saw the door in its original place. In 2021 the front building that hosted Tubby's 4-track studio was gutted. The building behind it with the carved mahogany door remained untouched.

12 Anthony Red Rose – "Tempo", 7" Firehouse 1985.
13 A young four-piece band that Tubby had discovered.
14 *King Tubby The Dub Master. The Official Biography* Dread Editions, France 2020
15 ibid p. 10.

You said you were fascinated by Tubby, a fascination that gripped many, even those who didn't know him personally, and remains unbroken to this day. That's why so many legends surround his work. Like the story that he recorded his digital productions in the new studio. This has led to questionable views on the history of dub.

YES! Because he's become a symbol, an icon.

Like Bob Marley...

Exactly. It's the perfect analogy. He was what he was and he did what he did, and it was very, very important. As far as I'm concerned, he's still the best engineer, with all due respect to the others. There was something about that sound he created on that board, the fact that he customized those units. At the height of his creativity his best dubs are his cooler dubs. Understated, just beautifully restraining. Magnificent. The dubs that Augustus Pablo did with Tubbys, particularly "Cassava Piece", "Up Warreika Hill", "King Tubby meets the Rockers Uptown". When I first heard that Island Records 7-inch, with "Baby I love you so" on the B-side, I thought I was in heaven. It was beautifully pressed and the sound was amazing. It was like a nirvana.

Perfect remarks to close, thank you very much. Let's just briefly talk about *Rockers Arena*[16], the LP that came out under your and Tony Williams' name.

A complete rip-off. This guy Larry Lawrence (1947–2008) was a cavalier kind of character and had a very strong, dominant personality. A Jamaican who had a close friendship with some of the Wailers, particularly with the Barrett brothers. When they came to England, he would record them in sessions. And he would release some of these sessions with junior British artists often singing on his Ethnic Fight label. Now the label alone told you about Larry Lawrence: Ethnic FIGHT.

With the boxing gloves logo.

He was a colourful character, but he could be very demanding. He was a clever operator, always wanted his records played on the radio, this is in Radio London days. A tough guy, but I actually liked him. He ran a record shop in Brixton and he came up with this dub album. Now he didn't really ask permission, didn't pay any money.

He put your name on the cover without asking?

Yeah, he said he was promoting us. He was, like, doing us a favour, ha ha!

"Us" means you and Tony Williams? You used to have a radio show together...

In the beginning he and I shared the show. We alternated. Williams was Jamaican, I was English. No one had seen me, they only heard me. They presumed that I was black. What happened was listeners were talking 'bout Rodigan's better than Williams, Williams' better than Rodigan. A talk on the street. Jamaicans love to comment, you know: Bwoy Rodigan badda than Williams, Rodigan have the baddest tunes... Williams was a friend of mine and I still have occasionally contact with him. But Larry Lawrence been active and came with this *Rodigan versus Williams* album.

16 *Rodigan-v-Williams – Rockers Arena*, 1980 on Ethnic Fight according to the cover, according to the label on Exclusive.

I can't remember any of those riddims. They would have all been riddims from Larry Lawrence. I had nothing to do with it. When I saw the album, I was embarrassed. I don't even have it, I didn't keep it... Let's stop talking about it, please!

Ras Craft HiFi Sound System, Germany.

The Story of Fatman: Three The Hard Way at King Tubby's

> "Everything was mixed in one take most times because time is the essence. You had no time to sit on a whole day business."
>
> (Roger Lewis)

He owed his nickname to the impressive belly that surrounded his torso when he was young. Everyone called him "Fatman", except Tubby, who called him "Jackson", since he called everyone that, a hip slang expression that had been circulating among New York's jazz musicians since the 1940s. Both Tubby and Coxson took the moniker up. Leroy "Fatman" Thompson was one of those figures in King Tubby's circle who are notoriously underrated by history, which often does not even remember their last names, just like Barry (Williams), who used to build amplifiers for Tubby, or Ervin, whose last name was probably Robinson, who came from Jones Town and was able to fix anything slightly fixable. Fatman was a solid studio craftsman, without the glamour of engineers like Scientist or Prince Jammy. For four years he had been doing his work with passionate dedication and mastered all the processes perfectly. Confusingly though, he was not the only Fatman on Tubby's territory. There were three, each with a role of their own.

Most obviously, guitarist Roger Lewis embodied the name. At the end of the 1960s, together with brother Ian, who played bass, he founded Inner Circle. Three decades later they scored a worldwide hit with "Sweat (A La La La La Long)". With the brothers as the core of the band, Inner Circle still exists as an independent reggae act. In their first two decades, however, they operated primarily as a backing band and as producers under the name Fat Man Riddim Section. Among other things, they recorded the riddim of "Stir It Up" for Bob Marley and released a series of spectacularly powerful dub albums on their own label Top Ranking: *Baldhead Justice*, *Israel Tafari*, *Heavyweight Dub*, *Killer Dub* (all 1978), *Tough Guys In Dub* (1979), *Is*

It War Or Is It Peace? (1980) as well as *Wagon Of Dub* and *Tribulation Dub* (both 1982). Apart from *Killer Dub* none of these were mixed at Dromilly Avenue.

At Tubby, only the odd *E-E Saw Dub* from 1976[1] was created, a fun project by keyboard player Bernard "Touter" Harvey, which Tubby mixed casually without the intention of releasing it.[2] Touter had just bought his first synthesizer (an ARP Odyssey) and checked out the monophonic, electronic instrument while playing over some riddims by Jacob Miller, which came from the Fat Man Riddim Section and to which Augustus Pablo had also contributed. Pablo introduced Roger "Fatman" Lewis to King Tubby, and Roger subsequently used to sit next to "the don man" at the desk to watch him mix. "I never really turn the knobs", he swears, "but I would say: Bwoy Tubby, dat bad man!"

The next Fatman was Kenneth Gordon, who lived up to his nickname. Growing up in Waterhouse, he emigrated to London in 1963, and started building a sound system in Tottenham, north London, in 1967, which was named "Fatman HiFi" in 1974. Like all Jamaican sound men active in the UK, Fatman Gordon produced material in Kingston to release on his own labels in the UK. He maintained a close relationship with Prince Jammy, who acknowledged his great influence on the British reception of dub. "Fatman was the one who really got the dub music popular in England." Gordon visited Tubby frequently and had Jammy mix dubs, which he first used as dubplates for his sound system, and later compiled for LPs like *First, Second & Third Generation Of Dub* (1981) or *Unleashed Dub From King Tubby's Studio* (1991) for his own labels KG Imperial and Fat Man. In 1979 he released *Fatman Dub Contest: Crucial Bunny Versus Prince Jammys* on the British Star label.

Neither Lewis nor Gordon ever mixed a dub themselves; both were just occasional guests, unlike Leroy Thompson. When still a young boy, Leroy lived within walking distance of Dromilly Avenue, and attended Pembroke Secondary School on Ken Hill Drive. When students wanted to look for a summer job, they received a letter of introduction from their school. Armed with such a document, Leroy presented himself to Tubby to ask for an internship, but Tubby sent him away, as he didn't want apprentices, he needed professionals. Leroy was disappointed, after all, he had taken a class in electrical installation at school and was taking part in a correspondence course at the National Technical School in Tennessee. He financed his further education in the States with the lunch money he got at home. However, in 1980, with the Jamaican dollar rapidly losing value after the change of government, Leroy was no longer able to pay for his classes, so he returned to ask Tubby a second time, only to get the same answer, no apprentices, only professionals. Four years later, when he had just finished his education, he tried a third time, but alas in vain again.

At the time of his last attempt, Peego and Professor were the masters at Tubby's console. However, Professor wanted to move to the US with his family, so Tubby needed a successor. He remembered the inquisitive and persistent young man who had repeatedly requested to work together, and, one Monday morning in the spring of 1985, summoned him to his studio through a mutual friend. Just recently, Prince Jammy had dropped the "Under Mi Sleng Teng" bomb, and Tubby was about to respond with Anthony Red Rose and "Under Mi Fat Thing". The vocals had already been recorded, Professor was just taking care of the mix and Tubby put Leroy by his side to assist him. He welcomed him with the

1 Also released under unclear circumstances as *ABC Dub* on the Penetrate label.
2 The LP, pressed in a small quantity, was officially released in 2006 with detailed background information by the English Motion label as *King Tubby meets Jacob Miller – Ina Tenement Yard*.

words "Youth, I'm leaving here Thursday, so you have to learn everything between now and Wednesday!"

When the song was finished, Leroy "Fatman" Thompson had got the job. He was just 19 and had achieved his dream of working for King Tubby. Quickly he got into the day-to-day studio processes, which remained as if nothing had happened, even though Jamaica was going through a seismic musical change. The evolution from ska to rocksteady and reggae was nothing compared to the upheaval triggered by "Sleng Teng". The sound of reggae was changing radically, and with it, the beats. There was no programming yet, but digital tone generators were increasingly replacing conventional instruments. Fatman Thompson represents a time of change. He experienced the transition from analogue to digital, in which reggae by musicians like Steely & Clevie, Asher, the Firehouse Crew and Mafia & Fluxy was now played on synthesizers and drum machines in the studios.

When you finally got to work with Tubby, did your expectations come true?

Fatman: Yeah, it was King Tubby's studio and I always wanted to work there. Honestly, I didn't know what. [But now I] record songs and mix. I can't wait in the mornings for as I see little bit of lights I man just check there. I will walk to the studio and will walk back home. It was such a pleasure.

Compared to today, was it difficult to learn how to work in the studio? With four tracks, it shouldn't have been too complicated.

Tubbys a great teacher, man! He always said: "When you think you have it balance, call me." Sometime, because it was only four tracks, he need just come and maybe push one fader a bit up and push a fader down a bit an' him say: "Yeah, good Jackson!" Hehe, and that's it. He taught me what to look for when the needle [of the vinyl cutter] chip. You can see it on the dub. When you're cutting a dub, the needle is warm. Tubby's machine could increase [the heat]. On Jammy's machine the voltage to warm the needle was set. So, if the blank is too old the acetate is tough. Is harder to cut. What we do is we just increase it, so the needle is a bit warmer, so it cut it easier. In those days [with four tracks] we didn't have a full multi-track. What actually mean the riddim was laid at Channel One studio. They were laid on 16-track and they bounced it to 2-tracks. We had drum and bass on one track, and the riddim section, that's the piano, the organ, the guitar, and the horns, on the other track. What we did, when it came to King Tubby's, we transferred from 2-track to 4-track. So, we only had one track for lead vocal, one track for background vocal.

You got a quarter-inch 2-track tape from the other studios and transferred it to one of your 4-track machines?

Right.

On dubs and dubplates, however, you sometimes hear the bass, sometimes the drums alone. So, they couldn't have been on the same track together.

For a dub mix, we take the drums alone on one track, the bass alone on the other track, the riddim section on the other track and the horn section on the other track. So, you have four tracks to play with. Sometimes when we record vocals we're out of tracks. So, the person is singing while we're mixing the tracks.

On the fly?

Yes! He he he. So, there was no room for errors.

To be honest, you can hear mistakes here and there, in the mix as well as in the vocals.

Exactly. We know, but you see it was hard to redo it. Ca' we do it on the fly. We just said "Let it go". It's no too bad at that time. That's the difference between the music then and the music now. The music now is always too perfect, too computerized.

And everything sounds similar.

Because now everybody is buying all these bag a plug-ins. All we had was a AKG spring reverb. It had a door, when you open the door there was a big spring. And we had three tape machines. A 4-track specifically for recording, and a 4-track for mixing. The same one we use to record we use for delay. So, without all these plug-ins we had a AKG for reverb and a tape for delay. And we had a 2-track to record the mix.

You voiced some of the dubplates directly onto the cutting machine?

When we're doing dubplates, there was no more free tracks.

And because no one cared about mistakes.

'Member the plate itself is important. Because the artist was hungry to make the cash and they was good in what they are doing in those times. When we say ready, they are ready. Once you spoil it, it's not like the digital world you can press undo, or you erase.

What did the digital development mean for dub and reggae?

(Fatman thinks for a long time) Well, alright. It is easier now and less creative. In my time, you had to use your engineering techniques in order to create the sound. Now you have plug-ins to create the effect you want. Any effect now you can find a plug-in to give you what you want. In comparison to our time, we had the reverb, the delay and the high pass filter, and that created magic. The beauty between then and now is the difference in ideas. Because now you have one man playing the riddim, so it's just one idea going in the recording. At that time, the drummer, the guitarist, the bassie, piano, organ, horn section... say about eight different ideas going in the one riddim. With one likkle man idea creating, the mix started get cheaper, [but] there's no dynamics, there's no feel. When you have eight or ten musician play, everybody put in their thing, it must sound better!

Let's talk about Tubby some more. After Professor left, you and Peego remained.

I had three days with Professor. After that, Peego and I alone. We trained Banton. When I left after four years, Banton took over. Peego was in the studio basically more than I. I represented Tubbys on the road, run the sessions [for his productions] at Channel One or Tuff Gong where we recorded *Two Big Bull Ina One Pen*[3]. Tubbys never go nowhere. Once he went to Dynamics [and] everybody go like crazy. Tubbys [stayed on] Dromilly Avenue. When he drives in, his routine was basically the same. He takes off his shirt, he's in his undershirt all day. He sit down in the office, listening to his jazz and designing the circuit.

He was planning his second studio, that's all he was interested in?

Yes. The board was actually installed, a bigger MCI. He was sticking to the brand. A few outboard equipments came, the Urei boxes... He also had a pirate radio station with the large antenna in his garden.

To play his tunes?

Dubs all night...

Tubby's studio was a few steps from a border between JLP and PNP territory. It is known that this has had an impact on some of the tracks of his dubs. U-Roy also sometimes made comments in the dances accordingly. How did Tubby position himself in this?

It was hard to say. He doesn't speak politics. Spanglers and Shower were the main posses at the time. You have to give them the recognition, gi dem "big ups". The studio was on the PNP side, near the border (of the JLP area).

People say they often heard gunshots fire outside, while they were in the studio, and that they didn't dare to go out. But

3 Anthony Red Rose & King Kong, Firehouse 1986. The full title is *King Tubby's presents Two Big Bull Ina One Pen*. The album, as well as its dub counterpart *Two Big Bull Ina One Pen Dubwise*, was mixed at King Tubby by Fatman and Peego.

when Tubby got into his car and drove off, there was a moment of truce.

Right. Nobody who comes to Tubby's studio was ever been interrogated by anyone. When you say "I'm going to Tubby's studio," they say "alright, go there, turn there..."

Strange times.

Yes. (Fatman is silent and dives into memories.) It was nice times! Me and Peego make the music then, we mix "Tempo". Tubbys was the executive producer (in the sense of financier). We didn't have to go far for food, because you had this little guy with his little buggy. He came [with] all different kind of food. You just place your order, and you get your food.

What happened after the four years at Tubby?

When I left Tubbys, I went to Jimmy Cliff. It was a step up in terms of tracks. Because Jimmy Cliff was 8-track. [He had] a nice little TASCAM board and a live room, so we could actually do live drums. We did rehearsals there, too, and sometimes miked it up. That's where I started practicing live sound. Bunny Lee took me from Jimmy Cliff to Jammys. At Jammys all was computer. Drum machine, keyboards... A few times we used live bass.

Fatman worked at Jammy for nine years. At the same time, he started live engineering. When Bounty Killer came to Europe for the first time in 1997, he demanded him as engineer. Leroy Fatman toured into the 2010s with Jimmy Cliff, The Wailers, Cocoa Tea, Junior Kelly, Sanchez, Ky-Mani Marley, Baby Cham and many others.

Sightiva Hi-Fi Sound System, Germany.

King Shiloh Circle Of Sound, Netherlands.

Pat Kelly: The Demythologization of Dub

> "Dub is a jargon which Reggaemakers use to describe the essence of the roots. By adding 'Wise' to dub – DUB-WISE – the music takes on a new meaning."
>
> (Mikey Dread[1])

He was called Jamaica's Sam Cooke and his official date of birth is September 6, 1944. However, that was not his actual birthday but the day his father registered him. In fact, Pat Kelly had been born a month earlier. The inherent contradiction between document and fact, between appearance and reality, would play a constant role in his life.

For a long time, Pat Kelly led a double life professionally. He had studied electrical engineering and sometimes worked as a studio technician, but above all, thanks to his falsetto voice, he was an extremely successful rocksteady singer, one of the greats from the Jamaican voices hall of fame. Nevertheless, he called singing just a hobby that had taken on a life of its own. In 1967, he was persuaded by Bunny Lee to succeed the legendary Slim Smith in The Techniques, Jamaica's most popular vocal trio at the time. Right at the start, Kelly took on lead vocals for their giant hit "You Don't Care", but didn't stay long. After just one year, having recorded other big tunes like "Queen Majesty" and "Love Is Not A Gamble", all of which became classics, he decided to continue his solo career. In 1968, he sang "Somebody's Baby" for his friend and discoverer Bunny Lee. It was the first recording with a one drop, the drum pattern in which the snare and bass drum are hit at the same time, which would become the most significant reggae beat. It was created by Winston Grennan, Sly Dunbar's drum teacher, who played one drop on this song for the first time on record. In 1969, Kelly sang "How Long Will It Take" for Lee, which in Jamaica became the best-selling single of the year. In the meantime, he transformed Curtis Mayfield's "Little Boy Blue" into a rocksteady evergreen, and three years later, gave producer Phil Pratt "Talk About Love", another timeless hit. The Beatles' label Apple then made him a lucrative offer, which came to nothing because British Pama Records wouldn't release him from his contract. Kelly had signed with brothers Harry, Jeff and Carl Pama for a year, and they did not want to let him go, not even for compensation of £25,000.

1 Liner notes of the LP *Dub Merchant*, Dread At The Controls 1983

Disappointments of this kind, as well as the fact that over the years others have received particular recognition and financial gain through his skills, made Pat Kelly appear disillusioned. Despite countless hits and more than 20 albums, there were often periods of downtime in his life, which he used for his true passion, studio work. However, nowhere did he achieve the status of resident engineer because it could not be coordinated with his career as a singer. No matter who he worked for, throughout his life Pat Kelly remained the unknown engineer in the shadow of his clients. He still sat at the desk at Randy's, Joe Gibbs or King Tubby. For the latter, he was involved in numerous dub productions, but was rarely mentioned in the credits. Sometimes he was even confused with Tubby because Kelly, unlike the other engineers working for Tubby, wasn't interested in creating something new but had a sound almost identical

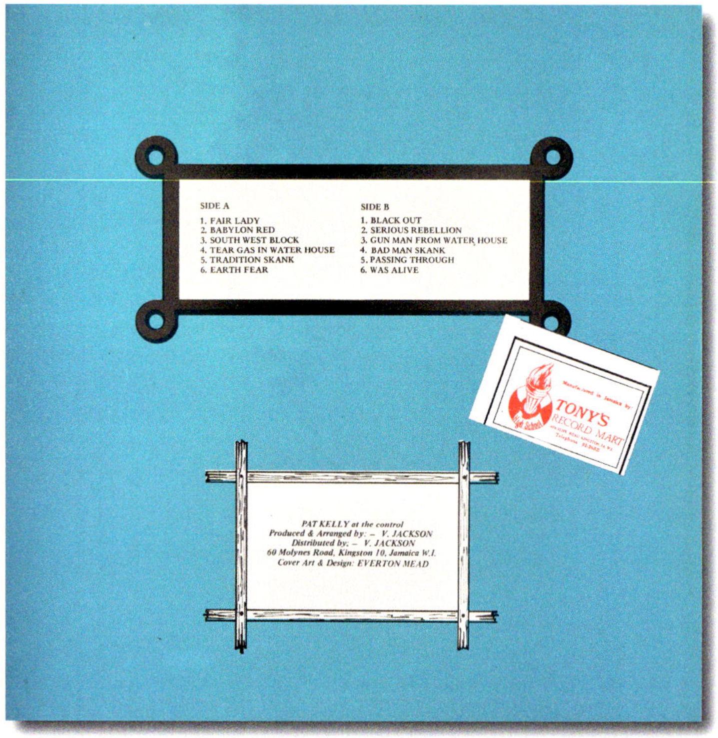

to that of his boss. As a result, singles are now being traded as alleged Tubby dub, such as the Palmer Brothers' "Stept It Out A Babylon" [sic], despite its label explicitly indicating "Engineer: Pat Kelly".[2]

Only in rare cases did Kelly contribute to a distinctive dub language of his own. He achieved this most effectively with the mix of *Bunny Lee & The Aggrovators Presents Super Dub Disco Style*[3]. This album is a small masterpiece of dub art, with recordings coming from Channel One, and which benefited from the sub mix of Barnabas, the local engineer. If you compare the sound of the mix and the application of the effects, Kelly could also be credited for *Page One – Rock A Dub*[4]. Kelly himself couldn't help clarify this issue, as he had no memory of any album he had mixed. What is certain, however, is that he created one of the most spectacular LPs in dub history, the title of which, tellingly, did not have his name on it, but rather that of the studio owner: *The Prophets – King Tubby's Prophecies Of Dub* appeared in 1976 as the only release in a small edition on the Jamaican Prestige label. Today, this pressing is a highly sought-after collector's item.[5]

2 The single, produced by Brent Dowe with singer Clifford Palmer aka Junior Ross and the note "Engineer: Pat Kelly", was released in 1975 on the Jamaican Sweet City label and did not have a dub on the B-side, but an alternative vocal mix. The A-side vocal mix appeared a second time under the artist name The Palm Threes on the Canadian Maica label with the title "Step It Out". This time with a dub on the B-side which could be by Tubby but just as easily also mixed by Pat Kelly along with the vocal tracks. When The Palm Threes single was repressed by Hawkeye in 2008, Pat Kelly was no longer mentioned on the label.

3 Jamaica Sound 1979.

4 Jamaica Sound 1979.

5 There was a second LP from the same year, mixed by Tubby and with a similar title: *King Tubby's Prophesy Of Dub*. To complete the confusion, in this case the label was called "Prophets". It belonged to the singer and producer Yabby You, from whom the songs on the *Prophesy* album came. The *Prophecies* album, on the other hand, is based on riddims by Bunny Lee. He had stored his tapes at King Tubby and so Vivian Jackson aka Yabby You got access to the material. Only one of the 12 *Prophecies* riddims came from Yabby You. A sticker on a large portion of the LPs with a reference to "Prince Tony" Robinson's International Record Mart Shop at 45 Slipe Road sugge-

You did not plan on becoming a singer but studied electrical engineering at Kingston Technical High School.

Pat Kelly: Three years (in the early 1960s), later (1966) in Springfield, Massachusetts. I wanted to become an electronic engineer. That's my real career. Entertaining to me is like a hobby which took off. I didn't set out to be a singer. Engineer was my whole focus as a youth growing up. Until I made my first record. It kinda changes the whole picture. I was engulfed into this new career.

But have you always worked as an engineer on the side?

I really went into operations as an engineer after I became an established entertainer. I started out with King Tubbys.

After Philip Smart stopped there...

I went there and saw King Jammys and Tubbys, they were tightly knitted friends, right? I didn't know anything about Philip until I went to the United States. That's how I knew Smart. He said he was working at King Tubby's, but I didn't know him from Jamaica.

How did you experience Tubby? Was he already more interested in repairs and amplifier building than in studio work when you were there?

Well, I think the whole focus was making this dub. He never go out and do his own records. That came later. When he heard a song, from Bunny Lee or from other producers, and he liked it, he said "Do you like to have a dub of that?"

Are we talking about dubplates for sound systems or dub versions for B-sides?

Dubplate, dub version, the whole thing was going side together. Originally, we used to make the dubplate. Then Bunny Lee get some mix and was putting out one or two songs in England before the dubplate came out [in Jamaica]. That's how he really get famous, by having these hit records abroad.

Were there any differences for the mixes of dubplates and dub versions for singles? For example, were effects used differently?

sted that the pressing was financed by Robinson. In 2019, the album was reissued by Pressure Sounds.

It's the same identical thing. It's just that one was released and one was made solely or exclusively for a sound system. Dubplate is slightly different because it's a different version (of a tune or an instrumental). Dub is basically drum and bass.

... with interjections of offbeat or melodies...

Occasionally. But the old format of that is drum and bass. When we singers make a vocal side and they mix a version, it is flavoured with the vocal and a little of the riddim section (offbeat). Now when most men make dub albums it's basically drum and bass. Well, anybody has different ways of doing things. I couldn't mix a dub like Scientist, neither could Scientist mix a dub like me, so he has his own identity. Just like King Tubbys, he had his own identity. But it's the same format.

Your sound was a lot like King Tubby's. The way you used the high pass filter...

Yes, because...each studio has a different sound, Dynamic, Randy's, Joe Gibbs, they all make dubs, but Tubby seems to be the one that the people liked. The filter was there, and you had to use it. Scientist, Jammys, me, we all used it. But I think the main effect came from the (second) reel to reel tape. That's how we used to get the echo reverb. (Note: an audio signal was recorded on a second tape, from there brought back into the console via the tape monitoring and sent directly back to the second tape. The feedback loop created this way resulted in echoes, the length of which could be controlled with the channel fader. The echo time was controlled by the speed at which the tape ran.) Now I don't find any echo effect like that. In other words, whoever engineered at Tubby's you'd hear the same effect. You'd hear a different style but you'd hear the same effect.

As an engineer at Tubby, did you try to create your own sound? Was that even desired?

I don't think you try to find your own sound, the sound is already there. The only thing that differs is the style of the mixing. If you want a King Tubby sound it doesn't make any difference which engineer. The sound remains the same, because the studio have that particular sound. You cannot change a studio's sound, you change the style. The way you manipulate the sound was what makes a difference.

The recordings that were mixed at Tubby, were done in other studios. Didn't that affect the sound? Ultimately, only vocals were recorded at Tubby's, apart from horns every now and then, or guitar overdubs like with Carl Harvey[6].

All the songs come from another studio. Some come from Dynamic, some from Randy's. They come from all over. [They all] sound the same [when they've gone] through Tubby's board. You wouldn't know [if the song was recorded at] Joe Gibbs or Dynamics. You would know if it was coming from Channel One because Channel One uses a different drum pattern. Most studios in Jamaica used Neumann. That was the best microphone (expensive and high quality). Tubbys used ordinary AKG microphones. But you get fantastic sound. It was the board. Haven't seen a board again like Tubby's board.

Which wasn't tinkered with much until it sounded good. It was like an assembly line. A tape was put on and as soon as you heard the intro roll, the mix began.

What is gonna set? Tubby's board is a simple board, you know? The simplest of all boards I have seen. It doesn't carry a lot of features. It has this nice effect (the high pass filter), but it's not complicated. It's very, very basic. I guess great things are simple things, maybe. You have high pass in every studio. Except that this one is rotary, which was our advantage. The others have to punch.

... and were not variable in frequencies...

A rotor high pass works more effective, you can twist [the frequency] up. It's a different effect than one you have to punch.

Was there a difference between a vocal mix and a dub? Did you approach it differently?

It's different. Dub was created because it's unique to a sound system, and it should have something that no one else has. That was dub.

Did you have a specific idea in mind when mixing or did you leave the result up to chance?

When I was mixing, I mixed the way I feel the song. The energy that the song gives me, that's how I mix. But every mix is gonna be different because it's a different time you mix it. You couldn't mix all the mixes the same. Nature does not supply that. So consciously or unconsciously each dub is gonna be different. I don't know why people want to make a big issue out of it, but that's the way it is. No two dubs sound the same.

But two vocal mixes can definitely sound the same.

Exactly. If you are doing a vocal it's generally quite simply because every little error you have to hear. A dub is already recorded so you're just playing back. Dub is when you drop the instrument out and bring it in. The time factor is different. Every day is a different pattern. The way you feel, the way a thing presents itself to you. It's the same with dub.

Does dub have a spiritual vibe?

Spirituality is something individual. You get your spirituality listening to something, now I listen to the same song, maybe I don't get the same energy. We feel it different [but] it's the same thing. The same God that works the same way. It's not a miraculous feat or anything. I didn't create the music. [As engineer] I reproduce the energy from the music, how I feel it. That's why it's different from yours. You could never sit down and copy the way I did it, because it's not the same energy you get from it. Dub is your own expression at the time.

Do you recall the three albums *Harry Mudie meets King Tubby in Dub Conference*[7]? You are not mentioned on the LPs, but in the booklets of the 1994 CD versions you are explicitly named by Harry Mudie in the credits as one of the mixing engineers.

I know I did some things with Tubby. And me have done some tracks in it, Scientist may have done some, maybe Jammy himself or Tubbys himself. We as engineers, we're signed to the studio. So, whoever bring the work the studio pays us. Now a lot of these engineers when they make the dub, they said it's their work. So, I don't know... when it said "Tubbys meet whoever", we just work as an engineer. Is Tubbys who get the credit. To tell the truth, we didn't take it as anything how you're looking at it. That big fuss that people talk about this dub thing, it's foreign. We

6 In January 1978 for the album *Carl Harvey – Ecstasy Of Mankind*, produced by Bunny Lee, which was first officially released on Makasound in 2005 after various bootleg releases.

7 Released between 1976 and 1978 on Moodisc, were repressed several times.

Vol. 2
DUB CONFERENCE
HARRY MUDIE MEETS KING TUBBY IN CONFERENCE
HM
DUB
SIDE 1 (a) WORLD DUB CONFERENCE (b) MARIJAUNA DUB
(c) HEART LEAP DUB (d) DUB INSIDE OUT (e) MELODY IN DUB
SIDE 2 (a) JUNGLE WALK DUB (b) MAKA BACK DUB
(c) DONT PLAY WITH DUB (d) PLANET DUB (e) DRIFTING DUB
All titles written by: H.A. Mudie Produce & Arranged by: H.A. Mudie
MOODISC

Vol. 3
DUB CONFERENCE
HARRY MUDIE MEETS KING TUBBY IN CONFERENCE
HM
DUB
SIDE 1 (a) WHERE EAGLES DARE (b) WITH YOU IN MIND
(c) DO THIS IN BED (d) PEACE OFFERING
SIDE 2. (a) NINTEEN LOVE IN DUB (b) CONFERENCE THEME
(c) TRIBAL RECIPE (d) MUDIE'S SERENADE (IN DUB) (e) DUB IN PARADIS
Publish M.C.P.S. All titles written by: H.A. Mudie. Produced & Arranged by H.A. Mudie
Engineers: King Tubby & Harry Mudie
℗1978 ©1978
Art: DUNCANSON, MOODISC RECORDS 44 Young Street, Jamaica W.I.
Phone: 984-2595 (DISTRIBUTORS)
MOODISC

know it works and it sells records but that's it. This big energy that is creating, it's all abroad. There was a lot of dubs and we just mix it like we'd be doing ordinary things. Nobody didn't come and say: "We want it a particular way." Nobody tells an engineer how he wants it. We know what a dub is. 80, 90 percent is drum and bass with very little other instruments in it. And it's unique to whoever is getting it, because regardless of doing how many dubs a week they never sound the same. Fatman from England telling me about this fantastic dub that I mixed [for him], I just mixed it like any other song. But when he play it at the dances it creates an impact, I was told.

When you were mixing, did you have any idea how it would work in the dance?

No. I didn't know this thing was out there.

Didn't you attend any dances?

I didn't go to dances in Jamaica. When I did, it was Bunny Lee who took us out. I particularly don't smoke or occasionally have a beer; I wasn't brought up like that. This thing with smoking in the studio throughout the day, I never joined. Never. One guy asked me one time: "No wonder why you sing so great because you smoke weed." I didn't trouble the argument. I don't burst bubbles, I am not like that.

When and how long did you work at King Tubby?

(Kelly runs his hand over his head, as if searching the corners of his brain for the correct year.)

Let's see… I could be there… early 70s… for about five or six years on and off.

Then you went to Randy's and Joe Gibbs.

I worked at Randy's for a long time on and off, too. Then my singing started develop again, so I was in and out of Randy's. In and out of all studios.

Did you also work at Channel One?

I didn't work at Channel One. I go there all the time and they wanted me to work there as an engineer, but I didn't take the offer. Somebody else was there and I figured it would cause some conflict.

Wouldn't it have been financially lucrative to work there? After all, the studio became the most influential production facility of the 80s.

I dunno if I could say it was for money, I guess it was something to do. Nobody was making money. The singer of a lot of songs never got paid. I don't know how we existed. There weren't any shows around, you only have [public holidays like] Christmas Morning, Valentine's Day...

So it was a passion?

I liked it. It's how I'm making some money. My philosophy is "You can have what Mr. Brown has, maybe not in quantity, but you can still have what Mr. Brown has."

The interview took place on August 31, 2010. Shortly before his 75th birthday, Pat Kelly died of complications from kidney disease on July 16, 2019. The *Jamaica Observer* wrote "He was believed to be in his early 70s".[8]

8 "Singer Pat Kelly is dead", *Jamaica Observer* July 16, 2019.

I-Livity I-Fi Sound System, Germany

Bunny Lee's studio and and shelves of master tapes in Duhaney Park, 2014.

Bunny Lee: The Kingmaker

> "Bunny Lee breaks all the rules, honestly speaking. Bunny should be credited for a lot of things that other people taken credit for. Bunny could go to King Tubbys, get the key and we go down by the studio. Tubbys wouldn't do that with anybody else."
>
> (Pat Kelly)

Edward O'Sullivan Lee was born on August 23, 1941 in Greenwich Town, in the west of Kingston, the sixth of ten children of a shoemaker. After finishing school, he began training as an electrician. In his early 20s, he earned a living repairing motorcycles and selling car parts. "With his winning personality and good manners, he could certainly have become the most successful car dealer on the island if it hadn't been for his love of music"[1], is how the young man called "Bunny" because of his friendly, bearlike appearance, was described. Later, the nickname "Striker" was added, a reference to the 1953 film "The Hitch-Hiker". As Bunny gained success in the Jamaican music business, the phrase "Striker strikes again!" became a household expression.

Lee started out as a promoter, taking care of airplay for new productions by Coxson, Duke Reid and Leslie Kong. In return, he received free studio time. In 1967, with the last £20 he had earned as a car mechanic, he paid guitarist and arranger Lynn Taitt and his small band for a handful of playbacks. During the session, Roy Shirley's "Music Field" and Lloyd Jackson & The Groovers' "Listen To The Music" were created, among others. One tune reached number 5 in the national charts, and the other went to number 1. After this, Bunny was awarded the title of "Jamaica's Top Producer" four years in a row. In a remarkably short span, then, Bunny had reached the pinnacle of the Jamaican music industry, a position he was to keep for decades. He won the title of best producer four more times, keeping in good contact with musicians and artists, hanging out with them, and acting as an affable, friendly business partner. He had a sure instinct for successful records and set trends instead of following them. In the late 1960s, Bunny had his own radio show called "Bunny Lee At Randy's A Go Go", and established around 20 labels for his own releases for both domestic and foreign markets. Label names ranged from Agro Sound and Attack, to Explosion, Hatchet, Hot Stuff, Jackpot, Justice, Rude Pigeon, Soul, Total Sound and Unity. He licensed his recordings to Trojan, Island and PAMA in the UK, and also managed the interests of other producers and musicians during negotiations, including Bob Marley. In gratitude, Marley gifted him the song "Mr. Chatterbox" in 1970.[2] Bunny chose Slim Smith to be his favourite singer and had one hit after another with him. "Let Me Go Girl", "Everybody Needs Love", "Ain't Too Proud To Beg", "My Conversation", "Love And Devotion" and many more. In 1969, he had his first British top ten hit with "Wet Dreams", although it did not receive any airplay because it was declared indecent. Lee himself wrote the lyrics and had to search for a long time until he found a singer who was willing to do justice to what, from today's perspective, was a harmless but rather raunchy text. It was Max Romeo who took up the vocal challenge. The recordings took place at Studio One, but because Coxson didn't want his name associated with lines like "Lay down girl, let me push it up", he only provided him with an apprentice to do the final mix. His name was Errol Thompson.

In 1971, Lee produced Eric Donaldson's "Cherry Oh Baby" and clinched victory in the annual Festival Song Contest, a government-supported event that has been held since 1966 to the present day. He was responsible for Delroy Wilson's "Better Must Come", which became the PNP's election campaign anthem, outclassing the ruling JLP in 1972. Two years later he developed the aforementioned Flyers style with drummer Santa Davis, which made Johnny Clarke a star, Bunny Lee wealthy and Tubby's way of dubbing famous. In the mid-70s he sparked a verbal battle between two deejays that entertained the entire island by publishing a microphone check accidentally recorded at Tubby's. During the sound check, I-Roy joked about Prince Jazzbo, also present: "Jazzbo man, if you were a juke box, I wouldn't put a dime into your slot!" Jazzbo didn't think it funny but had no choice. He had to react and a week later responded with "Straight To I-Roy's Head", also produced by Bunny Lee. So, the Striker staged a clash[3] that lasted over many singles, with Derrick Morgan later joining in. Morgan had already been involved in a similar

1 "Bunny 'Striker' Lee – Reggae Gone International" German Reggae print magazine *RIDDIM* 02/2012 p. 54ff.

2 Bunny Lee pre-released the song in Jamaica on the Lee label, and in the UK on Jackpot.

3 The entire story can be found on the album *Once Upon A Time At King Tubbys*, released by Pressure Sounds in 2009. It contains the most famous tracks from this dispute plus the associated dubs, which was only the official part of the production. There were also other mutual accusations that were pressed as pre-release or dubplate.

dispute with Prince Buster back in 1963, although it wasn't nearly as serious.

Bunny Lee was a permanent guest in Tubby's studio. Here he voiced most of his productions, and had them mixed by one of the engineers working there. He is the one who proclaimed Philip Smart and Lloyd James princes and contributed to Osbourne Ruddock becoming internationally worshipped as King of Dub with the albums *Dub From The Roots* and *The Roots Of Dub*. Lee had the gift of turning the coincidences of studio work into success. "Every spoil is a style!" Following this motto, he gave the young dub genre decisive input, especially after Tubby had installed the discarded 4-track equipment from the Dynamic studio in his electronics and dub cutting workshop, thus enabling him to mix and record vocals as well. However, Jamaican singers didn't always hit the right note, which in the past meant the recordings weren't suitable for release. Bunny Lee took advantage of multi-track technology here, and suggested removing the revealing melodic instruments from the mix at problematic points where the vocals and harmony clashed. "Tubbys would say 'It can't work man!' Yeah Tubbs! When you reach there just drop out the guitar and bring in the drum and pure noise (effect), and then drop out the bass and chiiinnnggg! ... Just pure madness! ... They didn't know it was through the singer was off key. But with the pure drum track alone it nah really go off key! They thought it was a style and everybody followed we, and started the dropouts. ... Singing on pure drum and bass, and if it ran too long you'd bring in the echo."[4]

The trick with the variable use of the offbeat not only helped the 4-track dub to its first structure. The dubby background of singing or toasting also soon created the sound of an era that interpreted dancehall as a musical genre. It wasn't long before a new style emerged from the Hoo Kim brothers' Channel One studio that took Jamaica by storm. Producer Junjo Lawes dominated the scene with his "Volcano Sound System" and the Roots Radics as riddim suppliers, while the British label Greensleeves opened the European market for trimmed reggae, with its fusion of roots, dub and dancehall. This development was imminent, and the groundwork for it was laid here.

Bunny Lee continued to focus on the original reggae market and always kept an eye on the Jamaican communities outside the Caribbean. He became one of the first producers to record in the Channel One studio and with numerous dub LPs fueled the emerging competition between Channel One and King Tubby. When Scientist moved from Tubby to the Hoo Kims, the competition took on a particularly spicy note, which Bunny also knew how to exploit.

In 1977, he released the LPs *Ranking Dellinger Superstar* as well as *Johnny Clarke – Superstar Roots Disco Dub* in Jamaica on Weed Beat, the Dynamic Sounds label, and sold himself as the inventor of the vocal & dub combination in LP format. Although similar LPs had already been released the previous year[5], he wrote in the credits of the Johnny Clarke LP "Produce [sic] by Bunny Lee with a new trend six vocal and Six Dub on side B the very first of ist [sic] kind in Jamaica". He began to produce a considerable number of dub albums, indulged his preference for extravagant titles and released them, sometimes several at a time, on his own and licensed labels in the UK, Jamaica, the US, or Canada as follows:

- **Greatest Hits Super Dubb – Wise Doctored For Super Sound** (Hatchet JA 197X)
- **Tommy McCook & The Agrovators – King Tubby Meets The Agrovators At Dub Station** (Live And Love UK + Striker Lee JA, both 1975)
- **Rasta Dub '76** (Grounation UK + Attack JA, both 1976)
- **Agrovators Meets The Revolutioners At Channel One Studios** (Third World UK + Justice JA + Gorgon JA, all 1977)
- **Kaya Dub** (Third World UK, 1978)
- **Agrovators Meets The Revolutionaries Part II** (Micron CAN 1979)
- **Jack Ruby Hi-Power vs. Gemini Discotheque** (Tad's US 1980)
- **Dub War: Coxsone vs Quaker City** (Attack, Imperial CAN 1981)
- **Dub War Vol. 1** (Vista Sounds UK 1985)[6]

4 *Reggae Going International 1967–1976. The Bunny 'Striker' Lee Story* ibid p.133.

5 See chapter "Prologue".

6 Often listed under "King Jammy" because his name is on both label stickers and many times on the cover. However, it only ran under *Dub War Vol. 1* and according to the credits was mixed by King Jammy and Scientist. Who actually mixed it is unclear.

RASTA DUB '76

KAYA
DUB
4

VISTA SOUNDS
VSLP 4039
DUB WAR
VOL. 1

Dub War
coxsone vs quaker city

Lee enjoyed taking on the role of MC on the albums and spoke intro jingles for the tracks, for example:

- **Allied Dub Selection** (Tad's USA, 1980)
- **King Tubby Studio verses Channel One Studio** (Bumb USA, 1980)
- **King Tubby – Majestic Dub** (Star UK, 1983)[7]
- **Sly & Robbie – Masters Of Ceremony Dub** (Imperial Canada, 198X)

Also, he was portrayed or depicted on the covers, either alone or alongside others:

- **Bunny Lee The Version Master presents Creation of Dub** (Total Sounds JA 1975)
- **Bunny Lee & The Aggrovators Presents Super Dub Disco Style** (Jamaica Sound UK 1979)
- **Sly & Robbie – Masters Of Ceremony Dub** (Imperial Canada 198X)
- **King Tubby's and The Agrovators – Dubbing In The Back Yard** (Black Music UK 1982)
- **King Tubby The Dubmaster With The Waterhouse Posse** (Vista Sounds UK 1983)

In the 80s, Lee withdrew from the business, which was now involving new artists, although still produced the debut LP by Beenie Man[8], a 10-year-old prodigy. Lee was now primarily on the road as a sales representative in the countries where his records had been released and was rarely seen in Jamaica during this time. One of his last LP productions was an attempt to participate in the worldwide success of Gussie Clarke's "Rumours/Telephone Love" riddim with the various artists/one riddim sampler *More Ideas 1988*[9]. From now on, he focused on evaluating his immense back catalogue. After all these years, he was in possession of what was probably the largest contingent of recordings from Jamaica, chaotically stored unsorted in former Joe Gibbs' studio building in Duhaney Park. In 1972, Lee had bought the property for $30,000 after Gibbs had moved his location to 20 North Parade. Since then, the premises have housed not only Lee's own master and multi-track tapes, but also recordings he has dealt with on behalf of others. On March 9, 2015, a fire destroyed the upper floor containing computers and tape machines, where Lee also had tapes sorted and some of them remastered. The fire did not reach the archive with the historical recordings on the floor below. The extent to which soot, heat and extinguishing water had caused damage becomes apparent from case to case.

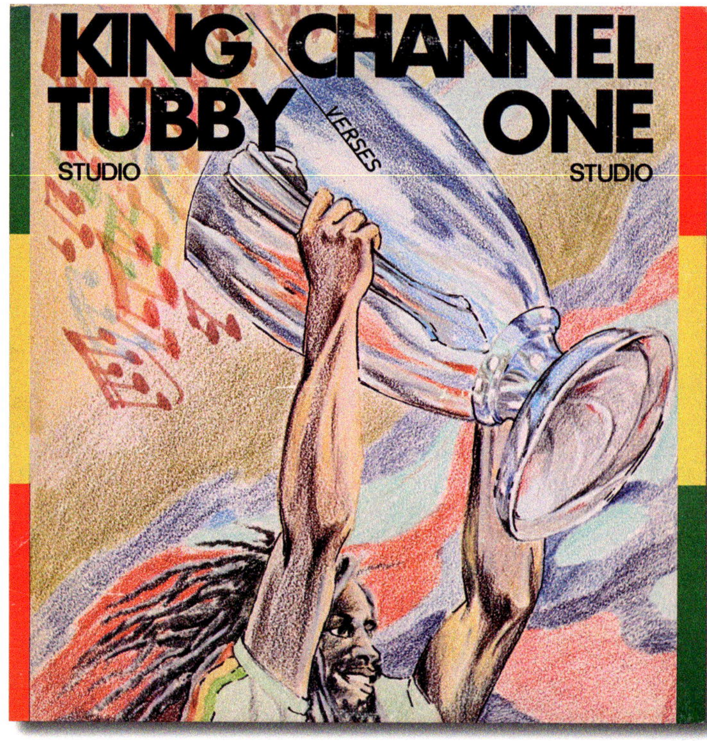

Some of what has been and is still released from this collection is dubious. The Jamaican Recordings and Kingston Sounds labels, which operated from the UK and presented themselves as "Jamaica's Best Kept Secrets", "Original Jamaican 1970's Dub Specialist" and "Outstanding Artists In Their Greatest Performances", played a particularly deceptive role here. More than 200 compilations have been released since 2001 and 2003, earning the operators the reputation of being a "bogus company", a counterfeit workshop. Alongside regular re-releases, you can find great oldies and goldies on both labels, although you are well ad-

7 Mono version of *Jack Ruby Hi-Power vs. Gemini Discotheque* Tad's US 1980.
8 *The Invincible Beany Man – The 10 Year Old D.J. Wonder*, released on Justice in 1983.
9 Released in 1988 on the British label World Enterprise Records, with Vin Gordon, Delroy Wilson and Beany [sic] Man among others.

MASTER OF CEREMONY "DUB"
Sly and Robbie

BUNNY LEE
The Version Master
presents
CREATION OF DUB

Dubbing In The Back Yard
King Tubby's and The Agrovators

VISTA SOUNDS
VSLP 4015
KING TUBBY THE DUBMASTER
WITH
THE WATERHOUSE POSSE

vised to approach them with skepticism. Song titles were often altered, and details regarding timing of recordings, as well as the musicians and engineers involved, were not uncommonly embellished for promotional purposes. The information content was particularly bold in the case of some dub albums that were declared as "lost & found" or as "previously unreleased". In most cases, both sound and composition made it clear that these dubs were not created in the 70s, but with digital help in more modern times.

In these matters, Bunny Lee washed his hands of any involvement, although in the past he had indulged in similar practices himself. Back in 1980, the *Jack Ruby Hi-Power vs. Gemini Discotheque* LP wasn't what it claimed to be on the cover. It was neither a clash between two sound heavyweights, with deejays Nicodemus and Welton Irie on the microphones, nor did the Roots Radics record the riddims with bassist Flabba Holt on drums! In addition, the mix was not by "King Tubby himself", but was mixed by Scientist, with recordings by the Soul Syndicate band. Bunny Lee himself spoke the intro on one track. Three years later he released the mixes with other titles in the UK as *King Tubby – Majestic Dub*[10].

The reputation of the man who had made the captain's hat his trademark remained unaffected by such obfuscation. In his homeland, clever businessmen like him were revered as "Gorgons". On October 20, 2008, Jamaica presented him with the Order of Distinction for his contributions to the national music industry. Bunny Lee appeared at the awards ceremony dressed in a gold-striped colonial three-piece suit, complete with frock coat and top hat, whereupon the press hailed him as "the most dapper" gentleman present.[11]

By this point, the Gorgon had already shed the Striker moniker, and taken on a new role in reggae. Until his death on October 6, 2020, he toured the world, accompanied by his children, as a walking encyclopedia, telling his audiences what had happened and when, where, and how, and who recorded or produced what with whom and why! No interview request was rejected, no opportunity to tell his stories was turned down. Bunny Lee was blessed with a phenomenal memory and benefited from the fact that he had had a hand in every reggae trend since the '60s, as long as it was analogue. He knew everyone and anyone and those with whom he had done business over the years recall him as a fair partner. Everywhere he appeared, he was celebrated as a welcome guest. Even

if Bunny Lee wasn't always the guarantor of established facts, he was still a sure bet to provide an entertaining look into the past. Since he had publicized the incident with Ruddy Redwood at Treasure Isle studio, it remained essential to have him recap the events.

Bunny Lee: Ruddy was a popular sound in Spanish Town ("The Supreme Ruler Of Sound"). He and another guy named Stereo[12] – Seymour Stereo we called him – those guys used to rule in Spanish Town. The main sound in Kingston was Coxson, Duke Reid and "King Edward the Giant". Stereo was a very quiet person, he built sound systems. To me, he built a better amplifier than even Tubbys, with better bottoms. Stereo's sound was heavy. When the bass come in, man... Ruddy used to come to Duke Reid or Coxson. He had the money to back it up and pay. So, he always looked

10 Star UK, 1983
11 http://jamaica-gleaner.com/gleaner/20081021/ent/ent1.html (last accessed on October 15, 2014).

12 This refers to Seymour Williams, owner of the "Stereo" sound system.

for some strange tunes and thing that never came out yet. When Ruddy cut a dub at Duke Reid's studio everybody always listened his selection. Tubbys himself was up there, too.

But not to operate the cutting machine?

No. Tubby used to go there to get tunes from Duke Reid to cut. Coxson don't give him cuts no more. Coxson used to give away riddim on 2-tracks, the voice over here and the riddim over there. He thought that was stereo. No, it's not stereo. If you have a good stereo set you could lock off the voice side, then you have a riddim. Tubbys took it and put other artists on it for his sound. Coxson couldn't understand that till I tell him. He didn't know 2-track recording was different from stereo. So, Coxson kinda vex that Tubbys put other artists on Studio One riddims. Now everybody stop go to Coxson and flock Tubby's place 'cause he had Coxson riddims and sounded wicked. Duke was a smarter man than Coxson by far. He always mixed it like a record, you never get no 2-track. That record is not released, you get it a couple weeks or months till it releases. It advertises the record... I am telling you now the real thing that started the version...

The year is 1968...

Yeah man. What I'm telling you is gospel, because I was there. Tubbys, Smitty, Ruddy, the whole of we talked about some sound system business. They cut a dub and Smitty forgot to put in the voice. I think it was a Paragons tune. It's pure riddim and Smitty said "Rahtid, the dub is spoiled", but Ruddy said "No man, make it play." Smitty cut the whole riddim and then Ruddy said "Cut it again and put in the voice".

Back then it wasn't officially called "dub", but rather "version".

They said "Now play part one, now play part two". U-Roy come with the new name "version". The deejays then just said "version 1, version 2", it's shorter. So, the name version came on.

That was when Linford Anderson began the first version experiments.

Linford Anderson, you could class him as a pioneer. He did all of Clancy Eccles versions and mixed tunes [for me] like "My Conversation". He was coming from 2-track, you know. He used to be a big engineer at RJR[13], one of the big radio stations. In Jamaica he's a good engineer, later worked with United Nations. He lives somewhere in America now, he retired.

After RJR he started at Dynamic...

Dynamic was WIRL. WIRL was bankrupt so Byron Lee pulled strings and get it. He enlarged the control room, but he never touched the inside of the studio because he would lose the sound. Dynamic has the best sound in the Caribbean, 'cause the bass, the closest thing to it was Studio One.

Was it the room acoustics?

Yes. Byron never troubled it. If you go in there now, all of the acoustic remain the way that West Indies Records (WIRL) built it. Because the bass. You have bass on a tune built at Dynamic and you turn it up, it never distort. It will blow your speaker but you can hear every note clear. The other studios are kind of muddy sometimes, when you go up on it, it distort. Dynamic was clean.

Maybe the quality came from the fact that the best engineers in Jamaica worked there at the time. Linford Anderson, Sylvan Morris, Graeme Goodall...

Morris wanted to build a 3-track to have an extra track for voice. But it wouldn't work because the tape was 2-track (¼ inch). Graeme Goodall was one of the greatest engineers that ever lived. He came from Australia, but he used to live in England.

And he was involved in the founding of Island Records.

He was involved with everything, right. He was a man that helped everybody, for a start. Duke, Federal, Coxson, every studio. He worked at the radio stations, used to run his own label named Doctor Bird and had a contract with West Indies. Anything that West Indies Records put out automatically Doctor Bird put out [in the UK]. Byron sent for him to fix up the West Indies studio when he acquired it and named it Dynamic Sounds. Graeme Goodall was brilliant.

Tubby also had employees who contributed a lot to his fame. Some of them weren't even known by their last names. There was Barry who showed him how to build amplifiers, or Ervin,

13 RJR (Radio Jamaica and the Re-diffusion Network) was a subsidiary of the London-based Rediffusion Group and first broadcast from Kingston on July 9, 1950.

of whom it was said "If Tubby cyaan fix it, make Ervin fix it. If Ervin cyaan fix it, throw it in the basket."[14]

Oh man, Ervin. He is dead now. Ervin was a genius. He could fix anything that broke down, any amplifiers. Plenty of these guys were better than Tubbs electronic wise, though I boost Tubbs on my radio program. You see advertisement can make you be the greatest man, and at the end of the day there are others that are better. Even Jammys build amplifiers, Jammys bass was heavier than Tubbs. Both were apprentices of a guy named Barry (Williams), he teach them how to build amplifiers. Barry, we called him God. He built that amplifier for "King Edwards The Giant". When God turned on Hercules Unchained it was a disaster. It have the separation for the frequencies and the bass alone killed everything. But if I was building a sound in Jamaica, who would build my sound? The man Stereo from Spanish Town. Even up to now, he is an old man now.

What happened to Barry?

Barry get famous [in Jamaica] but he left and went to America. He used to convert cars and go race. God is a man that liked the fast-lane thing. Sometimes he got above the law and started experimenting with drugs and all that.

When Tubby owned his own dubplate studio soon after the Ruddy Redwood story, he started playing with the vocals in the dubs. When did he start his studio?

I don't remember the year now. Tubbs had his little dub cutting room, with a little board that he built. We had a riddim named "Proud to Beg" with Slim Smith.[15] It was 2-track recording. [When] Tubbys cut some soft wax of it he start with the voice, he then take off the voice and just lick in the riddim and bring back the voice in a later part. The people started tell everybody "Tubbys has an amp, wha' can drop the voice out." Randys (Randy Chin) come and say "Bwoy Bunny, what is this amp wha' can take out the voice out of the riddim?"

The inspiration for Tubby's experiments with the high pass filter came from Randy's studio.

Randy's studio did "Have Some Mercy" with Delroy Wilson. Randy had some equalizer thing and Niney started playing with it (and produced a similar sound effect to Tubby's filter). People said "madness that". [At the time] Byron Lee change out the 4-track and wanted space and I said "Byron, I carry it to Tubbys." That board now had a high-pass filter on it where you can change the sound. I made a tune with Tommy McCook named "The mighty gates of Goza"[16], on Slim Smith's "Everybody Needs Love" riddim. I said "Let me try it out Tubbs, you balance it up, [start the tape] and I play with it." We did it and it was the same sound! The killer sound! I started calling it the "Squawki" and then Tubbs started using it. The rest is history. Some of the tune, when you touch the "Squawki", sounded like you have a knife that cuts into the riddim. Especially when it comes with the flying cymbal through the [sound system] tweeter.

Today I see Tubby's albums all over the place. [But] Tubbys only made three personal dub albums where he sit down at the board and mix: *Roots Of Dub*, *Dub From The Roots* and *Brass Rockers* with Tommy McCook. You see the *Shalom Dub*[17], Tubbys mixed it as B-sides not as a dub album. So, you can call that a King Tubbys album, too. All other King Tubbys albums you see out there are fraud.

Good point. *Shalom Dub* was re-released on Jamaican Recordings in 2010. A label that contained a lot of things that one would honestly have to call counterfeit. Take for instance *Augustus Pablo Dubbing On Bond Street*[18]...

That's Treasure Isle riddims.

Yes, but it's never Augustus Pablo playing there.

Between me and you, some of them might be Pablo but some are Pablo Second. This guy used to go on tour with Pablo, we called him Keysie. Glen Brown play the thing like Pablo, Peter Tosh too, Joe White... you had a lot of people. I saw a guy from Venezuela, he sounded like Pablo. If I didn't see him playing, you would think

14 Scientist in a conversation with the author.

15 "Ain't Too Proud To Beg", officially released in 1969 on Lee's Unity label.

16 Here, as with Slim Smith's "Ain't Too Proud To Beg", Bunny Lee speaks of dubplate mixes. The official version of "The Mighty Gates Of Goza" can be found on the LP *Tommy McCook & The Aggravators* [sic] – *Brass Rockers* (Total Sounds and Striker Lee), released in 1975.

17 1975 on the British Klik label, 2010 re-released on Jamaican Recordings.

18 2012 on Jamaican Recordings.

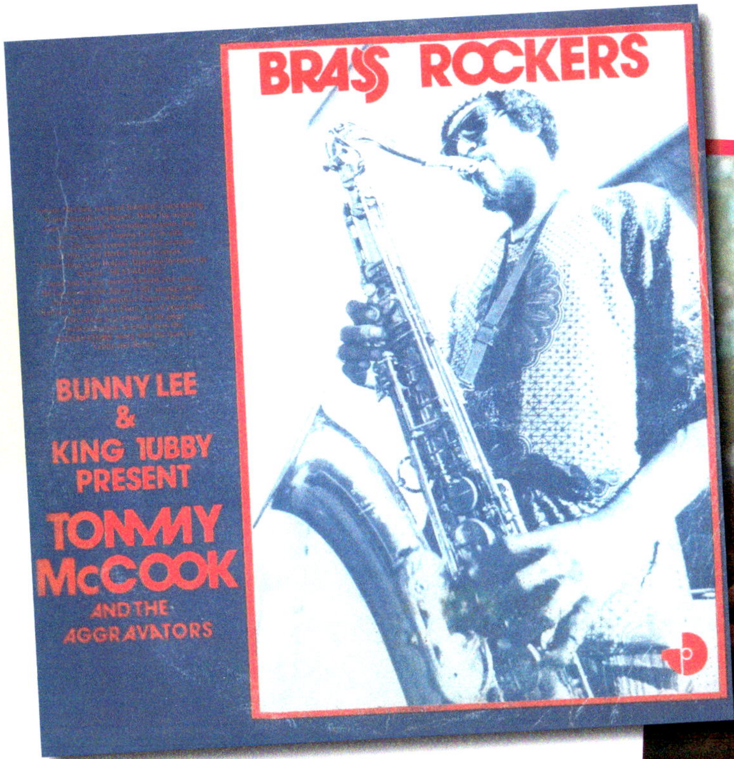

it's Pablo. Pablo was a good friend of mine, played piano on plenty of my tunes. Nobody did know Pablo was going to get so big.

Bunny Lee indirectly owed the band name The Agrovators – sometimes spelled with two gs and sometimes as The Aggravators – to Larry Lawrence, the producer of Ethnic Fight Band's dub albums *Out Of One Man Comes Many Dubs*[19] and *Music Explosion*[20], previously mentioned by David Rodigan, among others. Initially, The Agrovators started as The Hippy Boys, then became The Upsetters and ended as The Wailers. Bunny Lee was so enamored with the name that he not only named a label and his record shop at 101 Orange Street "Agro", but also called "The Agrovators" whatever constellation of musicians were playing for him at the time. He came up with the idea in a conversation with Eddy Grant, the former front man of pop group The Equals, and singer of worldwide hits such as "Gimme Hope Jo'Anna" or "I Don't Wanna Dance". Grant had made a deal with Lawrence for his Torpedo label and whined: "Bunny, your friend Larry, he's causing me aggro, man." – "I said: what is this word?" – "He's causing me problems." – "I liked the name and when I went back to Jamaica, I start calling a bunch of musicians The Agrovators."

Bunny Lee and the author, France 2012.

19 UK 1975.
20 UK 197X.

Community Rockers Sound System, Germany

Errol Brown: Dub as a Musical Event

> "That now is dub, playing with the control, in and out with the guitars and steady bass, drum and bass coming at you. That is really dub."
>
> (Coxson Dodd[1])

When I entered his hotel room, Errol Brown was ironing a white sweater, which he then carefully folded. He was planning to wear it later that evening, while mixing Ziggy Marley's live concert. Marley's son was performing at a big European festival, and Errol knew that there were going to be no sound checks at an event like this. His only option would be to preset the channels during the band changeover. In such situations experience helps, and Errol had already practiced this blind flight hundreds of times. When the concert began, he made a sensational acoustic start, going from zero to one hundred in a few seconds, and well above the permitted noise limit of 93 dB.

The man who knows how to transform volume into pleasure was born in Kingston on September 26, 1950, one of four children of a butcher and a saleswoman. In the music business, he is one of those outside the spotlight, valued by insiders and connoisseurs, but hardly noticed by the majority of music consumers. As a recording and mixing engineer, Errol Brown has mixed countless dub albums, his name mentioned on the back covers only in the fine print. His status as a dark horse didn't change even when his abilities led him into the concert business. He initially toured with Culture, following his work on their album *Harder Than The Rest*[2] and then made a career as the Marley family's personal engineer. In April 1980, Brown made his debut as Bob Marley's live engineer during a concert to celebrate Zimbabwe's independence. Following this, he embarked on multiple world tours, continuing his role as a live engineer, first with Bob until the last day of the "Uprising" tour, and later with sons Julian, Stephen, and Ziggy Marley. After decades of service for Jamaican employers, he was poached to join the American reggae league, just like Soljie Hamilton[3]. Both have been at the mixing desk for US top scorers for a long time, Soljie with SOJA, Errol with Rebelution, two white bands that in the States far outpace Jamaican acts in terms of audience

response, concert volume, sales figures, and chart rankings. In 2019, at Buju Banton's comeback concert at the Kingston stadium in Jamaica, Errol Brown mixed the live sound in his homeland again.

Brown learned his craft when his uncle Arthur brought him to Treasure Isle studio. The latter was producer and studio owner "Duke" Arthur Stanley Reid (1923–1976), Errol Brown was his nephew, Reid and

1 *Studio One Story*, Soul Jazz DVD 2002.
2 Frontline/Virgin UK + High Note JA 1978.
3 See chapter "Soljie Hamilton & Groucho Smykle, Dub Design for Sly & Robbie".

Brown's mother being siblings. Reid owned the Treasure Isle Recording Studio, ran the "Trojan" sound system and managed a liquor store at 33 Bond Street, not far from the infamous Back-O'-Wall[4] ghetto. The start-up capital for all these ventures came from his wife Lucille, who had won the lottery. At the beginning of 1966, Reid opened a studio on the floor above the shop. Initial equipment consisted of an Altec 250 SU tube mixer from the 1950s, fitted with palm-sized bakelite knobs – still legendary and highly traded for its rich sound – an Ampex tape recorder and a Pultec equalizer. He took over the equipment from Lyndon O. Pottinger, who had just separated from his partner, a woman who would later take over Reid's business, although at the time that was of course neither planned nor foreseeable. In 1961, the Pottingers had set up a small production facility behind their house on Molynes Road, including a record press, which Reid also acquired.

One of the first LPs recorded with this equipment was the sampler *Greatest Jamaican Beat*, subtitled *Rock Steady Baba-Boom Time*[5]. On the back it showed a photograph of the control room, and the caption under it read "Well designed and boosting the modern recording studio equipment in the island is Treasure Isle Recording Studio".

In October 1963, just a mile away, Coxson Dodd opened Studio One. Although friends in private, in public Coxson and Reid were bitter rivals, both in competition for Jamaica's attention in the days of ska and rocksteady. They feuded with sound systems, dubplates, and music production, for which both initially rented the Federal studio before creating their own recording facilities.

Looking back, Studio One was reverently and rightly described as the home of good music. The longest-lasting riddims, the most beautiful melodies, and the greatest voices in Jamaican music history were said to have come from the Brentford Road production house. Objectively speaking, however, more technically and musically sophisticated productions emerged on Bond Street during the rocksteady era. This was not only because the reflections from the wooden cladding in Treasure Isle recording studio had a major influence on the sound quality. While Studio One worked more according to the assembly line principle, with microphone setups and mixing console settings, once established, remaining unchanged for months, Duke Reid was a perfectionist, constantly looking for the perfect sound. He did not learn the music. The former police officer was simply an obsessively meticulous worker, with exceptional musical intuition. He directed his musicians all over the studio, experimented with microphone distances and persistently gave new instructions until the recordings sounded the way he wanted them to. His absolute will to focus only on the best possible result led to recordings of timeless class. In the first few years after it was founded, Treasure Isle studio sound quality was clearly superior to the Brentford Road productions.

Nevertheless, around 1973, Reid left the field to his opponent Coxson. He disliked the varieties of roots and dub, as well as the growing influence of the Rastafarians with their lyrics. In addition, a cancer diagnosis curbed his fighting spirit, and it became apparent that he would have to give up the Treasure Isle operations.

Three years previously, Duke Reid had liberated his nephew from telecommunications company Cable & Wireless, where Errol had been earning his living since completing his schooling, alongside pursuing studies at Kingston Technical High School. "We're a family," he persuaded him, "come to my studio and learn this stuff properly." The studio engineer Byron "Smitty" Smith took over the training, and his uncle, the former police officer, took over the drill, which wasn't always easy for Errol. It was obvious that Reid wanted to get rid of Smitty and replace him. Errol felt uncomfortable with the situation. "I didn't like that idea. Byron was teaching me and I don't want to push him out of the work. I just go out and never go back."

Four months later, Smitty threw in the towel on his own. Like Reid and many others, he also wanted to set up his own liquor store (which he did, on Molynes Road). Besides, he took on mastering for Alvin Ranglin's "Record Specialists" pressing plant. Unexpectedly, the Treasure Isle studio found itself without an engineer in 1973. Duke Reid intervened with his sister. When Errol came home, his mother just said: "Mr. Smith left." The son became reconciled with his uncle, and "decide to go back, of course."

Reid had since moved his shop across the street and upgraded the studio with a 12-channel mixer. Errol couldn't remember the brand but was sure it came from Germany. Connected to it were an Ampex 2-track and an 8-track tape machine, some Pultec equalizers and compressors, a Fish-

4 The Back-O'-Wall ghetto was considered the scariest slum in the Caribbean. Many of the socially ostracized Rastafarians had retreated there. On the morning of July 12, 1966 Prime Minister Seaga evicted the residents, bulldozed their huts and began building concrete structures there. The district was named Tivoli Gardens and is still characterized by poverty and crime.

5 Appeared in Jamaica in 1968 on Treasure Isle, in the UK on Doctor Bird.

er reverb and, temporarily, a Roland Space Echo[6] which was brand new and had just come on the market.

Errol Brown's return to Treasure Isle studio, for the meager weekly wage of JA$100, which was roughly equivalent to US$70, went hand in hand with Reid's knowledge of his health. The Duke wanted to keep the business in the family, and hoped that Errol would take over the company, but it did not get to that. Ultimately, Reid didn't trust Errol to pay him his monthly allowance of US$2,000. In 1974, he sold the studio and the rights to his production catalogue to Sonia Pottinger. On September 26, 1976, Duke Arthur Reid died in St. Joseph's Hospital in Kingston.

Before the takeover, Sonia Pottinger (1931–2010) had already established herself as the first woman and producer in the Jamaican music business. Not only did she own several successful labels such as Gay Feet and High Note, but she also had a retail location on Orange Street (not far from Bond Street), with her Tip Top Record Shop. She also had contacts in the UK, where Trojan Records had established a well-running sub-label called High Note for her.

After the purchase, the successful entrepreneur Sonia showed little interest in preserving for posterity the illustrious past of a studio that she had not founded herself. In this way, Duke Reid's early demise had left a gap in reggae historiography that was difficult to fill. This was in complete contrast to the knowledge accumulated at Studio One, where Coxson Dodd, almost 30 years after his studio's heyday, was obliged to hone his legend through re-releases, interviews, and documentaries.

Errol Brown was deeply affected by the sale to Pottinger. Driven by disappointment, he gathered up all the important master tapes, dragged them to his house and waited. However, the new owner wasn't looking for a fight. She wanted to cooperate, came to visit him, and asked how the back catalogue could be monetized. Errol recommended compilations

6 The "Roland Space Echo" is a tape echo device from Roland with the abbreviation RE-201. Released in 1974, it worked with a ¼ inch tape loop passed through multiple record, playback, and erase heads, each of which could be controlled individually. Roland released several similar devices, but only the RE-201 achieved lasting fame.

and especially dub albums, which he had already suggested to his uncle, but to no avail. Mrs. Pottinger immediately agreed, so Errol took all the tapes back to Bond Street, curated *Treasure Isle Hottest Hits Volume 1 – 3* and began to do what Duke Reid had vehemently refused to do, i.e., he mixed dub albums from his productions. For the first LPs *Treasure Dub Vol. 1 + 2*[7] and *Pleasure Dub* he used hits from Duke Reid's rocksteady catalogue. Since these tracks now belonged to Sonia Pottinger, she was credited as producer, even though she had only commissioned the dubs. Only from the fourth album *Medley Dub* did Errol begin incorporating playbacks that Sonia Pottinger had recorded as a client at Treasure Isle in 1968–'71, before taking over. He also mixed dub LPs for the former Gaylads singer and producer Harris "B.B." Seaton (1944–2024), who preferred to produce at Treasure Isle, and called Errol "Roots Brown" on his vocal and dub covers.

As with the regular productions, in terms of sound and finesse, the rocksteady dubs from Treasure Isle also trump the simultaneously released rocksteady dub albums from Studio One. They also demonstrate the high quality of Duke Reid productions. Errol Brown skillfully incorporated their musicality into his dubs, using the well-crafted playbacks from Tommy McCook & The Supersonics, who served as the in-house band until the studio was sold. In addition to brilliant mixes on B-sides[8], he released at least 11 dub LPs during his time on Bond Street, between 1974 and '79:

- **Treasure Dub** (Treasure Isle Records 001 Dub Series 1975)
  Producer: Sonia Pottinger, Riddims: Duke Reid
- **Pleasure Dub** (Treasure Isle Records 002 Dub Series 1976)[9]
  Producer: Sonia Pottinger, Riddims: Duke Reid
- **Treasure Dub Vol. 2** (Treasure Isle Records 002 Dub Series 1976)
  Producer: Sonia Pottinger, Riddims: Duke Reid
- **Medley Dub** (High Note 1976)
  Producer: Sonia Pottinger, Riddims: Sonia Pottinger
- **Dubb Everlasting** (High Note 1977)
  Producer: Sonia Pottinger, Riddims: Sonia Pottinger

7 Repressed with different artwork as *Treasure Isle Dub Vol. 1 + 2*.
8 A small selection can be found on the DoCD *Dub Over Dub: 27 Track Dub Extravaganza*, Heartbeat 1996 or among the 25 bonus tracks on the DoCD *Errol Brown & The Revolutionaries – Culture Dub & Medley Dub* Doctor Bird 2019, as well as the DoCD *Errol Brown & The Revolutionaries – Tip Top Dub* Doctor Bird 2021.
9 Re-released in 2009 by Pressure Sounds UK as *Tommy McCook & The Supersonics – Pleasure Dub*.

Orthodox Dub
Orthodox Dub

DUB
EXPRESSION

DUBB
EVERLASTING
HIGH NOTE
007
DUB SERIES

Medley
Dub

- **Dub Expression** (High Note 1978)
  Producer: Sonia Pottinger, Riddims: Sonia Pottinger
- **Culture Dub** (High Note Jamaika 1978) or **Culture In Dub** (Sky Note UK 1978)
  Producer: Sonia Pottinger, Riddims: Sonia Pottinger/Culture
- **Orthodox Dub** (Magic Fire Records JA 1978)
  Producer: Harris Seaton, Riddims: Harris Seaton

Orthodox Dub is an album of mysterious provenance that only saw an official release in 2016 through the Japanese Dub Store label. Undoubtedly, it features playbacks recorded and mixed by Errol Brown for B.B. Seaton at Treasure Isle. However, who compiled or produced and released the LP remains a mystery. In the late 1970s, it somehow found its way to New York, where individual copies surfaced bearing the Wackies[10] imprint. Producer Clive Hunt said[11] he put the LP together, pressed 1,000 copies in Jamaica and sold it to the British label D-Roy without the cover. The number of copies that surfaced in the years leading up to the re-release indicated a print run of less than 1,000. Possibly some copies also made their way to New York. Somewhere along the line the LP was given a printed cover that credited Errol Brown as producer. When the Hunt compilation *Bad Bad Bad*[12] was released in 2020, the liner notes stated that Hunt had produced *Orthodox Dub* and released it "in a very limited pressing" on his Magic Fire Records label. Well-preserved copies of this white label pressing are now selling for four-figure prices. It remained unclear who produced the LP. Hunt described himself to me as "not a friend of B.B. Seaton" and referred to him as a "manipulator" who ensured that Duke Reid did not sell to Errol Brown. In any case, in addition to *Orthodox Dub,* Errol Brown has mixed other dub LPs for B.B. or Jah Seaton, which, despite small numbers, received an official release with exceptional cover artwork, becoming high-priced treasures on the collector's market.

- **Gun Court Dub** (Love, UK 1975)
- **Revolutionary Dub** (Trenchtown UK 1976)

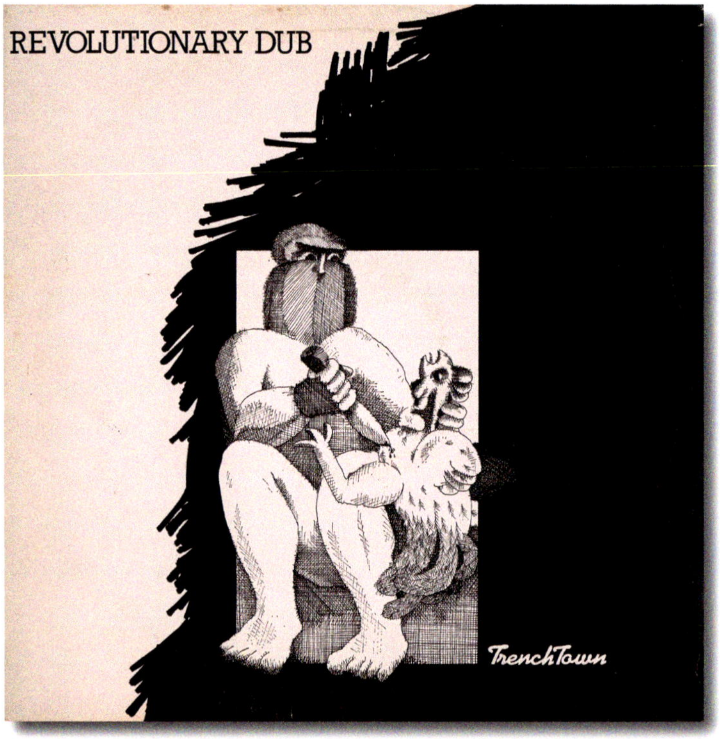

10 Studio and label in the Bronx run by the Jamaican Lloyd "Bullwackie" Barnes, who emigrated to New York, where Barnes produced more than 10 dub LPs besides vocal and showcase albums.
11 2017 during an unrecorded conversation in Kingston.
12 *Clive 'Azul' Hunt presents Bad Bad Bad*, VP Records 2020.

Enticed by the positive reception of the repeatedly reprinted first edition (which can be recognized by the fact that "Vol. 1" is not yet on the cover), Seaton compiled old material from 1976–'78, 19 and 26 years later, into two additional *Gun Court Dub* LPs with mixes by Errol Brown:

- **Gun Court Dub Vol. 2** (Soul Beat UK 1994)
- **Gun Court Dub Vol. 4** (Soul Beat UK 2001)

Errol Brown was not involved in *Gun Court Dub Vol. 3* on Seaton's Soul Beat label, which is out of the ordinary with digital riddims and divergent artwork. On the other hand, he probably also mixed the LP *Bag-O-Wire,* which was circulating in Europe in the late 70s. The task had been assigned by producer Sydney Crooks, who is likely to have been responsible for the overdubs of an unknown harmonica player[13], adding expressive drama to the playbacks of the Revolutionaries. Crooks was the founder of the vocal trio The Pioneers, who have recorded frequently on their own account at Treasure Isle since the studio opened, and worked with Errol Brown early on. In 1975, he released *Bag-O-Wire* on the British Klik label. Two years later he licensed it to France via CBS/Epic, where the title track, a remake of Burning Spear's "Marcus Garvey", was released as a single. In 1978, *Bag-O-Wire* was released in the Netherlands on the Roots Music International label as *Marcus Garvey* with identical mixes, other titles, and different cover art. Since then, the album has usually been attributed to Sonia Pottinger under this title. However, although undoubtedly mixed by Errol Brown Sonia released the *Bag-O-Wire* playbacks, including the harmonica, on her High Note label in 1977 together with other versions, entitled *Dubb Everlasting*.

13 Probably Stephen Wiest aka Chicago Steve, a blues harmonica player from Milwaukee, who played on a few tracks during a stay in Jamaica in 1974/75.

Have you ever been paid for one of your dub albums?

Errol Brown: I never get royalties. I engineered the dubs but they never put "Errol Brown" or my picture on an album. When I was doing these dubs, I don't know nothing about the business. Probably if they take my picture at the board and put my name on the sleeve, I would be getting royalty. But it only said *Treasure Dub*. And even though it was my creation, it would just say "mixed by Errol Brown" on the back. Same with Burning Spear's *Living Dub* (*Vol. 2*, 1982) at Tuff Gong.

It even said "arranged by Winston Rodney" on the cover. Your name was only written on the vocal counterpart *Hail H.I.M.*

It's because... I just like who I am. I'm kinda in myself and Treasure Isle got away long time...

Aside from recognition and payment, what was it like when you dubbed back then?

It was competition. Dub used to be big in Jamaica, big, big! Everybody come and everybody get a different dub. I do it live, I don't have it on tape. I mean the sound systems in Jamaica... King Tubbys, Jammys, Stereograph... we cut dub for all of them. That time Tubbys never start do anything like that. All them talking about Tubbys, these guys come after me. I did cut dubs for Tubby. I cut dubs for a lot of different sound systems, Tubby's was one of them. I don't really brag. But even Channel One people they come and look how I mix my dub. JoJo, Ernest (Hoo Kim) used

to come to Treasure Isle, watch me and learn. In those days we did singles. I would start to do dub in the early 70s. Before that we'd put two different songs [on one 45], and then we always do the version on the B-side. In the beginning Treasure Isle had a little 2-track radio mixer, later we got this German board and a lot of outboard gears. Pultec equalizers, limiters and all of that shit. What I really like bout that board, it have a little speaker (for orientation purposes, you could hear tracks on it without them going into the mix). Those days I wasn't into music that much, that's why I would put the voice in the little speaker while doing a dub. So I know when to come in and when to take off. I loved that board. I don't remember the name but I had that board until I left Treasure Isle. It had a three-band equalizer. Sweepable mid-frequency, the highs and the lows was fixed. I usually boost the mid-frequency when I do my dub and sweep the different frequency to get [a sound effect]. Then we have spring reverb, you just spring a little and pooow... get the reverb effect.

It often sounds like you've been playing with the return of the reverb.

Yeah, yeah, sometimes I do it. We don't have no [other] technology, we [only] had spring reverb and Space Echo.

You actually worked with the Roland Space Delay? Apart from Lee Perry, no one in Jamaica seriously used it.

Yeah, a couple times but afterwards it got boring to me, and I bought a 1-track Ampex machine, and keep looping till I get different delays.[14] Treasure Isle was a small room. Not big like this [hotel room]. The speakers were right there, I sit on the mixing board in the middle of them and the cutting machine is right behind me. Everything was straight. Just like how I hear it in the studio, same way I cut my own master and send it out to do the stamper.

... the stamper was made from the acetate from the cutting machine. The plates were pressed with the stamper...

I cut it on the thing, so I get my sound. I liked the dub with the music in it and I can affect the music. If you just leave the drum and bass, it is not doing nothing for it. The middles is the life of the music, not just drum and bass. And tweeters bring out the clarity, the hi-hat sound, you know? I like my hi-hat defined and that is the problem I have with all those oldtime music, [it has] no high-end.

Because the technology couldn't do it yet.

Yeah probably. We didn't have [the right] microphones. I went there and changed it; I was fighting for that. I was crying... I used the equalizer to bring up the highs. I remember we were doing some various artist. No hi-hat was on the songs. Enough bass and kick drum but you don't even get the rimshot. So, my uncle usually repair it. He went in and play hi-hat and I recorded. Like on *Alton Ellis Greatest Hits*[15].

Duke Reid on hi-hat? Added later?

Duke, yah man. My uncle leave the catalogue to me, he said: "Generate those things like overdub and get everything in the

14 It is the same setup as described in the chapter "Pat Kelly, The Demythologization of Dub".

15 Count Shelly UK 1973, was repressed by Sonia Pottinger as *Alton Ellis – Mr Soul Of Jamaica*.

right place." But the greatest thing he leave with me, [is] the knowledge. I get a lot of drilling [from him]. Every time I have to cut a dub I walked over to the liquor store cross the road and played it. Sometimes he get upset: "Listen man, start mix the music!" I said "alright", and when I think it sound good now, he say "no!". I remember one time I frown [when leaving], and by the time I reach upstairs it's him that come in the control room and shout: "Master, when I say something don't mix good I mean it don't mix good!" This man no easy. He walk with three gun, two on him side and a shotgun. He come in with the shotgun and Boom! Boom!

He fired inside the control room?

In the wall. To frighten me.

Was that just attitude, or was Duke Reid a dangerous man?

No, he was not pointing at me. He was pointing the wall, pointing the studio, pointing some bottle. We had a lot of tables outside [the store], with whole heap of bottles. He always bring those things to the sessions. Sometimes, when he feel like it, he just fired a shot inside the bottle while the music sweet.

What made you go to Tuff Gong? Was that because of Sonia Pottinger?

Well, Mrs. Pottinger... I'm doing all of these things at Treasure Isle. Producing, holding up the studio, everything. I was in all of the productions, made [two albums[16] with] Marcia Griffiths. The Culture album (*Harder Than The Rest* s.a.), I produced it, and some other artists. I don't get a recognition as producer.

Even though you were not only an engineer for them but also musical director?

Yeah. If I don't like, I tell the musicians to go back [and play again]. I get a whole heap of cursing from the horns people, because sometimes the horns were not so nice, and I would tell them. One time, I will never forget, we were working on a Culture song, and Cedric Brooks, the saxophone player, was blowing like Woody Woodpecker, BaBaBaBa! I stopped the tape and said "Listen man, that Woody Woodpecker is not working." He gave me some bad word and rae rae and pack up. He walk to Mrs. Pottinger record shop which is about three miles from the studio. I locked off the studio and drive down there. Him reach the record shop before me to complain like "This young boy here telling me I'm playing like Woody Woodpecker and disrespect me". I just said: "Mrs. Pottinger, this is how I feel." I don't care how big you are. We're paying you to play, you're not doing me a favour. So, if I don't like it, I don't like it. And when it sound like Woody Woodpecker I tell him. Since I took care of all these things I asked for an increase. There was this saxophonist from Tommy McCook days, Herman Marquis. He was playing alto. Duke knew he had the ear for the notes and harmonies, and used him for the voicing. When Mrs. Pottinger take over I said: "Listen, we need to employ Marquis." I never learned music, you know, and he had the musical ears. So, she employ him as assistant engineer. When I asked for the increase she said she have to let him go and give me his salary. Wrong answer! So, I look for a next job. Hard ting to leave cause Treasure Isle was a part of me.

After the upset over Smitty and the sale to Mrs. Pottinger, Errol Brown left Treasure Isle in anger for the third and ultimate time in 1979, with fatal consequences for the studio. It largely ceased operations and finally closed in 1985. Errol, on the other hand, met Bob Marley, Marcia Griffiths had arranged the meeting. She had been raving about her Treasure Isle engineer for quite some time, who, since the two joint LP productions, had also been at the mixing desk at her concerts. It came to a meeting at the new Tuff Gong studio, where Errol was confronted with a large, modern mixing console for the first time. "I said 'wow' within myself. When I see the board, I was frightened. Leaving this little board [at Treasure Isle] with 12 channels and go to this big MCI 500 which had 36 channel, computer and everything. I was confused, was scared, but I don't even let anybody know and tried to figure out [how it worked]."

The studio was brand new, not yet in operation and was having problems with the bass. Errol found out that this was being caused by the elevated position of the mixing console, a discovery which convinced Bob Marley of Errol's value. A carpenter moved the speaker boxes, and Errol joined Tuff Gong, initially as Alex Sadkin's assistant in the production of *Survival*. He mixed Israel Vibration's *Unconquered People* LP[17], including a dub

16 *Naturally* 1978 + *Steppin'* 1979, both on Sky Note, UK. Two elaborate productions with doubled brass sections and mixed in stereo.

17 Tuff Gong 1979

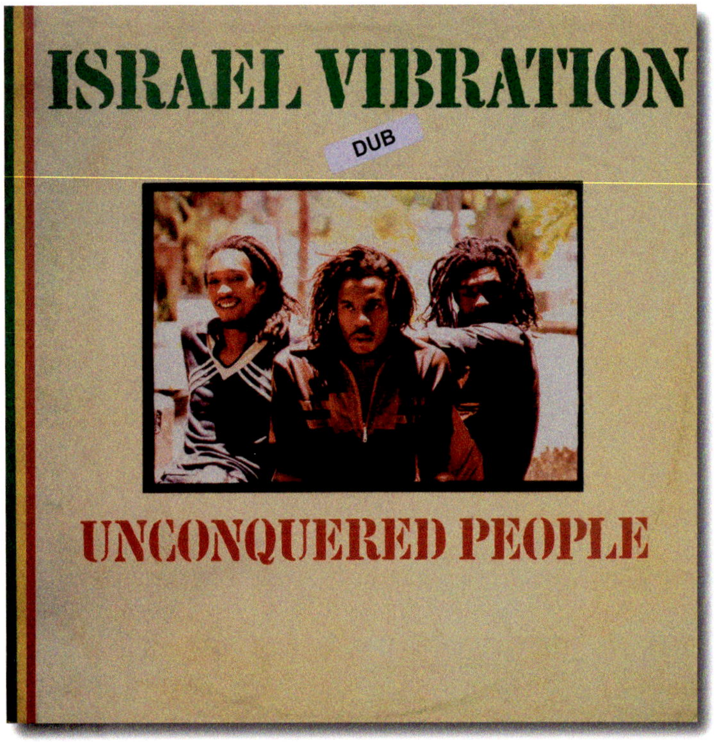

version with eight of the ten tracks. The dub came in the original cover, marked only with a handwritten note or sticker.[18] It was a little masterpiece mixed in stereo, with the Barrett brothers on drums and bass. And, despite the noisy off-center pressing, it sounded fantastic. Errol then independently took over work on Rita Marley's *Who Feels It Knows It* LP from 1980. When Bob Marley had listened to the finished result, he asked "How come I ain't got this sound in my music?" and assigned Errol to work on *Survival*'s successor, *Uprising*. Directed by bassist Aston "Family Man" Barrett (1946–2024), the Burning Spear LP *Hail H.I.M.* was subsequently produced with the Wailers musicians and led to the dub LP *Living Dub Vol. 2*[19] previously mentioned by Errol.

18 An album with an irritating history. The dub version was only released on Rave Music Ltd years after the vocal album, but it stated 1980 on the label. Shortly after the vocal LP, however, a dub LP appeared in the UK with a neutral sleeve and a label sticker on which the original writing "Yabby You & Michael Prophet Meet The Scientist – At The Dub Station" was crossed out..

19 *Living Dub Vol. 2* was reissued countless times, the dubs were mixed several times. Only the first edition from 1980 certainly contains Errol Brown's mixes.

After his departure from Treasure Isle, Errol Brown contributed to the albums *Dub Out Her Blouse & Skirt Vol. 1* and *Cultural Roots Dub* by Donovan Germain, later founder of Penthouse records. However, although he also regularly mixed dubs for productions at Tuff Gong, the big surprise remained elusive. After Treasure Isle, the stylistic changes in reggae prevented the magic of his dub mixes from continuing. Nothing has been released under his name, and some works have only appeared years later when the big dub hype had long since faded. Examples are the following:

- **Chinna Smith presents... DUB IT!** (Nature Sounds US 2004) (Counterpart to Mutabaruka's 1983 LP **Check It!**)
- **Familyman In Dub** (Heartbeat 1999) (Counterpart to the compilation **Aston Familyman Barrett – Cobra Style: Productions From The Wailers' Musical Director** Heartbeat 1999)

Errol Brown remained connected to the Tuff Gong studio even during his temporary departure to the States. In 2012, the LP *Busy Signal – Reggae Dubb'n Again*[20], the counterpart to his album *Reggae Music Again,* was mixed here. Despite the analogue equipment shown on the cover, he had long been an ardent supporter of modern technology. He dreams of a digitally mixed dub album from the material recorded with Bob Marley, which was something Marley always rejected during his lifetime. This was because, as Wailers keyboardist Tyrone Downie revealed to me years later, dub "was a different culture" to him. A different culture? – "Dancehall culture. Bob was not interested in that." Errol is convinced that a digital mix would make the old recordings sound better today than when they were made. "It was the better days of our music." Even if "people don't dance slow and laidback anymore", he emphasizes, "in dub music we use live music and musicians, nothing programmed."

20 VP Records 2012

Cpt. Yossarian's Dubtrain One, Germany.

Channel One Studio ruin, 2018.

Channel One: Vorsprung durch Technik*

(* Progress through Technology)

> "Channel One helped the whole music industry in Jamaica by setting the highest standards of professionalism in audio recording, which made the music more marketable on a global scale. The sound of Channel One is a gold standard in reggae to this day."[1]

In 1971, construction of a recording studio began in Kingston, which would subsequently significantly change the coordinates of the dub landscape. The builder was Joseph "JoJo" Hoo Kim. So far, he and his brothers Ernest, Kenneth, and Paul (or Paulie) had earned their living as vending machine operators. JoJo had purchased slot machines, so-called "one-armed bandits", and jukeboxes, from Issa's Company, which also employed Randy Chin, when it began to withdraw from the business in 1960. In 1970, the government banned gambling machines; jukeboxes also hardly made any profit anymore, as the increasing popularity of record players led to private house parties replacing celebrations in the rum bar. The Hoo Kims had to realign themselves. JoJo (1942–2018) was the eldest, so it was up to him to decide what to do. By chance, he witnessed a recording session at Dynamic studio; the singer John Holt, a good friend since childhood, had taken him there. Fascinated by the atmosphere, JoJo decided to venture into the production business.

The parents of the four brothers met in China. The mother, a Jamaican of Jewish descent, had emigrated to his homeland with her first Chinese husband. After he passed away, she remarried a Chinese man and returned with him to Kingston during the Second Sino-Japanese War (1937–1945). The couple first sold ice cream in Papine, then moved to Spanish Town Road and ended up on Maxfield Avenue, a route from Half Way Tree to Greenwich Town along the ghetto districts of Trenchtown to the east and Whitfield Town to the west. In the corner house at number 29, the pair opened an ice cream parlor with rum bar attached named "Cool Paris". They had purchased the property in 1966. JoJo now aspired to establish a studio within this building – one equipped with the latest, finest technological amenities.

JoJo knew that there were a lot of things that could go wrong. So, he sought advice from a Canadian technician: "We took him to Duke Reid, we took him to Dynamics, we took him to Harry J. He was looking at the racks [with the outboard equipment], he said all what they have in the racks wasn't really necessary. I was wondering what he was talking about because every studio I go I see this hell of a rack with all sorts of equipment in it. He said buy a console that is good like an API."[2] JoJo trusted the man, committing a substantial sum of US$38,000, a considerable amount at the time. Using this investment, he acquired a modern 16-channel API console in Miami that made additional preamplifiers or equalizers unnecessary.

The crucial parts of the API console were developed in 1967 by US American Saul Walker. A year later he founded Automated Processes, Inc. (API). The console was based on a modular system and equipped the individual channels with innovative high-end preamplifiers and semi-parametric 3-band equalizers. Every band had five selectable frequencies (seven in later versions) that could be filtered. The technology was not new; Tubby's MCI console also had selectable frequencies on its high pass filter. The assertion made by Barrow & Dalton in their book *Reggae. The Rough Guide,* stating that the Channel One studio was also equipped with an MCI high pass filter[3], is, however, a misconception and may be due to confusion of the MCI and API acronyms; both equalizers used similar technology. King Tubby's MCI only had a single selectable filter for the entire console, whereas the API used the principle for the highs, mids and bass ranges of each individual channel strip. In combination with the input amplifiers, it delivered an unprecedented sound quality, the richness and warmth of which was unique. The API quickly found its way into American television and production studios. Frank Zappa, Stevie Wonder, Marvin Gaye, Bob Dylan, to name just a few, recorded on it, Lauryn Hill and Rick Rubin still do today. API consoles with the "old" analogue technology continue to be developed and manufac-

1 VP Records in the obituary for JoJo Hoo Kim September 21, 2018: https://www.vprecords.com/vp-records-celebrates-the-life-of-producer-and-businessman-joseph-jo-jo-hoo-kim/ (last accessed October 10, 2018).

2 Cover notes *Hitbound! The Revolutionary Sound Of Channel One*, Heartbeat LP/CD 1989. JoJo mentioned here "someone from Canada, he was an engineer". Other sources stated it was Bill Garnett, but Ernest Hoo Kim denied this. Garnett came into play later.

3 Steve Barrow & Peter Dalton – *Reggae. The Rough Guide*, London 1997 p. 213.

tured, although first-generation consoles are still in circulation, often fetching many times their original value.

The console JoJo had purchased had 16 input channels that could be directed to eight individual outputs when recording, and two stereo outputs when mixing. In dub literature, the assumption that JoJo started with a "4-track API console" is frequently encountered, appearing in works by Michael Veal[4] and in some of the typically well-researched booklets by Pressure Sounds[5]. This is a mistake, as Channel One was only ever a 4-track studio in its early years. The API-16in8in2 mixer was part of the equipment from the start, and was never replaced, the reason being it was for years the best desk on the island.

After six months of construction, JoJo flew in technician Bill Garnett from New York. Garnett had already wired Randy's studio, and had been involved in building Harry J's studio at Roosevelt Avenue and also Joe Gibbs' facilities in Duhaney Park. He stayed for two weeks and installed all the equipment, consisting of a half-inch 4-track tape machine and two 2-track ones, one for mixdown, the other for echoes, all Ampex 440 series models. There was also a Fisher spring reverb unit, the same one Tubby had used at the beginning, and that was it. This was rudimentary but exquisite standard equipment, and, combined with a high-performance console incorporating two Keypex noise gate modules, preventing bleed from other instruments, would later become important for the typical Channel One snare sound. In 1972, the studio opened its doors to the public, but the beginning was difficult. None of the brothers knew how to work in a studio, and JoJo didn't plan to rent it out, but wanted to use it mainly for his own productions. However, hoping to learn from others, he adopted the motto "free try before you buy" and hired Sid Bucknor as a permanent engineer. Among the first to accept the offer of a free test session were producer Phil Pratt, who scored an immediate No. 1 with Gregory Isaacs' "All I Have Is Love", and the omnipresent Bunny Lee. He recorded Delroy Wilson's "Can I Change My Mind" with the Soul Syndicate band on Maxfield Avenue but reported problems.

In-house engineer Sid "Siddy" Bucknor had been an integral part of the Jamaican recording landscape since day one. We don't know when he was born, but he died in London in 2010. As cousin of Studio One owner Coxson Dodd, he started in the latter's company and stayed until Sylvan Morris replaced him, subsequently going on an odyssey through the Kingston studios. In the end, there wasn't one where he hadn't worked. Musicians and singers appreciated his calm personality. He had met all the greats on the island, was involved in recording Bob Marley's *Natty Dread* for Island Records in 1974, and then emigrated to London. He also worked at studios in the British capital, at the Roundhouse, Island's Basing Street and at Chalk Farm[6], where he mixed, among other things, Keith Hudson's *Nuh Skin Up Dub* LP[7]. Occasionally, he provided cousin Coxson with recordings of British reggae artists. In the second half of the 70s, Bucknor had a handful of LPs pressed at Dynamic Sounds with an unprinted logo, put them in a neutral cover and stamped them *Dub Sensation*.

The dubs, including an overly bass-heavy version of Channel One's Jackie Mittoo track "Cold Blood"[8], were an obscure hodgepodge from his stints in Kingston and London. 40 years later, the LP has become a collector's item, valued at four figures.

Sid Bucknor had one problem, he worked very thoughtfully. Said Bunny Lee, "Sid was so slow, he and Coxson fell out. He was a good engineer, too, but he was slow. When the versions came, he took out a stopwatch and tried to drop out the voice. By the time a man should mix a version, Sid go into the drum and bass part, the straight riddim. The man spent the whole day, and nobody wanted to work with him."

In addition, at Channel One, Sid Bucknor had a second, much more serious problem, which was that he couldn't handle the desk, and the semi-parametric in particular was a mystery to him. "Those are decorations on the board, psychedelic lights", he claimed, projecting his incompetence onto the manufacturer. Bucknor disassembled a channel strip from the board and had JoJo fly to Miami with it. He should complain to API that the sound control was not working properly. However, having arrived, JoJo was laughed at! "Which flipping engineer you have? He must be mad. These things are parametric equalizers, if he don't know, tell him!" They showed him how to operate it so he could pass it

4 Michael E. Veal ibid p. 135.
5 E.g., in *Channel One – Maxfield Avenue Breakdown. Dubs & Instrumentals 1974–79*, Pressure Sounds 2001 or *Drum Sound – The Revolutionaries. More gems from the channel one dub room*, Pressure Sounds 2007.

6 A 24-track studio on Belmont Street, that existed 1968–'82 and was frequently used for reggae productions.
7 *Nuh Skin Up Dub* was the counterpart to Keith Hudson's's LP *From One Extreme To Another*, identical to *Black Morphologist* on KEJA. Both vocal and dub were mixed by Bucknor at the Chalk Farm and released in the UK on Joint International in 1979, the dub with a neutral cover. In 2007 it was reissued on Pressure Sounds.
8 The mix could also be found on the B-side of the Jamaican I-Roy single "Proud Black" on Well Charge from 1974.

on to Sid, but when JoJo came back, Sid was watching TV and didn't want to be disturbed.

Bunny Lee was not the only one who complained about the weak sound, also many of the "free sessions" failed, and the reputation of the new studio was suddenly at stake. "Studio not good" was already a rumour. JoJo had a full LP production with singer Alton Ellis that he couldn't release because it wasn't recorded properly. They had the most expensive mixing console on the island, but didn't achieve good sound with it, so consequences were drawn. After about a year, the collaboration with Sid Bucknor ended.

What to do? To make himself independent of outside staff, JoJo wanted Ernest to fill Bucknor's place. Ernest, born in 1948, was the youngest of the brothers, a passionate slot machine mechanic and totally unenthusiastic. "I know electronics, but I didn't know how to operate a recording." The parametric was apparently not the problem. "You go by your ears, right? But I don't know nothing about bringing the instruments on the console." Ernest had Errol Thompson show him the basic knowledge of recording technology, and while JoJo took care of the business side of things, Ernest eventually took over the desk. He read up on drum miking in American studios, and tried to do the same thing. Support came from Sly Dunbar, who for many years afterwards respectfully referred to him as his "ex-boss", and was also constantly looking to improve his drum sound. Whenever time allowed, the two would spend entire days on equalizer settings, microphone positioning and absurd-looking drum skin taping and sound attenuation, as seen on the cover of *Sly & The Revolutionaries – Go Deh Wid Riddim*[9]. The experiments lasted almost two years, and in the end, the drums emanating from the loudspeakers sounded better than natural, without amplification. Previously, due to limited technology, the entire drum kit was recorded with just one single microphone. Ernest now used individual microphones for each drum and cymbal, filtering the signals separately in dedicated channels of the mixing console. This made his sound significantly more differentiated than in the past. "Ernest's mix was brilliant", raved Roots Radics drummer Style Scott, "the heights sound crispy and sweet, the rimshots were coming, cutting through proper, the bass drums got stomach." For the bass, similarly meticulous work was undertaken, earning even the approval of Bunny Lee, who was usually critical of most Jamaican studios. "The bass came like a lead guitar, that's the bass closest to Dynamic Sound." The sound of bass and drums became crucial to Channel One's rise. "Ernest Hoo Kim has never got the recognition", lamented singer and producer Roy Cousins, years later. "When he took over at Channel One, he revolutionized the whole reggae sound, and moved it twenty years forward!"[10] Also, from 1975 onwards, the replacement of the Fisher reverb unit with an AKG BX10 contributed to Channel One's ability to transform the reverb sound in the dancehalls.

In the meantime, reggae had changed. The close association with the Black Power movement in the USA, the experience of neo-colonial occupation by the IMF and the World Bank, the increasing spread of rebellious ideas hatched by Rastafarians and Pan-Africanists Marcus Garvey (1887–1940) and Walter Rodney (1942–1980)[11] all brought about long-term change. Last but by no means least, we must also mention the visit of Ethiopian Emperor Haile Selassie in 1966. Reggae was moving away from the rude boy habitus of ska and the euphoria of rocksteady, towards a roots & culture, bass-driven offbeat. It had become a cultural export. The British record company Island Records signed the Wailers in 1971, and the following year saw the release of "The Harder They Come" with Jimmy Cliff taking the lead role in the film. It laid the foundation for a worldwide success story, showing that reggae had developed into the sound of a cross-border collective consciousness, global prayer versus global player.

The new content was not happening on Jamaican radio, but was distributed via sound systems, where a new generation of spokesmen had established themselves. They brought to the people the burning issues of self-confidence, African heritage and repatriation, and from this perspective commented on the liberation struggles of African states that were being closely followed in Jamaica. While Bob Marley and Jimmy Cliff conquered the world with a slightly different reggae sound, infused with rock and pop, dancehall continued to dominate events at home. The Hoo Kims reacted. They hired the deejay I-Roy as an in-house producer to incorporate the trends of the dancehall more prominently into their productions. "We were selecting some riddims and I-Roy was the selector of what we should record", is how Ernest described his task. Roy

9 Released in Jamaica on the Derrick Harriott label Crystal Records in 1977.

10 From the booklet *Drum Sound – The Revolutionaries. More gems from the channel one dub room*, Pressure Sounds 2007.

11 Walter Rodney came from Guyana. He studied in Kingston, then taught African history and wrote the standard works *Grounding With My Brothers* (on the Black Power movement in the Caribbean) and *How Europe Underdeveloped Africa*. Rodney was in demand internationally, including teaching in Hamburg, Germany, for a semester in 1978. In October 1968 – when he was 26 – he was denied re-entry to Jamaica, which led to serious riots in Kingston with deaths and millions of dollars in damage. Rodney was murdered in Guyana in 1980 at the age of 38.

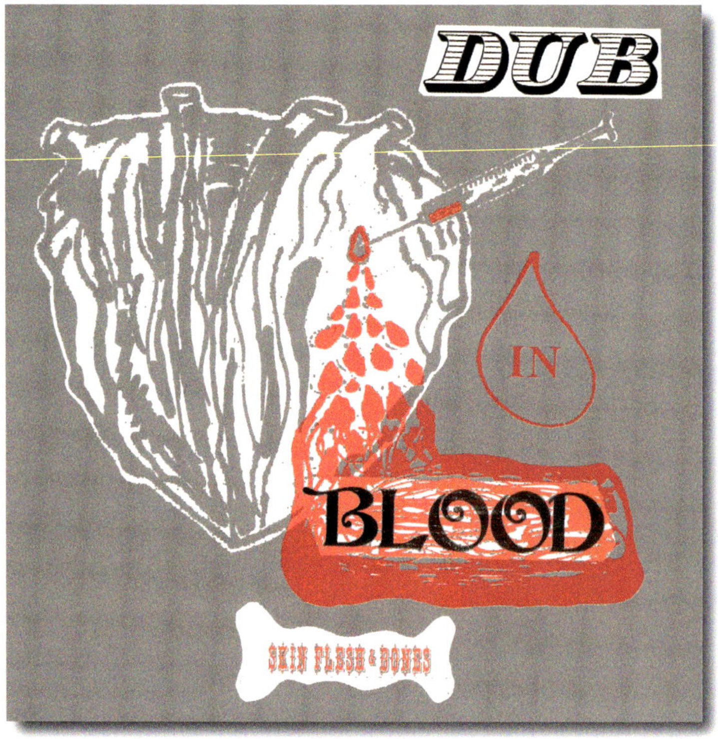

Reid (1944–1999) was a civil servant before daring to take to the microphone as I-Roy in 1966, becoming the eloquent top deejay in Spanish Town for the "Surpreme Ruler Of Sound" and "Stereo". Before joining Channel One in 1975, he spent several months in London, so was aware of the spread of Jamaican culture in the diaspora, as well as the growing European interest in Jamaican music. A year later he signed a contract to release five LPs with Virgin Records, but ultimately there would be eight.[12]

The same year I-Roy began working on Maxfield Avenue, pianist and organist Ossi Hibbert was brought on board as a member of Channel One's creative team. Hibbert (1951–2012) was a sought-after musician who was highly regarded among Kingston's producers, since his organ playing helped Big Youth score a huge hit for Keith Hudson with "S90 Skank", the biker anthem, in 1972. Hibbert was a member of the Soul Syndicate band, worked a lot in Joe Gibbs' studio and played for Bunny Lee in the Aggrovators. In the spring of 1975, JoJo asked Bunny Lee to guide Hibbert to Channel One. He joined the Revolutionaries and, together with Sly Dunbar, arranged a great many tunes that, on release, were credited as productions by JoJo Hoo Kim. Hibbert also fell victim to Kingston studio's practice of calling the paying commissioner the LP producer. Impressed by his musical flair, Ernest turned the musician into an engineer, and gave him the desk seat for third-party bookings he didn't want to do himself. Hibbert was enticed by the way Errol Thompson approached dub, and wanted to try something similar. The Hoo Kims had no problem with it as long as it didn't hinder business operations. In 1975, Ossi Hibbert mixed his first dub LP. He started at 6:30 in the morning, and had roughly three hours before clients arrived at 10 a.m. In two early shifts he created an album, which he named *Earthquake Dub,* after his label, and initially pressed them in small numbers as a pre-release, without cover or title. However, since he had his eye on the car that Thompson cruised through Kingston with, he traded the album in exchange for the vehicle, along with a handful of songs he had produced at Channel One

12 *Crisus Time* (1976), *Musical Shark Attack* (1976), *Heart Of A Lion* (1978), *World On Fire* (1978), *Ten Commandments* (1978), *Cancer* (1979), *The General* (1979), *Whap'n'Bapn* (1980).

with Dennis Brown, Gregory Isaacs, Earth & Stone, Freddie McKay and other artists. An official release on Joe Gibbs' label was agreed upon. Some of the vocal versions were released as *United Dreadlocks Vol. 1* on Joe Gibbs in 1977, with *Earthquake Dub* following a year later.[13] During his time at Channel One, Hibbert mixed the ultra-rare, coverless LPs *Meditation In Dub* for the US label Flames and *Crueshal Dub* for Earthquake as well as *Dub In Blood* for Phil Pratt (all 1976) and *Guerilla Dub* for Burning Sounds in 1978. In the same year, the LP *Leggo Dub* was released on Cash And Carry, mostly containing dub versions of the Gregory Isaacs LP *Mr. Isaacs*, produced by Hibbert. Its noise applications used everything the archive had to offer, from barking dogs to cuckoo clocks, and snippets of other people's music, showing how strongly Ossi Hibbert was influenced by Errol Thompson.

In 1976, the Hoo Kims' personnel decisions and investments began to pay off. Following the recommendation of producer, deejay, and singer Pat Francis (aka Jah Lloyd aka Jah Lion), JoJo and Ernest produced the debut album of a vocal trio that represented the new spirit of reggae. Although their cultivated harmony singing in the Phillisound tradition of the Stylistics suggested otherwise, the Mighty Diamonds were radical representatives of the Garvey and Rastafari movement. They chanted "Natty Dread will never run away", had a militant view of history, and denounced the country's ghetto policy in their songs. Their album *Right Time* became the Hoo Kims' biggest success to date and set the course for the next few years. Virgin Records licensed *Right Time* and released the corresponding mono LP *Vital Dub* onto the international market in the same year but did not miss the opportunity to decorate the dub with an image of a weed-smoking Rasta.[14] The Jamaican *Vital Dub* pressing was different, being placed unspectacularly in specially made standard sleeves, with a four-pointed star and the imprint "Well Charged". Both writing and star became the logo of the Hoo Kims' highest-output label[15] of the same name. Both went back to brother Paulie, who ran the Channel One sound system with this name and logo. The title of the LP was written around the star or in its centre, as was the case with the albums *Revival Dub Roots Now* (1976) and *Satta Dub Strictly Roots* (1978). A small part of the *Vital Dub* edition previously appeared in a cover with the "Super Boom Super Charge" imprint, which was probably used for test pressings and pre-releases. This was indicated by other Channel One dub LPs, which also first appeared with this sleeve. When asked, Ernest could only cautiously confirm "That might be JoJo works".

Meanwhile, Ernest Hoo Kim had taken on as an apprentice an inquisitive boy from the neighborhood named Stanley "Barnabas" Bryan. "These guys coming to the studio, we observe how interested they do things. (If they) show the interest, we teach them, show them." Hoo Kim's nephew Donovan Philips also worked temporarily in the studio, but the 24-hour operation required the employment of more engineers. Lancelot "Maxie" McKenzie and Anthony "Crueshal/Crucial Bunny" Graham aka Bunny Tom Tom came from Paulie's sound. One helped build the amplifiers, the other was a selector. Ossie Hibbert was permanently involved; Sly & Robbie relied on Soljie Hamilton. Later, when Scientist came over from King Tubby, he also met a curious youth named Donovan, who accompa-

13 In 1979, Ossi Hibbert released the album himself as *Satisfaction In Dub Strictly Yard Music* in New York on Flames and in London as Satisfaction in Dub on Live & Love

14 The Mighty Diamonds were discovered by Jah Lloyd (1947–1999). In return for his referral to the Hoo Kims, the track "Shame And Pride", which he produced for his own Teem label in 1974, was included on the Hoo Kims' LP. The track was missing on the subsequent dub LP *Vital Dub*, but can be found on the Jah Lloyd LP *Herb Dub* (Micron + Teem Records, 1975), which is identical to *Kaya Dub* (Kaya Records, USA).

15 Besides Well Charge, the Hoo Kims also owned Cord, Disco Mix, Vital, Hitbound, J & J, Channel One and Empire labels

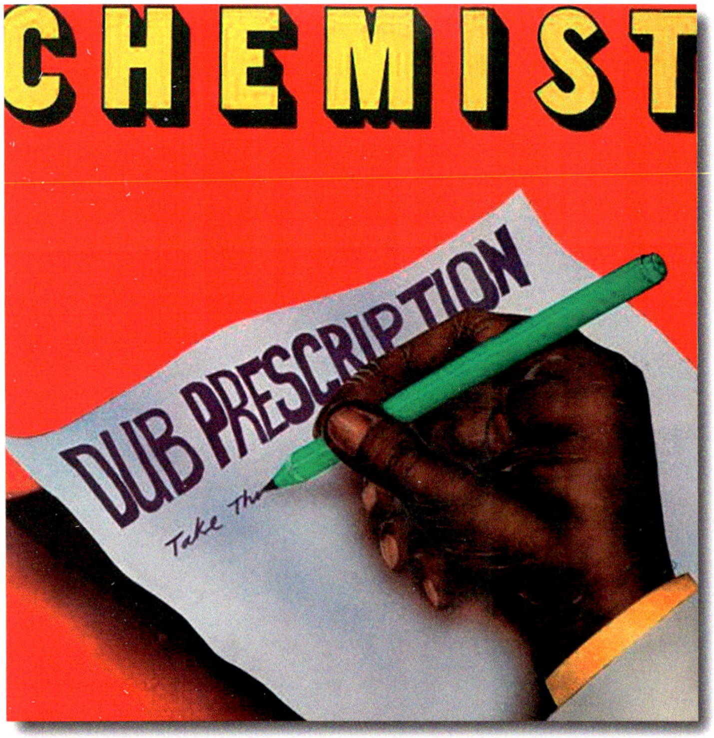

nied his mother to the studio when she was cleaning there. The boy with the family name Thompson, later known as "Peter Chemist", operated the mixing console with a purist, edgy flow. Nobody else crafted dub in such a minimalistic way, stripped down to bass, kick and snare, the hi-hat relegated beneath the threshold of perception. In addition, there were singular offbeat accents with modernistic electronic effects and echoes, which, while doubling or halving the tempo of the repetitions, he froze using the hold function. This technique enabled Peter Chemist to deliver his most striking dub act by firing volleys from the echo device between the lyrics "illegal gun fires more than the licensed one" on the Midnight Riders' song "Illegal Gun"[16].

With this permanent staff, the Channel One dub factory began work. Having the dancehall in mind, every in-house produced single now received a custom-made dub or instrumental B-side; overdub versions with brass were particularly popular. The 12-inch single was introduced to the reggae export market[17] and its extended running time was used for 4-track dub EPs[18], such as "Fatal Dubs"[19], "Scanking Dub"[20], the "Hertz" dubs[21] or the so-called "Painful Disco Dub"[22] EP by the Revolutionaries. The attempt to launch EPs in the 7-inch format with 33 rpm failed, however, because the sound quality compared to the 12-inch was not convincing and diminished the studio's now excellent reputation.

The *Vital Dub* LP enabled the Jamaican remix to conquer international territory. Foreign countries were craving dub, and the Hoo Kims delivered. In the following years, more dub LPs spilled out of their studio than from any other place in Kingston. Channel One dubs were becoming mass-produced, and a product for the masses. The Hoo Kims produced the first big wave themselves, and on their own account with their in-house band, the Revolutionaries.

- **Vital Dub – Well Charged** (Well Charge + Virgin UK 1976) Mix: Ernest + Ossie Hibbert
- **The Revolutionaries – Revival Dub Roots Now** (Well Charge 1976) Mix: Ernest
- **The Revolutionaries – Revolutionaries Sound** (Well Charge + Channel One 1976) Mix: Ernest + Barnabas (in later editions some song titles changed, and it said: Mix: Ernest + Ossie Hibbert)
- **Don't Underestimate The Force. The Force Is Within You** (J&L 1977 + Channel One) Mix: Ernest + Barnabas + Maxie
- **The Revolutionaries – Jonkanoo Dub** (Cha Cha 1978) Mix: Ernest + Barnabas + Maxie
- **The Revolutionaries – Reaction In Dub** (Cha Cha 1978 + Channel One) Mix: Ernest + Maxie
- **The Revolutionaries – Satta Dub Strictly Roots** (Well Charge 1978) Mix: Ernest

16 1985 on Thunderbolt, a version of the Joe Frazier riddim.

17 1976 with the Jays and their remake of the '68 Studio One single "Truly" by Marcia Griffiths, plus dub and deejay version by Ranking Trevor.

18 EP = "Extended Play".

19 "Cardiac Arrest", "Heart Failure", "Rigor Mortis", "Post Mortem". The tracks can also be found on the showcase LP *Errol Scorcher – Rasta Fire* (LP and 12" Ballistic 1978)

20 Scanking Dub 1978: "Rema Scank", "Dunkirk", "Jungle Scank", "Tivoli Scank".

21 Crown 1977: "Mega Hertz", "Geiger Hertz", "Killo Roit", "Herz".

22 Released in 1978 as "Disco Dub" and as Island 12" with the title "Headache". The name "Painful Disco Dub" was just an unofficial name due to the titles "Heartache", "Bellyache", "Toothache" und "Headache".

Don't Underestimate The Force The Force Is Within You
Chapters
1 GENESIS 1:11
2 JOHN 2:7
3 ROMANS 8:4
4 MALACHI 1:11
5 EZEKIEL 29:13
6 JAMES 1:19
Recorded • Remixed at CHANNEL ONE Studio 29 Maxfield Ave. Kingston Jamaica
• Richard (Dirty Harry) Hall
Drums: Sly Dunbar
Percussion: Scully Simms
Bass Guitar: Ranchie • Robbie Shakespeare
Rhythm Guitar: Robbie Shakespeare
Lead Guitar: Rad Bryan
Keyboard: Ansell Collins
Synthesizer: Robbie Lyn
Chapters
1 EXODUS 1:9
2 SONG OF SOLOMON 5:11
3 PROVERBS 22:17
4 PETER 1:24
5 PSALM 23:2
6 REVELATION 8:11
Engineers: Ernest Hookim
Les McKenzie • Barnabas
Artwork Jamaal Pete
• Sticky Thompson • Lloyd Parkes
Piano: Errol Tarzan Nelson
Trumpet: Bobby Ellis
Alto Sax: Herman Marquis
Tenor Sax: Tommy McCook
Available at J-J Records
365 Utica Ave Bklyn N.Y.C 11213
Phone (212) 773-1100
Stereo
LP-031
J&L Records
DON'T UNDERESTIMATE THE FORCE
THE FORCE IS WITHIN YOU
I CAME
I SAW
I CONQUERED
I CAME
I SAW
I CONQUERED
Side A
Round One
Round Two
Round Three
Round Four
Round Five
Side B
Round One
Round Two
Round Three
Round Four
Round Five
Recorded + Remixed at CHANNEL ONE Recording Studio 29 Maxfield Ave. Kingston Jamaica
Engineers: Ernest Hoo Kim Les McKenzie + Barnabas
Available at J-J Records 365 Utica Avenue Brooklyn N.Y. 11213 (212) 773-1100
• Richard (Dirty Harry) Hall
• Sticky Thompson
• Lloyd Parkes
• Artwork Jamaal Pete
LP029
Stereo
Drums: Sly Dunbar
Percussion: Scully Simms
Bass Guitar: Ranchie
Robbie Shakespeare
Rhythm Guitar: Robbie Shakespeare
Lead Guitar: Rad Bryan
Keyboards: Ansell Collins
Synthesizer: Robbie Lyn
Piano: Errol Tarzan Nelson
Trumpet: Bobby Ellis
Alto Saxophone: Herman Marquis
Tenor Saxophone: Tommy McCook

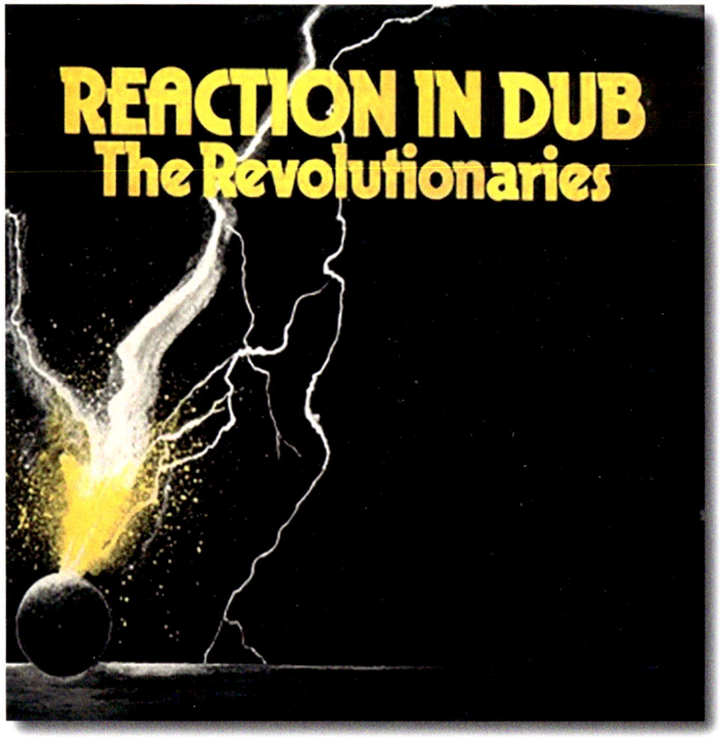

- **The Revolutionaries – Revolutionaries Sounds Vol. 2** (Ballistic 1979) Mix: Ernest + Barnabas, 1st edition with Che Guevara poster
- **The Revolutionaries – Dutch Man Dub** (Burning Vibrations 1979) Mix: ?
- **Back To The Channel** (free LP with **The Mighty Diamonds – Deeper Roots,** Virgin 1979) Mix: Ernest
- **Spider's Web** (free LP with **I Roy – The General**, Virgin 1979) Mix: Ernest
- **The Revolutionaries – I Came I Saw I Conquered** (Channel One 1980 + J&L 1981) Mix: Ernest + Barnabas + Maxie

The design of Hoo Kim's dub productions reflected the attitudes of the national zeitgeist. Increasingly, Rasta symbols spread in Jamaica, flanked by a militant aesthetic inspired by the African liberation struggles and the Vietnam War. In April 1976, B.B. Seaton came out with *Revolutionary Dub*[23] and titles like "Riot In Soweto", "Dread In Johannesburg" or "Forward The Battle Dub". Keith Hudson released *Rebel Dub*[24], the Fat Man Riddim Section *Is It War Or Is It Peace* with a tank behind soldiers wearing steel helmets[25]. Roy Cousins presented two dub LPs under the titles *Freedom Fighters Dub*[26] and *Liberated Dub*[27] in an armageddon and battlefield look for his dub project The Force Of Music. Deejays juggled with the "militant" attitude, calling themselves Militant Barry[28], *Militant Dread* (Prince Ras Murray[29]) or *Militant Man* (Errol Dunkley[30] and Big Joe[31]). Images of weapons became socially acceptable, as did

23 Trenchtown 1976.
24 Third World 1976.
25 Top Ranking International 197X.
26 Ballistic UK 1978.
27 Ballistic UK 1979.
28 LP *Militant Style*, Rasta Connection, Belgium 197X, with pictures of Ayatollah Chomeini and Ronald Reagan on the back.
29 Third World, UK 1977.
30 Lovella International, Kanada 1980.
31 "Natty Dread is a militant man", line from the deejay version of Delroy Wilson's "Have Some Mercy", Hot Disc 12".

uniforms and combat scenarios. The dancehall rehearsed the uprising and staged it as a "dubocalypse". However, no one presented the genre in such a consistently "revolutionary" way as Channel One. "There was a communist change all over in the country. Seh we were going socialism, revolution was the in-thing" Ernest described the time. He and JoJo named their tracks after political slogans ("Leftist", "Angola", "MPLA"), or used biblical terms or type names of handguns. Their covers were decorated with weapon-like designs and images of Che Guevara and Haile Selassie. Although the appearance was very martial, the mixes were benign. Ernest's dubs were staid instrumental versions with echoes as sound applications, far from the fader virtuosity of King Tubby, the creative nonsense of Lee Perry or the absurd noise additions of Errol Thompson.

The Hoo Kims saw their production facility as a contemporary legacy of the Studio One tradition. What Coxson had been in the 60s they wanted to continue in the 70s. To cement their claim, they had chosen the name Channel One and revitalized, you could also say copied, the tried and tested riddims from Studio One, benefitting from the non-existent copyright laws in Jamaica. Coxson was furious and confronted JoJo, becoming violent and being barely restrained by singer Leroy Smart. He countered the riddim theft by having drummer Leroy "Horsemouth" Wallace modernize his old recordings with syndrums. However, this did not diminish the success of the Channel One remakes, nor did it decrease the demand for their dubs. Despite the conventional mixes, almost all of them lived from the Revolutionaries' interpretations and Sly Dunbar's innovative drumming, which was referred to as "militant" or "Rockers" style. Bassist Lloyd Parks gave the band its name after he and Sly had played together with a variety of musicians, first as Skin, Flesh & Bones at Randy's studio, then as The Professionals at Joe Gibbs'. At Channel One, the Revolutionaries became Dunbar's band. When Parks formed We The People Band and was taken on by Dennis Brown, guitarist Ranchie McLean (1948–2012) temporarily took over on bass, until Robbie Shakespeare (1953–2021) filled the position permanently. Now with Robbie Shakespeare on board, the Revolutionaries became Sly & Robbie. The two founded the Taxi label under the moniker "The Riddim Twins" and increasingly pursued their own interests. As Word Sound & Power they became Peter Tosh's backing band, then joined Back Uhuru. The Hoo Kims had to realize that the former Revolutionaries no longer gave their all when they were hired for recordings, so they looked for a replacement. They found it in the Roots Radics. This band had emerged from the Morwells, with bassist Errol "Flabba" Holt (born 1950) and drummer Style Scott (1956–2014) and began as an exclusive ensemble for Gregory Isaacs but had long since been in demand by other producers. When the Radics recorded at Channel One, which was becoming increasingly common, the Revolutionaries initially received preferential treatment, being the in-house band. Sly got a brand-new Ludwig drum set with a large 24-inch bass drum, but Style had to play on an old drum kit. Scientist finally put an end to it. "Style get mad. From we get the new drum set we killed everything. Radics started playing bare hit tunes" boasted Flabba Holt.

Flabba Holt and the author, Kingston 2012.

Ernest and JoJo continually improved the equipment, gradually replacing their microphone park with high-quality condenser microphones made by Sennheiser, Sony and Neumann. Ernest preferred to use Sennheiser, as the Neumann phantom power was not really compatible with the console. In 1979, they expanded their studio from 4 to 16 tracks with a 2-inch Ampex MM1200 tape machine and replaced the reverb device with the larger AKG BX20E version with remote control. Together with the Roots Radics as their new in-house band, these measures cemented Channel One's supremacy.

The expansion to 16 tracks, the API console, the modern microphones, and the monstrous reverb generator implemented the global technical evolution of studio technology into the music of Jamaica. It gave the change an acoustic equivalent in the dancehall, and made the sound of reggae more internationally compatible, from the soundtrack of the rude boys to the holy wrath of the Rastafarians. As Jamaica's producers lined up to use their facilities, the Hoo Kims had only Sundays left for their own productions. During the week they had the studio running non-stop, renting it out 24 hours a day. To their advantage, the studio was in an area where no one wanted to be out at night.

The Roots Radics, as playback suppliers, recorded as if on an assembly line; every producer wanted them. At the end of the 1970s, singer and producer Linval Thompson brokered a distribution deal with Greensleeves, a new independent British label. He brought in Henry "Junjo" Lawes, born 1960, a mysterious businessman who was shot dead in a drive-by killing in London at the age of only 39. Lawes had spent six years in New York's Riker's Island penitentiary for criminal activity at a time when Jamaican gangs like the Shower Posse and Spanglers Posse were active in the highly lucrative crack/cocaine business on the American east coast.

Lawes became the big profiteer from the distribution deal. As the beneficiary of the Roots Radics/Channel One/Greensleeves connection, he would temporarily dominate the national, international, and especially European reggae landscape, amassing a gigantic musical legacy. Lawes was a man full of biographical secrets. He emerged as a hustler in downtown Kingston and evolved into the impresario of a production-oriented musical hybrid, now known as foundation dancehall, which represented the heyday of the pre-digital phase. Under his aegis, artists such as Barrington Levy, Cocoa Tea, and Yellowman became the main stars, flanked by Scientist's powerful sound eruptions. He recorded at Channel One from 1981 onwards, but continued to go to King Tubby for the final mix until 1983. Junjo had an instinct for finding successful artists and brought in the money. In the first half of the 80s, Junjo Lawes, operating as a financier and talent promoter, achieved remarkable success with his "Volcano" sound system and other productions that left the competition struggling to catch up. He reserved the Channel One studio for days but left the musical proceedings to his "most lethal weapon"[32], the Roots Radics. They were also booked by established acts such as the Heptones, Sugar Minott and Bunny Wailer, in order to adapt their new albums to the change in style. Whoever was recording during this time, whether newcomer or established, singer or deejay, could not ignore the Radics. The band worked incredibly quickly. They had internalized the new style to such an extent that fifteen minutes were enough to draft and record a song or riddim. Often, the next LP was recorded in four hours. Over the following years, they turned out hundreds of albums, representing a rate of output never seen before or since. The number was high also because the dancehall style introduced a swarm of fresh deejays, and versioning (or remixing) was made much more effective by the possibilities of multitracking.

The new sound was characterized by a dubby mix aesthetic, designed and perfected by Channel One engineers such as Barnabas, Peter Chemist and Scientist. As a result of this trend, dub LPs flooded the international market, including six LPs with the Roots Radics, produced by Linval Thompson or Junjo Lawes, which Greensleeves released in the UK under the Scientist name. Subsequently, over these albums, a bitter legal dispute arose between the record company and Scientist, which continues to this day and is reported on in the chapter "Scientist vs. Jammy vs. Greensleeves. The Everlasting Showdown". Regardless, with this six-pack, the Channel One studio was now perceived as a dub station beyond the reggae world, even though the mixes, with one exception, still came from Tubby's studio. From now on, everyone who recorded at Channel One also wanted a dub LP. Producers such as Roy Cousins, Jah Lloyd, Jah Thomas, Bunny Lee, Linval Thompson, Don Mais, Philip Fraser, Roy Francis, Mandingo, Al Campbell, Phil Pratt, Alvin Ranglin and Mikey "Dread At The Control" all wanted one. The same goes for British companies like Trojan, Greensleeves Records or Burning Sounds, the label with the eye-catching colored vinyl, or bands such as the Fat Man Riddim Section and Sly & Robbie. In fact, anyone who came to Channel One at Maxfield Avenue didn't leave without a dub master tape under their arm! Sometimes LPs were released under the name of the engineer (not necessarily the one who actually mixed it), sometimes without any personal reference, simply being called *Burning Dub*, *Guerilla Dub*, *Green Bay Dub*, *Beware Dub*, *Heavy Metal Dub*, *Dawn Of Creation*, *Phase One Dub-Wise*, *Afrikan History*, *Star Wars Dub*, *Black Foundation Dub*, *Three Dreads From Zion Dub* etc. While the Revolutionaries had previously been the namesake attraction, dub LPs were now also released under the banner of Roots Radics.

- **King Tubby Meets Roots Radics – Dangerous Dub** (Copasetic 1981) Producer: Jah Screw & Ranking Joe, Mix: at Tubby's
- **Scientist Meets The Roots Radics** (Selena 1982 + PicDisc 2014) Producer: Flabba Holt, Mix: at Tubby's
- **Roots Radics Meet Mighty Revolutionaires – Outernational Riddim** (FORM 198X) Producer: Burning Sounds, Mix: Scientist, Crucial Bunny, Danny Allen
- **Roots Radics – Radicfaction** (Cha Cha 1982) Producer: Bingy Bunny & Blacka Morwell, Mix: Scientist
- **Roots Radics Live At Channel One Kingston Jamaica** (Live And Love 1982 + Abraham 1982) Producer: Jah Thomas, Mix: Tubby, Barnabas, Scientist

32 "The law according to Junjo", Howard Campbell in the *Jamaica Observer* November 2, 2012.

- **Roots Radics Featuring Gladstone Anderson – Radical Dub Session** (Solid Groove 1982) Producer: Gladstone Anderson, Mix: Barnabas + Maxie
- **The Roots Radics – Roots Splashdown** (Body Music 1983 Producer: Jah Thomas, Mix: Barnabas, Scientist, Soljie, Peter Kemist [sic]
- **The Roots Radics – Roy Cousins Presents The Kings And Queens Of Dub** (Tamoki Wambesi 198X) Producer: Roy Cousins, Mix: Scientist
- **Roots Radics – Roots Dub Style** (Scorpio 1984) Producer: The Heptones, Mix: Scientist

Shortly before its collapse due to its overuse of the limited variable sound spectrum, Channel One's success story came to an unexpected end. Machine sounds had been permeating the music, and technological progress, which had previously been Hoo Kims' safe bet, suddenly spelled the studio's death knell. The turning point came in 1985, when

King Jammy's "Sleng Teng" opened a pandora's box. Immediately, music played with traditional instruments was no longer in demand in the dancehall.

At this point, however, JoJo had long since withdrawn from active participation. Paulie had been murdered in 1977 during a nighttime domino game on Greenwich Town beach, and the loss had taken its toll on JoJo, who moved to Brooklyn, there setting up both a record store and the "Hitbound" pressing plant. He would only come to Kingston to take care of business matters. Brother Kenneth (1947–2013) joined later, producing with Frankie Paul, among others, and mainly supervised compilations such as the in-house Showdown series[33] initiated in 1983, but only playing a supporting role in the Channel One structure. Ernest had taken over the management of the studio but disliked the on-going musical developments; digital sound was too weak for him. He had also increas-

33 Barry Brown & Little John, Sugar Minott & Frankie Paul, Don Carlos & Gold & The Gladiators, Yellowman & Fathead & Purpleman, Frankie Paul & Little John, Wayne Smith & Patrick Andy. Further "Showdown" albums were released by Channel One but were not produced by the Hoo Kims.

ingly lost interest in the production process. Yes, he was happy to mix, but the constant repetition of recording and correcting individual passages by dropping them in and out annoyed him. He longed to go back to his workshop, where he could tinker, solder, and repair all by himself. He was also tired of the constant rivalry with Joe Gibbs, whose relationship with Channel One resembled that of Mohammed Ali to Joe Frazier. In 1984, with the reopening of Tuff Gong studios, a serious competitor had appeared, equipped with 24 tracks and the latest technology. Tuff Gong was also more conveniently located, being on Marcus Garvey Drive, whereas Channel One was still in the heart of a ghetto.

"I wasn't interested no more", Ernest explained the end of the family business, "JoJo was away, and then the violence thing..." The Channel One complex closed its doors in the early 1990s. Unlike at Randy's, the technical inventory was being removed and temporarily stored, neatly lined up at JoJo's. At some point most of it went up for sale. The only things JoJo didn't want to sell were the piano, the API desk and an British made NEVE digital desk, purchased shortly before closing but never used. By 2017, these three remnants were rotting in a side room of Ernest's workshop and were left to their fate, just like the former studio

building. Decaying into a ruin, it became a refuge for the homeless and a place of pilgrimage for reggae tourists, who recorded its progressive deterioration on numerous pages on the web.

In the ruins of Channel One Studio, 2015.

Ranking Barnabas: The Boy Next Door

"You take an hour or less to balance the vocal mix, the dub mix take four or five minutes."

(Phil Pratt[1])

Businesspeople of Chinese descent in Kingston faced hostility on multiple occasions throughout the 20th century. There had already been serious riots in 1918 and 1938; in 1965, they erupted again when a rumor spread that a Chinese store owner had beaten up his Jamaican cashier. Riots downtown simmered for three days. Vehicles burned, bars went up in flames, and their owners were threatened. Some fled the country, like Mister Ten, who ran a wholesale business on Maxfield Avenue. After his departure, the building stood vacant, the power lines were severed, and the house withered away. Based on a 1970s film title, the ruin became referred to as the "House Of Dark Shadow" by local Jamaicans. This B-movie, like the TV series of the same name, told of an undead who, during renovation work on a disreputable house, where a witch had trapped him because of unrequited love, was accidentally freed. It's a story tailor-made for children, who, illuminated by the pale light of the street, reenacted it in the shadows of its dilapidated walls. 10-year-old Stanley Brian from the local neighborhood liked to play the role of the main character, and so became Barnabas, the bloodsucker. Since he took great pleasure in scaring little girls, he was soon called Barnabas at school too, and the name stuck.

Born in 1960, Stanley lived with his mother at the top of Maxfield Avenue. On a Friday night in 1972, a woman who ran a bar there sent him down the street to Channel One. Her jukebox had stopped working, which was a disaster for a bar on a weekend, and Stanley should let them know down there. When he arrived, it was late. Anyone who could help was already off work. The bouncer let the boy through and told him to speak to JoJo directly.

When he entered the studio for the first time Stanley was only 12; they were working on Boris Gardiner's "Every Nigger Is A Star". After making his request, he left the studio deeply hooked because, like all children on the island, he loved Jamaican music. As luck would have it, shortly after this his mother moved house, and suddenly Stanley was living directly opposite Channel One! He went to the All Age School on Whitfield Avenue, located over in the next street. Every day, after completing his homework, he hung out at the studio, with hustlers and gamblers, domino players and artists all posing in the street. "Channel One was the place where all the musicians met," was how Finnish photographer Pekka Vuorinnen described the scene. "In front of the studio was a huge crowd of hopefuls. On the small door there was a gateman who let in only the lucky ones."[2] This included Barnabas, who became the little

Barnabas and the author, Kingston 2012.

1 Booklet *Skin Flesh & Bones – Dub In Blood*, Pressure Sounds reissue 2016.

2 Pekka Vuorinnen "A conversation with..." Midnight Ravers blog "Legendary Reggae".

studio boy, valued as an honest youth who could be sent out to run errands, and who always gave back the change.

Barnabas soaked up everything that was happening inside the studio. He watched Ernest record and mix. Like all Jamaican youths, he imitated the deejays. He watched Sly Dunbar play and practiced on the drums when the studio was not recording. It was only a matter of time before he would become active in front of or behind the mixing desk.

At the age of 15, on the recommendation of Ansel Collins, for a recording by his friend Earl Zero, he sat at the drums for the first time. At 17, he dared to play publicly, and drummed at a concert for Hugh Mundell (1962–1983), who was two years his junior. A year earlier, he had had his deejay premiere, where his initial tune, entitled "Sister Fay" was a toast to the Chantells' "Effort in Yourself".[3] At around the same time, he mixed his first dub, but was still very reserved, and only faded the vocals in and out. It became the B-side of the Earth & Stone single "In Time To Come"[4], which he also mixed. Both debuts were released on 7-inch in 1976.

Stanley "Barnabas" Brian was now part of the Kingston recording and dancehall scene. After completing his studio work, the all-rounder switched to the dancehall, and improvised live with the "Ranking" suffix on sound systems. As a deejay, in the following years he released around 20 singles, maxis, and album contributions. It remained a manageable amount; no one wanted to produce an entire deejay album with him, just a spontaneous version here and there. If necessary, he played drums, such as for the Fat Man Riddim Section[5] or on various Gladiators' LPs[6]. But his main occupation was the production process of recording, mixing, and

3 The Chantells were a vocal trio and, like the Barnabas version, were produced by Roy Francis, on whose Phase One label both titles were released. Prince Buster had previously released the riddim under the name "Yusuf Ali & The Revolutionaries" as an instrumental with brass overdubs entitled "Uganda" on his Prince Buster label.

4 Released on the Channel One label Disco Mix.

5 *Fat Man Riddim Section Meets Downtown Horns At Channel One* and *Jacob Miller – Mixed Up Moods*, both Top Ranking 1979.

6 1982 *Back To Roots* and *Symbol Of Reality*, 1984 *Serious Thing*, 1985 *Country Living*, all recorded at Harry J's studio.

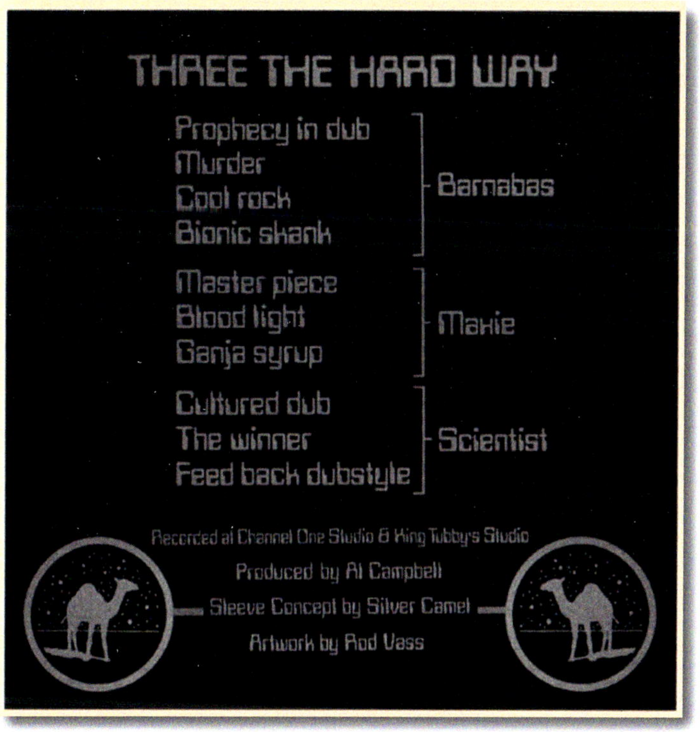

dubbing. The mixes he created were characterized by a striking rhythmic structure because the drummer's spirit controlled the faders. Barnabas became the anonymous creator of countless dubs on Greensleeves maxis and, in addition to the in-house Channel One productions, was also involved in dub LPs by external producers, including the following:

- **King's Dub** (Manzie, JA 1980) Producer: Dudley Swaby
- **Scientist & Barnabas & Maxie – Three The Hard Way** (Silver Camel, UK 1981) Producer: Al Campbell
- **Heavy Metal Dub** (Clocktower, US 1982) Producer: Brad Osbourne
- **Roots Radics At Channel One Kingston Jamaica** (Live & Love, UK und Abraham, CAN 1982) Producer: Jah Thomas
- **The Roots Radics – Roots Splashdown** (Body Music, UK 198X) Producer: Jah Thomas

- **King Tubby & Scientist & Bunny Tom Tom & Barnabas – Universal Dub** (Zola & Zola, NL 1995)[7]

"He was a killer dub man," was how Pat Kelly praised his colleague. As a sign of recognition, Kelly called the dub version of his single "How Long", produced for Yabby You in 1976, simply "Barnabas"[8]. However, the highly acclaimed Barnabas was rarely mentioned in a title on a cover; and if so, then not alone. His name was exclusively emblazoned on an LP sleeve only once, which was *Ranking Barnabas – The Cold Crusher,* a dub album from the late 70s, produced by Phil Pratt for the US label Express. The only other album featured on the label was *Dial M For Murder in Dub Style*[9], mixed by Bunny Tom Tom at Channel One. Barnabas was not a recording star, but more of an assistant, taking care of day-to-day business wherever he was asked. After Ernest Hoo Kim had trained him, Junjo Lawes, the great maestro of the era, initially preferred him at Channel One as an engineer. On his behalf, he recorded, mixed, and dubbed the Eek-a-Mouse classic "Wah Do Dem" in 1981. In just one day of work, the track became a hit two days later in the local dancehalls, and shortly afterwards throughout Europe. When Scientist arrived, he became Junjo's favorite, and without a murmur of resistance, Barnabas retreated into the background again.

With the end of Channel One, Ranking Barnabas' mixing desk and deejay career also faded. He focused on drumming, toured the world with the Gladiators, Sugar Minott and Max Romeo, and lived in New York City for a few years. Upon his return, in the new millenium, at the time of the conversation which follows, he was living back in Kingston in the yard of Sugar Minott's (1956–2010) Youth Promotion under modest but not unfortunate circumstances.

7 These were mixes from 1979. The original recordings were made between 1974 and 1978 at Randy's and Channel One studio. The dubs remained unreleased until published by the Dutch label.

8 Prophets 7-inch 1976.

9 Also produced by Phil Pratt, re-released in 2011 by Pressure Sounds.

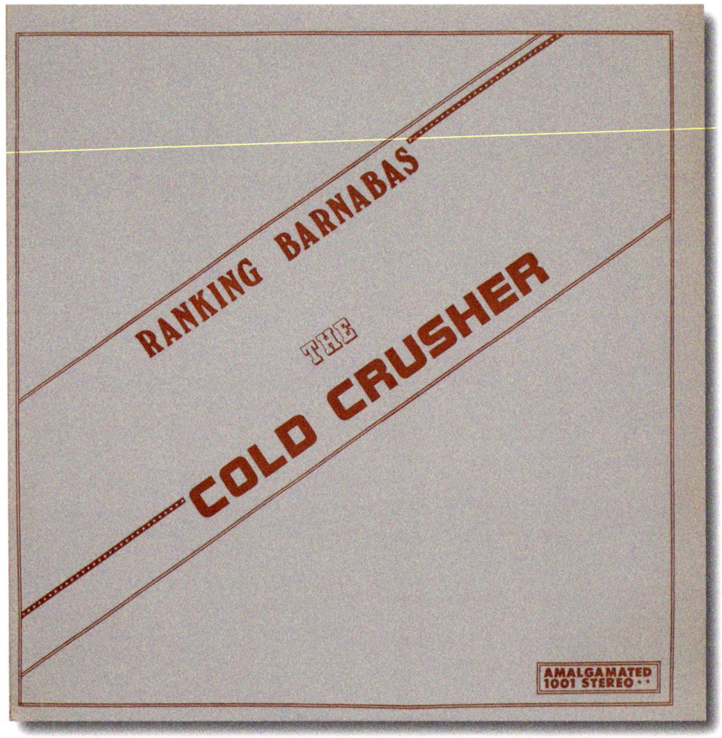

Of all the things you have done, what has been your favorite? Deejay, drummer or engineer?

Barnabas: To tell you the truth, I was having fun with all of them. Sly (Dunbar) one day said to me I got to decide on one of them. He was kinda giving me a little more knowledge [of drums], he was letting me know. But in the course of time the system changed to the computer age now, and I kinda dropped the engineer a little [and] decided I'd stick more to the drums.

How did you go from "best boy" to engineering?

I was a young kid at that time of my early career. Ernest Hoo Kim was the main engineer in the studio. He would balance [the equalizer and level for] the Earth & Stone song "In Time To Come" for me, so I was the one who was mixing the instruments in and out, you know? That was my first experience, and it was so loveable.

You learned everything from Ernest?

By just observing him. After I come from school I'm right there in the studio, every day. I watch and learn mostly. How to plug in the jack chords for the mics and all that. I'm a pretty quick learner. They always credited me for that back in my early years. Over the years by knowing it a little more, the experience got better and better. [It helped] being around people like Sly, Robbie, Ranchie. Revolutionaries and all these people... I started out from the 70s. Been around there from '72, but like about '76 I would say, professional as an engineer.

When it comes to sound, you had a very good teacher in Ernest, one of the best of this time. But when it comes to dub, he was very reserved. With him, dub became more of an instrumental version.

You are right about that, he never really mixed much dub, he was not the man of that kind of thing. He would do the A-side. Whenever you needed a dub version, he would call me.

At what point did you start working alone and mixing the A-sides?

[It started] when JoJo created the 12-inch.

However, they were not made for the domestic market, but as export products.

At that moment it wasn't for Jamaica, it was really for export. JoJo created that in the music. The first 12" was a song by the name of "Truly" with the Jays and Ranking Trevor (1976). Ernest, my teacher, mixed the original and I was the engineer who mixed the dub part where Trevor is deejaying. [Until that day] Ernest balanced the whole thing really, cause I was too young to do the balance. But by just watching him, I mastered it so good he started telling people to let me do the work. With me developing so much over the years, he said "Damn, this kid is even better than me." He tells the producers I'm the man now. He really drifted from the studio and started working on these [slot] machines more often.

This allowed you to develop your own style.

Back in the days, I was the first engineer that really started doing a little delay on the riddim section and on the vocals for the A-sides of the records. And I do a little splash on the drum, I created that in the music. A lot of people may not know that. The main reason for that was, we used to mix dubs from our Channel One productions for sound systems which had such an impact in the dance. And then JoJo wanted me to mix some of the [regular] 45s (7-inch singles) like this. So, it really reach in from the dancehall. It's a lot of issue with me. After I finished doing the dubs at the studio I would go home, have a shower and (soon after) I'm in the dance deejaying on those same riddims I just mix in the studio. Through that experience the dub thing really take on more on 45s. It blew up, people really did go crazy. Especially when they hear this reverb I splashed on the drum. I created also that slow 7 ½ delay on the drum. It sound like a horse. But it only fit on a certain tempo. I know which songs to use it cause we were experimenting.

You mean the slow tape speed of the tape recorder that was used to make the echoes back then.[10]

Yes, that's where it started. You know no (adjustable echo devices such as) Lexicon wasn't around at that time. The tape-recorder got two speeds, it got 15 and 7 ½ (ips[11]). When we wanted a slow delay, we would put it on 7 ½, when we want a little faster delay, we put it on 15.

Was bouncing used at Channel One?

Well... when I started engineering it was 4-track. Drum and percussion on one track, the bass on one track, and the whole riddim section – piano, organ, the two guitars – on the third track. You had to be listening really good and have a good riddim section balance. Most of these recordings you hear the riddim section sounds so good it's by a good balance. Most of the time we only have one track for the vocals. So, harmony and lead vocals always record on the same time.

10 Echoes were created via audio tape as described in the chapter on Pat Kelly.
11 ips (= inch per second) is the length the tape traveled in one second.

What about the horns? Or the deejay versions? How did you organize that recording-wise?

After a while we had two 4-track machines, JoJo bought the Studer from Switzerland. Now we would do transferring, most of the time when we were doing horns. We would tie the drum and bass on one track, the riddim section on one track and the vocals on the third track. So, we have one track for the horns.

Which were then recorded all together at once.

You gotta balance those three horns in one track. We all learned a lot from Lancelot McKenzie (i.e. Maxie). He was like a big brother to us. People like Maxie would help me in my early years of engineering. He would set [the channels on the console] for the voice and the harmony. And he help balance the horns. I look, listen and learn.

Later, with 16 tracks, you could say: "There's no problem I can't fix, cause I can do it in the mix."[12] But that was still impossible in the early days. Everything had to be recorded carefully. Subsequent corrections were not possible.

Exactly. You have to be right on top of the game, you have no second chance. Like even before me they used to record on two tracks. Nobody in the band can make a mistake, [cause] everybody gotta go all over again. You see, it's stages.

You didn't work as an engineer in other studios?

I would go to another studio – Tuff Gong, Harry J, Dynamics – and play a little drums, but the engineering part not much at another studio. Actually, I didn't get much time to do that at another studio. I was so busy, people they had me so busy, everybody just want me to come. Back in the day it was all fun, so I would still come. Sometimes I would really get a little upset, cause I need some rest, man.

And when it came up, you also voiced the deejay version yourself?

I still do a little deejay, like that song "Tumbling Tears" by Gregory Isaacs. I was just smoking a chalice next door, and Jah Thomas was supposed to be doing that deejay on it. But he couldn't really manage it pretty well, so they called me because I was a person

12 Indeep with rapper Genius in "Last Night A DJ Saved My Life" 1981 US.

on the sound also.[13] Back in those days most of the [deejay] vibes was coming from what the singer was singing about. That's what I used to rap mostly about. It's just an on-the-spot-creation.

What was it like working with Scientist? Was there competition?

We didn't look at it as no kind of competition. It was a new ball game for him. He needed me more then I needed anything from him. He was an engineer who was used to 4-track, just recording voice and mix. When he came Channel One 4-track was long gone, it was 16-track. [At the beginning] we've been around each other. His first [solo] session I was over my house sleeping, cause I was working all night. He's supposed to be recording the Roots Radics band, but they had to come and wake me. The drum alone is taking him nearly two hours and he can't even get the drum proper yet to the sound standard that we set. I came over, was

13 In 1977, the combination Gregory Isaacs/Ranking Banabas [sic] appeared as 12-inch on the Alvin Ranglin labels Hit and GG's Records.

still a little tired but I came over, balanced it up for him and he learned from that day. After that he started recording riddims a little quicker.

Didn't he also try to replace parts of the desk and transformers?

He was trying to do that, yeah. He did a lot of experiments. He just loved to experiment. Even the way he lost his job at Channel One it was by experimenting also. Whenever he's mixing a song in the studio he would blow the tweeter very easy. They had to put a protector on the speaker because of Scientist.[14] I used to even get upset with him sometimes and say "Damn! What's wrong with you man? You're the only engineer that comes in here and bwoy, you quit the speaker! No [more] treble is in the speaker." But he loved that, that's how he got the name. A scientist is always experimenting. It's a person who really lives up by his name. But he really loved music.

Scientist did a lot of work for Junjo Lawes. However, before he came to Channel One, you did everything for Junjo.

Junjo was one of my favourites. Actually, he was one of the only producers who could get me into the studio on a Sunday. I'm working Monday to Friday around the clock so I have to start restricting people: Oh no, Saturday and Sunday are for me! Cause Saturday I listen to the racehorses, that's my little game... Junjo was a great producer. Differently. He was really a vibes person, not just as a person who was spending the money. Brought a lot of vibes to the table. He would just come in, have a seat and everything else is getting done. Then Junjo start dancing, going around the studio and say "Yeah man, dem kind of vibes are the right vibes!" That alone is a hype for the musicians.

Still, he was more the producer with the money and the right instinct than the musical director.

Well, now and then he would come with a little [musical] thing. But you're right, it was really the engineers and the musicians doing most of the producing. But we didn't look at it like that at the moment. We didn't even know then; it was just the love for the music. I do a lot of those works in the business, cause it's my passion. It wasn't about the money thing. When I started engineering at Channel One, I started getting 12 dollars an hour. 12 Jamaican dollars, until it went to 15, to 20 Jamaican dollars and then I migrated to America. When I came back it's 300 dollars an hour [for recording] and much thousands of dollars to mix a song. Back then I was mixing all those songs for free. Producers would still give you a little pocket money but it wasn't really like: "I'm gonna charge you this and I'm gonna charge you that". It was all fun [cause] we're the creator of a sound and brought quality into reggae music.

Let's say a new quality. Randy's also stood for quality already.

That's true, you're right about that. But we take it to another level. Coxson created the music, we turned this into reggae. Doing over a riddim track from Studio One and having a singer do a new melody and original lyrics on that riddim track, we invented it at Channel One.

Can you explain how this new sound came about?

Because the building was a studio [construction]. They pad the wall... that made a special acoustic sound. And we had parametric equalizer, no other studio had something like that. [That's why] Sid Bucknor never used that EQ back in the days, I heard. He just take the music flat.

He didn't know any different. In the early days it was common practice to work in studios without equalizers. Coxson also resisted using the possibilities of sound filters for a long time.

So, Ernest, my teacher – I still call him teacher every time – he went in there and he started experimenting by just turning those EQs. From ten in the morning way back to like seven in the night just experimenting on the EQ and listen how the sound would sound. [Finally] we came up with this great result you [can still] hear in reggae. I'm telling the world, we created it.

14 Ernest Hoo Kim confirmed this and laughed heartily: "Very often! Man, we used to chain him like crazy with ALTEC limiters [on the monitors]. He dwell with feedback sounds and that will cause the tweeters to real blow. Is not the volume, is feedback burn the coils [in the speakers]".

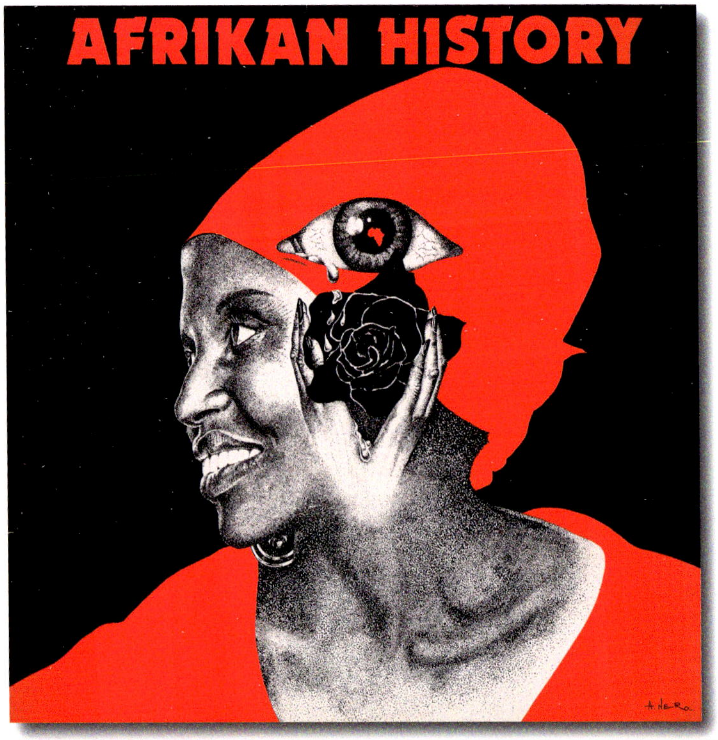
AFRIKAN HISTORY

XTERMINATOR IN DUB VOL. 1
XTERMINATOR ALL STARS
NO CABBON
..FEATURING XTERMINATOR ALL STARS-
SLY & ROBBIE, DEAN FRASER
AND MANY MORE

1 18
99
free
at
last
XTERMINATOR PRESENTS
MLKDUB
FEATURING
LUCIANO SIZZLA
+COCOA TEA

Soljie Hamilton & Groucho Smykle: Dub Design for Sly & Robbie

> "The whole combination of the effects and the pluses and minuses… it takes you on a journey."
>
> (Mad Professor[1])

In the mid-70s, a new name appeared on the scene. Spelled in a variety of ways and appearing on the backs of Jamaican LP covers were Soldgie, Sodjie, Solgie, Sogie, Soji, Sojie, Solje, Solijie and even Sol Jie, sometimes with a surname, more often with the attribute "brutal" attached. A distinction for the powerful mixes that swiftly elevated him to the status of heavyweight among Jamaican engineers. In private, Cegrica Anthony Hamilton was a reserved, gentle man whose aliases date back to his time as a soldier in the Jamaican Defense Force.

Soljie Hamilton didn't like to reveal anything personal, including his age. When he did divulge it, he asked for it not to be published. Fending off all questions, Soljie stated "I've kept myself private in this entire music business; all people know about me is what is out there on records and LP jackets." We learned about his sound system past from the notes on the cover of the dub LP *Rebel Soldier*[2], the only one ever released under his name. Soljie was part of the "Echo Vibration" sound from Greenwich Farm that was popular from the mid-70s. Deejay Ranking Jerry was on the microphone there, together with singers Michael Prophet and Sammy Dread. Soljie produced their album *Road Block* in 1982 for Hitbound, the Channel One sub-label. His love of music, he said, had existed since he started a hobby disco called "Village Soul Merchant" with two school friends. After school, he enlisted in the army and stayed for nine years. Strolling by Channel One one day, he became curious and knocked on the door. From 1973 onwards he hung out there regularly, observing how work was done in a studio. Ernest Hoo Kim told him a lot about frequencies and signal separation, and Crucial Bunny and Barnabas let him watch, but his main instructor was Lancelot "Maxie" McKenzie. In 1983, he shared the red-soaked *Afrikan History* LP with him on behalf of producer Martin Williams for the latter's Mandingo label. It's an album

that is not easily accessible and unique of its kind, and not the usual compilation of dancehall templates, but rather a statement created at the mixing desk in the revolutionary tradition of Channel One dubs. Not least thanks to the involvement of Neil Fraser aka Mad Professor, *Afrikan History* provided a blueprint for the later British dub aesthetic, with its radical mixes and sound applications. Dub became Hollywood. Experimental body cinema full of sproings, echoes that fall out of beat, reverberation rooms that have never been entered before, unimagined depths, synthesizer overdubs, shots, and the cries of seagulls.

Soljie was not one of those egos often found in Jamaica who like to point out that they were the ones who had invented this or that. The

1 Bassline Of A City, Museum of London 2020.
2 Published under the name Sojie, released in 1982 on Taxi.

Brutal One preferred to take a back seat, although had valid reasons to emphasize his contributions towards the evolution of reggae and dub. Whether tape or hard drive, studio or live, Soljie Hamilton was a master of all trades. Since the late 1970s, he has worked on hundreds of albums, both as recording or mixing engineer, and as producer. However, the resulting dubs were rarely attributed to him. "You do dub mixes and they put you as recording engineer" he said and shrugged. With the dubs it always depended "on which engineer [currently] is the peak of time because the name will sell." Soljie dubbed French chansonnier Serge Gainsbourg's reggae recordings[3] and survived the digital turning point unscathed. Afterwards, he was involved in the careers of internationally successful artists such as Supercat, and in 1999, when Jamaica's dub art was already languishing in neglect, he designed the modern roots albums *MLK DUB*[4] and *Xterminator in Dub – No Gabbon*[5] for Phillip "Fatis" Burrell (1954–2011) at the Anchor studio. When working on the songs by Luciano, Sizzla and Cocoa Tea, he was one of the first to recognize the problems arising from the legacy of analogue dub technology interacting with programming processes and digital recording media.

When computers brought a new generation of engineers to the control rooms of the studios, Soljie switched to live engineering, which subsequently became his main activity. He toured with Bunny Wailer, Ini Kamoze, Sly & Robbie & The Taxi Gang, Shabba Ranks, Buju Banton, Luciano and Sizzla, among others, but was also still booked for studio work. Like in 2013, when he mixed the song "Steamers A Bubble" on behalf of NuRoots singer Jah9 and provided a "Solji Mix" for the B-side of the Hitbound single. In 2010 he provided the live sound on Gentleman's *Diversity* tour. The opening act for the tour was the US reggae band SOJA, which Soljie also mixed. He had been traveling worldwide with the Americans since 2005. In 2013, JaRIA, the Jamaican Reggae Industry Association, honored him for his achievements as an engineer.

Soljie Hamliton's sound design for Sly & Robbie left the biggest impact in the world of dub. After the end of the Revolutionaries, the duo wanted dubs for their own productions other than the conventional elaborations of Ernest Hoo Kim. It should thunder out of the speakers in a more hypnotic and brutal way. Their entire dub catalog followed this maxim, starting with *Raiders Of The Lost Dub*[6] and *A Dub Experience*[7],

3 To be found on the DoCD *Serge Gainsbourg – Aux Armes Et Cætera*, 2003 Mercury/Universal Music, among others.
4 RAS Records.
5 Charm Records.
6 Island 1981.
7 Island 1985.

through the joint projects with Bill Laswell and up to their 2012 dub comeback with the albums *Blackwood Dub*[8], *Underwater Dub*[9] and *Dubrising*[10]. Sly & Robbie became the man-machine of dub. These were technically hypothermic, emotionless and antiseptic, continually alternating between brilliance and monotony. Island in-house engineer Paul "Groucho" Smykle took the next step towards this "different" sound when, on behalf of the Riddim Twins, he mixed three of their productions. First, he exaggerated Ini Kamoze's self-titled showcase debut[11], recorded by Soljie, into an inferno of orchestral effects. Then he mixed Black Uhuru's *The Dub Factor*[12] and approached the remix of *Anthem*[13], their vocal effort, for international release, as if it were a dub album.

8 Groove Attack 2012
9 Groove Attack 2014
10 Tabou 2014
11 Island + Taxi 1983
12 Island 1983
13 *Anthem* was first released in Jamaica in 1983 with a standard mix and was published internationally a year later with a different cover and a new Groucho mix

Seemingly out of nowhere, Groucho, a new type of dub engineer, entered the business in 1983 at Island's Fallout Shelter studio in London. *New Musical Express* compared him to a world-class boxer and wrote "Step aside Scientist and all you great pretenders. Groucho is poised to return dub to the prestigious state of an art form."[14] Smykle's style of mixing was new and completely different to what had previously come out of the Kingston dub headquarters. He mixed loudly and aggressively, pushed reverb and echo beyond the maximum, and manipulated stereo effects to emerge from the very edges of the speakers. He made no distinction between the vocal part and the dub version; nothing was safe from his grasp, and even the bass drum fluttered in the echo chamber. However, as suddenly as Groucho had emerged, he disappeared again, because the digital evolution had swiftly changed reggae and the need for dub. It wasn't until 30 years later that he returned, with *Sly & Robbie – Dubrising*[15] and *Sly & Robbie + Brinsley Forde – One Fine Dub*[16]. By adding additional instruments, Groucho was now actually mixing the soundscapes that inspired Michael Veal's title of his book.

Soljie had been there at the beginning with the *Sly & Robbie – Disco Dub*[17] and *Sojie – Rebel Soldier* LPs in 1978 and '82, becoming the first sound designer for the Riddim Twins. When asked about this, he downplays his role. "The engineer can add his things, but generally, it's not just one person that generates the sound. Each individual has a sound. The combination of all creates an [overall] sound. My technical skills were limited at that time. What I had in me I added to it, but it wasn't me alone that changed the sound."

Sly & Robbie recorded at Channel One studio just like the Revolutionaries did before them. It was the same technique, and yet the sound changed extremely.

Soljie: As I said, it's a combination of things. You know, sound is frequencies...

... and timing; the way an instrument is played...

Yes! Sly and Robbie is a unique blend of drum and bass. Definitely they know what they want. They compare [the recordings] and

14 "Paul 'Groucho' Smykle – Surgeon Of Dub" *New Musical Express 1983*
15 Tabou, France 2014
16 Tabou, France 2016
17 Gorgon Records 1978

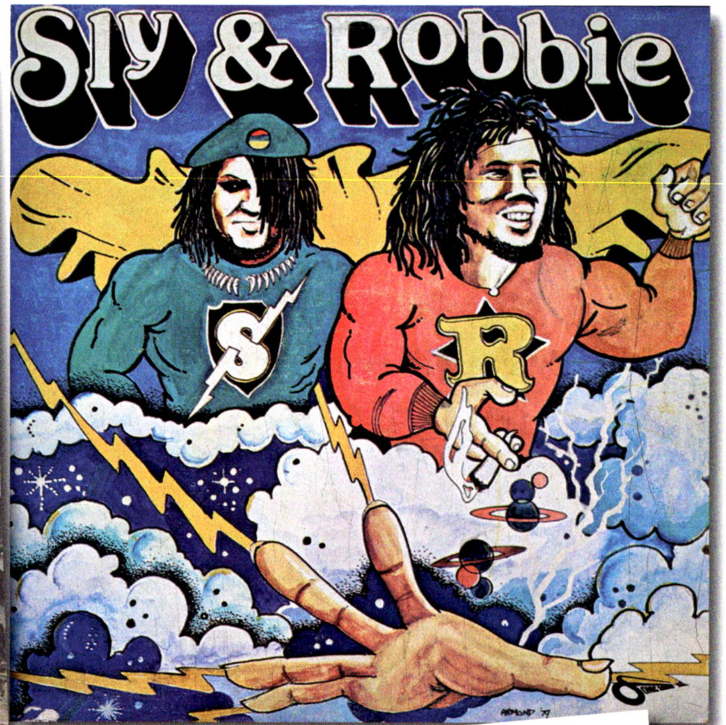

say: ok, this is what I want. I want it to be right like this. Maybe somebody just left out something (laughs). That's it.

"Leaving out something" was certainly a factor. Sly & Robbie played the riddims more pointedly. Less breaks, more patterns. That created a different feeling right from the start.

Yes. Sly was doing experiments with his drums. I was thinking: Sly, I think we overdid something, and Sly was "No, Soljie, we are on the right track. Try to forget what's happening out there. We are creating something new. This is new, totally new." You know it opened me up to other things.

Is that why your two dub albums for Sly & Robbie had this different character?

As an engineer just go for your sound, your duty, your job is to create something new. The idea with *Disco Dub* was that Sly

Soljie Hamilton, Germany 2010.

and Robbie said "Soljie, give us something tough! You know, different from what is going on there. We don't want it to be like what's out there already. Jus' a different thing..."

A new thing ...

A new thing, yes. So, I came up with some something (laughs).

This meant you let the riddims run longer without effects, pure and steady. This way, when the effect came, it had much more impact.

Yeah. Doing music is always a test [to find out] what the listener gravitates to. The unusualness of the sound will make you listen. So, one should not be afraid to venture for new sounds. Don't try to sound like somebody else. Come with something new, [even if] it isn't right. But there is something groovy with this bass like a winter cloak, keeping you warm. We were not going by the rules. We never used to check for bars and beats, we do the things out of the norm, and we don't rehearse it. Dub is just a feel. We're into this creative mood and just put it where you feel it. When it came down to where it was accepted [people] put it in the standards.

What exactly did you do differently? Boosting certain frequencies or use compression?

Well, we didn't have a lot of outboard gear to work with at Channel One...

But a very good desk, one of the best of the time.

Yeah, it was a great console. You just had to put yourself into it. It's like you are the outboard gear (laughs). Everything is in you, so put it in the music. Forget about your personal feelings and let the music flourish. There are no barriers. The only fence around music are the [melody] lines and spaces and their expressions.

Does dub have a spiritual aspect?

Yes, there is a spiritual thing about it. [It's] the spirit of the forefathers within the music.

... which carries over from the original onto the dub?

Yeah, yeah. The music has its spirit in it from the original and onto the dub. You feel it and it let you create. That's how you know the music has a soul.

Some say an "African" soul.

In some ways I would agree. We project a lot of drums, a lot of bass, the horns... it has that African thing about it. Even though... no matter what type of reggae it is, whether it was played for lovers' rock or whatever, you can go in and transform a dub version of it. You'd only recognize the line, but the total flavour of it will be changed, because dub is about you, your creativity. Like you watch a movie and the producer's copy is different from the editor's copy. Dub music is the engineer's cut.

There are now new styles that are based on dub and are called that. They are created in computers and come from people who are less engineers than programmers.

Hyper dub and dubstep and all of that, these things come with the new generation. They want to stay in contact with the original, right? So, they just add that other little name and keep the original name, that's all they are doing. That name alone they're interested in. Taking it away from dub somebody is going to wonder what is really this now? As I said, it's a new generation. They are going to do things how they feel it. Anybody now can be an engineer, anybody. Because you're working on a computer and it's all there. You just add some effects to it. But your inner self is not in it. Is not in it at all. I don't just sit there and use the regular delay, I try to create a delay, you know? Their music is like fast food. It's easy to get and it looks nice. It tastes nice at the time you eat it. If you put it down and it gets cold, you cannot eat it again. [I know] because I've tried to mix dub on a computer.

What makes the difference between a computer mix and an analogue mix on a desk?

Computer take away some things from you, it's like you're too mechanical. The flexibility is not there, because using analogue you do things on the fly. It hits your mind and you're spontaneous with it, while on the computer you have to stop, edit this, edit that...

Technical developments have always influenced reggae. Why doesn't this work in the dub and computer connection?

Yeah, reggae changed with the technology. There are only a few engineers now that work off frequencies, that can relate frequencies to. [On the computer] the mix is just a balance. There's no real separation there of frequencies. It's a cost of work. Everybody is looking at the time and it takes time to sit down and try to get this right. So, the new standard [is] you just balance. They say Pro Tools (for recording) is the industrial standard now and bla bla bla. I [still] record my tracks on multitrack (tape machine) and then put them on a hard drive. Because I still need that tape sound and the noise.

And you need a console to mix a dub?

If I was supposed to do a dub LP, I don't think I would go digital for that. Dub is a creative thing. You have to have your feeling work on it. Doing it on a digital thing, like mixing on Pro Tools, you set things and you set it to be done. You sit there, programme your mutes, and do the action on the console that is on the computer and then let it run. [But] dub is not an electronical thing. I want to be in it, not out of it.

Dub is the moment it happens. Dub needs empathy.

There's no feeling, yeah. I don't want faders to do it by themselves for me. Just sit and watch? No!

On December 24, 2022, Soljie Hamilton died unexpectedly of a heart attack; he was 69.

Reggae Roast Sound System, UK.

Linval Thompson: Dub Exporter to Europe

"There are no facts in Jamaica, only versions."

(Jamaican saying)

Born October 12, 1954, Leval Thompson grew up on the west side of downtown Kingston 13, near Waltham Park Road, an area with lots of shops and bars, a high crime rate and a thriving sound system culture. In this sociotope, Leval, who only became Linval in 1975 through a misprint on a single, went to school with Jacob Miller, Johnny Clarke, Al Campbell and Chinna Smith, first at Maxfield Park Primary, then at Melrose All Age, and finally at Kingsway High School. His parents ran a small grocery store, so the boy was born into a family with an instinctive business sense. At the age of 14, he was already distributing flyers and organizing equipment for dances with Percival Tibby's "Sir Percy Sound", with Ken Boothe and sometimes U-Roy on the mic. Leval really wanted to be a singer, like his friends.

In the second half of the 60s, Thompson's mother left Jamaica for Queens in search of a better life, with father and son following in the early 70s. Leval stayed in New York for almost two years. During this time, he decided to tackle his singing career, right then and there. In a small studio, he recorded two songs on his own account with a group of musicians who called themselves The Buccaneers, who included the later Third World singer, Bunny Rugs. He founded a label called ELSA Records, pressed 500 singles of one of the tracks ("No Other Woman" in 1974), sold some of them, but after his return to Jamaica mainly used them to promote himself. The plan panned out. The first person to make a record with him was Stamma Hobson, a downtown producer who also hired himself out as a bodyguard for Keith Hudson when needed. Stamma took an already finished backing track and had Leval sing "Ma Ma Saya"[1] (aka "Westbound Plane") over it at Randy's. The second person involved was Phil Pratt. Leval sang "Jah Jah Redder Than Red"[2] for him, a successful tune that he re-recorded three years later as "Jah Jah Dreader Than Dread". Afterwards, Lee Perry made two tracks with Leval, one of which – "Kung Fu Man"[3] – caused a sensation in Jamaica, the US, UK, and Japan as part of the martial arts/Bruce Lee craze in the mid-70s.

1 Big Style 7-inch 1974.
2 Sunshot 7-inch 1974.
3 Jamaica: Globe Intl. 7-inch, UK: Ackee 7", USA: Clocktower 7-inch, all 1974–75.

Bunny Lee had no choice but to let him sing on one of his trendy riddims too, and Leval, who had become Linval in the meantime, sang "Don't You Cut Off Your Dreadlocks"[4] despite not yet having any himself! It was the heyday of militant, pan-African Rasta consciousness, and the song hit a nerve and marked his breakthrough. In response, Bunny Lee produced an album of the same name with him in 1976, mixed by King Tubby[5].

Linval Thompson now lived in Whitfield Town, not far from Trenchtown, and now he was well established as a singer. However, he quickly realized that in the reggae business only producers made real money, and he learned that riddim backing tracks were a profitable form of exchange currency. If you sing me a song, I'll give you a riddim, and we incur no costs other than studio time. Following this transaction model, Linval voiced dubplates for the former "King Attorney Sound", which now called itself "Socialist Roots". In exchange, he received a new recording of the "Death In The Arena" riddim, over which he sang "Train To Zion" in the Channel One studio. This became Linval Thompson's first self-produced hit. When he followed it up with "Jah Guiding Star"[6], the single featured a previously unknown co-producer named Henry Junjo Lawes. The man was a colourful character, a flashy styler from the Olympic Way district in West Kingston. Linval and Junjo became friends and each other's constant companion. "I wanted to have somebody with me who everybody know, cause in Jamaica it was rough that time" Linval explained. "[Junjo] was coming to the studio all the time. He like the business and I say: I'm gonna put your name on this label, so people can see that you is a producer, too. But he really produce nothing yet. We put that on the label trying to make him into a producer."[7] They repeated the action with the single "I Love Mariguana" [sic] for Linval's new label, which was simply called Thompson Sound. The song became the title track of his second album in 1978, the first of his own accord, produced with the help of Ossie Hibbert at Channel One. Linval licensed the *I Love Marijuana* LP to Trojan in the UK. People immediately asked for more material, so Linval promptly submitted *Big Joe – African Princess* with deejay cuts, and the

4 Jamaica: Justice 7-inch, UK: Attack 7-inch, both 1975.
5 *Don't Cut Off Your Dreadlocks*, Third World 1976, in the US as *Cool Down* on Clocktower.
6 Mr. Danamic 7-inch 1977.
7 Liner notes *Linval Thompson – the early sessions 1974–1982*, Thompson Sound 2006.

dub album *Negrea Love Dub*. Trojan released all three together and ran ads showing the LP covers under the headline: "Dope... Sex... and Dub". These were not the only albums with which Linval began to penetrate the international market that year. The timing was good, reggae was selling well in Europe, and even made it into the national charts. Foundation dancehall was consolidating its position, while dub was conquering new audiences. Bunny Lee's flying cymbal riddims, combined with Tubby's mixes, stimulated interest. Now Channel One was also in the game, the maxi single was on the horizon as an innovative sound medium, and Scientist was raring to go. Major players, independent labels, and countless small and micro labels, most of them Jamaican-owned, served customers' needs. A volcano erupted in the UK, pouring reggae and dub like lava across the mainland.

Among the many independent label operators in London was I.M. Rana, a merchant from India, not a reggae aficionado, but someone who saw reggae as a worthwhile investment. No one knew where this man came from. In 1976, he had set up Burning Sounds, his headquarters with record store and office at 379 Harrow Road, in the west of the city. People went to see him, put a master tape on the table and collected cash. Rana did not ask if the material might have already been published elsewhere under a different name. He bought albums from Channel One on a large scale, from producers like Phil Pratt, Junjo Lawes, Jah Thomas and Linval Thompson, including rootsy lovers' productions specially designed for the UK market.

Mr. Rana enjoyed a good reputation, paid cash on delivery for finished productions and conveyed the feeling of trust and a fair deal. He owned a record pressing plant in Ireland, where he manufactured LPs on demand, although the quantities remained unclear due to the lack of sales accounts. The only thing that seems certain is that he released the first edition mostly in colored vinyl and re-pressed it in black. Burning Sounds installed six sub-labels (Burning Rockers, Burning Vibrations, His Majesty, Dread Hot, FORM and Caribana, the last two registered in Dublin), and quickly published around 150 releases. Almost half of them were LPs, the rest being maxis and singles. Mr. Rana didn't advertise but bought and pressed, sold, and pressed still more vinyl. The records with the red-yellow-green stripes and burning notes logo were a sure-fire success. Unfortunately, after four years, the flame went out, and at the end of 1980, Burning Sounds went into liquidation. Rana withdrew to Dun Laoghaire on the east coast of Ireland, and the label was taken over by Clive Stanhope of CSA Records, who released another 20 albums under the original name, but then sold the catalogue to Colin Newman of Trojan in 1987. After that, business stopped and the Burning Sounds albums became sought-after collector's items. This was until 2015, when Secret Records Limited began repressing the catalogue's highlights, leading to a drastic drop in the price of the originals.

Mr. Rana never showed up again. Since his disappearance in 1980, memories have faded. Today there is no one left to tell true and valid facts about him and his labels, no artist, no producer, no collector. Since the record covers at the time were also short on information, all that remains of Burning Sounds is a mysterious black hole of colorful vinyl containing a considerable number of exceptionally good albums. In addition to maxis with dub versions and showcase albums, this included a high percentage of dub LPs, which helped the message of dub to spread from Swinging London:

- **Black Foundation Dub** (Burning Sounds 1977) Producer: Gussie Clarke
- **Slum In Dub** (Burning Sounds1978) Producer: Gregory Isaacs

Linval Thompson: Dub Exporter to Europe

- **Star Wars Dub** (Burning Sounds 1978) Producer: Phil Pratt
- **Guerilla Dub** (Burning Sounds 1978)
- **Variation On A Theme** (Burning Vibrations 1978) Producer: Revelation
- **Burning Dub** (Burning Vibrations 1979) Producer: Junior English
- **Dutch Man Dub** (Burning Vibrations 1979)
- **Red Hot Dub** (Burning Vibrations 1979) Producer: Elroy Bailey
- **Green Bay Dub** (Burning Vibrations 1979) Producer: Linval Thompson
- **Dread Lion Dub** (His Majesty 1979) Producer: Patrick Francis aka Jah Lloyd
- **Black Magic Dub** (FORM 1980)
- **Outernational Riddim** (FORM 1980)
- **Soul Man Dub** (Burning Vibrations 1981) Producer: Junior Soul

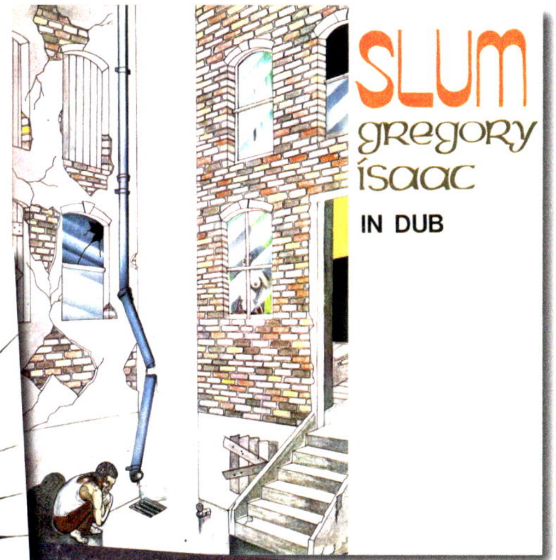

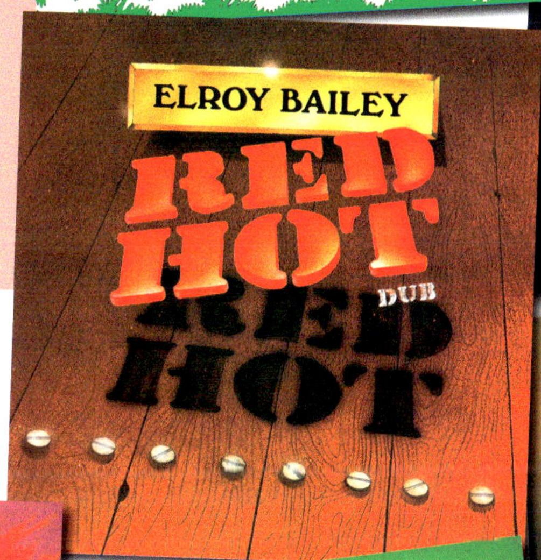

The same year he signed his first deals with Trojan, Linval Thompson also sold *Love Is The Question* and *Rocking Vibration*, the first two LPs, to Burning Sounds. Without even thinking about it, the singer had turned into a businessman. Looking back, he said "it just happened. I never know it was so easy." He marketed his records himself, hardly ever went on tour and instead began to produce other artists on a large scale[8]. At Trojan he released ten albums, on Greensleeves seven LPs and countless maxis, and at Burning Sounds six productions with other artists, in addition to two more of his own[9]. However, he was only involved in one release for Burning Sounds' range of dub LPs.

In 1979, Thompson responded to the 12" boom by founding a label in the UK specifically for maxi singles, on which he released the current dancehall trends with combinations of his own songs, deejay versions and dubs. He took the name of the UK platform from the LP *Strong Like Samson*[10] that he had just released in Jamaica in small numbers, with a printed label only and no cover. He had previously sold the same mixes to Trojan under *The Revolutionaries – Outlaw Dub*. He also pressed an untitled LP with dubs of other productions, again without a cover and dispensing with a label imprint, but it didn't go beyond the status of a test release. The number of copies of the white label pressing number 0023 was so small that the LP became one of the most expensive dub LPs in history.[11] It wasn't until 2013 that it was officially released as *Linval Thompson & The Revolutionaries – Boss Man's Dub*[12]. In addition to the two double-issued self-pressings and the debut *Negrea Love Dub*, Linval Thompson released another eight dub albums between 1979 and 1982, six of them on London-based labels:

- **The Revolutionaries – Green Bay Dub** (Burning Vibrations UK 197X)
- **Train To Zion Dub** (Tuff Gong JA 1981)

8 Barrington Levy, Johnny Osbourne, Eek-a-Mouse, Horace Andy, Freddie McGregor, Dennis Brown, Gregory Isaacs, Ranking Dread, Ranking Trevor, Papa Tullo, Al Campbell, Cornell Campbell, Meditations, Trinity, Prince Mohammed, Viceroys, Wailing Souls, Mystic Eyes, among others.

9 *I Love Jah* on Burning Sounds and *Follow My Heart* on Burning Rockers, both 1979

10 Thompson Sound 1979. The LP had the full title *Strong Like Samson Linval Thompson In Dub*, but the new maxi label received an additional "p" and was called "Strong Like Sampson".

11 A German importer found 20 copies of the LP in London at the time and stamped them with "FOTOFON DAB23". In 2015 one of them was sold for 699 €.

12 With the addition *The Lost 1979 Dub Album* Hot Milk UK, CD 2013, LP 2014.

- **Scientist In Dub Volume 1** (Jah Guidance US 1981)
- **Scientist – Dub Landing** (Starlight UK 1981)
- **Scientist Meets The Space Invaders** (Greensleeves UK 1981)
- **Scientist Encounters Pac-Man** (Greensleeves UK 1982)
- **Scientist and Prince Jammie – Dub Landing Vol. 2** (Starlight UK 1982)
- **Scientist And Jammy Strike Back!** (Trojan UK 1982)

Two obscure LPs appeared on the Canadian Abraham label after 1982:

- **Linval Thompson Meets King Tubbys – Ina Reggae Dub Style, Dis A Yard Dub**
- **Sly & Robbie Meet King Tubby – Reggae Rasta Dub**

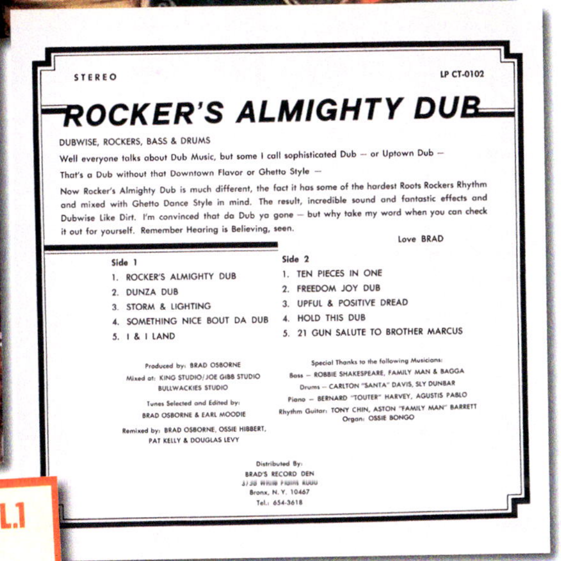

The Abraham label succeeded Brad Osbourne's New York Clocktower label, which had been the main US base for Jamaican productions from the mid-70s. Osbourne bought tapes or produced them himself, including major dub albums such as *King Of Dub*, *Rockers Almighty Dub*, *Macka Dub*, *Heavy Metal Dub*, *Scientific Dub* and others. Thompson also licensed material to Osbourne[13] and said about him that "he was maybe the only man in New York who pay you as you come. I couldn't give him no bad name for that." Osbourne had a shop in the Bronx where he was shot during an argument in 1986. Abraham took over the label and has since released a series of disreputable dub albums under dubious titles and compilations. Linval Thompson referred to the albums Abraham released under his name as bootlegs. "Everybody is trying to make money of our

13 His own albums *Six Babylon* and *Cool Down* among others, as well as material by Barrington Levy and Freddie McGregor

stuff. [Even] Bunny Lee never tell nobody nuttin. So he alone earn money. If we [artists] do it it's a problem."

In 2002, Thompson followed up with the compilation *Phoenix Dub*[14]. Bunny Lee's compilation *Dub Story*[15] from the same year, on the other hand, was not authorized by him and was partly mixed after 2000 without his knowledge. Thompson's riddims came almost exclusively from the Channel One studio, sometimes recorded by the Revolutionaries, sometimes by the Roots Radics. The vocals were recorded either at Harry J or King Tubby, where mixing was also carried out, initially by Tubby himself or Prince Jammy. This lasted until Scientist became his preferred engineer because "[that] echo slap, only Scientist could give you that mix at King Tubby's"[16]. Accordingly, Thompson released six of his dub LPs under his name (see above), all of which Scientist considers illegal.

On this topic, Thompson waved his hand. "Well, we make Scientist, you know" he countered. "If we wasn't, you'd never hear about Scientist"[17], a statement that is as accurate as it is exaggerated. When asked about this, Thompson immediately started an argument.

Scientist claims he had no idea what was being released in the UK under his name. Did he really not know?

Linval Thompson: No, he never know. Look! Is an important ting. Who make Scientist get popular? Who? Which producer? I am asking you who? Which special producer? In that time? We need to find out that. Who was licking out those song in London in that time? Which record company was pushing those [dubs]?

Are you alluding to Greensleeves and Junjo?

Ahh! Talk again! Who bring Junjo? Who was first before Junjo?

Well, you.

Done the argument! I am the founder. So, who make Scientist get popular?

You..?

Not me alone.

... and Junjo and Greensleeves..?

Alright! Done the argument! We make him where he is now. Without our style no Scientist. We booked him to do what I want him to do. If it's him alone he wouldn't do that. He never come to England to hear what the people them want. Tubbys [also] never come to England. I come to England, I hear what they want. So, me tell him give me that sound, that heavy bang! Stick with that sound more than once. B-L-O-W! Tubby say is a distortion and I say, no, make it stay. Is not a distortion. Bang! Bo! That echo they love it.

How did you know what people were into in the UK?

(Laughs) I don't know... When I come to England the companies always want dubplate from me, dub, dub songs. They always pay less money [than for the vocal album]. But it was selling crazy. I never know that it was so important in Europe, in France or Germany. Me never know that it was so strong.

If you didn't know, then why did you produce it?

Because the company want it. We never know it was selling so much. We didn't know the truth. I only know the company was gonna pay us a likkle more money. That's what I was really interested in, to earn a likkle extra money. We didn't know it was a big ting for the white people.

So, you're saying you only did it because the companies wanted it?

England was waiting to do business with dub. I was doing my own thing. I used to press my songs in London, on my Strong Like Sampson label and on Thompson Sound label. I wasn't waiting for them; they sent for me. The sound that I come with, they love it. It was different from the Bunny Lee sound, from the Lee Perry sound, from the Coxson sound. I think they wanted a different sound. When you listen to the *Negrea Love Dub* album, it's a different style. From there it started to fly, dub was going crazy. People were waiting for me to come with dubs. I have to come with more than one LP.

14 Motion Records UK/Nocturne France 2002.
15 Jamaican Recordings UK 2002.
16 Liner notes *Linval Thompson – the early sessions 1974–1982* ibid.
17 Interview Reggae-Vibes "Can't Stop A Natty Dread" by Peter I 2004.

Who got paid for the dubs? The engineer, the producer or the artist, whose songs were dubbed?

The artist never get pay, no. Greensleeves used to pay Scientist royalty, beca' we use his name. So, him title get royalty. And the producer. Greensleeves was willing to pay anybody, I'm telling you. Chris Cracknell always pay, me know that.

Then why did Scientist sue Greensleeves?

Scientist want to sue that he own the tracks. He is trying, [but even] though Junjo die, them really Junjo tracks, you know.

The dubs were part of a contract between Greensleeves and Junjo?

Yes. Scientist supposed to get pay for royalty still, as long as it selling. But he can't own Junjo tings them. The rights on his productions have his kids. Junjo made no will, that's the real problem. Scientist vex with us now, he say we go against him at Greensleeves. Greensleeves pay us royalty and they pay Scientist too. So, I don't know what the problem is.

Scientist wasn't the only one whose mixes were released without his knowledge. Other engineers also thought they were mixing specials for sound systems until they found out that the mixes were being released as LPs in the UK.

That's true. They never know about that, fi true.

Often the producers also put engineer's names on the cover that they assumed would sell better than those who actually mixed.

Sometimes a true that! (laughs). It's true, it's true, true, true... (Linval can't stop laughing).

Pressure Sound System by The Bug.

Sightiva Hi-Fi Sound System, Germany.

Scientist: Anarchy and Anger

> "Dub is where the engineer becomes like the person in the orchestra that gives the commands to the musicians, what to play (and) where to play. The only difference is instead of we waving a stick telling the musicians when to come in or when to play soft we'd use a volume control (i.e. a fader)."
>
> (Scientist[1])

Hopeton Overton Brown grew up with his grandparents in Harbour View, a fishing settlement on the lowest tip of Kingston. It was the last inhabited stretch of town before Norman Manley Highway which leads to the airport. Jamaica gained independence in 1962, and the community of Harbour View had been established two years previously. In the same year, Hopeton was born on April 18. Afterwards, his mother decided to emigrate to the United States, and when Hopeton was eight years old, tried to file for her boy to follow, but the plan failed because Hopeton could not learn anything from her that he was interested in. He returned to his father, who did TV and radio repair work, and this sparked his passion for electrical engineering. At the age of 16, he was not only assisting his dad, but was also building amplifiers for small sound systems. To test their functionality, he used dubs mixed by King Tubby and was impressed by their extraordinary dynamics. He decided he wanted to get to know this man and wanted to talk shop with him. At the age of 17, he checked off school and headed to Dromilly Avenue, about 11 miles away. He was introduced to Tubby by a friend named Francis who installed window grills there. Hopeton was at the beginning of his successful journey as an audio engineer specialist who gained the reputation of a scientist.

At first, the work in the studio was out of reach, and Tubby only let him wind transformers, which didn't bother Hopeton. Above all, he sought exchange with Tubby to present his vision of an automated mixing board. The idea of a console specifically designed for the requirements of dub has stuck with him to this day. By the late 1970s, however, thoughts like these were like stargazing. To the witnesses of these conversations the youngster appeared like a prophet speaking of the future.

In one of these situations, he was given the moniker "Scientist" by Bunny Lee. Suddenly the name was there, and it stuck. In a country like Jamaica, where duppies, obeah, spirituality and magic are part of everyday life, it seemed natural to associate him with the necromancy of voodoo, were science stands for the inexplicable. Yet, it's absurd. Hopeton Brown had as much to do with voodoo as dub has to do with dubstep. He was a clear-headed electrician who realized early on that there would soon be much more than just four audio tracks like at King Tubby, and that automation would be possible in the studio environment, that there would be faders that move on their own, and pots that turn by themselves. With such thought experiments, he met a congenial spirit in King Tubby. And while listening to the two of them and their visionary ideas about the future of electroacoustics (with no one else understanding a word), it was even more obvious, that this youth had to be an actual scientist.

He didn't lack self-confidence. At every opportunity he bragged that the processes in the studio would not be a problem for him. David Rodigan recalled their first encounter thus "there was this young boy [at King Tubby's], producing literally nuts and bolts on the lathe. And I said to him 'What's your name?', he said 'My name is Scientist. I'm doing this but actually I want to be in there.' (pointed to the studio door) – 'As a singer?' – 'As an engineer. And one day I will be.'"

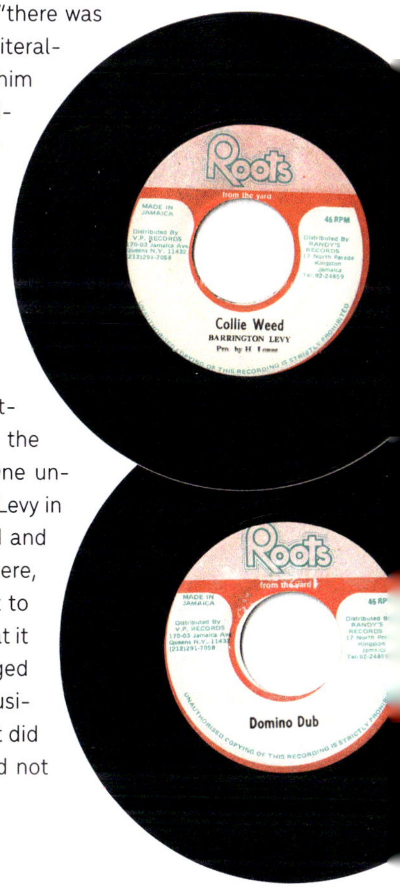

The day he went "in there" came in 1978. Tubby had retired from the studio, with Prince Jammy now doing most of the work. Scientist often boasted that he could do better. One night, Junjo Lawes showed up at the door, with an instrumental from Channel One under his arm, and a singer named Barrington Levy in tow. He had a song that had to be recorded and mixed, right there and then. Jammy wasn't there, neither was Pat Kelly, and Tubby didn't want to do it himself. "You always said you've got what it takes, so show it now!" These words challenged Scientist. Neither Junjo nor Levy we're enthusiastic, but they had no choice. Either Scientist did it or there was no song that day. They could not

1 "Return Of The Rub-A-Dub Style", DVD Walking Road Films 2009.

avoid agreeing, and for the first time in his life, Hopeton recorded vocals and mixed vocal & dub. "Collie Weed" was the single they created; it shot straight to number one, marking Levy's international breakthrough.

The success had got Scientist a new job. He had made it now, he worked "in there", in the studio. He didn't try to copy Tubby but had his own ideas for sounds which he also tried to create and develop at Coxson, where he was now also allowed at the mixing board. Here, in the same year, he entered with a mix of Sugar Minott's "Oh Mr. DC", the tune that opened wide the door to foundation dancehall. Subsequently, he created sound brilliance for the production of Willie Williams' *Armagideon Time* that the studio had never heard before. He mixed Johnny Osbourne's "Truth And Rights" and Michigan & Smiley's "Nice Up The Dance", among others. However, when Hopeton tried to explain that the sound controls on the channels of a console could not only be used for correcting the mix but also for designing sound, already during recording, the studio owner spoke of sabotage. When Coxson learned that Scientist worked at Tubby on a permanent basis, the interlude at Studio One was over after just a few weeks.

Scientist revolutionized the sound at Tubby's studio. He was not just an engineer, but an instrumentalist who stamped the tracks with his mark at the mixing desk. With stoic physicality and tentacle-like movements of his fingers, he switched the faders and twisted the knobs. His settings banged out of the speaker boxes with unprecedented clarity, loudness blending with controlled aggressiveness. Every frequency was a raging wave, neatly separated between high, mid, and low. Scientist designed the acoustic equivalent of the new trends of the dancehall.

When it came to the version, the young man knew no boundaries, and left his colleagues with egg on their faces. You're never alone in a Jamaican studio, and when Scientist started to dub, turmoil was guaranteed. He shot the console's test tone through the effect devices, ignored all habits, pushed the sproing of the reverb to the limit of distortion, and refrained from the King Tubby style of sending treble-heavy signals through the high-pass filter. Instead, he modulated the bass, which turned the previous dub practice upside down. He dubbed past arrangements with virtuosity, created his own swing, left gaps, tore off voices in the middle of the word, or instruments in the middle of the theme, and drowned them in echo loops. Scientist dubs were radical experiments of symphonic anarchy, creaky science fiction from the effects universe, and all paired with relentlessly good sound.

Scientist: Anarchy and Anger

In the wake of the success of "Collie Weed" everyone scrambled to give Scientist work, everyone craved his dubs. The genre was only five or six years old when the tall beanpole gave it a lasting upgrade with his innovative mixing technique. In addition to dubplates and flipsides, the market overseas, apart from the Jamaican communities, was now enticing. From 1980 the long players came. The first to appear in New York – "straight from the Big Apple" – was the *Allied Dub Selection*[2], staged as a clash. Bunny Lee spoke, shouted and screamed intros for both sides of the LP and, like the cover, tried to suggest that one side was mixed by Tad Dawkins in the Bronx and the other by Scientist in Waterhouse. Doubts were justified. The consistently uniform sound as well as the effects suggested that the alleged clash was more of a publicity stunt. The album, which sounded exceptionally good due to the high-quality US mastering, was probably mixed entirely by Scientist at Tubby. During the same period, the London based label JB Music released *The Best Dub Album In The World*[3] including the note *Introducing Scientist*. It was the counterpart to the *Working Man*[4] LP, also mixed by Scientist for singer Al Campbell. The cover photo showed how young the man preparing to stir up the dub world was. The final breakthrough was looming with what was being brewed elsewhere in London by Greensleeves.

Chris Sedgwick and Chris Cracknell had moved their Greensleeves Record Shop from West Ealing to Shepherd's Bush in 1975, and ran a constantly growing mail order service, increasingly focused on reggae. After checking Daddy Cool, Dub Vendor, Trojan or Rough Trade, Jamaican producers who wanted to sell their productions in the city became regular visitors. Greensleeves assumed pole position in the favour of reggae producers. In 1977, Sedgwick, the accountant, and Cracknell, the music enthusiast, decided to become active in the record business as licensees. First with a few test singles, and after encouraging five-figure sales, in 1978 they ventured into LPs. The first single by deejay Dr. Alimentado was called "Born For A Purpose" and ended up in Johnny Rotten's selection on his visit to the John Peel show[5]. The first LP was Alimentado's *Best Dressed Chicken In Town*. The fourth LP was already a dub album entitled *Goldmine Dub* (1979). From 1980, six LPs followed within three years under the Scientist name, as follows:

- **Scientist v Prince Jammy – Big Showdown** 1980 (GREL 10), Producer: Junjo Lawes
- **Scientist Heavy Weight Dub Champion** 1980 (GREL 13), Producer: Junjo Lawes
- **Scientist Meets The Space Invaders** 1981 (GREL 19), Producer: Linval Thompson
- **Scientist Rids The World Of The Evil Curse Of The Vampires** 1981 (GREL 25), Producer: Junjo Lawes
- **Scientist Wins The World Cup** 1982 (GREL 37), Producer: Junjo Lawes
- **Scientist Encounters Pac-Man** 1982 (GREL 46), Producer: Linval Thompson

Hopeton Overton Brown was unaware of these releases. "Scientist had no involvement, he simply mixed them", Chris Cracknell confirmed[6].

2 On the TAD's label of Jamaican producer Tad A. Dawkins, produced by Dawkins and Jah Thomas.
3 A title Phil Pratt had already used for an LP four years earlier.
4 JB Music UK 1980.
5 See chapter "Prologue, Counteraction".
6 Al Fingers: *Greensleeves. The First 100 Covers*, Stüssy Deluxe UK 2010 p. 31.

Cracknell was the actual producer, while Junjo Lawes and Linval Thompson provided tapes with dub mixes. They were the producers of the vocal versions and sold to the label top performers like Barrington Levy, Eek-a-Mouse, Yellowman, Wailing Souls, Don Carlos, John Holt, Johnny Osbourne and many others. Always in the form of complete albums, and they also provided dubs corresponding to most of the tracks. Cracknell, a big fan of King Tubby, selected what he thought were the best mixes, came up with thematic concepts, found appropriate titles and commissioned Tony McDermott to design matching, cartoon-style covers. McDermott, born in 1958, was a recognized comic artist for *Black Echoes* magazine, and later designed the entire Greensleeves look, as well as the comic-inspired covers for Mad Professor's *Dub Me Crazy* series.

Cracknell's concepts for the Scientist LPs were tailored to the spirit of the times and the British market, and the dubs from Jamaica were edited accordingly in a small London studio. For the *Vampires* LP, he had the deejay duo Eastwood & Saint record creepy vocal and horror sound effects as overdubs, then spread the legend that Scientist had mixed the LP on Friday the 13th at midnight! Given the hero worship in reggae of African American boxers, as well as the strong dancehall affinity for boxing matches which aim to knock out the opponent in the fight for the clash crown, two albums were staged as boxing events. Jah Thomas took over the role of ring announcer on both *Heavy Weight Dub Champion* and the supposed *Big Showdown* between Scientist and Prince Jammy. Not a single dub on it was mixed by the latter. The fact that his mixes were assigned to the rival with whom he had been at loggerheads since the first days of King Tubby only served to rub salt in the wound, as Scientist knew nothing about these projects. He only found out about the albums when his cousin, who lived in London, called him and told him that records under his name were being sold in the UK. When he saw the *Pac-Man* cover, he felt like the victim of a conspiracy. On the back he discovered the image of Prince Jammy pointing at the Scientist LPs and angrily exclaiming: "Gnnaaarrrrr!! Jus the sight of 'im mek mi blood a gwaan boil up!" Scientist's opponents planned to destroy him with the help of the popular video game character Pac-Man, an omnivorous ball that had been wreaking havoc in the digital world for two years.

Legally speaking, the Greensleeves publications were in a gray area. On the one hand, they followed the decades-long practice of Jamaican producers, who rarely asked or informed their artists if they wanted to release records in the UK, and on the other, it was common practice for singers, deejays, and musicians to be paid only once for their recordings. There were no sales-dependent licenses. According to the same principle, Hopeton Brown was paid for his work as an engineer by clients Lawes and Thompson; Hopeton had no rights to this work. In the music business, copyright only exists for composers and lyricists; recordings, including mixes, belong to the person who commissions and pays for them, in this case, Junjo Lawes and/or Linval Thompson, who sold them on as owners. Be that as it may, the albums involved naming rights. The name "Scientist" belonged to Hopeton Brown and should not have been used without consultation or permission. The question also arises as to whether an engineer's dubs are not an art form that required special legal and financial assessment. Jammy also insisted if they "come for me to mix dub, they come for me because of my name, right? So, they got to pay for my name. If I create the mix, I have a percentage of publishing to get. I have to get some form of royalties. But I didn't know about that in those days."

The conflict has not been resolved to this day; the following chapter discusses it in detail. The sales figures for the albums, repressed countless times, were not disclosed anywhere; it was only admitted that, of the six LPs, *Space Invaders* was the biggest seller. Regardless of how many copies were ultimately sold, Greensleeves made a decisive contribution to making the "Scientist" brand profitable outside the reggae world. The LPs with their eye-catching comic-inspired covers made dub socially acceptable. Since then, cartoons have become the artwork typical for the genre, and it somehow stuck to Scientist. Although his early LPs (more or less without his intervention) in both visual design and title, just as often followed the warlike revolutionary aesthetic that has been widespread since the mid-70s. *World At War*, *Dub War*, *High Priest Of Dub*, *International Heroes Dub*, *Repatriation*

Dub etc. They were at the beginning of many publications advertised in the following decades with the Scientist name. Not everything was of convincing quality, but it was precisely in the initial phase that brilliant works of sound-technical improvisation were achieved, favoured by the connection between Roots Radics and the Revolutionaries with the Channel One studio. This was not just in the pure dub LP format, but also on legions of showcase sets (vocal & dub), maxis (a product with which Greensleeves had also been active since 1978) and, above all, on the backs of Jamaican singles that never appeared on any LP. Five albums show how the canon of dub music developed in the hands of Hopeton Brown in the early 80s:

- **Scientific Dub** (Clocktower US + Sarge UK 1981) Producer: Brad Osbourne, mixed at King Tubby on the way to a new dub sound of the studio, packaged in a painted cover with the image of a seven-handed wizard surrounded by futuristic electrical equipment
- **Dub Landing** (Starlight UK 1981) Producer: Linval Thompson, mixed at King Tubby, with varied bass modulations and even distortion
- **Radicfaction** (Cha Cha UK 1982) Producer: Maurice Wellington & Eric Lamont aka The Morwells, mixed at Channel One, with surprising sounds, great effect dynamics and effects partly in stereo
- **World At War** (Black Ovation Records US 198X) Producer: Jimmy Riley, completely in stereo, mixed at Channel One, with an exceptionally wide, delicate range of effects
- **International Heroes Dub** (Tamoki Wambesi UK) Producer: Roy Cousins, also in stereo and from Channel One, with echoes building up and mixed much more brutally

Let's not go into the fact that there are more LPs mentioned here that Scientist considered to be just as illegal as the "Green-Thieves"[7] albums, or that when Jimmy Riley recently joined Sugar Minott at Coxson Dodd's side, he accused the Hoo Kim brothers of stealing ideas. It wasn't long before that Riley had recorded a rude diss track against Channel One for copying Studio One riddims.[8] Now he produced a dub LP (*World At War*) in this same studio with Scientist, and had four Studio One relicks in his luggage.[9] Equally strange is that Sugar Minott, who owed the success of his"Oh Mr. DC" single to Scientist, among others, released a dub album around the same time in which he explicitly attacked him on two tracks.[10] The supply of Scientist dubs didn't seem to dry up. Forgotten tapes, lost recordings, old LPs in new packaging or new compilations of well-known material were constantly turning up. In 2014, two LPs that no one was

7 A slur for Greensleeves often used by Scientist.
8 "Channel One Crash", to be found on the LP *Majority Rule*, Burning Sounds UK 1978, among others.
9 Rockford Rock, Darker Shade Of Black, Sweet Talking, Why Did You Leave.
10 *Sugar Minott & The Black Roots Players Meet The People Inna Lovers Dubbers Style*, Black Roots UK 1981.

expecting were released in Brooklyn, both on the Jah Life label, owned and established by Hyman Wright (aka Papa Life) in the 1970s. These were:

The Dub Album They Didn't Want You To Hear, the counterpart to Flick Wilson's *School Days* LP from 1980, co-produced by Junjo Lawes and Papa Life, with mixes that no one knew existed.

Jah Life In Dub, an album with Barrington Levy dubs that was supposed to be released in 1980. The covers were already printed when Greensleeves launched *Scientist v Prince Jammy – Big Showdown*. Since four mixes on the albums were identical, Jah Life opted out in favour of the more potent company. In 1983, Donovan Germain bought a small part of the covers, and bagged an untitled dub LP from his own Revolutionary Sounds label without comment. This caused confusion for 31 years until the release of the originally intended Scientist LP solved the mystery in 2014, appearing in the designated sleeves. Two years later, Germain released his album, which until then was in its sleeve, in a new edition entitled *Revolutionary Sounds Pre-Release Dub*.

Also in the same year, a picture disc of the 32-year-old LP *Scientist Meets The Roots Radics*[11] was pressed in the US on the occasion of Record Store Day. As a reprint of the original cover, it showed a painted street scene in which the Roots Radics handed a tape to Scientist to mix. As Style Scott recalled "Scientist, he came the hard way! When we recorded at Channel One, the little youth is large, you know? He made some sounds with snare drums, bad! Even me as a drummer sometimes criticize him and say 'Bwoy, the drum too loud, the snare too loud.' But you know what, it was right! It was the right amount of levels and anything because he had it. Trust me, that run dancehall."

From 1981, Scientist worked as a recording engineer for the Hoo Kim brothers. He had already joined Studio One because he not only wanted to mix, but also record instruments. Now he shuttled between Tubby's studio, where he mixed, and Channel One, where he recorded. At first, he was thought to be a spy because Tubby had started building a 24-track studio. When Junjo made it clear that he preferred to work with Scientist, this was no longer an issue. In 1983, the Hoo Kims hired Scientist to be their resident engineer. From then on, he also mixed and dubbed at Channel One, and managed to improve the studio's already excellent sound still further, on the one hand by experimenting in stereo (the sound of the dancehall was usually mono) and on the other, by avoiding any form of compression, apart from the vocals. But he didn't stay long on Maxfield Avenue, as the spot was a hub for drug, business, and political gangsters. "Everyone was dealing drugs back then" Bunny Lee confirmed, "even the artists." Scientist got into trouble with a lot of people and no longer wanted to work for Junjo, who was clearly involved in illegal business. Besides, the story of Greensleeves had left its mark. After just one year, he moved to a supposedly better area and joined Tuff Gong, as the second man next to Errol Brown.

He felt comfortable in the Marley empire environment. The work there was professional and structured; Hopeton had the impression that Marcus Garvey Drive was not about exploiting artists like other studios. But the feeling of security didn't last long. "The ghetto haunts you" he realized, "you can't shake it off."[12] The thugs belonging to the political factions had mutated into internationally active, violent drug gangs, from whose presence Tuff Gong was also not immune. The relationship with his now arch-enemy Jammy also took on threatening characteristics, Scientist feared for his life, so in 1985 he fled Jamaica and never came back. He initially tried to cultivate his sound ideal in Washington, developing his own studio equipment, including a replica of the high pass filter from King Tubby's studio. In the early 90s, he moved to Los Angeles. To this day he never tires of emphasizing that the second phase of the dub era, particularly when it comes to mixing the drums, was sonically superior to the sound of American black music of that time. A direct comparison proves him right in many cases.

Even in the diaspora, the duppies of the past had a hold on Hopeton Brown. He was unable to let the old stories rest, and his opponents didn't give up, either. In interviews, discord was spread, truths were manipulated, lawsuits were initiated. The man who was one of Jamaica's greatest, most innovative and talented sound and dub engineers, the "Master of Drum & Bass", and a "genius between reverb & echo" was in danger of fading away from recognition in the fog of complaints and accusations.

After emigrating to the States, the name Scientist has sunk into oblivion in his homeland; the disputes had not helped his reputation. Accordingly, participation in the rest of the reggae scene was marginal. Apart from *Scientist Dubs Culture Into A Parallel Universe*[13] in 2000 and a combination album with Mad Professor[14] two years later, little of note happened. He now found recognition in a new environment as a remixer. He creat-

11 Selena UK 1982.

12 Translation from the German French TV documentary TRACKS, ARTE TV September 7, 2013.

13 RAS Records US, reissue by Diggers Factory 2022 with holography 3D cover and coloured vinyl.

14 *Mad Professor Meets Scientist At The Dub Table*, Ariwa UK 2002.

ed adaptations of Marvin Gaye's "What's Going On" and Bob Marley's "Lively Up Yourself", among others. In 2003, the British band Death In Vegas commissioned him to remix "Scorpio Rising", a track which they had recorded with Liam Gallagher. This was in addition to a series of inconspicuous reggae collaborations like

- **The Scientist Meets Ted Sirota's Heavyweight Dub** (Liberated Zone Records 2013) with Chicago jazz drummer Ted Sirota
- **Dubiterian meets The Scientist – Tribute to Augustus Pablo** Digital 2014 (LP MIR Mirumir 2016)
- **Scientist & Dubiterian – Classeek Riddims** Digital 2018

Scientist achieved another big success thanks to the so-called Reggae Revival in 2017. He had already mixed a few tracks from the Hempress Sativa LP *Unconquerebel*[15], and showed on the dub version *Scientist Meets Hempress Sativa In Dub*[16] that his anarchic skills at the mixing desk were still effective.

Two years later, another supposedly unreleased album mixed by Scientist appeared. This was *Roots Radics – 12 Inches Of Dub*[17], but it was not what it claimed to be, being playbacks of the 1980 Greensleeves LP *12" Of Pleasure* by General Echo. The basis of this were artistic dubs that Scientist had created at Tubby's studio from Rod Taylor, Flick Wilson, Heptones or Barrington Levy tracks, which had, however, been lost behind the lyrics. Freed from the crude overdubs, almost 40 years later these mixes were freshly remastered as a supposed counterpart to the General Echo album. However, they were not the counterpart, as it was the same album, just without the vocals. At that time, Scientist was at the peak of his craft, resulting in *12 Inches Of Dub* attaining a quality akin to his best works for Greensleeves. However, due to the feud between him and the label, one must refrain from naming it as such. That's

15 Conquering Lion Records 2016.

16 Conquering Lion Records 2017.

17 Greensleeves/VP Records, appeared in a limited edition for Record Store Day 2019.

why the record was under Roots Radics; for Scientist it was further evidence of the rip off by the old record company.

In London, where the depth of old sound systems paired with the coolness of young dance programmers gave birth to one bass-tard after another from the jungle of drum'n'bass, Scientist was celebrated outside the reggae scene as the forefather of deeper club music, because he was the first to manipulate, shift and modulate the bass frequencies. Decades after his Jamaican retirement, he continued to influence the sound of British dance underground, and is considered the inventor of minimalism. The fact that reduction was not minimalism, but rather a form of expression of the early dancehall years was overlooked. Spokesmen of the scene, such as Kode9, who is university lecturer Steve Goodman[18], emphasized the minimalist nature of "bass & space" in dubstep. Mala, referred to as the "Bruce Lee of Dubstep"[19] explained "electronic music in general has a lot of respect for people like Scientist, King Tubby, Lee Perry."[20] Both Mala and Kode9 were involved in a project that brought Scientist to London at the end of 2010. Rob Ellis from Bristol, known as Pinch and owner of the dubstep label Tectonic, came up with the concept of a "visionary fusion of roots and future"[21] for which Scientist should remix, or dub dubstep tracks. He was flattered and happily agreed. A year was spent designing, programming, mixing and reworking in various studios, then the double album entitled *Scientist Launches Dubstep Into Outer Space* was created; one CD with 12 originals by renowned representatives of dubstep, and a second one with remixes by Scientist.

Opinions about the project varied. The Brit Shackleton, who was involved in the album and places the physicality of dub above the metaphysical, pointed out contradictions. "You're asking Scientist to take on a project which is made in a different way to classic dub, in that there are not real musicians playing real instruments. For me, the ones that worked best is when there was actually a vocal or musician element that could be dubbed. [It] reminded me of what was going on maybe six or seven years before there was dubstep."[22]

For the release of *Scientist Launches Dubstep Into Outer Space,* the Red Bull Music Academy was won as a sponsor, flying the godfather of the scene from the States to London for a demonstration of his art. On November 18, 2010, Scientist arrived at the city which has always been the center of wild speculation about dub. The admired star enjoyed the attention and, during a conversation in the sponsor's premises, couldn't help but express favorable sentiments about the symbiosis of dub and step, and the influence of Jamaica's sound system culture on the British club scene.

Is dubstep a next step in the Jamaican dub tradition?

Scientist: Undoubtedly yes! We have a new generation here in London. They love the dub music and I endorse them and encourage them to keep doing it.

Even if they do things completely differently? While you improvise at the mixer, they dub by editing on the computer.

You can call it improvisation on the computer, too. In the end, people are listening and don't know what you do.

A reggae dub is always preceded by a vocal track or an instrumental as the source material. Dubstep exists on its own, as a bass-heavy sound structure.

So what? It still produces the same results. (laughs) You know, there's many ways to skin a cat.

What is dub for you? A functional mix for the dancehall or a remix?

Dub is the original remix. We had dub, we had couple other genres and then we had the remix. It's not just a Jamaican thing anymore. All those people in America and the UK who are doing dubstep, they kinda redefined "remixing".

18 Steve Goodman is, among other things, the author of a study on the use of sound waves in war conflicts: *Sonic Warfare – Sound, Affect and the Ecology of Fear*, The MIT Press, Cambridge 2010.

19 http://de.paperblog.com/mala-bruce-lee-des-dubstep-75435/ (last accessed January 2, 2022).

20 *Scientist On Dub*, Red Bull Music Academy 2010.

21 Release info of the DoCD *Scientist Launches Dubstep Into Outer Space*, Tectonic 2010.

22 In a conversation with Olaf Karnik for the radio feature "Dub Not Dub", as part of the "Open Frei Raum" series of Westdeutscher Rundfunk on April 9, 2011 on WDR 3.

Not rather reinterpreted?

Of course. We have so much different interpretation alive. Look at me and look at you... One of the draw backs with digital [is] you can't really tell what was made where from what wasn't made here. Back in those times in Jamaica every studio had its own unique sound. You could always tell where what [was] recorded.

The sound of a studio through room acoustics or individual technology is becoming increasingly less important. At the end of digital development, everything will sound the same.

Yes, without a doubt. However, analog mixing consoles will die out. They are like dinosaurs. None of the console [currently] on the market is physically set up to do dub or remixes. None of the engineers who were to design a console were thinking of doing what we have been doing with it. I'd like to link up with a company to show them how to physically lay out a console [suitable for dubbing].

This is what you wanted when you went to Tubby. At first it wasn't about dub or remix, was it?

After listening to King Tubby's *Roots of Dub*, I wanted to build a console. I could sort electronics because my father was a TV repairman. I could imagine what needed to be done and wanted to go to a studio to see if my theory was right. Now, when I met King Tubby's, all my theory that I had in my head wasn't 100 percent right. It was more like 90 percent. I started talking to King Tubby's, pretty much about everything like what you see in the modern world, moving faders and all of that. Back in those time a lot of people thought I was crazy, because I was foreseeing all these things that happened 20 years later. When I went to King Tubby's, at first, I was just a TV repair guy winding transformers. I made him a bet: "I bet I could go inside [the studio]" and he: "Oh no, you should be in school, kid. You smoke too much of that green stuff, you should leave that alone, blah blah blah..."

He wasn't entirely wrong about school, was he?

Here is what, the whole school and education system is shit. I was bored listening about Christopher Columbus and all that foolishness. If I was trying to become a historian, yes. But I don't wanna become a historian, I'm an electronic engineer. It's good having a broad striped picture about different topics. But I got bored in

Scientist and the author, London 2010.

Jamaica of these teachers talking to me about things I had no interest in. And as a result, right here in the modern world, you find more and more kids dropping out of school because they have no interest in what the teacher is teaching.

Then the day came when Junjo showed up at the door with Barrington Levy.

The regular engineer who used to be there (i.e., Jammy) was not there. Junjo didn't want me to mix his record because I never mixed a record before. The singer didn't want me to record his voice because I never record a voice before. He begged and begged Tubbys and Tubbys repeatedly tell him: "No no no no no! The only choice that you have to get this tune recorded is him." [To me] he says: "You're always talking you can mix mix mix mix. I bet if I send you inside, you don't know the first thing to do."

And – did you?

Well yes. After the electronic experience and being around the studio and watching Tubbys mix, everything came automatic after that.

Do you recall that tune?

It was "Collie Weed" (by Barrington Levy[23]). His first song and number one.

Do you agree that there is a connection between African heritage, reggae and dub?

What I would agree on (is) in reggae some of the beats have an African influence. But damn, I don't remember any people running around with bones in their nose dubbing (big laugh).

That means the original has African reflections, but the version, the dub or the remix doesn't?

I would agree on that. No African influence exactly with dub. In Jamaica the only time they talk about a dub is probably a dub-plate for sound systems. Dub right now is coming out from everywhere. Dub even came from Red Bull Studio. But I couldn't tell when I heard a dub last time come anywhere from Jamaica. Here is what one of the reasons are: it is very important to view history. This is where I blame the Jamaican government. They should have preserved the history, but they have no interest in preserving the history. They are doing a very poor job. It's a disgrace when King Tubby's console somebody in Seattle, Washington, went and bought it. It should have been in Jamaica in a museum. They say a king never really get any respect in his own country and that's true. Look at me and look at you. I come [from] 5000 miles away, and somebody completely different than me is all into dub more than the people in Jamaica. I am really upset with politicians. I don't trust any politician anywhere around the world. Look what they are doing. They all use the same language; they all dressed the same way. Isn't it like a secret society? Educated in Hartford and Oxford with the end result that all of us is witnessing. They're all settling their disputes with violence and their countries going bankrupt. I don't really have any more confidence in politicians. I am not a fan of violent people, and I don't want violent artists near me. I don't want no gun business.

Is that why you left Jamaica?

Dem kill my friend Tubby; gangster took over the business. More and more records were being released with my name on them and I didn't know about it. Some of them I don't even mix. I was fed up and didn't feel safe anymore...

23 1979 on Roots From The Yard, was pressed very often. The dub was mostly called "Collie Weed Version", on some pressings it bore the title "Domino Dub".

Scientist vs. Jammy vs. Greensleeves: The Everlasting Showdown

They never became friends. From the very beginning they were competitors, rivals, adversaries, and envious opponents who later became enemies. There have now been over 30 years of strife, with no end in sight.

Hopeton Overton Brown was just a teenager when he came to King Tubby. At the time, Lloyd James, thirteen years his senior, was working there as a resident engineer. He was friends with Tubby, and they had known each other since their childhood on Dromilly Avenue. Jammy's position was undisputed. He took the pressure off Tubby, created a distinctive sound inside the studio, and was endorsed by Bunny Lee. Then suddenly this little rascal showed up and peed on his leg.

As soon as Scientist had joined Tubby, he started bullying Jammy. Scientist complained about Jammy's mixes and all the time insisted he could do better. When the 17-year-old's first studio work immediately had a massive impact, Jamaica's producers began to favour him, even though Jammy was already established as an engineer and successful as a producer.

Dancehall as a barometer of the Jamaican spirit had found a new favorite in Junjo Lawes and his "Volcano Sound System". But Junjo didn't want to work with Jammy, even though he had initially wired his sound for him. "They were friends" commented Bunny Lee, but then the taste of success got to him, and "one of the time the t'ing it go to Junjo head, him get bigheaded." Junjo asked for Scientist because the latter's anarcho-dub mixes as basis for the new deejays gave an additional boost to the enthusiasm in the dances. Tubby therefore gave Scientist the keys to the studio, although probably not, as Scientist later claimed, saying "here are the keys, just don't give them to Jammy. Don't leave him here alone. Don't let him touch anything, not a single cable."[1] Tubby had no reason to behave like that; his childhood friend Jammy was specifically employed by him as an engineer. Jammy now had to watch as the relationship between Tubby and Scientist became ever closer. Tubby's mother cooked for him, and Hopeton Brown became a family friend. With this new

1 Translation from the German French TV documentary TRACKS, ARTE TV September 7, 2013.

standing, Scientist continued to tease Jammy. The close unity of king, prince and heir to the throne suggested by the photo on the back of the *King Tubby Prince Jammy And Scientist – First, second and third generation of Dub*[2] LP never really existed. Around 1980, Jammy withdrew, as he had built his own studio. Behind closed doors, it was said that he was tired of the constant arguments with his adversary. But Jammy just decided to avoid him, and he was far from giving up.

Scientist, however, had gained a new opponent. He stormed against the dubs Greensleeves had published under his name. He had not been informed, asked, or paid. While the first two points were undisputed, opinions differed when it came to renumeration. "Scientist was working for Tubbys when we come to the studio" Linval Thompson recalled. "We have to pay Tubbys, Tubbys have to give us an engineer. So, Scientist was there, we have to use [him as] the engineer." For his work, Scientist's wages came out of the amount Thompson paid for studio rent, so it was money coming specifically from a person he could not stand. "I was in charge" Jammy said, "I was the person who used to pay Scientist."

According to Linval Thompson, Scientist also received a share of the proceeds from the dub albums. "We (i.e. Junjo and Linval) take the dub albums to Greensleeves. They pay us and they pay Scientist, too. Greensleeves show me paper that they are paying Scientist, but he's not saying that. Scientist say he own the songs."

When the video game "Grand Theft Auto III" was released in 2001, the conflict escalated. Five tracks from *Scientist Rids The World Of The Evil Curse Of The Vampires* LP were part of the violent gangster/mafia game's soundtrack, but without Hopeton's knowledge or consent. So, he hired a lawyer to fight it, reaching an out-of-court settlement with Rockstar Games, the US video game publisher, who subsequently demanded proof from Greensleeves that the British had the rights to the titles. Greensleeves presented two contracts clearly showing Junjo Lawes had been the producer. Since there was no contract between himself and Junjo, Scientist questioned the validity of the papers concerning him, and in 2003, sued Greensleeves. Negotiations took place in New York which went on for three years, and although Scientist could not prevail with his position that the dubs belonged to him, Greensleeves ultimately had to bear the costs of the legal proceedings due to an agreement they had made with Rockstar. Two years later, the Greensleeves label was sold to VP Records. One can only speculate about a potential connection.

In court, the judges were trying to understand the business processes of Jamaican record production because inconsistencies were emerging all the time. For example, the question of whether Greensleeves took advantage of the fact that Junjo Lawes was illiterate when making the contracts. When questioned in court, Hyman "Papa Life" Wright confirmed in Scientist's favour that Junjo was, in fact, never present at his productions. The key witness for the other side was a certain Lloyd James, now known to the world as King Jammy. James stated that Scientist was paid to work in the studio, but was far too young to make any claims beyond that. "Scientist came there as apprentice" he explained. "[Later,] he tried to steal the rights from dead people. Tubbys, Junjo, he tried to steal [their] rights. I represented Greensleeves in that case. Scientist never produce a song for himself. Never!"

To that, Scientist said "Greensleeves paid Jammys to come to court to tell a lie."[3]

The fronts were relentless, each side recruiting its allies and comrades. On March 19, 2006, Hopeton's phone rang. At the other end was Toops, a man devoted to Jammy since childhood, who had joined him in 1962 when putting together his first sound. Toops insulted Scientist loudly, and made death threats against him and Papa Life. Hopeton remained calm. "You want kill me, 'member you said that tonight. You threaten me. Jammys is a liar! Put your boss on the phone." He was able to record the hysterical screaming and posted it on his website. Who initiated the call remains unclear, but the threat of death was certainly out there. Despite that, Scientist had to remove the recording of the screaming from his website.

Although he had lost the case, Scientist managed to prevent Greensleeves from publishing his mixes further, even if this turned out to be a Pyrrhic victory. Nonetheless, the albums were reissued for a short time between 2014 and 2015, even in their original design, but as a bootleg by an obscure Moscow label with the addition "©1980 Scientist ℗2014 Mirumir Music Publishing issued under exclusive license for the world excluding North America by Hopetown [sic] Overton Brown".

In 2015 there was also a dubious, remastered re-release of *High Priest Of Dub*, the first pressing of which had come from the British Kingdom label back in 1982. This time, the LP came from Seattle on Zion's Gate

2 KG Imperial, UK 1981 Producer Fatman.

3 In an interview with Angus Taylor for United Reggae 2008

Records, with different artwork, limited to 300 copies and in colored vinyl. Half of the tracks were swapped for dubs from the *The Force Of Music – Liberated Dub*[4] LP.

Scientist asserted that he had sympathy for small labels, and for shops that repress his records in order to make a little profit for their own living. "I support them and don't want anything in return. I only fight against Greensleeves." He consistently resisted coming to an agreement, an attitude which turned out to be fatal, because by doing so he took himself off the market by banning Greensleeves and VP Records from publishing his work. He was left out when VP or other reissue labels re-released old dub albums. Between 2009 and 2013 alone, eight CD boxes were compiled, each with four albums from the history of dub under the motto *Evolution Of Dub*, but Scientist was not taken into account. His "own initiative" was commented on at VP by an insider who wishes to remain anonymous thus "Scientist is on a crusade to try to destroy the evil VP Records and its vampires."

In spring 2016, the empire struck back, as VP Records responded to the Mirumir label's bootleg campaign and deleted the Scientist name. His face was neutralized on the covers and everything that pointed to him was crudely covered up to the point of defacement. If you compare the original and the rework, you will find more than ten surgical interventions in its visual design, a perfect template for the picture puzzles in the daily newspapers. In the new version, the controversial dub albums came as "official reissue" under the producer's name; Scientist was only mentioned as "engineer" on the back pages. The records were enriched with a "giant cover poster", remastered and highly tuned with a second LP containing the vocal versions from which the dubs were created. The records formerly known as "Scientist" were now called the following:

- **Junjo presents: Wins The World Cup**
- **Junjo presents: Big Showdown 1980**
- **Junjo presents: The Evil Curse Of The Vampires**
- **Junjo presents: Heavy Weight Dub Champion**
- **Linval presents: Space Invaders**
- **Linval presents: Encounters Pac-Man**

While VP Records prepared to attack, Hopeton Brown, now referred to himself as "The Scientist", was taking action on other fronts. He remastered the Linval Thompson releases *Dub Landing* and *Dub Landing Vol. 2* (which were then reissued by VP under "Linval presents…" in 2018) and *Scientist In Dub Volume 1* as well as the Jimmy Riley production *World At War* at 45 rpm, and released them with a bonus CD version via MIR, briefly after the first VP backlash. In 2023, he

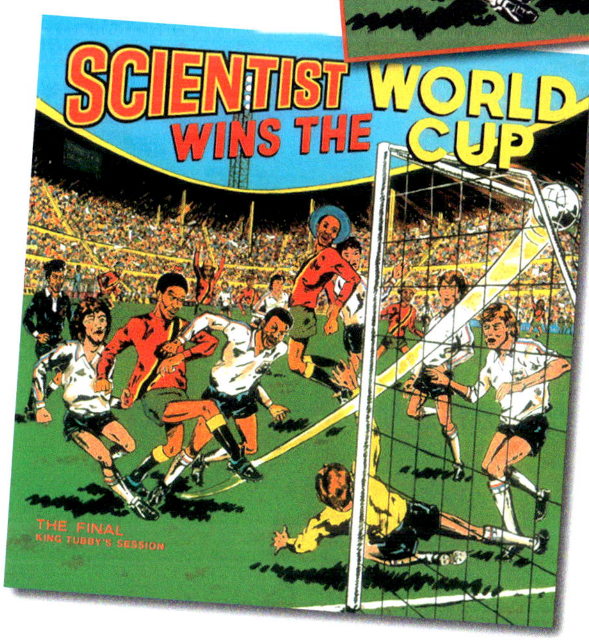

4 *The Force Of Music – Liberated Dub*, Ballistic UK 1979 Producer Roy Cousins.

reissued the *Dub War* LP, which was originally published in 1981 with excellent mixes under the obscure and inaccurate subtitle *Coxsone vs. Quaker City* by Bunny Lee in Canada, on the Berlin label Dubmusic Productions.

The final battle in this war over copyrights and hurt feelings is far from over.

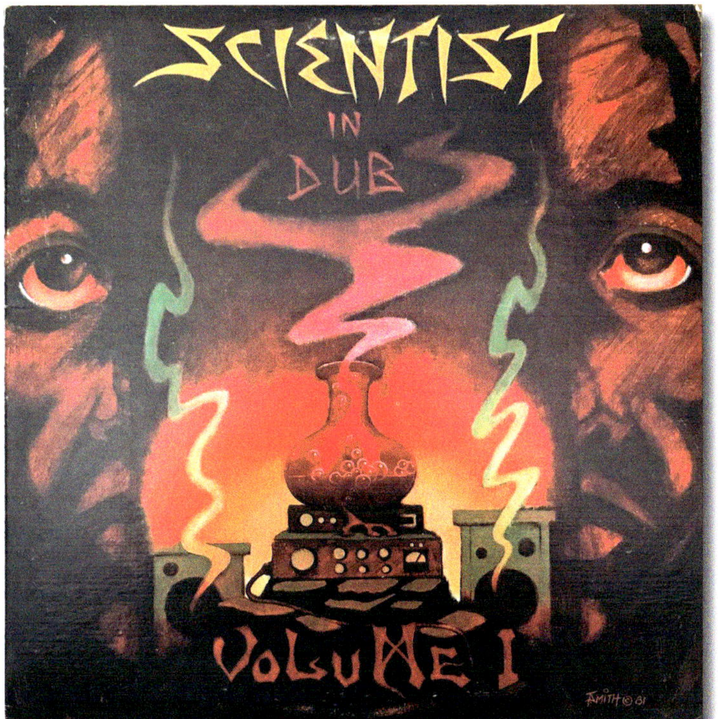
SCIENTIST
IN
DUB
VOLUME I

Dub War
coxsone vs quaker city

Scientist Dub Landing

LINVAL PRESENTS
DUB LANDING
VOL.1
SET BASS TO FULL AN' HOLD TIGHT... WE READY FI' DROP!

Painted record labels on the outside wall of Jammy's studio complex in KIngston, 2012.

King Jammy: Dub is Freestyle

"You must become a prince before you're king anyway."

(Prince Rogers Nelson[1])

The audience was held after sunset; I was about to meet King Jammy, and although everyone referred to him as "Jammy", he was also called "King", because his success and influence have made him one of the untouchables in the reggae business. The King, it was said, had the ability to recognize hits before they were written. Without him, roots artists like Black Uhuru might have never been discovered; without him, dancehall reggae of today would be unimaginable; without him, dub would have missed out on formative impulses.

We had an appointment in the heart of Waterhouse. The journey there was a trip into the unknown, especially at night. To slalom around the potholes at night seemed even riskier than during the day; the noise of the pulsating life here was louder, the scenery eerier. In the middle was a square, large, and brightly lit like a football field, flooded with light. An unexpectedly quiet oasis in the middle of Kingston's hustle and bustle. Lloyd James, the King, resides here. Two big white luxury jeeps with tinted windows were parked on the street in front of a concrete building complex. Its walls were decorated (and still are) with painted record labels as signs of success. The first floor presented an image common in Jamaica of half-finished walls, skeletons of buildings waiting for completion. Shops and bars were supposed to be built there, but then the laconic explanation was that the plans had changed. Jammy had the aura of a grandfather, a soignée elderly gentleman sitting outside the door with his wife and grandson. The dazzling light, the slow quiet amidst the hectic noise, and the unmistakable but discreetly staged power, all of this gave the square the touch of royal eminence in yard style.

"Life is hard in Waterhouse." In 2010, the Jamaica Gleaner summarized the decades-long history of blood feuds and gang terror, writing of a "culture of violence".[2] In this neighborhood, drive-by shootings were commonplace. In the mid-1970s, the main players, Spanglers and Shower Posses, the Buckers Gang, and the Yap Sam Gang (named after the JLP candidate Ferdinand Yap), had divided the Kingston 11/Waterhouse area between themselves into invisible demarcation lines. In the wrong place, expressions of sympathy for a certain party could mean death, and childhood friends could suddenly become enemies. Even after the declaration of a state of emergency, political gangsters and drug dealers could not be stopped from brutally criminalizing the district, and turning it into a battleground during the 1976 and '80 elections. There is a strongly held belief here that Jammy's sound, his studio, and productions had helped to pacify Waterhouse.

Lloyd James was born October 26, 1947 in Montego Bay, and came to Kingston ten years later when his family moved. His father was a construction worker and his mother a seamstress. He owed his nickname "Jammy" to Trevor, his elder brother. The James family settled at 92 Dromilly Avenue, just a stone's throw from 18, where young Osbourne "Tubby" Ruddock repaired electrical equipment, constructed amplifiers, and would later set up his own studio. The ten-year-old Jammy became friends with Stagga, Ruddock's brother, and used to hang out around the yard of number 18, watching with fascination how amplifiers were built. The boy's curiosity soon began to revolve around music, records, and sound engineering. He loved strolling around Federal studio two miles away, sifting through the reject pressings and discarded records dumped in the yard, and maybe even catching a glimpse of the musicians in the studio. The route to school took Jammy and Stagga past a garbage dump, where the repair shops from downtown disposed of their electronic waste. Here the two boys dug out still functional components, and tried their hand at building radios. "That was our main action as kids" Jammy remembered[3], still recalling how in 1963 they heard about the assassination of John F. Kennedy on a home-made shortwave receiver, even before the news was reported on the Jamaican radio stations. After leaving school, Jammy began an apprenticeship at "Chin's Radio Service" at 48 Church Street, more than four miles away, an 80-minute walk twice a day. Pat Kelly also worked in the shop where mento records used to be produced.

In 1962 Jammy soldered his first amplifier; it had just 20 watts. Somehow, he got hold of two speakers, borrowed a record player, and had

1 "My Name Is Prince" 1992.
2 Waterhouse: *Terrorised By Gangsters!*, Gary Spaulding in: *The Gleaner* April 25, 2010.
3 Jammy's In His Own Words 2006 in: *King At The Controls*, in: *King Jammy's Roots Reality And Sleng Teng* VP Records/17 North Parade DVD 2014.

someone explain how to generate electricity from batteries. Jammy was 15 and owned his first modest indoor sound system which he used at house parties and weddings, playing American music, rhythm and blues, Otis Redding, Louie Jordan, Chuck Berry, Dionne Warwick... A friend named Franklyn took care of the wiring. Another youth from Jammy's neighborhood and still just a kid wanted to be the disc jockey and juggle the records, but to reach the tone arm he had to climb on two beer crates! His name was Devon Gardener, called "Toops", born in 1953, who would remain Jammy's selector for the rest of his life.

Since he felt like he wasn't getting anywhere, Jammy didn't stay long at Chin's Radio Service. He preferred to spend his time with the six-year-older Tubby and his technician Barry Williams. Because of his powerful amplifiers and the live gimmicks with reverb and echo, Tubby was considered the "King of the Dancehall" at this point but didn't yet have his own studio. With the knowledge he gained from Tubby, Jammy expanded his sound, and was no longer just playing at indoor parties. He was well on his way to establishing himself in the Waterhouse sound system scene when his girlfriend left for Toronto. That this was his future wife Iris is a legend that spread widely through copy and paste gossip. No, said Jammy, it was a different woman, without going into detail. In November 1970 he followed, intending just to visit her. The visit turned into five years, even though the relationship had soon ended. He supported himself as a radio and television technician, worked part-time at a swimming pool equipment company, and took an electronics course at "George Brown Technical College". He helped Jerry Brown, who had emmigrated from Jamaica, set up the Summer Sound studio, using it for his first self-made production[4] and made demo recordings with Jamaican artists visiting the country. He seriously tried to settle in Canada and even had his amplifiers sent to him to build a sound there too.

Jammy and Tubby stayed in touch, so Jammy heard about Tubby's plans to set up a dub cutting studio in his mother's house, and got him a vocals microphone in Toronto. He learned that Tubby was expanding the studio to four tracks, and knew that Philip Smart was working as his assistant. At the end of 1975, unexpected visitors in the shape of Bunny Lee and Robbie Shakespeare arrived from back home; it was not beyond the bounds of possibility that the initiative had originated from King Tubby. In Toronto, they reported that Smart was about to immigrate to New York, and tried to sell Jammy the idea of taking over the vacant position, with Bunny Lee clinching the argument. Lloyd James moved back to Kingston, and in January 1976[5], took up his position as Tubby's right-hand man, whereupon an enthusiastic Bunny Lee spread the word across the island. "New engineer round a Tubby's named Jammy. Him wicked!"[6]

From day one, Jammy was involved in the dub business. At Tubby's no playbacks were produced, the space didn't allow that. Vocals were recorded there, and, above all, mixing was done. There was a dub version for every mix, which was standard by then, and dubplates were cut. Studio work at King Tubby meant assembly line work, 200 dubs per week were not uncommon. Especially before weekends, producers and sound men frequented the studio. Without a break, mixing was done, almost always as a one take. "Time" said Roger Lewis of the Fat Man Riddim Section "is the essence. You had no time to sit on a whole day business."

4 "Single Girl" by Nana McLean. The song only became successful when he later recorded it again in Kingston.

5 This is how Dave Hendley dated it in *The Crowning Of Prince Jammy*, Pressure Sounds 1999. According to "King Jammy's – The Godfather" in the German print magazine *RIDDIM* 03/2017, Jammy wasn't back in Jamaica until the end of 1976. What speaks for Hendley is that Jammy had already produced "Born Free" by Michael Rose in the spring of '76. Jammy spoke to me about "'round 1976".

6 Booklet *Jammy's From The Roots 1977–1985*, Greensleeves Records 2010.

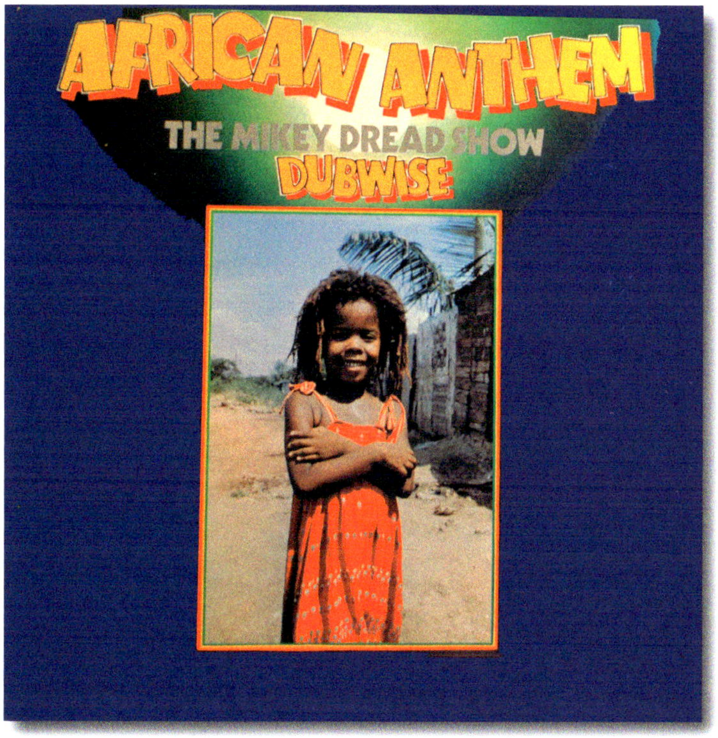

Tapes were put on and started, and with the first audible signal the mix or dub began. No repeat, no second try. All of this was only possible because with four audio tracks the effort was manageable, and once the settings on the console or effects devices were found, they were hardly changed. As British photographer and journalist Dave Hendley (1952–2016), who often witnessed hour-long sessions during this period, has said "I've never seen anything mixed with more than one take at Tubby's."[7]

Hendley is considered a reliable chronicler of events during the analogue years at 18 Dromilly Avenue. He was a close friend of Jammy, and briefly ran the Cruise Records label in the UK, where the Mikey Dread LP *African Anthem Dubwise*[8], mixed by Jammy, was first released, as well as Sufferer's Heights, on which seven 12-inch maxi singles from Tubby's studio were released in 1979, five of which Jammy had mixed and dubbed. After Hendley's death, Jammy dedicated a requiem to him entitled "Dub For Dave Hendley" on his 2017 *Waterhouse Dub*[9] album.

Jammy often worked half the night. His initial main customer was the man who had brought him there. "The first dubs I mixed is just Bunny Lee"[10] as he recalled, and went on to tell how he had been accepted into the royal family of reggae after Philip Smart's departure. "All the names that were given to people who worked at King Tubby's were given by Bunny Lee. He was the person who used to say: Tubbys is the king, but you are the prince now, because you are under him, you're working for him."[11]

In Jammy's hands, the MCI console, the studio's little miracle weapon, sounded different than it did under Tubby's direction. This was also because the recording quality of the Kingston studios, which brought their tapes here for mixing, had significantly improved. In addition,

7 Quoted from Michael E. Veal ibid p. 117.
8 *The Mikey Dread Show – African Anthem Dubwise* UK 1979.
9 Greensleeves/VP Records 2017.
10 *Jammy's From The Roots 1977–1985*, Greensleeves Records 2010.
11 *Soundtrack Of King Jammy*, WDR Funkhaus Europa 2015.

Jammy, like Channel One, benefited from the fact that reggae itself had changed. The time of the flying cymbals was over, the reggae beat had become rockier. "When we went on tour" Sly Dunbar explained the change "we found out that the one drop groove didn't have that energy. So, we figured out how the rock'n'roll would play. We wanted that same energy in reggae music."[12] The harder, slowed down beat changed dub. Jammy's mixes were groovier than the jazz-influenced improvisations on the mixing board by King Tubby. He placed the bass more prominently in the foreground, and created echoes with repetitions that seemed to be endless. His reverb came from the same AKG Echo Chamber that Tubby was now using, but erupted from uncharted depths where the snare sank while occasional offbeat licks crashed to the surface. Jammy's mixes didn't have the dark theatrics of Tubby's dubs, they were "more controlled and with more attention to detail"[13]. His use of the high pass filter was more reserved, but he also played with the test tone of the desk. He dubbed less virtuosically than King Tubby, but instead staged, with increasing confidence, large, orchestrated scales of effects through which endless echoes wound their way.

Even before Jammy had created his own publishing platform in 1977 with the instrumental single "Zambia" by Yabby You, he had already mixed his first dub long player for producer Everton DaSilva, and his Queens-based Hungry Town label. This was *In The Light In Dub*, the counterpart of a Horace Andy album, lavishly recorded by Sylvan Morris at Harry J and in New York's A & R studios. Jammy's mix took away the broad fluidity of the original, instead adding a rumbling world of reverb between kick and snare, and only allowed the rock guitar of the vocal versions to flash in little dabs. Vocal and dub LP were released both in Kingston and New York in small numbers, but sadly did not attract the attention they deserved. Also, because DaSilva passed away in New York in 1979, this LP only got to be released internationally in 1995 on the British Blood & Fire label.

12 *The Anthology Of Reggae Drumming*, documentary by Alex Domhoever, 2016.
13 Jeremy Collingwood in the liner notes of the re-release of *Prince Jammy Presents Strictly Dub*, Pressure Sounds 2010.

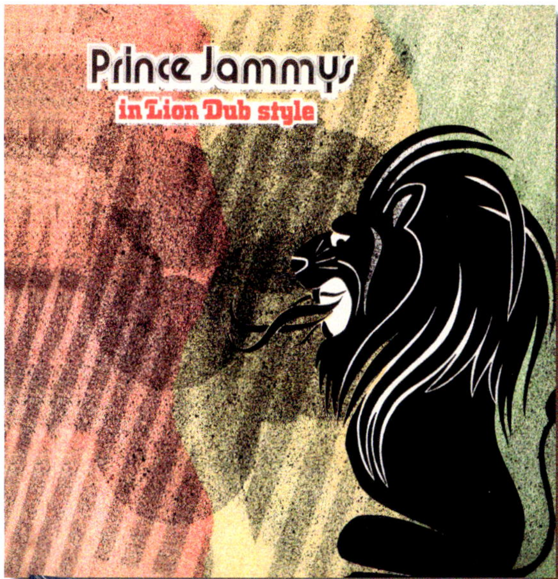

Jammy also mixed his second dub LP for Tappa Zukie in 1977. He gave him tapes of his productions from the Channel One studio, and initially released the dubs created from them without any further information as a white label with the imprint *Dub Master Musically Intemidaters*, before he officially released them on his Stars label as *Escape From Hell* with a skull on the cover.

In addition to these commissioned works and the day-to-day business at Tubby's, Jammy began to position himself more as a producer. In the spring of 1976, he had already recorded the title "Born Free" with the Waterhouse singer Michael Rose for the sound system operator Fatman, who had emigrated to London. When Rose knocked again, this time as part of a trio with Duckie Simpson and Errol Nelson, Jammy jumped at the chance. He became their patron, producer, and mastermind. The outgoing, committed attitude of the three together, calling themselves "Black Uhuru" or black freedom, fitted in perfectly with his self-perception as an engineer. His (dub) mixes thundered infernally from the erected sound system speaker walls tall as houses. The political climate in Jamaica was brutal, reggae marched against it and Prince Jammy was providing the soundtrack.

Love Crisis, the first Black Uhuru album, was ready in 1977. Shortly after, Jammy presented the dub LP *Jammies In Lion Dub Style*, which was essentially based on the Black Uhuru debut, on his own Jammy's (option ally also Jammy$) Records label. In the UK, where mixing boards experienced a sales promoting cult status[14] since "King Tubby Meets Rockers Uptown", the dubs appeared in a blue-tinted cover[15] that showed Jammy recording the LP at the console of Harry J's studio, even though he had mixed it at Tubby's. Four years later, Jammy revisited *Love Crisis*, and released the album a second time on Greensleeves, enhanced with overdubs, under the programmatic title *Black Sounds Of Freedom*. As chance would have it, the release coincided with a live concert on German television, which made the band, also now including Sly & Robbie, known across Europe and beyond. The broadcast of a "Rockpalast Night" from Essen on October 17, 1981, became the starting point of a

14 Winston Edwards even put the lover's rock maxis of his Studio 16 label in red sleeves with a picture of a white mixing board.

15 On Live And Love, including the addition *"The Agrovators"*.

PRINCE
JAMMY
PRESENTS
DUB
KAMIKAZE

Scientist and Jammy Strike Back!
ROOTS RADICS BAND
Produced by Linval Thompson
TROJAN

Close Encounters
of the
Third
World
Creation Rebel

20TH. CENTURY
DEB-WISE

INNER CIRCLE
KILLER DUB
when this music
you will feel no
PAIN
KILLER DUB
INNER CIRCLE
INNER CIRCLE
INNER CIRCLE

PRINCE JAMMY DESTROYS
THE INVADERS...

The REGGAE FILE
HARDER
NA RASS
THE RASS-ES BAND
A JAMMY'S MIX

ROCKERS ALL STARS
Chanting Dub
With the help of the Father

PRINCE
JAMMY
DUB
UHURU
DUB
PRINCE JAMMY PRESENTS 'UHURU IN DUB'
WITH SLY AND ROBBIE

global career for Black Uhuru. And what about King Jammy? He stayed at his job at King Tubby and mixed the counterpart to *Black Sounds Of Freedom* entitled *Uhuru In Dub* – freedom in dub. Only four years passed between the two Black Uhuru dub mixes, a period in which the number of dub albums mixed by Jammy increased more than tenfold.

- **In The Light In Dub** (Hungry Town JA 1977)
- **Escape From Hell** (Stars JA 1977)
- **Jammy's In Lion Dub Style** (Jammy's Records JA + Live And Love UK 1978)
- **Rockers All Stars – Chanting Dub With The Help Of The Father** (Rockers 1978)
- **The Agrovators – Kaya Dub** (Third World UK 1978)
- **Inner Circle – Killer Dub** (Top Ranking USA 1978)
- **Gregory Isaacs – Slum In Dub** (Cash & Carry JA + Burning Sounds UK 1978)
- **DEB Music Players – 20th Century DEB-Wise** (DEB UK 1978)
- **Creation Rebel – Close Encounters Of The Third World** (Hit Run UK 1978)
- **Kamikazi Dub** (Trojan UK 1979)
- **The Revolutionaires – Goldmine Dub** (Greensleeves UK 1979)
- **Prince Jammy v King Tubbys – His Majestys Dub** (Sky Juice JA 197X)
- **Africa Must Be Free By 1983 Dub** (Rockers JA 1979 + Greensleeves UK 1986)
- **Crucial Bunny versus Prince Jammy – Fatman Dub Contest** (Star UK 1979)
- **Prince Far I In Dub – Cry Tuff Dub Encounter Part 2** (Virgin 1979)
- **The Rass-Es Band – Harder Na Rass** (Warrior Records UK 1979 + Ballistic Records UK 1980)[16]

16 Counterpart of *The Rasses* (= Prince Lincoln Thompson) – *Experience* Ballistic Records UK 1979

- **Strictly Dub** (Jammy Records USA 1980)
- **First, Second & Third Generation Of Dub** mit King Tubby & Scientist (KG Imperial UK 1981)
- **Train To Zion Dub** (Tuff Gong 1981)
- **King Tubby's and The Agrovators – Dubbing In The Backyard** (Black Music UK 1982)
- **Prince Jammy Destroys The Invaders** (Greensleeves UK 1982)[17]
- **Scientist and Prince Jammie – Dub Landing Vol. 2** (Starlight UK 1982)
- **Scientist and Jammy Strike Back!** (Trojan UK 1982)
- **Uhuru In Dub** (CSA UK 1982)

Let's rewind back to 1977, when the Black Uhuru debut was ready for release: Jammy travelled to London for the first time. Ken "Fatman" Gordon paid for the ticket, Bunny Lee took him along and showed him around. He introduced him to Ephraim Barrett aka Count Shelly, who had taken over Sid Bucknor's Third World label two years earlier, which Bunny Lee frequently used to release his albums. A year later Shelly posed on the cover of *Agrovators – Kaya Dub* mixed by Jammy and produced by Bunny Lee. At their meeting, Jammy and Shelly agreed to license the *Love Crisis* album under the "Black Sounds Uhro" band name. Jammy collected £1,200. He invested part of the money in a small mixing console, a Ferrograph 2-track tape recorder[18] and some microphones. The equipment became the basis of his own studio, set up in the back room of the house that the mother of his new girlfriend Iris, his later wife, owned on St. Lucia Road. The equipment was still too limited for producing or mixing, but was enough to copy on music cassettes exclusive voicings of his productions from the studios at Harry J, Joe Gibbs, Channel One or King Tubby. The main customers for 25 Jamaican dollars each were the island's minibus drivers, who played music non-stop and thus brought Jammy's name onto the streets.

Jammy's main place of work remained the mixing desk at King Tubby, where the albums were created that increased his reputation in the UK. When he traveled to London for the second time in 1979, this time mainly to negotiate with Greensleeves about his productions, he was surprised to find that he was celebrated as a dub engineer. He owed his reputation to Bunny Lee, who immediately had dubs mixed of all the songs he had produced to put them on the B-sides of singles or to compile albums with them. On top of that, he benefited from the boom of maxi singles, with which labels like Attack and Sufferer's Heights used to publish their dub mixes. In 1980, Ballistic even put three to four dubs of Prince Jammy on three 12-inch B-sides, each with a track produced in the UK on the A-side. The releases, entitled "Jamdown Players" had nothing to do with the A-side, and put together would have made a complete album.[19] In Jamaica you didn't have a big dub market" Jammy described in retrospect, "like in Europe we used to have a lot of fans of dub music. So, we used to mix these music particular for those markets."[20]

Although Jammy enjoyed a reputation as an excellent dub engineer, dub, beyond dubplates, remained a fringe business for export to Europe. At home, he focused on productions with singers and deejays primarily from Waterhouse, and used the licensing advance from Greensleeves to expand his studio, in which he increasingly spent more time than at Tubby's. The latter wasn't very enthusiastic, but did have Scientist to fill the gap. In 1982, Jammy bought a 4-track tape recorder, decided to start his own business, and stopped working at Tubby's studio.

At the same time, he had been pursuing an ambitious, long term project that perfectly complemented his career as a producer: Jammy put together the most massive sound system Jamaica had ever seen. According to Bunny Lee, Jammy had always built better amplifiers than King Tubby. Now he bought bass amps with 5,000 watts, gigantic low-frequency scoops from which meter-long sound waves emerged, and tinkered with equalizers and crossovers with the same meticulousness he applied to fine-tune his productions in the studio. "You can't tell the king to stop turning knobs" echoed with reverence. "When Jammys come a dance, Jammy touch every button pon de sound. Even after six hours

17 An album unclear whether the mix was actually Jammy's. The LP was released one year after *Scientist meets the Space Invaders*, the most successful LP from Greensleeves catalog at the time under the name "Scientist". *Prince Jammy Destroys The Space Invaders* was obviously an attempt to repeat the success, only this time under a different name. As with the Scientist albums, sound effects and vocal overdubs were mixed additionally in London. Scientist claimed that the mixes were his, e.g. here: https://www.youtube.com/watch?v=NvPjXCULiQQ (in the comments). Greensleeves' approach to his dub albums suggests he might be right.

18 Modell Logic 7, came onto the market in 1974 and cost between £295 und £350.

19 Movement – "Money In My Pocket", Wolete Miriam – "Warrior", Third-I-Band – "Go Find Yourself Another Fool".

20 *Soundtrack Of King Jammy*, WDR Funkhaus Europa 2015.

he's still turning knobs. Him a turn up the tweeter, him a turn the midth, tune the bass. Same t'ing inna de studio."[21]

On February 23, 1985, the time had come. After a few test runs, Jammy set up his highly tuned speaker wall on Waltham Park Road, ready for a clash against Black Scorpio. In the end it wasn't the 45,000 watts of his sound system that decided the musical competition, but Wayne Smith's "Under Mi Sleng Teng". This was a riddim secretly produced by Jammy with a Casio keyboard, played publicly for the first time that night, and which changed the world.

The reggae world at least, in which nothing was as it had been before. Needless to say, this song and its versions decided the outcome of the clash. From that point on, Prince Jammy was the King, even though he wasn't officially called that until after King Tubby's assassination. He already had his territory firmly under control. He converted reggae into digital currency and ruled the island with "King Jammy's Super Power", the "heaviest sound in Jamaica – ever!"[22]

What no one yet knew was that when Jammy beamed reggae into a new era, a radical transformation befell dub. Not only the riddim and dancehall, but also dub was no longer what it used to be. While it was retained as playback for dubplates or sound systems, the independent experience of dub was lost in the quicksand of digital sounds. There were only a few attempts to carry dub into the future. Albums like Tubby's *Two Big Bull In A One Pen Dubwise*[23] or *Soundclash Dubplate Style Part 1 + 2*[24], like Jammy's *Computerised Dub*[25], demonstrated the limited expression of the new equipment. The dub community refused to follow digidub. It turned to new fans and other sources, Jamaica was no longer in demand and dub operations ceased.

It is absurd to realise that Greensleeves, with their six Scientist albums, first opened the door to the world of Jamaican dub, only to close it again in 1986 with *Prince Jammy's – Computerised Dub. Computerised Dub* became the tombstone marking the end of Jamaican dub for decades.

It would be hard to deny that, from a historical perspective, February 23, 1985 was the end of Jamaican dub music. Of course, the King saw it differently. It remains a cruel irony of history that Jammy, of all people, as a highly respected dub engineer, also became the genre's executioner. Early on, Jammy had made it clear that the role of engineer alone would not be enough for him. He had always wanted to produce. Just as Jammy, against the advice of his friend Tubby, had embraced Black Uhuru's militant style, he had also been the first to recognize the potential of digital instruments. The "Sleng Teng" coup shows that he had reached his goal. From that point on, the King determined the runnings in the dancehall. He knew what the people wanted to hear, and gave it to them. Jamaica was at his feet and voted him "Producer of the Year" six times in a row. Jammy enhanced his business, and in 1987 acquired a Tascam 8-track tape machine and a Studiomaster console. He started to build a second studio in the same building. After several stages of expansion, this eventually resulted in a 48-channel DDA mixing desk and a hard drive for storage. He was so busy with sound system and productions,

21 DVD *King Jammy's Roots Reality And Sleng Teng*, VP Records/17 North Parade 2014

22 "King Jammy's The Godfather" in the German print magazine *RIDDIM* 03/2017

23 Firehouse 1986

24 Both Firehouse 1988, 2014 released as DoLP on the Taurus sublabel

25 Greensleeves 1986

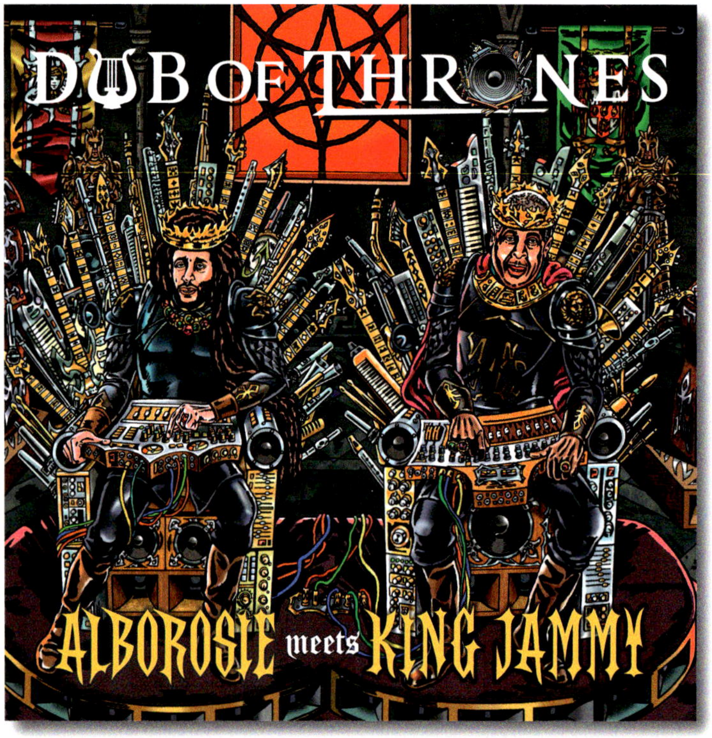

that he didn't even notice that his career as a dub engineer had come to a pause.

Only around the turn of the millennium did he return to the dub arena. A few albums with material from his back catalogue were re-released, he dubbed an album by the Japanese band Dry & Heavy[26] and collaborated with the Italian Alborosie for *Dub Of Thrones*[27]. For his 70th birthday, his ever-loyal record company let him dig through the archives to blast old recordings by artists like Dennis Brown and Junior Reid through reverb and echo generators for a new LP with the raw character of dub, just like in the good old days. Perhaps the expectations of the gift were too high, the 2017 *Waterhouse Dub*[28] lacked magic. The thrill was gone, also because the analogue charm of the King's new dubs was missing.

Jammy started digitizing his own back catalog early on, which inevitably changed his dub sound. Now he dubbed from digital sources using digital equipment. He no longer sent the tunes through breathtaking echo loops, but instead designed them with clear bass tones as grooving instrumentals with fades in and out. The reverb rumbled in dull basements and was often cut off by a gate, over which horn sections sprinkled sharp brass. The new sound design enabled even digital riddims to be organically integrated. They were no longer disruptive factors between the analogue playbacks.

In 2022, *Destroys The Virus With Dub*[29] proved this. Jammy was 74 years old, and his recent dubs had been staged effortlessly and age-wise. All mixes were based on a distinct attitude (in the titles) and the hook lines of the successful producer's well-known hit tunes[30]. But the tickle didn't really want to set in here, either.

Since Jammy had constantly upgraded his studios to digital technology, new opportunities arose. He could now stage dub as a show. "All their favourite music, like Dennis Brown, Frankie Paul, Half Pint, this an' that, people never see a live dub mix like this before" was how he described what was happening. He had his sons John John and Jam 2 put to eight tracks bounced songs from a hard drive onto an analogue mixing console, and practiced in public, something which usually took place behind closed doors in the studio. It didn't look very spectacular, but led to storms of enthusiasm. Several times he competed in dub clashes in Europe against the Brit Mad Professor, a master of live dubbing, who, because Jammy was able to draw from an unbeatable pool of his own productions, was hopelessly inferior. A solo performance at the French Garance Festival in the summer of 2013 was the stuff of legend. There was an area on the site for a group of visitors who were not interested in concerts. Instead, they used their marked area to bathe in brutally loud bass waves and echo showers from midday until late at night, creating a surreal scenery that could not be compared to Jamaican sound systems. Hardly anybody looked to the small stage where the selectors were operating. These controlled a busy crowd of people who, moving like a swarm of bees, stared into the loudspeaker walls set up around the square as if the dub queen lived in there. Nobody reacted to the announcement that King Jammy would now be dubbing live. However, as soon as he began, with dubplates from Black Uhuru and three then-unknown combinations of the old *Love Crisis* LP with Chronixx, Gentleman

26 *King Jammy meets Dry & Heavy – In The Jaws Of The Tiger*, Beat Records 2000.
27 *Alborosie meets King Jammy – Dub Of Thrones*, Greensleeves/VP 2015.
28 Greensleeves/VP.
29 Greensleeves/VP.
30 By Barry Brown, Sugar Minott, Patrick Andy, Hugh Mundell, Black Uhuru, Junior Delgado, Frankie Paul, Gregory Isaacs etc.

and Alborosie[31], the dub warriors all collapsed. Orgiastic screams rose to a hurricane that drowned out the music. Three tracks, skillfully placed, sent 2,500 people into ecstasy. Even as a senior citizen, the King still knew how to govern his people.

Even though you've transferred all your recordings to digital storage media, you're still dubbing on an analogue console.

King Jammy: I don't edit dub. I just dweet (do it) freestyle. That's not the real dub if you gonna edit, [it's] completely different.

Does improvisation influence the result?

Of course. As the music plays you create. Whatever comes to you, you just do it. Freestyle. It's like painting a picture. When I'm mixing a dub, I'm focused, well concentrated. Nobody can speak to me at that moment. I'm just into it with my whole body. My brain is feeling the dub, that's the technique.

Do you have a plan, or do you let things flow?

I know what I want to bring in at a time. But sometimes when you waan bring in the voice, something [inside you] says: No, bring in the horns. You just sit and create something different to the music.

Does ganja play a role in this?

Noooo, no! I wouldn't link ganja to dub music.

There are people who claim that.

Probably is the mood that they got from the dub music, the vibe you know. I don't smoke.

Others say that there used to be straight dub dances in the Kingston ghettos, where no vocal tracks were being played.[32]

Sometimes [they play dub] when they just were stringing up the sound. Not like when the dance was in full session, you know. They used to play dub music after they play the vocals.

31 The tracks only appeared three years later on the album *King Jammy presents New Sounds Of Freedom*, VP Records 2016

32 E.g. in the liner notes of *The Ring Craft Posse – St. Catherine in Dub 1972–1984*, Moll Selekta Germany 2004: "It was not uncommon for entire Dub dances to take place in Kingston's ghettos, whole evenings passing by without any singing."

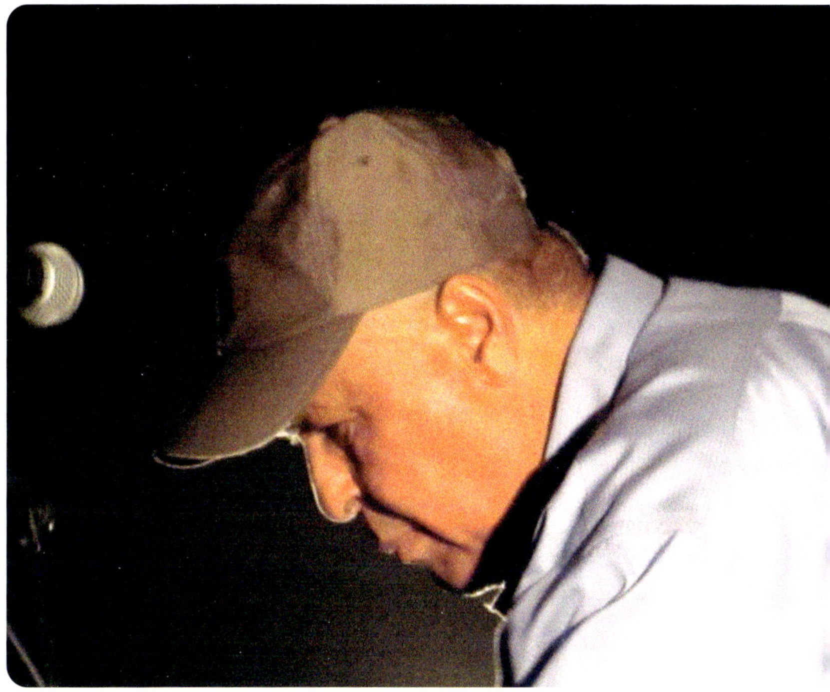

King Jammy dubbing live at Garance Festival, France 2013.

Dub alone hardly interested anyone in Jamaica.

Yeah, very likkle people would support dub music in Jamaica. When I mix a dub album they didn't sell in Jamaica. It was mostly for England.

For a white audience.

Yes, for a white audience. Because the distributor was Greensleeves, they distribute across Europe. Dub music is very popular in Europe.

... and a lucrative additional income. No costs because the recordings and the musicians were paid. And done quickly.

Yes, very quick. Like I could mix two dub LPs in four hours, five hours. Because you didn't have anybody to tell you, mix it that way. It was just a creation from you. You just do it the way you feel. You don't have to go by any rules or regulation. You just freestyle.

And when something went wrong, it was an effect.

Haha, yes, it could be an effect. Every spoil is a style. Everybody's saying so. The first time I heard it was from Bunny Lee. Because I was mixing a dub album for him one night and something went wrong. Some audio signal wasn't coming in right. It make some squeak and I was about to stop. And him say: "No King, don't stop it, every spoil is a style."

Have you ever had the feeling that dub was destroying the music? Some engineers of the generation before you felt that when the sound boys came and wanted only drum & bass. They felt like the music was being chopped up so that in the end you only had parts of it.

No, because dub is a different form of music. A different style. You know, we have jazz, we have soul, we have hip hop, we have reggae and rocksteady. The world is big enough, we can appreciate every music. [Also] in a vocal track you have several different mixes. Probably the one that you chose as the best don't having percussion or another instrument that was in the other mix. It's not cutting off the music, it's just creating a different style. Music is music. Even if it's just one drum playing.

In the early days of bouncing, not much more was technically possible with two tracks than reducing it to drum & bass.

Well, now, the real dub music started on 4-track. You can play around with four tracks. It's a more versatile way of making [dub] when you have four or eight tracks. [With] four separate tracks [you have] one for the drum [and bass], one for the riddim, one for the vocal, one for the horns.

Only with four tracks could the elements be separated. Taking vocals out of the music, separating brass…

… the riddim track out, drum and bass out…

There is a video from British TV. You're recording Johnny Clarke's vocals for "None Shall Escape The Judgement"…

Oh, at King Tubby's studio… (Jammy remembered immediately) Deep Roots…

Exactly. "Deep Roots Music"[33]. After recording the vocal you can be seen mixing the dub and, in the studio, a big party developed, chalice smoke obscured the view, Bunny Lee started to dance…

It was a show. Everybody knew that they should do that action. It was no spontaneous thing that they feel the vibes of the dub music. The person who was fliming it (who filmed), he wanted it to be that way. It was set for that. They were told to do that. They were acting.

Tubby didn't even appear in this event. Did he no longer feel like doing daily studio work at that point?

No, he used to build amplifiers and wine transformers. I was there and I was as good as him. He had confidence in me, said I don't need to do that anymore because it was hard work. You had right through the day to sit there. Sometime you don't even get up to eat. Especially when you're cutting dub for sound system. Live, you know. Playing the tape [with the playback], the artist there singing, and you mix it and cutting the dub same time.

Tubby was six years older than you and trained you?

We were friends, we grew together. Everything I learned while I was there King Tubby taught me. [But] I tell you this: I was like I was born this way. I didn't got much training. All I did was looking what was going on. Tubby's saw that thing in me from I was a youth. That is why he allowed me to be resident engineer of his studio. Most thing that I know it was self-taught. I used to work as electronic technician, I love these things from birth coming right up, so it developed in me. Probably God made me that way. (laughs)

What also becomes clear in the Deep Roots video, the dub technology was easier to control with four tracks than later with an increasing number of channels and therefore had a more effective dynamic for dub mixes.

Yes! The energy on a smaller board is more tighter, together, for reggae music.

Were the digital riddims perhaps the reason why Jamaican dub was suddenly no longer in demand? Because the music became very minimalistic and didn't offer enough for dub? (Although I don't mention "Sleng Teng", I feel like I'm treading on thin ice with this question.)

33 "Deep Roots Music" a 1982 six-part series, each episode one hour, produced by Channel 4 for British television. Has been released as a bootleg several times.

So, what would you say about "Sleng Teng"? "Sleng Teng" was the first digital and it went big, aiight? I don't think that was the reason for dub going down. The reason was that people [were] more attracted to vocals. More R'n'B was coming into the market, hip hop was coming into the market, you know. Older people that used to buy dub music probably they were getting outta music and just cooling down. I always have dub albums mix and not release [even when] the world wasn't craving for dub. Every new song I have, every riddim, I mix a dub cut from it.

Because dub and reggae belong together. Other musical genres, that experiment with dub, only play with echoes. They don't dub.

True, true, true! (the King is smiling again).

King Jammy and the author, Kingston 2012.

The audience was over. When saying goodbye, Jammy reiterated the last point. "The heartbeat of reggae music is important for dub. I don't think dub would work with other music. Maybe with soul or R'n'B..."

Basskateers Sound System, Germany.

Lee Perry: Dubstrumentalist

> "Music is not notes, not chords, music is atmosphere, and what you bring to it is your own life."
>
> (Joe Zawinul[1])

The decline of dub caused by the impact of "Sleng Teng" did not harm Lee Perry, on the contrary, he just had to reinvent himself. Relying on old talent helped. The studio wizard took a radical turn in his career and became a self-promoter. A bizarre appearance almost 30 years after "Sleng Teng" in a venue in Jamaica's capital also testifies to this.

The Redbones Blues Café on Argyle Road in the heart of New Kingston was, until its closure in May 2018, an open-air club with a sophisticated menu frequented by tourists and uptown residents. People sat at the bar, had a drink, or dined on the inviting terrace. From there, the view descended upon a semicircular area, designed in the shape of a small amphitheater. Readings, rock, reggae, and jazz concerts took place on its stage.

On the evening of April 5th, 2012, Inna De Yard, a variable ensemble of honorable veterans, were performing, reviving their glorious past over Nyabinghi rhythms with an acoustic set. The "Roots & Culture Unplugged" idea, initiated in 2004 by Makasound, the French label, had since 2011 continued under Chapter Two Records, and the event enjoyed an international reputation thanks to numerous albums and tours. In addition to guitarist Earl "Chinna" Smith and keyboardist Robbie Lyn, the line-up that evening included, among others, the jazz singer Susan Couch, the Congos' vocalist Cedric Myton, Kiddus I, who became famous in "Rockers" the film, and the legendary Studio One Nestor, Bob Andy. The number of reggae celebrities in the auditorium corresponded to the large number on stage, with Mutabaruka, Oku Onuora, Style Scott, Lloyd Parks all present, to name just a few. The average age was quite high; people celebrated each other and the good old days.

Suddenly, a wave of unrest spread through the crowd. Lee Perry, it was rumored, was at the door. The audience jumped up and rushed to the entrance. The musicians on stage were dismayed. When they realized what was going on, they dropped their instruments and hurried after the others. All composure fell by the wayside when everyone realized it was indeed the man himself. Lee Scratch Perry, now a shrunken old man of 76, was leaning against the admission counter, completely red, from the roots of his hair to the hem of his trousers, shoes and cap all decorated with tiny mirrors. Not just a colourful character, no, a living voodoo doll. Motionless. Speechless. Petrified.

The spectators pulled out their cell phones and everyone started talking to him. Perry didn't bat an eyelid. Then, suddenly and without warning, he yelled "Uaaah!". Eyes and mouth were wide open, hands raised like claws. Those surrounding him backed away in fright. Perry laughed! He knew what effect he would have. Without a word, he crossed the crowd, parting it like Moses the Red Sea, and entered the arena. He had himself photographed, but remained silent. Eventually the excitement died down, the concert continued, and Perry strolled to the bar. He ordered white rum and marched to the stage where Bob Andy was singing. Perry drew a circle on the floor around him with the rum. Most people understood this gesture to be a protection from evil spirits. While Andy continued to sing untouched, Perry offered him his hand with an expression that said "I did it for you, my friend. You are safe now. Nothing will happen to you." The crowd roared in approval.

Cedric Myton could not be stopped. He grabbed the microphone and sang "Out of Africa comes the Congo Man", a classic from *Heart Of The Congos*, a Lee Perry production and legendary album with which Perry had steered his Black Ark studio towards "psychedelic Africa" in 1977. This was an ultimate gem, for which no superlative can be found. The most frequently chosen attribute is "Best Roots Album Of All Time" but that is entirely insufficient. Perry didn't bother asking. He took a microphone and shouted "I am the Congo Man!" which made it clear to everyone. A fifteen-minute session followed, which attracted even Mutabaruka to the microphone.

Afterwards the situation calmed down, although discussions continued for quite some time. The audience was divided. Some said Lee Perry was the greatest, others that he was crazy. Apart from the tourists, no one here really took him seriously. Jamaica's relationship with the man who had been a significant influence on the development of national icon

1 *Joe Zawinul by People Plus* Vinyl Factory 2018 https://thevinylfactory.com/features/vf-mix-154-joe-zawinul-by-people-plus/ (last accessed on March 14, 2022).

Bob Marley by producing *Soul Rebel* (1970) and *Soul Revolution* (1971) is ambivalent. Many worshipped him, precisely because of Bob Marley, while others laughed because they had little use for his self-portrayal as a shaman. His role as a sound magician was also not without controversy in Kingston. In addition to the high recognition of Perry's musical ideas, there were numerous experiences of technical deficiencies in his studio.

The British journalist David Katz compiled anything and everything worth knowing about Perry for the book *People Funny Boy. The Genius Of Lee "Scratch" Perry*[2]; in 2006, an extended edition[3] filled the last gaps in the story. Since there is nothing to add to the book biographically, this chapter is limited to the question of Lee Perry's significance in the dub arena. The feature section as well as Perry's worldwide fan base respond to the question with adoration, even though his role within Jamaican dub was special.

Lee Perry's creative work could be divided into three periods, the phases before, during and after the Black Ark. Phase one initially saw him as an assistant at Studio One, responsible for whatever Coxson asked him to do. Every day, he washed his employer's Buick before Coxson used it to pick up his foster son, Freddie McGregor, from school. In 1963 little Freddie had moved into Brentford Road as a seven-year-old. Perry took the studio's master tapes to WIRL, later Dynamic Sounds, for record production, where he became friends with engineer Linford Anderson. Perry also picked up the pressed singles and distributed them to the public. He organized auditions and worked at Sir Coxsone Downbeat, his boss' sound system. He acted as the studio's best boy and was allowed to use time off from recording to sing himself. Although Coxson didn't think much of his vocal abilities, he had Lee Perry record more than 30 tracks, which he sometimes released as singles, sometimes licensed to the UK, sometimes used exclusively for his sound system. Like the ska title "Chicken Scratch", a homage to a popular dance at the time, which gave Perry his nickname "Scratch". In 1966, "Doctor Dick" and "Pussy Galore" (with harmonies by the Wailers trio) became veritable hits, whose success was owed primarily to Perry's suggestive lyrics.

Especially in view of these two hits, Scratch felt that his work was not sufficiently appreciated by Coxson and was being inadequately rewarded. As 1966 ended and ska was replaced by rocksteady, it was time to go. Perry left Studio One in discord, but, due to the diverse tasks he had completed at Coxson, was well connected. He joined Prince Buster, worked for Bunny Lee, Joe Gibbs, and Winston Holness, aka Niney the Observer. He recorded on his own account, and started to produce himself. He repeatedly met Linford Anderson at the Dynamic studio, with whom he concocted the proto dub shenanigans described in the chapter "Overture of a New Genre". Anderson was the executing force[4]; any reports that Lee Perry was already at the mixing desk at that time are based on misinterpretations. In a studio, it was normal for other people present alongside the technician to carry out minor tasks on the mixing console. This should not be confused with creative processes. We only saw Perry as an engineer on the Black Ark's command bridge.

In May 1969, after a fire, the WIRL studio was reorganized into Dynamic Sounds studio. Part of the building complex at 13 Bell Road was destroyed, but the recording rooms survived the fire unscathed. Byron Lee changed the number to 15 because 13 was bad luck. He travelled to New York with Anderson to purchase new equipment. They acquired a 4-track tape recorder and the history-making MCI console with the legendary high pass filter,

2 Payback Press Edinburgh 2000.
3 Omnibus Press 2006.

4 According to reports from contemporary witnesses such as Bunny Lee or the British journalist and Fashion label founder Chris Lane, e.g. in the liner notes of the album *Byron Lee & The Dragonaires – Uptown Top Ranking* VP 2015.

both of which Tubby later bought. During this time, Perry recorded on Bell Road with The Bleechers, a vocal trio, including the song "Ease Up". When released in 1969, the single had a second vocal track on the back. It wasn't until a year later that the instrumental version "Squeeze Up Part 1", the playback of "Ease Up", was released in the UK under the Byron Lee & The Dragonaires name, with a dub called "Squeeze Up Part 2" on the B-side. At the same time, parts 1 and 2 were pressed in Jamaica on Tiger, the Dynamic house label, called "Shortwave" and "Superior" respectively. On these versions, the high pass filter could be heard for the first time. The extent to which Perry was involved in the mixes cannot be clarified. Bunny Lee was sure Anderson was playing with the filter. The quarter-note-long rhythmic mutes in the riddim of "Part 2" could point to Perry, as later they became typical of his Black Ark sound. Maybe they came from Anderson, and Perry was inspired by them.

A little later, in the same year, Byron Lee followed this up with a cover version of Sly & The Family Stone's "Don't Call Me Nigger, Whitey" on Tiger, including a dub that also used the high pass filter. Perry folklore often claimed that Scratch was actively involved in this production, especially in the mixes, but this was speculative. The main argument here is that, as long as Perry did not have his own studio, he appeared only as producer, and did not work anywhere on the desk, apart from minor contributions here and there.

Street Sign Cardiff Crescent, Kingston, 2023.

Perry's productions began to pay off. When Trojan set up his own sub-label in the UK, he expanded his radius and no longer recorded exclusively at Dynamic. In 1969, Gladdy's All Stars created a riddim at Studio One that was actually intended as a playback for a vocal track. Because all attempts to sing on it had failed, Perry licensed the instrumental recording to the UK, where it reached number 5 in the pop charts as "Return Of Django". Around the same time, Perry began producing at Randy's Studio 17, which had opened the year before, also without ever operating the console himself.[5] Between 1970 and '71, the Wailers' *Soul Rebel* and *Soul Revolution* LPs were created at Randy's. These productions in particular increased his reputation enormously, and put him in a financial position to realize a dream he had had for a long time, i.e., to build his own studio in which he could do as he pleased. In early 1973 he began converting the carport of his home on Cardiff Crescent in Washington Gardens, a quiet residential area in Kingston, into a studio. More precisely, he had it rebuilt. The singer and guitarist Bobby Aitken built it,

5 See statements by Clive Chin in the chapter "The Story of Java Java Java Java".

Cardiff Crescent, view from Perry's Studio.

and Leonard Dillon from the Ethiopians plastered the walls. Perry invested more than £12,000 in the construction, a relatively large sum, of which the smallest part went into technical equipment. For just £35 he bought a used Alice radio console as a mixing desk in London, with only one VU meter, not actually designed for recording. At the end of the year, without being properly equipped, he began producing with two tape recorders – a TEAC 3340 quarter-inch 4-track and a TEAC AX300 quarter-inch 2-track as a master machine. Since he initially lacked microphones for vocal recordings, among other things, he first recorded the vocals at King Tubby's studio, almost two miles away, who had since taken over the MCI console and a 4-track tape recorder from the Dynamic studio. Most of Perry's debut *Upsetters 14 Dub Blackboard Jungle* aka *Blackboard Jungle Dub* was created there on this equipment.

In 1973, the now 37-year-old Lee Scratch Rainford Hugh Perry was on the threshold of phase two of his career. Coxson's former confidant had become a successful producer, and he now developed into a style-defining sound magician.

It was when Jamaica, always addicted to new trends, had discovered its latest obsession, kung fu. Martial arts films dominated the movie theatres, and Carl Douglas' global hit "Kung Fu Fighting" was blasting out from every corner. The island was reeling in an "Oooh! Haaah!" frenzy. Lee Perry was one of the first to take advantage of this mania. He featured roots singer Linval Thompson on a single entitled "Kung Fu Man"[6] and began recording riddims with his rudimentary studio equipment. In 1975, in addition to the vocal collection *DIP Presents The Upsetter,* he released three instrumental albums on the British DIP label, each in an edition of 300 copies, two of which as white label LPs with the "Upsetters" stamp. Both LPs revealed their titles and track names only when they were repressed in the second half of the 90s. One was the jazzy *Musical Bones* LP by trombonist Vin Gordon, the other turned out to be *Return Of Wax,* a spartan, raw, almost gimmick and effect-free instrumental hodgepodge of titles like "Kung Fu Warrior", "Dragon Slayer" or "Samurai Swordsman".

Only the third LP *Kung Fu Meets The Dragon* under the artist name "The Mighty Upsetter" was released with a regular cover; from artwork to the musical content, it served the kung fu hype perfectly. Both *Return of Wax* and *Kung Fu Meets The Dragon* were largely based on specially recorded instrumental tracks, so-called "designer dubs", a term that goes back to Michael Veal, and hardly used in dub perception. Following Adrian Sherwood, Veal used it for riddims or playbacks that were recorded for dub processing, without intending to voice them.[7] Perry indicated

6 Clocktower, US 1975.
7 Veal ibid p. 228. See also chapter "Dub in the UK"

that his understanding of dub was different. He was less interested in dubby riddim workouts of well-known songs than in theatrical productions. With minimal echo effects, sound overdubs of kung fu screams, clattering and clanging chains, he flattered the kung fu fever that had reached ecstatic proportions in Jamaica, also by adding whispered slogans like "this is karate skank" (on "Black Belt"). What Perry was presenting wasn't really dub, but more instrumentals from a gray area between independent titles and dub pieces. In 2005, Trojan Records described it most precisely when it combined the three DIP LPs on DoCD as "Dubstrumentals".

The DIP label belonged to immigrant Dennis Harris, a friend of Edward Seaga, who came to London from Clarendon and developed into an in-demand businessman. In the southeast of the city, he opened one of the first black-run supermarkets in the Brockley district, selling canned food, yams, and plantains. He then moved into the music business, building a small studio on Upper Brockley Road. The drummer of the one-hit wonder band Los Bravos ("Black Is Black" 1966) built him an 8-track recording device, but only seven of them worked. Harris called his studio "Eve". Later, Dennis Bovell's first dub LPs were created there, which we delve into deeper in the "Dub in the UK" chapter.

Perry had first met Harris in 1975. Harris had just taken over the single "Hurt So Good" from Larry Lawrence, which Perry had produced with Susan Cadogan and given to Lawrence to release in the UK. With Perry's permission, Harris licensed the single to the British pop label Magnet, which took the song to number 4 in the UK charts in March. That same month, Magnet also took over the Perry-produced Junior Byles track "Curly Locks" from DIP. Allegedly, a quarter of a million singles were sold, but without achieving a chart placement. Perry did not receive any royalties for either single. Harris had been duped in the Magnet deal, and therefore felt responsible. To compensate, he bought studio equipment for Perry, including a Soundcraft console, shipped everything to Kingston and installed it in Perry's studio.

The new 16-channel device provided Perry with more professional mixing options than the old Alice board, and he immediately began experimenting with it. The first result was the *Revolution Dub* LP, released in

the UK by Cactus/Creole in November 1975, a work of extremes, with two different sides. One side turned the dub world upside down, frightened certain reggae fans and received reviews that fluctuated somewhere between irritation and celebration, and the other was in comparison trivial, thriving on Perry's bizarre self-dramatization. The LP featured "revolution" in its name, but the cover artwork led in the wrong direction. The silhouette of a soldier sporting dreadlocks, carrying a rifle with a fixed bayonet and a tank under palm trees indicated a militant component, but what was really revolutionary about this album was the mix, which broke all the rules for the standards of the time.

Perry gave the LP the character of a concept album right at the start by announcing "this is dub revolution, music to rock the nation". In the first track he used the same beat from a rhythm box that Bob Marley had used a year earlier on *Natty Dread* on the piece "So Jah Seh". Accompanied by bass and guitar, Perry drummed on his cheeks, played facial percussion, and sang "shalala", "dududu" and "nanana", sometimes loudly in the foreground, sometimes buried deep in the reverb. This was followed by infernal arrangements of Jimmy Riley's "Woman Gotta Have It", Bunny Clarke's "Move Out Of My Way" and Junior Byles' "The Long Way". Nothing about these mixes was dancehall compatible. They were audio plays, interspersed with recordings from a British TV sitcom, arranged with own vocal overdubs, filter variations and wild right/left excesses that unrestrainedly overstimulated the split-stereo principle, which had been created in the past due to technical limitations. This was a spectacular event on hi-fi stereo systems that unfortunately fizzled out in the mono-polarized dancehall.

On side two, the over-the-top magic disappeared. After "Bushweed Corntrash" by Bunny (Clarke, later Rugs) & Ricky (I Kong) at the end of side one, the revolution had passed its peak. Perry warbled a childlike "lalala" while the drums banged and blared around him, and the bass meandered along the distortion line. Now the mixes became ordinary and staid. Perry was only offering harmless playbacks with vocal overdubs, the meaning of which was not always clear, and even enriched them with vomiting and gagging noises! While the A-side was a mix of innovation and radical "ex-perry-ments", the B-side retreated into the banal.

When *Revolution Dub* was released, no one suspected that the LP marked a turning point in Perry's output. The sound of his studio was about to undergo a profound change. In late fall of 1975 in New York, Perry bought a Mu-Tron Phasor and a Roland Space Echo. He was the first to bring these effects devices to Jamaica, and in the long term, he remained the only one who actually used the Roland echo, which, is revered like a holy relic in dub today. In conjunction with the existing Grampian spring reverb, which according to the manufacturer was only semi-professional quality, Phasor and Space Echo became the crucial building blocks for an unmistakable sound world that was soon emerging from the Black Ark.

By the end of 1975, the new equipment had taken the studio to a significantly improved level, although it was still a long way from the technical standard available at Harry J or Channel One. Perry also had a drum booth installed, which changed his drum sound tremendously, the cymbals now sounding bulbous and long, while the bass drum became more clearly audible, with a buttery-soft attack. This gave a particular swinging boost to the stylistic device of "four-on-the-floor" beats, adopted from the disco music of the 70s, and accentuating every quarter note, the latter Perry liked to use for his arrangements.

Perry continued to work with the two tape machines he had owned from the start.[8] He wired them to the 16-channel mixer[9], to the phaser, the reverb and echo devices. He connected everything with everything, sometimes in unconventional ways. He knitted the connections so that he had constant access to the individual elements. At any time, he could mix (bounce) four tracks into two or one, then route them back and run them through the effects on both the send and return paths. It was also set up so that he could spontaneously mix in his own vocal effects or percussion using a microphone from the mixing desk. No one but him understood the wiring. Much of what happened from then on in the Black Ark was based on intentional coincidence.

The unconventional inter-connection of all devices led to unpredictable things during recordings, but even more so during mixing. Crosstalk from the edges of the individual tracks created ghost sounds, similar to ghost notes when playing an instrument. They were there, but were perceived only subliminally. In addition, bouncing and repeated copying back and forth between two tape recorders increased tape hiss, which in turn triggered independent impulses in the effects devices, and became an effect in itself. The magic of the Black Ark sound was partly self-generated. Inspired by what was happening in his studio, the magician spontaneously fired explosive shots into the sound structure by causing the reverb's spring to roll over by hitting the casing.

Only Perry himself could steer the Ark. He alone was able to direct the ghosts in the cables, meaning that hardly any other engineers worked in his sound laboratory. When the Gladiators recorded the single "Jah Vengence" with Yabby You in 1975, he asked in surprise "if he workin' obeah, cause no one supposed to come into Scratch's studio and get them sounds, except Scratch!".[10] Obeah, the Caribbean version of voodoo, is deeply rooted in Jamaican folk beliefs. Rituals such as sprinkling rum around to appease spirits, rubbing with white rum for protection among the Maroons, or pouring the first sip from a bottle for the ancestors can be observed everywhere, and are neither questioned nor commented on. Unsurprisingly, Lee Perry wasn't unaffected by this cult, either. Early on, there were clues, like the stories Clive Chin told about Randy's studio.

In the Black Ark, the mixing board became a voodoo altar. Objects piled up around the workplace which were typical of the spiritual connection to the afterlife, such as pictures of Marcus Garvey and Haile Selassie, pages from *Hustler* and *Penthouse*, paintings of slaves in chains, the Super Ape with a spliff, polaroids… a shrine, horseshoes, a vase, Star of David, rattles, ratchets, tambourine, triangle, cowbells… a fish, a white owl, cables, cassettes, singles, a book on human anatomy, the Pan-African tricolour… and symbols were everywhere. The reels of the tape, the effects devices, the percussion instruments, every free space on the wall, everything was covered with graffiti. Even the pictures and photos were painted with characters. "In the midst of this apparent chaos, every little sign is a message."[11]

The spiritual aura of the Black Ark took effect. The location in Washington Gardens became a hot spot for Orthodox Rasta artists, and members of the Bobo Shanti were continually hanging out there. "Mister Perry was a more rebel kind of person, he was more into the Rasta movement. Scratch was a man that would read his bible a lot in the studios, he would have little meetings" was how singer Earl 16 described the on-site situation. The studio developed into a revolutionary Rastafari cell because Perry, logged into the zeitgeist, gave the singers uncompromising space for spiritual visions and political agitation. In 1976, during the state of emergency imposed in the country due to electoral unrest, his yard was an enclave. The Bobos presented themselves as radical representatives of the Nyabinghi theocracy, with the stated goal of changing Jamaican society through music. They appointed Perry their "Minister of Music" because they saw him as a harbinger of Rastafarian rule.

From a secular perspective, the skipper of the Black Ark was heading towards the peak of phase two of his career. He entered a handshake deal with Chris Blackwell, and within a very short time, a series of epochal albums were released that changed the perception of dub, even though

8 A one-inch 8-track TASCAM later donated by Chris Blackwell was not used by Perry because he couldn't get it to work.

9 In his book *Bass Culture – When Reggae Was King* (German edition p. 289), Lloyd Bradley made the same mistake that also occurred in dub literature about Channel One when he equated the number of tracks on the tape recorder with the number of channels of the console and spoke of a 4-channel mixer. He also named a wrong echo device (Echoplex) and credited King Tubby with the Black Ark's technical design. Bradley's comments on Lee Perry tended to hit the mark but were full of errors.

10 *Yabby You – Dread Prophecy*, Shanachie 2015 booklet p. 6.

11 *Vodou. Kunst und Kultur aus Haiti (Vodou, Art and Culture from Haiti)* Berlin 2010 p. 94.

there wasn't a single dub album among them. Seven of them came via Island Records, as follows:

- **Jah Lion – Colombia Colly** Island 1976
- **Max Romeo & The Upsetters – War In A Babylon** Island 1976
- **The Upsetters – Super Ape** Island 1976
- **The Heptones – Party Time** Island 1977
- **Junior Murvin – Police And Thieves** Island 1977
- **George Faith – To Be A Lover** Black Swan/Island 1977
- **Various – Scratch On The Wire** Island 1979

At the same time, Perry released four LPs on other labels because they were rejected by Blackwell:

- **Prince Jazzbo – Natty Passing Thru'** Black Wax UK 1976 aka **Ital Corner** Clocktower US 1981
- **The Congos – Heart Of The Congos** (Version 1) Black Art JA 1977
- **The Congos – Heart Of The Congos** (Version 2, remixed & overdubbed) Congo Ashanti JA 1978, Jah Live France 1979, Go Feet UK 1981, VP Records US 1994, Blood & Fire UK 1996 (remastered plus bonus),
- **The Congos – Heart Of The Congos** (Version 1 & 2 anniversary edition plus bonus) VP Records US 2017
- **Lee Perry & The Upsetters – Roast Fish Collie Weed & Cornbread** Lion Of Judah JA 1978
- **The Upsetters – Return Of The Superape** Lion Of Judah JA 1978

Perry recorded relentlessly and mixed like a machine. In addition to the LPs mentioned, there were masses of singles and maxis released in Jamaica and especially in the UK with other artists, some of which later appeared on compilations such as *Heart Of The Ark Vol. 1 + 2*[12] or the

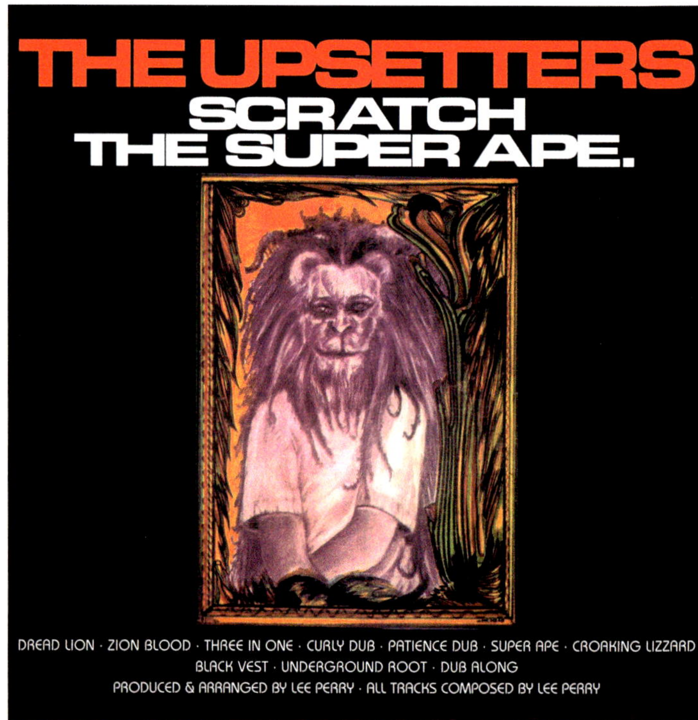

12 Seven Leaves, UK 1982 + 1983.
13 Much of this can be found on the vinyl only series *Disco Devil Vol. 1...* Studio 16 UK, started by Colin Young in 2018, with restored recordings from the Black Ark, some of them edited into extended mixes.

Trojan boxes *Open The Gate* (1989) und *Build The Ark* (1990).[13] At the same time, he produced records that only came to light years later:

- **Aura meets Lee "Scratch" Perry – Full Experience** Blue Moon Production, France 1988
- **Sekje Molenga & Kalo Kawongolo with Lee "Scratch" Perry – From The Heart Of The Congo** Jolie Zaire, Belgium 1991[14]
- **The Jolly Brothers – Conscious Man** Roots UK 1993
- **Lee "Scratch" Perry presents Candy McKenzie** Trojan/Upsetter UK 2011

Like a carver, in his studio Perry created one sound sculpture after another. Virtuously, the dubstrumentalist played the keyboard of his low-fi equipment. While dub-like versions were found on the B-sides of the singles, the tunes on maxi or LP were symphonies of emotions, sound, and effects. Acoustic landscapes transported into a never-before-heard psychedelic state of suspension by echo and phaser. The term "dub" only trivialized his sound images. This was especially true for *Super Ape*, perhaps Perry's greatest work of art, which was incorrectly referred to as a dub LP. Rather, he used overdubs and effects to condense new instrumental and vocal versions from existing playbacks into an independent magnum opus that was light years away from the dub in the dancehall. Nevertheless, Perry owed his reputation as the Salvador Dalí of Dub[15], as Dub Wizard, Dub Alchemist, Dub Daddy[16] or whatever names he would acquire in the future, to what he created during this time. Thanks to the deal with Island Records, a growing white following in Europe celebrated him and his fame, while Jamaica reacted cautiously. His mixes were not dub in the classic sense, and certainly not vocal or deejay playbacks for the sound systems, which is why they didn't appear there. "His productions were simply not ramming the dancehalls" as his biographer David Katz also admitted.[17] From the very beginning, Perry's music design sought a different audience.

With success came trouble. Anyone who makes money in Jamaica is asked to "let off supm", and Perry was no exception. Musicians and singers, idlers and hustlers, thieves and beggars, everyone held out their hands to beg from him. The Bobos demanded support; local gangs wanted protection money. On top of that, Island's refusal to license *Heart Of The Congos*, which was considered a masterpiece by all sides, supposedly because it might jeopardize the status of top seller Bob Marley, led to massive resentment. Not just between Perry and Blackwell, but also with the dreads in the camp, where it escalated into the absurd accusation that the host had covertly mixed pork into the Rastas' food. Perry was in a state of constant stress, increasingly worried about his finances, and began to despair about his stance on Rastafari. He resorted to drinking rum more and more often, which made him unpredictable. In 1978, the situation led to drastic mental breakdowns. During the recording of Ras Michael's *Love Thy Neighbour* album, Perry stopped the session and began painting the letter "X" over pictures and walls of the studio. "Upsetter get mentally deranged" was how Yabby You described the progressive change in character[18] that remained hidden from no one.

At some point, Perry had serious arguments with everyone he was interacting with. Fewer and fewer people hung out in his yard, it was getting lonely around him. Even his wife fled, whom he had been together with since Studio One days, and had had three children with, and who for years had managed his business and sold his records in the UK. By January 1979, he had driven everyone out of his yard; the studio was idle, but still functional. It was the moment that marked the abrupt end of phase two of Lee Perry's career, after five years of exceptional productivity.

Long after the Ark lay aground and had ceased operations, fascinating recordings from its legacy found their way to the public. Not everything had the class of the Island albums or *Heart Of The Congos*, and a lot of it only attracted attention because the legend spun around Lee Perry had a sales-promoting effect. Apart from *Blackboard Jungle Dub* (1973) and *Revolution Dub* (1975), it was only after 1979, long after Perry had since stopped mixing, that albums which aggressively associated Lee Perry with the term "dub" came onto the market. Not everything that now appeared had the quality of his official releases of the previous three years. The first so-called "dubs" in fact came from the Black Ark, but were compiled by Perry's ex-wife Pauline "Isha" Morrison, or by Tony Owens, the owner of the Seven Leaves label who had emigrated to the UK and whom Perry had often collaborated with:

14 First released in France on Sonafric in 1979 only as *Sekje Molenga & Kalo Kawongolo*.
15 Lloyd Bradley, German edition ibid p. 292.
16 ARTE Tracks December 15, 2011, a portrait full of absurd information.
17 David Katz: *People Funny Boy, The Genius Of Lee "Scratch" Perry* 2nd edition p. 301.
18 Yabby You – *Dread Prophecy* booklet ibid.

The ruins of Lee Perry's Black Ark Studio, 2023.

- **Black Ark Players – Black Ark In Dub** Black Ark International/Starlight UK 1980 with two mixes by King Tubby and synthesizer overdubs recorded in the UK
- **Lee Perry – Megaton Dub** Seven Leaves UK 1983
- **Lee Perry – Megaton Dub 2** Seven Leaves UK 1984

Perry knew nothing about these releases, as he was busy reincarnating as Pipecock Jackxon. He distanced himself from Rastas and dreads and wanted in the future to work only with white musicians. The attempt to produce an album for a Dutch label with a group of British musicians in his studio failed, due to desperate circumstances. Nevertheless, fragments of the sessions, without his knowledge, unfinished and without his mixing, appeared in 1980 as *The Return Of Pipecock Jackxon*[19]. In 1981, on the initiative of Chris Blackwell, he flew to New York. At a concert by the Terrorists, a white wave and reggae band, he took the stage and freestyled. This resulted in a short live and studio collaboration, which ended with a maxi produced, sung, and possibly

19 Black Star Liner, NL 1980

mixed, by Perry in Manhattan.[20] The Terrorists were succeeded by the Majestics, another white reggae band from New York. Heartbeat, the US label, financed a session for Perry and the band in a Kingston studio. Since it was no longer possible to work in the Black Ark, they went to Dynamic. There they created the *Lee "Scratch" Perry and The Majestics – Mystic Miracle Star*[21] album. After Pipecock Jackxon and the Terrorists, this marked the third artistic revelation of shortcomings. Nothing remained of the sound that had made Lee Perry famous. Instead of a magical atmosphere, there was cloudy recitation and slovenly lyrics; it was vulgar, ostentatious, gaga.

Perry had reached rock bottom. The man formerly known as The Mighty Upsetter had fallen mightily himself; his creative muse had come to an end. Four years after he had closed his studio, he still remained deeply bitter about the artists he had worked with there. Accompanied by excessive rum consumption, he staggered through severe mood swings. He actually wanted to bring Black Ark back to life, although, given his financial situation, it was clear that this would remain an illusion. After he had already thrown musical instruments and parts of the sound equipment into his cesspit, suddenly, in the early hours of the summer of 1983, the studio burst into flames. The cause remains a mystery. Had Perry started the fire? Given his mental confusion, this wouldn't have been surprising, or had it been caused by a short circuit?

The fire destroyed his old life completely, just swept it away, but Perry rose from the ruins of the Black Ark like a phoenix from the ashes. The Upsetter mutated into a self-promoter in a production as Madman. He would never mix anything again, never turn the knobs on a mixing console again, even if there are images that suggested he had. He had sung and toasted over riddims before, but from now on, he would only talk, and as a vocal acrobat, live off the fame he had earned. Lee "Scratch" Perry reinvented himself as an event artist, and the event was himself.

Perry "made a very conscious decision to become an artist", Adrian Sherwood confirmed. "He didn't want to sit behind a mixing desk that he wasn't familiar with, one mixing desk this day, a different one the next, and trying to emulate what he had done at the Black Ark. He left behind the period with the iconic imagery of him at the Black Ark mixing, and went on to become the artist."[22]

We're witnessing the transition of Perry's career to phase three, which eclipsed everything that had happened up to that point. While the output of singles, maxis and LPs produced before and during the Black Ark period was difficult to quantify, what was published with his name after its demise could only be represented in linear meters. The fact that Jamaican dub came to a standstill during this time because of "Sleng Teng" didn't stop him. The dub scene moved from Kingston to London and, starting in Europe, found a new worldwide following. In this environment, Lee Perry became a cult figure. Over the following 35 years, around a hundred LPs were released, as well as singles, maxis, and DVDs, some of it of dubious origin. Lee Perry was advertised on the front cover, often with the addition of "dub", while on the back you found out who was actually responsible for the mix.[23] It was not Lee Perry at least, not even if they claimed it was for sales promotional reasons. His name became a bond, or stock, whose value on the dub market was continuously increasing. All of this was fueled by past fame and a changed perception, in which two books played a major role.

20 *Terrorists and Lee "Scratch" Perry – Love Is Better Now/Guerilla Priest* 12-inch Spliff Records US 1981.

21 Heartbeat US 1982.

22 "Adrian Sherwood on Lee Perry" in: *I feel everything you say I feel everything you hear*, Published by Weekend Fest, Strzelecki Books, Cologne 2022 p. 108f.

23 Three examples from recent times, representative of many: *Lee Perry And Friends – Back To The Ark* Upsetter label UK, Record Store Day Edition 2019 feat. Dennis Bovell, Vin Gordon, Sylford Walker et.al., mixed by Daniel Boyle. Or the single "The Invisible Man" by the psychedelic funk band Solid Bronze from Delaware, Schnitzel Records, Rough Trade 2019, allegedly with a "Lee 'Scratch' Perry Dub Mix", that was done by Mad Professor. Or *Jack Johnson – In Between Dub*, Brushfire Records 2023, where the tracks were mixed by Subatomic Sound System engineer Emch.

In 1984, William Gibson, American science fiction author and cyberpunk pioneer, had published his novel *Neuromancer*, which expressed the spirit of the times, and sold millions worldwide. The central location of the story was a space station called "Zion", operated by Rastas. Zion circled the earth while non-stop "bass-heavy dub" pulses through its corridors. In the wake of *Neuromancer*, British music journalist David Toop published a music theory treatise entitled *Ocean Of Sounds. Aether Talk, Ambient Sound And Imaginary Worlds,* some eleven years later, which was highly acclaimed by pop critics. In it, he sketches a rough representation of dub history, which in many places did not withstand fact checking. Toop was the source of an intellectual, naïve, blue-eyed interpretation of dub, and played a major role in transfiguring Lee Perry. He quoted Perry speak extensively; typical explanations were "I was getting help from God. I got support through the weather to make space music. When I cut a Stench-Furt, it so loud that it bring up volcano lava, and is more dangerous than a hurricane." Impressed by Perry's comments, Toop concluded "dub music is like a long echo delay, looping through time. Spreading out a song or a groove over a vast landscape of peaks and deep trenches, extending hooks and beats to vanishing points, dub creates new maps of time, intangle sound sculptures, sacred sites, balm and shock for mind, body and spirit. Dubbing, at its very best, [is] turning a rational order of musical sequencies into an ocean of sensation."[24]

By the time *Ocean Of Sounds* came around, Perry had long since admitted that he no longer had "direct contact with the mixing desk"[25]. Nevertheless, around 20 new albums had already been released under the Perry brand, a good half of which had the term "dub" in the title. Many of them came from a white background, and were ideologically closer to Woodstock than to Kingston. Perry was now a busy performance artist who appeared around the world. He had bands backing him everywhere. His aversion to dreadlocks was gone. But true to the motto "I had an experience with Jamaican artists and I wish not to get involved with things not to my suit any more"[26], these bands – unless they were Mad Professor's Robotics or On-U Sound's Dub Syndicate – consisted exclusively of white musicians.[27] His audience reflected these requirements. African Americans or people from the Caribbean hardly made it to his concerts, and if they did, told him directly, as Paul Zasky recalled, "What the f*** are you talking about, dude?". In the US and Europe as bassist, Zasky had played more than 200 shows for Perry with both the American Subatomic Sound System, and Dubblestandart, his Austrian band. He explained that "Lee Perry works very differently in front of a white audience than in front of a black one. White people don't understand a lot of things, and have a different understanding of reggae. But when you play in front of African Americans or in France, different codes apply, so it becomes more difficult with Lee Perry."

24 David Toop: *Oceon Of Sound. Aether Talk, Ambient Sound And Imaginary Worlds* Profile Books, London 1995 p. 115f.

25 1992 in an interview with René Wynands, which the author was a witness to. To be found in »*Do The Reggay!*« Piper 1995 p. 226

26 1995 in an interview with the Grand Royal magazine, Issue 2 p. 68, published by the Beastie Boys 16 years later, however, the rude rejection had faded. In 2011 Perry performed with Max Romeo and The Congos at Summerjam in Cologne, Germany; in 2015 he shared the stage with Jamaican musicians at the Stepping High Ganja Fest in Negril as well as at the aforementioned appearance at the Redbones Blues Café in Kingston in 2012.

27 These included renowned names such as The Revolution feat. Jah Wobble & David Harrow from the UK (1990), but also regional groups like Soon Come from Germany (1993) or The White Belly Rats from Switzerland (2004, 2008, 2016). With musicians from the Austrian band Dubblestandart he played 114 shows in the US, from 2010 mostly in combination with the New York Subatomic Sound System, in 2013 with Easy Riddim Maker from France, 2015 with Pura Vida from Belgium.

With Perry, white dub fans kept to themselves. Not entirely uninvolved in this development was On-U Sound, the British label. Adrian Sherwood, its chief ideologist, confessed the following to journalist David Katz "a lot of the white smoky bears were all smoking spliffs, listening to dub music, which was us, so we were making records for ourselves."[28] Sherwood practiced this with the band Dub Syndicate especially, which, according to Style Scott their drummer, tried "to bring Dub Syndicate close to the Pink Floyd sort of thing."[29]

Perry's big break came in 1998 when the Beastie Boys cited him as one of their influences, inviting Perry to voice a song for them[30]. Perry had had previous contacts with the pop mainstream, among other people, in 1977 a failed liaison in the Black Ark with Paul and Linda McCartney[31], as well as a successful folk-rock production with British singer, songwriter and guitarist John Martyn[32]. Ten years later, in London, he created remixes for Simply Red and Terence Trent D'Arby, which essentially consisted of strange overdubs. They received little attention, but the recording with the Beastie Boys was of a different quality, showing Perry in his new element as distinctive spokesman, adding his voice to playbacks that hadn't come from him. The Beastie Boys, international hip hop superstars thanks to their mega hit "(You Gotta) Fight For Your Right (To Party!)", threw the door to the global (pop) market, previously only slightly ajar, wide open to Perry. Two collaborations with the electronic project The Orb in 2012 and 2013[33] further increased his popularity, but also contributed to the rampant dilution of the term "dub" in mainstream publications. Wherever it said Perry, there had to be dub in it. The pinnacle of feuilletonistic idealization was the German documentary *Lee Scratch Perry's Vision Of Paradise* in 2015.[34] This colourful film followed the same fictional narrative that had been created and nurtured by whites for decades. Efficient promotion thanks to public funding meant that the film spread throughout the world the historical misconception that Lee Perry had invented dub.

Accolades like that of the Beastie Boys, as well as a never-ending flood of reissues and compilations from Perry's past, obscured the fact that, after 1979, many of the records made with him at the microphone had little to offer musically. Exceptions almost only occurred when Adrian Sherwood or Mad Professor took him into their care. The further the development of sample technology progressed, the more both worked with samples from Black Ark productions, recycling Perry's old echo and phaser sound, without the original inventor contributing anything new to the playbacks. He contented himself by providing eccentric wordplay. This could be interpreted as a continuation of the talk-over tradition by the toasters in Jamaican music. In terms of content, as long as Perry could talk about himself and his relationship to the universe, it amounted to egocentric poetry that stopped at nothing. He spoke in rhymes, described himself as a "talking machine", announced that he would take over the World Bank, characterized himself as a Black Jesus or African shaman, resorted to obscenities, and glorified his flatulence and excrement. If there was an audience or a camera nearby, he would change clothes and slip into the role of the Madman. Many of those who worked or spent time with him knew the difference between the official and the private Lee Perry. Others were unsure to what extent the role of the otherworldly figure was playacting. There were reports that Perry behaved differently, not to say "normally", in familiar surroundings. However, "once somebody new comes in, he gets off into that different area. He does more crazy stuff".[35] Mad Professor went on to confirm this in his obituary "I don't think he was any madder than most. After a time, it became a kind of performance for the press, for white people generally. He realized they would take more notice of him if he put on an act."[36]

The neverending topic of voodoo returned and with Perry developed into a demonstrative obsession. Album titles like *Voodooism*, *Who Put The Voodoo 'Pon Reggae* or *Dub Take The Voodoo Out Of Reggae*[37] flirted with this passion. The older Perry became, the more often he brought the term back into play. He attacked bystanders who dared to step on his shadow in the sunshine, wanted to defeat the British Queen's voodoo[38], sang "I Do Voodoo"[39] and reinforced the request with his flam-

28 "30 Jahre On-U Sound" ("30 years On-U Sound") German Reggae print magazine *RIDDIM* 06/2011.
29 2004 in an interview for the online magazine Reggae-News.
30 "Dr. Lee PhD" on *Hello Nasty*, Capitol 1998.
31 This resulted in the titles "Sugartime" and "Mister Sandman", which can be found on various McCartney compilations, e.g. *Wide Prairie* MPL 1998.
32 "Big Muff" Island 12-inch 1977.
33 *The Orb featuring Lee Scratch Perry present The Observer in the star house* 2012 and *More Tales From The Observatory* 2013, both Cooking Vinyl.
34 A film by Volker Schaner, Fufoofilm, Germany 2015.
35 The New York producer Lloyd Barnes, operator of the Wackies label and producer of several albums with Lee Perry, in: *Waxpoetics* 20, Brooklyn 2007.
36 "Lee 'Scratch' Perry remembered by Neil 'Mad Professor' Fraser", *The Guardian* UK December 12, 2021.
37 All three released in 1996 in the UK. Voodooism was a Pressure Sound compilation, *Who Put The Voodoo 'Pon Reggae* and *Dub Take The Voodoo Out Of Reggae* were new productions by Mad Professor for his Ariwa label.
38 Under the title "10 Commandments" he explained in an interview with Q Magazine in 2019: "I will conquer all the voodoo that the Queen is doing in Buckingham Palace with my poo-poo and my golden chalice."
39 On the album Dubblestandart, *Lee "Scratch" Perry & Ari Up – Return From Planet Dub* Collision/Echo Beach Germany 2009.

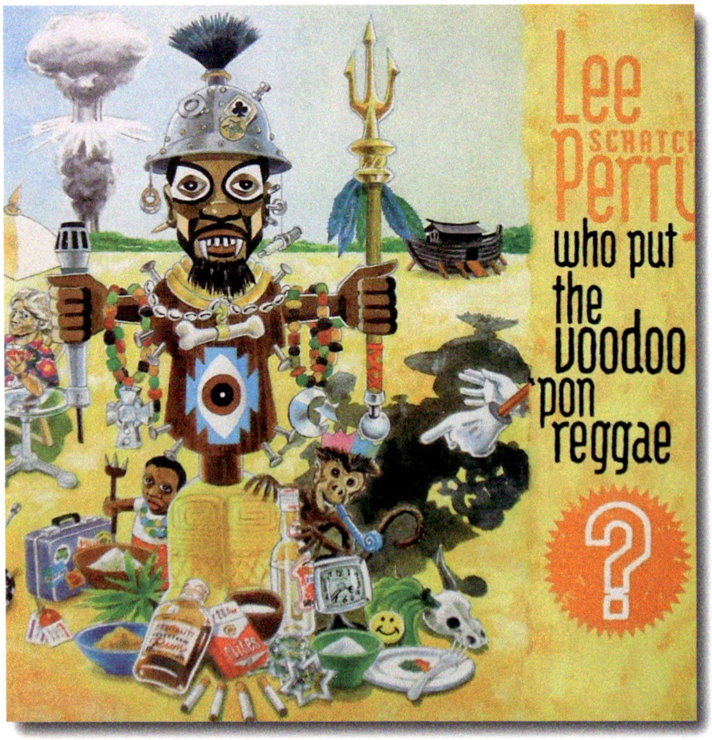

boyant appearance. This included the colourful outfits, the red hair as well as the symbols, tarot cards and mirror reflectors on his clothing that were supposed to ward off ghosts.

While the Upsetter used to juggle with music and technology, he now played with mirrors, candles, chains, signs, and words – and with his listeners. Perry's alter ego as the god of chatter lived the dub version of his former producer life. An eccentric, Afrofuturistic art form, entertaining and profound, which could have provided plenty of material for one's own consideration. Dub as a derivative of the dancehall remained pure fiction here. Nevertheless, the term was constantly equated with his person.

Anyone who brought Lee Perry into the studio witnessed obscure spirit and energy conjurings. Perry decorated the desk with feathers, hung pictures and lit candles. Kevin Metcalfe, London mastering engineer reported on a meeting in 1987 at Townhouse studio. Adrian Sherwood had produced the *Time Boom X De Devil Dead* album with Perry, and brought the Voodoo man with him to the mastering session. The latter carried a thick notepad full of symbols, images and rhymes, and asked Metcalfe to sit on this piece for the entire session, seven hours. Perry had the wiring in the studio explained to him and set up an altar above the cable duct, consisting of a small camera and something undefinable wrapped in silver foil. He was looking at the patch panel that connected all the studio technology and wanted to know whether the music was going through it. When the question was answered in the affirmative, he removed a cable, and the left channel was gone. He pulled out a hair, twisted it into a small ball, stuffed it into the opening and reconnected the plug. That the channel then stopped working, and it took a lot of effort to get the system up and running again didn't bother him. Later, during the vinyl cutting process, he threw razor blades at the machine's graver. Neither Metcalfe nor Sherwood could hold him back.

Despite occasional disagreements, hardly anyone treated Perry's legacy with as much respect as Adrian Sherwood. He succeeded in transposing the basic dubby-esque sound of the Upsetter's studio with new technology. Using samples and atmospheric reminiscences, he prepared platforms for complex playbacks for the artist to add odd spoken words, which, after the Black Ark fire, made their joint albums stand out from the mass of releases:

- **Lee "Scratch" Perry & Dub Syndicate – Time Boom X De Devil Dead** On-U 1987
- **Lee "Scratch" Perry – From My Secret Laboratory** Mango 1990

- **Lee "Scratch" Perry – The Mighty Upsetter** On-U 2008
- **Lee "Scratch" Perry and Adrian Sherwood – Dub Setter** On-U 2010[40] (Dub version of **The Mighty Upsetter**)
- **£ee $cratch Perry – Rainford** On-U 2019
- **£ee $cratch Perry – Heavy Rain** On-U 2019 (Dub version of **Rainford**)

Doubts as to whether the Upsetter consciously staged his crazy otherworldliness and perhaps wasn't "mad" at all were given new fuel in 2019. Sherwood had been following Perry for two years to record his mystical and mysterious statements. He then sorted them into order, and gave them a musical setting in his London studio. Once again, he incorporated sources from the Black Ark, such as Perry's single "Bionic Rats" from 1977, or Bobby Ellis' "Ska Baby" from 1975. Based on Perry's middle name, he called the powerfully grooving sound and effects legacy *Rainford*. It was an album full of autobiographical lyrics and Afro-futuristic visions. This audiophile testament was sealed by Sherwood with *Heavy Rain*, the dub counterpart. The subsequent album was ennobled by a contribution by Brian Eno, and there were analogies to the split-stereo experiments of the *Revolution Dub* LP 45 years previously. Although not mixed by Sherwood or Perry, *Heavy Rain* showed how far dub could stray from its origins without losing its essence.

After *Rainford* and *Heavy Rain*, the 83-year-old Lee Perry did well to stay away from any further records. It wasn't planned, but fate wanted it that way. *Rainford* and *Heavy Rain* became the perfect finale to the life's work of an innovator of sound who, in an earlier phase, had traveled through unheard dubstrumental galaxies on board the Black Ark with anarchic skill and with the help of the universe. On the morning of August 29, 2021, Lee Perry passed away at Noel Holmes Hospital in Lucea, Jamaica. He was 85 years old. The legend that he had been the inventor of dub was spun in the obituaries of the feature sections, although the moniker of dub wizard attributed to Perry never fitted properly; it had been destroyed in his flagship fire long before. After that, he never used a mixing console again himself. The Black Ark's ethereal soundscapes have since been managed by other, but they remained unreachable.

40 Before, in 2009, in Japan on Beat Records

Reggae Roast Sound System, UK.

Dub in the UK: Variation on a Theme

> "Dub is really when the engineer drop out parts of the rhythm, the rhythm section, and stick in some effects and then create a whole new atmosphere that takes the listener somewhere between here and outer space. This is music that explores the mind and the soul. And the thing about the good dub you could play it a million times and every time you listen, you'd hear something different."
>
> (Mad Professor[1])

On June 22, 1948, a former German troop ship captured by the British during the war and renamed "Empire Windrush" brought the first 493 Jamaicans to the UK. It was the start of a wave of migration from the Caribbean that lasted until 1971. The newcomers were not refugees; the British government had officially invited them to come from the colony to the motherland to help rebuild the economy after World War II. Those who followed the call back then were part of the "Windrush Generation". However, they were not welcome. The country viewed those arriving as foreigners, and often maintained rigid racist attitudes. Behind signs reading "No dogs – No blacks – No Irish", the British preferred to keep to themselves. Work and housing were difficult to find for Jamaicans.

In 1955 the government tried to counteract this. In the newsreels in the cinemas, images of those arriving were full of pathos and advocated a rethink in attitude. "In 1954 around 10,000 [immigrants] came to Britain from the Caribbean, and in 1955 another 15,000 will make the long journey. We cannot reject them. Because as British citizens they have the same rights as everyone in the Empire. [They are] a sorry sight, but they don't want pity. Just the recognition that all people are born free and equal in dignity and rights. Does the answer to these issues lie in the UK or in the West Indies? If we dig deep enough, we might find the solution in all our consciences."[2]

Duke Vin arrived in 1952, Daddy Vego in '54, and Wilbert Augustus Campbell, aka Count Suckle, three years later. They later independently reported that it was bitterly cold, dark, and foggy when they disembarked in London, and that they wanted to return to the sun and warmth of Jamaica immediately. But there was no return ticket.

Count Suckle, Duke Vin and Daddy Vego brought Jamaica's most original achievement at the time – aside from rum – to the UK, i.e., sound system culture. Duke Vin already had relevant experience; he was a selector for "Tom The Great Sebastian" back in the 40s. In London he discovered that there was no opportunity in his new home for black people to go dancing; the whites' clubs did not allow access. As a result, Vin built his first sound system in 1955, called it "The Tickler", and began DJing at so-called blues dances in apartments and basements. At the beginning, it was private house parties. Furniture was moved, rooms were emptied, speaker boxes and bars were set up, and Jamaican food served. "The people who lived next door must have gone through hell." said Daddy Vego[3], especially since the speakers were getting bigger and bigger over time, because in the UK too, the Jamaican competitive spirit of "Bigger! Better! Bass!" immediately played an important role. Vin's most successful competitor was Count Suckle, who became the first sound system resident in 1962 at the "Roaring Twenties Club" on Carnaby Street in London. Rhythm and blues and related music was being played everywhere, but when the first ska records arrived from Jamaica, the sounds quickly changed to, as Daddy Vego called it, "strictly Jamaican business."[4]

Sound systems in the UK were what they were in Jamaica, a leisure activity, but they wouldn't stay that way. Over time they developed their own, British identity, which went through many stages. They sprouted like mushrooms and formed the breeding ground for a counterworld to which white people had no access. The imported dancehall culture became a refuge for unwelcome immigrants. There for a few hours you could escape racism, unemployment, and the fear of not being able to pay your rent. In London alone, there were around 500 sounds in the 1970s. When the first dubs from Tubby's studio arrived in town, the mood became more dramatic. The blues dances became drum & bass

1 Bassline Of A City, Museum of London 2020.
2 Translated from the German version of the Dutch documentary *Gelobte Länder* (Promised Lands), Interart 2013.
3 DVD *Duke Vin and the Birth of Ska*, Gus Berger, Hackney Film Collective 2011.
4 ibid.

events, an outlet to let off steam in the face of the pervasive, racist hostility of British society.

"When dub first came out it was very, very black" Mad Professor told me. "No white guy was in there because it was deemed a very threatening music. Dubs like Augustus Pablo stuff, the "Java", the *Ital Dub*, they were aggressively menacing. It was a heavy mood, a heavy time. Most white people were not really checking it. Don't let anybody fool you. Dub was very, very black and the whole mood was very aggressive. I'm talking about '73, '74. White guys weren't welcome in the dance. I remember being in a couple of dances when a white guy just come in and suddenly some guys would be jumping on him."

With the sound systems, those who were unwanted in the country were able to immerse themselves in an acoustic cocoon of self-assertion. Dub was the militant folklore of their urban underground until the mood changed in 1976. Bob Marley's legendary London Lyceum concert had taken place the year before. The live version of "No Woman No Cry", the comparatively harmless but powerfully moving song, taken from his dynamic set, became an international chart success, and softened the feeling of isolation. Reggae was becoming a global phenomenon, especially in the UK. Dub and sound systems started to expand their musical spectrum, and white visitors were no longer turned away. The culture, which until then had been spread almost exclusively among immigrants, conquered the British mainstream. Frequencies replaced the message, bass became the new god in temples of loudspeaker walls. In addition to reggae and dub, the musical medium was now also soul, funk, and dance music.[5] From the end of the 70s onwards, sound systems were part of the fabric of society and no longer its opposite.

Once dancehall was no longer a purely exiled Jamaican phenomenon, selectors like Jah Shaka formed a countermovement with an apodictic Rastafarian identity. As Sister Stella of the Rastafari Movement UK put it "dub highlights and defines key moments of my youthful self in the 1980s. Racism was literally in your face and at the time it was intense. The A-side of a record spoke of politics, race, class, humanity, justice, and injustice, of love and of sorrow. But it was the B-side of dub that gave me a profoundly deeper inner, almost electric surge of strength. The bassline pushes out all negativity and allows space for magnificent ideas, of hope for my people."[6] Shaka & Co changed the dances in favour of a spiritual sublimation as a danced "Chant Down Babylon" rebellion against still rampant racism. This was primarily reflected in racial profiling, and the application of so-called sus laws[7], according to which people behaving suspiciously could be searched and arrested without specific charges being brought against them. Bredda Neil of the Amsterdam "King Shiloh" sound system described the change. "Sound systems is like a result of certain social conditions. In Jamaica, it's a different vibe. England was colder and wet out there. It was rougher and tougher. There was certain oppression going on. The police was chasing up the people all the time. We're talking about times like the Brixton Riots, Handsworth Riots.[8] People was sick and tired of the way government was dealing with us. Out of all that madness and jail sentences and crime and things came spirituality. That's the way to get ourselves out of it. And then Jah Shaka came along and said we got to look to Africa. We have to uplift people.

5 The rise from underground to integration has had a huge impact on British pop and club music. Bass-driven styles such as jungle, drum'n'bass, grime, dubstep etc. were essentially influenced by sound system experiences.

6 Quoted from the materials for the exhibition *Dub London: Bassline of a City*, on view at the Museum of London from October 2020 to January 2021. Sister Stella co-curated the exhibition.

7 "sus" was officially short for "suspected person", but unofficially it also stood for "stop and search".

8 In April and July 1981, Liverpool, Manchester and Leeds also saw serious rioting.

Not crying people down. Not fighting against government or whatever. No, we do it by music. That's where Rastafari make its impact in dances."

The British director Steve McQueen[9], himself a descendant of the Windrush Generation, made a series of feature films for the BBC in 2020 about the lives of Caribbean immigrants between 1969 and 1985 in London. Entitled *Small Axe*, the films showed bluntly how British society was dealing with the Caribbean immigrants it had brought into the country. Among other things, he documented how white police officers played cards to determine who had to chase and beat up migrants, and depicted the atmosphere at a private blues dance. This was at the end of the 70s, when the song "Silly Games", composed by Dennis Bovell and produced with singer Janet Kay, became the biggest success in the history of lovers' rock. Samson, the MC of "Mercury", the imaginary sound system playing at the party, commented on his song selection with jive talk rhymes. "We're about to move into outernational selection, without further objection, [to] give unno spiritual protection!" The spiritual protection emerged when Samson shouted "Babylon, we're not afraid!" into the crowd, and put on Sly & Robbie's "Kunta Kinte Dub", a militant mix by Barnabas from the Channel One studio, which could only be heard on sound systems until 2007[10] as a dubplate, and which sent the male members of the audience especially into ecstasy.

By the early 1980s, reggae in London was no longer limited to sound systems and licensed imports. Productions from Jamaica had been conquering the national charts for a long time, and Jamaican artists had discovered the UK as a prosperous market for tours and record sales. The Windrush Generation and their descendants gave rise to bands such as Steel Pulse, Aswad, Cimarrons, Matumbi, Tradition, Black Jade, Black Slate, Motion and many more. They built studios, produced albums, recorded dubplates and singles, released them on their own labels, and sampled reggae radio shows. Reggae in the UK spawned an independent chapter, distinct from its country of origin, which flourished particularly well with the lovers' rock variant, creating a unique and immensely successful offshoot. Caribbean immigrants had settled in the music metropolis of London and, although foreign to the country, found ways to produce their music there, which also included dub.

"Suddenly the B-sides became more popular than the A-sides" Mad Professor recalled. "Those tunes had something else underneath. Because the separation [of the tracks] wasn't that clean. You could hear there were tunes. It was such a new phenomenon. Never before have you heard something that is like a song but it's not a song. It's like an accident but it feels good."

The psychedelic-mystical aspect of dub was to an extent inherent in the productions coming from Jamaica. But the British bands didn't have any comparable studios that were exclusively focused on reggae. Although London, more so than Kingston, was dotted with recording facilities of all sizes, it was not easy to find the right sound, and an understanding of reggae in them. The big studios were unaffordable, the more budget-friendly ones didn't give the riddims the power they needed. Productions from Kingston lived from what Pat Kelly called the dirty, rough downtown roots and ghetto sound[11], while the music from London ema-

9 Steve McQueen has made films such as the Oscar-winning *12 Years A Slave* (2013) and *Widows* (2018).

10 In 2007 Pressure Sounds released "Kunta Kinte Dub" on the compilation *Drum Sounds – The Revolutionaries. More gems from the channel one dub room*.

11 See chapter "Errol Thompson, Joe Gibbs and the first Dub LPs".

nated a cosmopolitan, pop-infused tone. It was cleaner, tidier, and less bulky than the Jamaican records.

Despite having Jamaican engineer Sid Bucknor in the city, who, in addition to mixing the aforementioned *Nuh Skin Up Dub* LP, had also worked as a recording engineer on albums like the Creation Rebel debut *Dub From Creation*[12], the London dub of the second half of the 1970s was characterized by a quartet of engineers who did not hail from Jamaica. Mark Lusardi and Adrian Sherwood were originally Londoners, Neil Fraser aka Mad Professor, came from Guyana in 1968 as a 13-year-old; Dennis Bovell, born in 1953, moved from Barbados in 1965, while his father had already arrived seven years earlier. The four of them sometimes worked at the same studios, often crossed paths, yet each developed their own individual, groundbreaking style. When in February 1985 "Sleng Teng" buried Jamaican dub, international dub perception focused on the UK. Three of the said quartet achieved worldwide recognition and success on a scale that no Jamaican dub had previously achieved, when the fourth, Mark Lusardi, was no longer involved. Although he in particular created a dub language that was clearly different from the Jamaican aesthetic, and played a major role in the fact that, in London, dub developed, as it was said in a production by Dennis Bovell, "a little way different"[13].

After finishing school, Mark Lusardi, born in 1955, found a job at DECCA, the traditional record label, founded in the 1930s. There was no training given with the employment; you learned through careful observation. To his advantage, Lusardi had acquired classical guitar skills during his teenage years, and possessed a well-trained ear. He quickly rose from tape copier to tape operator in the large studios of DECCA's pop department. He was there when stars like Peter Sellers and The Moody Blues recorded; when Thin Lizzy's Phil Lynott made his first solo attempts, Lusardi was sitting at the desk, learning to work with 24 tracks.

In the mid-70s, Lusardi left DECCA and moved to the smaller Gooseberry studio. Peter Houghton, the owner originally built it in London's West End in 1968 as a 4-track demo studio in the basement of a dentist's office on Gerrard Street in Soho. When Lusardi started working for him, Dennis Bovell was already working there as an engineer. The studio was equipped with a 2-inch 16-track Ampex machine, and was expanded to 24 tracks in 1980. But even then, Gooseberry remained a small, inexpensive studio that didn't have enough space to mike up drums properly. Nevertheless, it was appreciated for technically high-quality, low-budget productions until it closed in the mid-90s. The Sex Pistols recorded there, Tubeway Army's successful album *Replicas*[14] with their hit "Are 'Friends' Electric?" was created there, as was the reggae version of "Caught You In A Lie"[15] produced by Lloyd Coxsone, with the 15-year-old Louisa Mark, a song which triggered the lovers' rock hype in 1975. With the exception of the drums, all the instruments on it were played by Dennis Bovell, on whose "Sufferer's Sound" Louisa Mark occasionally sang live.

Bovell and Lusardi shared shifts at the Gooseberry, Bovell working at night and Lusardi during the day. Although 19 Gerrard Street was not in one of the Caribbean immigrant neighborhoods but in London's Chinatown, reggae productions made up the majority of the commissions. In addition to favourable daily rates, a fruitful collaboration developed between Bovell and Lusardi. Both were excellent musicians, and one knew more about reggae while the other more about technology. "I basically introduced him to mixing, and how the gear worked." Lusardi said. "I liked the heavy way he equalized things" Bovell stated. Years later, mutual appreciation could still be felt.

Dennis Bovell succumbed to the fascination of dubplates and sound systems early on. His school in Wandsworth relied on intensive music lessons, and Dennis learned drums and keyboard there. He had already picked up the guitar on his own in Barbados. When the school set up a small recording studio in 1970, 17-year-old Dennis recorded the instrumental version of the then current Bob & Marcia hit single "Young, Gifted & Black"[16]. Using the technology available there, he separated four bars with two chord progressions, copied the part several times and combined the sections into a three-minute loop. He had a friend play the melody from "Guantanamera" with trombone and flute, and mixed everything together into a new song. At school he was warned that it was piracy, you couldn't do that. "It earned me the name of Blackbeard the Pirate. They started calling me 'Blackbeard' because I had a beard as well!" Blackbeard did not fear any copyright issues. "It wasn't the obvious loop of the tune" he added laughing but "it had the sound of Jamaica, haha. As you know, the trombone has been a favourite instrument in reggae." He had his new creation cut as a single-sided 7-inch acetate. "In dem days we never used to call it dub, it was called wax. In Jamaica they called it soft wax. We took the soft off and called it wax. A hard wax,

12 Hit Run UK 1978.
13 Errol Dunkley, Arawak 12-inch UK 1978, produced and mixed by Dennis Bovell.
14 Beggars Banquet UK 1979.
15 Originally a soul track by Robert Parker from 1967.
16 The cover version of the Nina Simone song by Bob Andy and Marcia Griffiths reached number 5 in the UK Charts.

Dennis Bovell and the author, Vienna 2020.

you know, hehe. I went to a sound called 'Jim Daddy' and sold it to him for three pounds. With that three pounds, we drank beer and took a taxi home. 'Jim Daddy' was one of my favourite sounds, I didn't mind him having it. At that time, I was not yet with 'Sufferer's Sound'."

Bovell continued to create loops from records in the school studio, and cut new tracks from them. "I was good at editing and importing. I took a piece from here and a piece from there and made it together. The I would take maybe a drum roll from somewhere else." Soon Errol Francis called him. An employed electrician who, on weekends, replaced power lines on his own initiative in old houses bought by migrants. Dennis was one of a group of young people who accompanied Francis on such work. "We were like his posse. He would get a house to rewire, and all of us would be sent on it. One day we got a job to rewire the Barbados High Commission, that was a big job. Out of the profits of that, he started 'Jah Sufferer'[17]." When the sound was ready, Francis visited Bovell: "He came to my house and said 'I hear you got some dubplates, let's hear them.' And I played them to him and he went: 'I want them all. We're starting a new sound, is gonna be crazy.' And I: 'Do you have a deejay?' He was like: 'No' and I: 'Well, that's me!' My part was MC and selector, all at the same time."

17 Optionally also "Sufferer Sound", "Sufferer's HiFi" or "The Mighty Sufferer".

Joining "Jah Sufferer" only motivated Bovell to experiment even more with dubplates. He began recording tracks, often on his own, as a one-man band. After Matumbi formed in 1971 with him as guitarist[18], Bovell became increasingly better connected. If necessary, he now recruited musicians from his inner circle. He mostly recorded in DIP label operator Dennis Harris'[19] Eve studio, who used it only for his own productions and did not rent it out. Bovell worked for him as an engineer and was able to use the studio for his own purposes. The dubplates created at Eve were mainly for "Jah Sufferer", but Bovell also sold to Count Shelly and others.

In the Jamaican tradition, dubplates were exclusive versions of official songs that were either already successful, or were intended to be pro-

18 The line-up initially also included Nicholas Bailey, who stormed the European charts in 1979 under the name Nick Straker with "A Walk In The Park".

19 See chapter "Lee Perry, Dubstrumentalist".

moted in the dance. There were also a smaller number of titles that were exclusively recorded or voiced for dubplates. Bovell mixed both variants and went his own way around 1976. His tracks, originally only recorded for sound systems, enabled him to check out what the audience was gravitating towards in the dances and, using this knowledge, he began to mix special versions from his dubplate recordings for albums. Four LPs were created under the name 4th Street Orchestra and released on RAMA, a DIP sub-label. Bovell had some editions pressed in Jamaica to create an authentic impression.

- **Ah Who Seh? Go-Deh!** 1976
- **Leggo! Ah-Fi-We-Dis** 1976
- **(Scientific) Higher Ranking Dub** 1977
- **Yuh Learn!** 1978[20]

Although he even had singles pressed using a fake Kingston address[21], Bovell didn't try to sound Jamaican. On the contrary, he swapped the heaviness of Rasta and roots for the lightness of British lovers' rock. Cover versions of Bob Dylan's "Man In Me" (with Matumbi in 1976) or George Harrison's "My Sweet Lord" (on *Higher Ranking Dub*) demonstrated how keen Bovell was to achieve "the balance between the pop sound of lover's rock and the roots reggae music on the same track. Lover's dub was always about matching the *Jamaicanicity* with sound and arrangements that made it palatable to the British ears".[22] When a double album was compiled 25 years later with excellently restored highlights from the 4th Street Orchestra's four LPs, it had a picture of "Empire Windrush" on the cover.[23] In the blurb, Jeb Loy Nichols from folk dubbers The Fellow Travellers summed it up. "Bovell's music wasn't Jamaican, it wasn't Channel One or Coxone Dodd [sic]. This was interpretation and invention. Reflections in a cracked glass. Uprooted and anxious. Roots music filtered through the streets of London, the English weather, the pop charts, pie and mash (the traditional English workers' meal), Enoch Powell (the health minister who agitated against immigrants), riot and affray." Bovell added at the same point: "We introduced a lot of things, English stuff and sounds they didn't use in Jamaica."[24]

Bovell's un-Jamaican approach was not shared by everyone. Sound operators like Lloyd "Lloydie" Coxsone (who came to the UK in 1962) and Fatman (arrived a year later) spoke out against a British dub version. They relied on dubs and dubplates from Kingston.

Nevertheless, Bovell pursued his path undeterred. He didn't know that his *Leggo!* album had received a Golden Award in 1976 for "Dub Of The Year". When I showed him the cover with the corresponding print confirming this decades later, he was astonished: "Really? I remember Tony Williams[25] had started an award scheme. Musician of the year, record of the year, supm else. I won quite a few times..." The British Reggae Industry Awards, founded by Tony Williams, only existed from 1981. For this reason, the list of awards on the cover of the *Leggo!* LP ("USA, Eastern, Jamaica, Barbados, Canada, Trinidad, Europe") led to the conclusion that the alleged "award" was merely a publicity stunt.

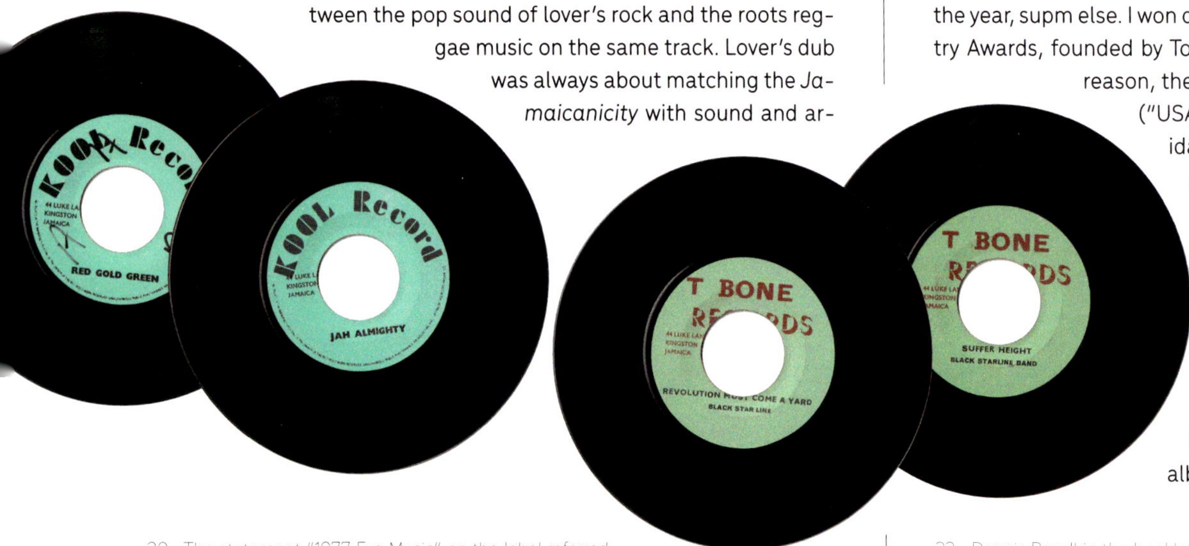

During the recording of *Yuh Learn!* there was water damage in the Eve studio, so they moved to Gooseberry. Black Echoes Magazine had meanwhile outed the fake with the Jamaican pressings so that the musicians involved were mentioned for the first time on the cover of the fourth and final album. Among them were musicians from Ma-

20 The statement "1977 Eve Music" on the label referred to the publishing rights; the LP was only released a year later.
21 1976 Black Starline Band – "Suffer Height/Revolution Must Come A Yard", 1977 "Red Gold Green/Jah Almighty", without artist credit, an instrumental cover version of Audley Rollen's "All That Glitter Is Not Gold". Both singles were released on Kool Records with a supposed address of 44 Luke Lane, Kingston.
22 Dennis Bovell in the booklet of the CD reissue *Dennis Bovell presents 4th Street Orchestra: Higher Ranking Dub + Yuh Learn!* EMI 2006.
23 *Dennis Bovell – Decibel. More Cuts & Dubs 1976 to 1983* Pressure Sounds UK 2003
24 ibid.
25 Deejay at BBC Radio London between 1977 and 1987, see also chapter "David Rodigan. Memories of King Tubby".

tumbi, who had been suspicious of Bovell's solo projects for quite some time, not only because he recorded a lot of things completely on his own, but also, encouraged by Dennis Harris, he had formed a successful duo with Aswad's Drummie Zeb, in which Zeb played drums and Bovell did everything else, including the vocals. The two had already recorded "A Little Way Different" together and collaborated on songs for Harris, released under pseudonyms such as African Stones, and credited "produced by Dennis & Harris" (= Dennis Bovell & Dennis Harris). Matumbi were close to a deal with EMI, which included the 7- and 12-inch single "Point of View". Bovell had produced it himself, along with Drummie Zeb, the uncredited Deejay I-Roy and the singer from Matumbi – but without the rest of the band members. They subsequently confronted him. "What you're gonna be? A solo artist or you gonna be in a band?" Bovell decided "alright, I'm gonna stop. But I wanna make dubs [where] the band is not in. So, this is how I started making dub albums instead of singing albums."

The first dub LP had already achieved resounding success, and led to its release by a major company. Bovell recorded the entire album by himself, from start to finish at Gooseberry studio. 40 years later, Mark Lusardi still remembered the sessions with admiration. "[Dennis] played every instrument. He did the drum track first, just imagining the rest of the song. Doing all the rolls, everything exactly in the right place. Then the bass line, the guitar, it was perfect. He could pick the parts out that he decided he wanted to do in his mind. Do them one at a time. And I recorded that. I was quite impressed, 'cause back in that day, without any computers or anything, he'd actually manage to form the whole production in his mind."

Dennis Bovell released his first three solo dub albums under the Blackbeard name. His debut *Strictly Dub Wize* was first released in 1978 on Tempus, the indie label, in a black cover with white lettering, but was taken over by Ballistic Records that same year, given a new, coloured cover, and distributed by United Artist Records. Dennis Bovell already enjoyed a high reputation in the music press because "Dub!" was now a successful formula in the UK, not only in the black music press, but also in magazines like *Sounds*, for which in December 1977 Vivien Goldman, the respected punk and reggae journalist, wrote an instruction manual: "Dennis Matumbi in dub: a step by step guide". Printing the article on the front cover, *Strictly Dub Wize* was given a third artwork in the year it was released.[26] On the back cover of all editions, Dennis Bovell's personal statement was retained. "This is a collection of my own music, mixed the way that I prefer. I hope you like them."

And how! Dennis Bovell had the hype on his side, and the trends were also working for him. Adrian Sherwood, Winston Edwards, Delroy "D-Roy" Witter, even Matumbi all wanted his dub mixes. In the following three years after *Strictly Dub Wize*, Dennis Bovell mixed seven dub LPs:

- **Creation Rebel – Dub From Creation** Hitrun UK 1978 (for Adrian Sherwood)
- **Cry Tuff Dub Encounter Chapter 1** Hitrun UK 1978 (for Adrian Sherwood)
- **Mawamba Dub (Warrior)** D-Roy Records UK 1978 (Bovell et.al., for Delroy Witter)
- **Blackbeard – I Wah Dub** More Cut UK + EMI Japan, both 1980

26 Five of the nine tracks appeared in France in 1980 on the LP *Very Ska . Very Dub* Tempus, which Bovell shared with John Francis (A-side John Francis, B-side Dennis Bovell).

- **Winston Edwards & Blackbeard – Dub Conference At 10 Downing Street** Celluloid, Frankreich + Studio 16, UK, both 1980
- **Matumbi – Dub Planet Orbit 1** Extinguish UK 1980
- **LKJ In Dub** Island 1980

In addition to his enormous output, Bovell found time to expand his radius. From 1979, he was both musical mastermind and bandleader of dub poet Linton Kwesi Johnson, who was born in Jamaica in 1952. He came to London as an 11-year-old and developed into an internationally recognized, important black voice in the UK during the Thatcher years. In June '79, Bovell produced and dubbed the ten-minute maxi by X-O-Dus, a short-lived group from Manchester. Their song "English Black Boys"[27] set a musical message against the propaganda of the right-wing National Front, who wanted to send all immigrants back to their home countries, naming this strategy "repatriation". He wrote the music for *Babylon*, a feature film[28] which dealt with the same issue. On top of that, he produced and mixed the debut LPs of the female punk trio The Slits

27 12" Factory Records UK 1979.
28 The film premiered in November 1980, the soundtrack was released in the same year on Chrysalis, UK.

(*Cut*) and avant-garde band The Pop Group (*Y*)[29]. It is impossible to list all of Dennis Bovell's projects, commissions, and collaborations. The examples are only intended to indicate the range of how far dub extended its sphere of influence in the UK, and at what levels Bovell was involved everywhere.[30]

After the many indie labels in London, the big record companies, inspired by the recent boom, also discovered dub was lucrative. Punk and reggae were good friends, and the music industry couldn't ignore that. "In the UK, white working-class youths have always gravitated towards black music, with that spirit of rebellion" remarked journalist and music activist Don Letts. Letts came from the Windrush Generation, and was well positioned to describe the spirit of the times[31] that companies such as RCA, CBS, United Artists, Phonogram, Polydor and EMI were taking advantage of. Far away from the reggae and sound system field, not only Dennis Bovell, but also Mad Professor and Adrian Sherwood became active. While Jamaica saw dub as the domain of dancehall, from the late 1970s onwards, London increasingly saw it as an independent event. Dub mixes of pop, punk, avant-garde or jazz music were not made for the dancehall. They aimed for it to work on its own, regardless of the cultural connotation. At the end of the 1970s, this practice laid the foundation for dub to develop into an autonomous, ideology-free, interdisciplinary music genre, defined as a play with effects. Since then, dub has been in constant danger of drifting into regions of new age, minimal or ambient.

In 1979, the London reggae band Revelation released a dub album called *Variation On A Theme*. By choosing the title, the band had unintentionally revealed that, in the UK, the subject of dub was varied, and understood differently in the UK than in its Jamaican home environment. Perhaps Revelation was inspired by the term "variations" in classical and jazz. Here, variations mean compositional adaptations of musical themes with regard to their melodic, rhythmic and harmonic structure. It cannot be assumed that the band's use of the term meant to imply that British pop cultural influences were changing the nature and principle of dub. And yet the album title gave the dub scene in the UK an apt moniker.

29 On YouTube you can also find a live dub of The Pop Group 12" "She Is Beyond Good And Evil" @Rough Trade by Dennis Bovell: https://youtu.be/IkVInVneiCA. In 2021, a 40-year-later mixed dub of the 1979 album: *Y in Dub* was released via Mute.

30 Further examples: From 1984 Bovell was the live engineer for Fela Kuti in Europe, and in the 2010s for Alpha Blondy. In 2015 he produced and mixed a 6-track dub EP for the soul singer Joss Stone (10-inch Stone'd Records UK), in 2019 a 12-inch for the jazz singer Zara McFarlane ("East Of The River Nile", Brownswood Recordings UK).

31 *Duke Vin and the Birth of Ska*. Don Letts often emphasized that he was the one who had brought punk and reggae together. "All this punky reggae thing happened by accident... I was playing at a punk rock club (i.e. The Roxy, opened in 1976), but it was so early back in the days, there weren't any punk records to play. So, I played hardcore dub reggae, and luckily for me because of this tradition of white working-class kids gravitating towards black music, they would bang on it." Letts overestimated his influence. Skinhead reggae was already around long before the Roxy opened. The English working-class youth from which punk had emerged had long been partying to the Jamaican sound.

Variation On A Theme had been mixed by Mark Lusardi, whose list of references included acts such as OMD, Duran Duran, PIL, Killing Joke, Davie Bowie, Howard Jones, and Jah Wooble, to name just a few. Lusardi played on some records himself, sometimes programming, sometimes contributing compositions, which here and there led to copyright disputes, all of which he ultimately won. Lusardi was involved in *Cry Tuff Dub Encounter Chapter 1* and *Clint Eastwood & General Saint – Two Bad D.J.*[32]. His workplaces at Gooseberry and later at his own Mark Angelo studio were popular places for London reggae bands. He was valued for his expertise and support. Lusardi treated reggae like pop music, which

32 Greensleeves UK 1981.

suited the British reggae bands. Unlike in Jamaica, where bands primarily served to accompany artists, their arrangements were – no surprise in this environment – influenced by pop. They were richer in harmony and melody, not as intensely riddim driven but more song oriented. Both Lusardi and Bovell tried to take this into account when recording. "We wanted the thing being solid from the basis, and would make sure that everything was right in tune and in time. I don't think a lot of people paid much attention to that in those days. They kinda like the brand and roughness of it. But the British reggae, we wanted it to be right. We wanted our music that we were doing with these people to be as correct as other music would be, as other genres. So that paid dividends."

With Lusardi it was possible to produce under favourable conditions, whether pure dub LPs or vocal albums, to which dub versions were of course also mixed. Between 1977 and 1980, Lusardi mixed a series of dub LPs that contributed further interpretations to the reception of British dub. They were as follows:

- **Tradition In Dub** BPI UK 1977 (appeared in a neutral cover, was reissued with a cover in 1980 under the name **High Risk Dub** of Venture Records)
- **The Simeons – Dub Conference In London** Freedom Sounds UK 1978
- **Revelation – Variation On A Theme** Burning Vibration UK, distributed by EMI 1979 (Dub of **Revelation – Book Of Revelation** Burning Sounds UK 1979)
- **Creation Rebel – Rebel Vibrations** Hitrun UK 1979
- **Tradition – ... Tell Your Friends About Dub** RCA UK 1980
- **Tradition – Captain Ganja And The Space Patrol** Venture Records UK 1980 (Dub of **Tradition – Alternative Routes** RCA UK 1978)
- **Black Slate – Ogima** TCD UK 1981 (Dub of **Black Slate – Amigo** TCD UK 1980. After exchanging a few songs, the vocal album was repressed by Ensign in the same year and by Mercury outside the UK.)
- **Black Slate – Six Plus One** Top Ranking Records 1982 (A DoLP, 1x Vocal, 1x Dub, distributed outside the UK by CBS and Polydor)

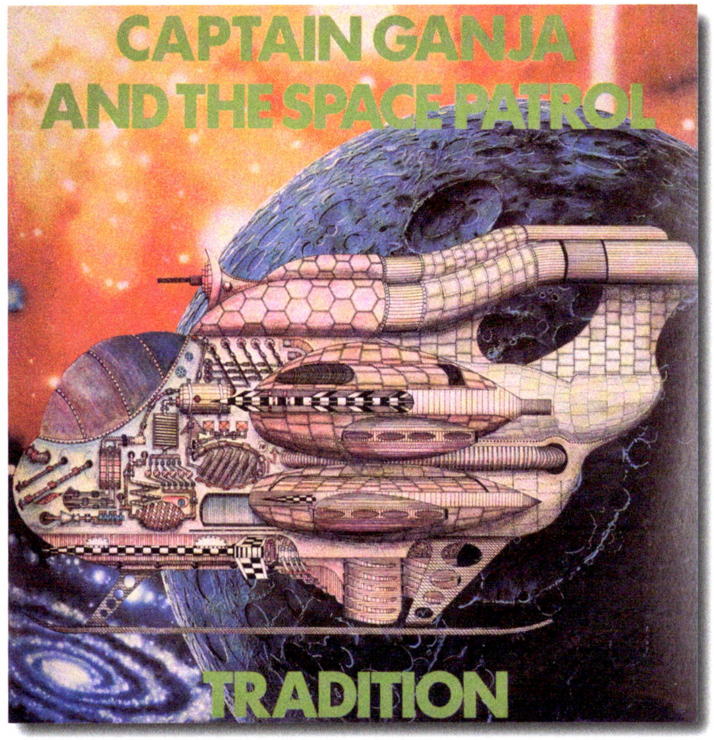

The Simeons[33] were one of the first to dub at Gooseberry. On the cover of their *Dub Conference* they put "this LP was created the way we see dub should be here in London" and described Mark Lusardi as "the hardest white engineer in London". His dub technique was vastly different from the way Jamaican engineers mixed. A lot in Jamaican dub arose from the limited technical possibilities of the time. It made a huge difference whether you had all the drums on a single, bounced track, and the entire offbeat of guitar, piano and organ on a second, or whether the instruments were spread across many tracks. The consoles and tape machines in London were more modern and larger than in Kingston and – because of the aforementioned pop influence – there was more on the tapes. For these reasons, muting individual instruments was more complicated than with four input channels at Tubby, eight at Treasure Isle, or sixteen at Channel One. Only the engineer mixed at the small consoles in Kingston. Lusardi, on the other hand, involved the musicians in the process: "I'd include the band, say when I press this button, press all those, so it turns off the cymbals, the hi-hat, the kick and the snare as this one I'm pressing is turning on delay on a guitar. We used to have to rehearse it. So, one of the tricks I found was to do dubs in sections. Wait for it to go wrong, then start again, wait for that to go wrong, and then edit the best bits together." Due to time constraints in Jamaican studios, it was unimaginable to select and edit the best parts from different mixes. It was taken as it came. Every take was a new dub, even when the result wasn't perfect. Here and there, chance produced the best results. Lusardi also knew the magic of every spoil is a style. "Sometimes, it would be what we call scientivity. It would have been of let going on, you know, make mistakes and some of them sound awesome. What happened there? Don't know, but we keep it."

Lusardi's ciphers consisted of briefly swelling echoes and almost full instrumentation throughout. His dubs were soft, without loud detonations. They floated in the song structure and didn't decimate the instruments down to drum & bass. At Gooseberry, Lusardi laid the foundation for a contemplative ambient reception that contributed to dub's cosmic image, not as conceived in the studios of Kingston, but in the offices of British record companies. After Virgin/Frontline presented *Planet Mars Dub*[34] in 1978, Lusardi mixed the dubby space trip *Captain Ganja And The Space Patrol* from the band Tradition's RCA album *Alternative Routes*, a year and a half before Greensleeves released the Scientist album *Space Invaders*. The LP experienced an irrationally excessive price development until its reissue 36 years later. Lusardi admitted with a laugh that, as a fan of both science and science fiction, he had perhaps unconsciously positioned his mixes between "Space Oddity" and ambient. "I wasn't part of the King Tubby/Scientist group of people. I probably was influenced by what I heard coming out of different radios and record shops, but without really thinking about it. Sometimes I was off my face, sometimes the music just sparks something in you. I don't know why I did what I did. Everybody was bringing in tons of spliffs. Some really mad stuff happened. Who knows why, hahaha."

Lusardi's mixes weren't suitable for the dancehall, nor should they have. "Mark never been to a sound system" explained Dennis Bovell, "he had different ideas, more ambient." This interpretation began to spread in UK dub, also followed by others, sometimes to an extreme extent.

In 1982, Adrian Sherwood a-dub-ted the term for the album *The Dub Syndicate – The Pounding System (Ambience In Dub)*. The producer, who was 24 at the time, experienced reggae socialization quite early. Born in

33 The Simeons were brothers Trevor, Ewan, and Paul Robinson and a guitarist. They later recorded two LPs with two other brothers under the name One Blood with Lusardi in the Mark Angelo studio before Paul began a successful solo career as a producer (for Maxi Priest, among others) and singer under the pseudonym Barry Boom.

34 *The Icebreakers with The Mighty Diamonds – Planet Mars Dub* Frontline UK 1978.

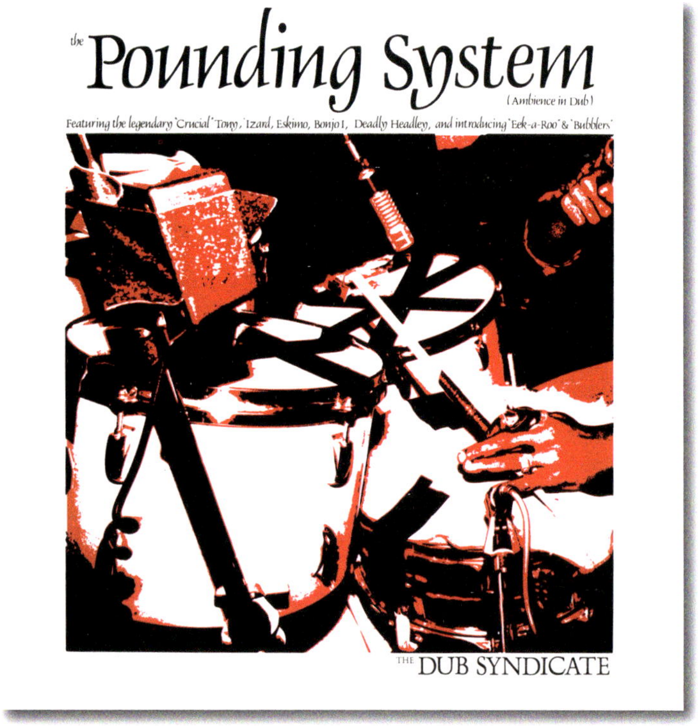

London in 1958, Sherwood grew up west of the capital in the small town of Slough in Buckinghamshire. As a kid he was invited to house parties and blues dances in the neighborhood. When his father died, Jamaican club owner Joe Farquharson took over the role. Sherwood has credited him with having the greatest influence on his life. As a tender 14-year-old, he was allowed to play in the afternoons at his "Newlands Club" in High Wycombe. "As the years moved on, I was getting more and more obsessed with the stuff coming from Jamaica."[35] Sherwood recalled. His surrogate father was well connected in the London reggae scene. Farquharson found the 17-year-old a job at Pama Records, where he encountered Jamaican musicians. At the age of 18, Adrian Sherwood moved to the Grounation label, and with Joe Farquharson founded J&A distribution. They brought the records from Grounation and other labels such as Ethnic Fight, Klik and Trojan to the most remote corners of the country. "The whole scene was driven by record companies and labels" Sherwood explained. "Reggae labels in London putting together a lot of B-sides and dubs because they're realizing a market (is) developing."[36] In a very short time, in addition to imports, and even before Greensleeves or Burning Sounds got involved in the business, the range of dub LPs specially released in London but from Jamaica grew:

- **King Tubby Meets The Upsetter At The Grass Roots Of Dub** Fay Music Inc. 1974
- **Augustus Pablo – Ital Dub** Trojan 1974
- **Leslie Butler – Ja-Gan**[37] Trojan 1975
- **Natty Locks Dub** Fay Music 1975
- **Bag-O-Wire** Klik 1975
- **King Tubby & The Aggrovators – Shalom Dub** Klik 1975
- **Sir Coxson Sound – King Of The Dub Rock** Safari 1975
- **Out Of One Man Comes Many Dubs** Ethnic Fight 1975
- **Music Explosion** Ethnic Fight 197x
- **King Tubby The Dub Master presents The Roots Of Dub** Grounation 1975
- **Tommy McCook – Horny Dub** Grounation 1976
- **Rass Claat Dub** Grounation 1976
- **Rasta Dub '76** Grounation 1976
- **King Tubby – Surrounded By The Dreads At The National Arena** Fay Music Inc. 1976

When Sherwood wasn't traveling, he was hanging out with friends at home. They smoked weed and listened to dub. In 1976, he became involved in the Carib Gems label, which was set up for licensing purposes. In 1978, still only 20, he founded Hit Run. The occasion marked *Dub From Creation,* his first own production, made within three days. John Peel played three songs in a row on his radio show and described the album as "the best dub record ever made in England". The next day, every record shop in town was asking for the LP. "That kinda got me go," Sherwood said "[but] it was tough in those days selling tunes because of

35 *Adrian Sherwood Boiler Room Collection* YouTube 2016.

36 ibid

37 Except for one track identical to *Sylvan Morris – Dub Wise Morris On Dub* Jaywax Jamaica 1975.

the volume of releases. You're competing with amazing records coming from everywhere. So, I decided to make my records sound different to the pack. I didn't want them to sound [like I was] copying a Jamaican record."[38] Hit Run became On-U Sound in 1981. The new label adopted a premise later taken up by people like David Foster Wallace in literature, and Banksy in street art, "disturbing the comfortable and comforting the disturbed". A year later *The Pounding System (Ambience In Dub)* was released, a classic today, a provocation back then. The sleeve notes made fun of the term "ambience" as "a mysterious kind of secret known only to a few". Ambience would simply be the sound of the environment. To prove this, the drums were recorded in the studio toilet and the reverberation from the tiled walls used in the mixes. Sherwood explored the extent to which the dubheads' listening habits could be burdened with radical reverb, echo, and stereo effects. The song titles attacked ("an open piss-take"[39]) Greensleeves' Scientist dubs, which were very successful at the time, and the latter's absurd titles like "Heavyweight Super Vampire Ninjas versus Alien Voodoo Cowboys Androids Chapter III".

Adrian Sherwood, 2011.

In fact, Sherwood was also infected by interplanetary space dub. As a follow-up to *Dub From Creation,* in 1978, he recorded the *Starship Africa* LP with Creation Rebel. It was released in 1980 on 4D Rhythm, another of his early labels, and was intended to be the soundtrack of a film by Don Letts about "alien dreads from beyond the stars", which was never made. In the meantime, before the release of *Starship Africa,* Creation Rebel recorded the *Rebel Vibrations* LP for Sherwood's Hit Run label, but without his active involvement. Now integrated into the On-U catalogue, the album, including the Lusardi mix, was described as "exploring the unique possibilities of space in sound within the disciplined structures of rhythm."[40] Space was the place, also for Adrian Sherwood.[41]

When *Pounding System* was released, no one thought that Dub Syndicate would ultimately release around 20 albums because they were less a band than a project with changing musicians. Although it was his hands and drum set on the cover photo, Roots Radics drummer Style Scott wasn't on the first album, not yet. He only joined afterwards, subsequently becoming the face of Dub Syndicate. With him as the groove guarantor, Sherwood converted the open-air climate of Jamaican dub into a hyper-technoid metropolitan sound that became characteristic of his label. Already on *Tunes From The Missing Channel* (1985), the band's second On-U album[42], repetitive sound samples appeared, the effects became more brutal, the staging more industrial.

Scott explained the difference to Jamaican dubs thus "we composed dub music. Our dubs were originals, not a version of anything. It was

38 *Adrian Sherwood Boiler Room Collection* YouTube 2016.
39 Steve Barker, host of the BBC program "On The Wire", in the liner notes for the 1998 CD release.

40 On-U Sound online store https://store.on-usound.com/release/61047-creation-rebel-rebel-vibrations (last accessed on March 15, 2022).
41 *Space Is The Place* was the title of a 1974 Afrofuturist science fiction film starring Sun Ra.
42 Before that, there were two productions that couldn't be more different. On the one hand, *One Way System*, an album that was only released on the US cassette label ROIR, and had its vinyl premiere in the On-U catalogue of 2017, which combined hard experimental material with effects from the test laboratory, and on the other, *North Of The River Thames* (1984), with melodica player Doctor Pablo (despite the allusion to the *East Of The River Nile* LP, not to be confused with the Jamaican Augustus

something that we intentionally went in the studio and made it like that." Sherwood described the process as "music designed as a work of dub from the beginning. We started making riddims and then adding different colouring and samples and things like that. It was a whole different way of working [than in Jamaica]."[43] Samples became an important factor. They helped Sherwood prepare his dub for a non-reggae audience.[44] He integrated songs from the British soccer stadiums (*Barmy Army* 1989), and melodies by the Indian sitar master Ravi Shankar, revered since his participation in George Harrison's "Concert For Bangladesh" (*Research And Development* 1996). He combined poems by Doors frontman Jim Morrison with Lee Perry (*Stoned Immaculate* 1991). In addition, vocal snippets from songs he recorded with Jamaican artists such as Prince Far I played an important role in connecting the On-U sound to traditional reggae listeners.

Dub Syndicate had the honour of being the first dub band in Europe. Live, they reproduced their sound in real time, with the help of a dubbing engineer at the side of the stage. He sent his effects into the audience as well as onto the stage so that the musicians could react to them. Until his murder in October 2014, drummer Style Scott was in two completely different camps; on the one hand with the Roots Radics in Jamaican dub, but on the other with Dub Syndicate in a neo dub variant[45]in the UK and the rest of the world. Scott would have liked to have performed in Jamaica with his British project, but he knew that Dub Syndicate "have an audience that is enthusiastic about world music and other music than reggae. In Jamaica you are not gonna find an audience like that. Unless somebody know of Dub Syndicate and expound it to the people before, people in Jamaica will say 'an instrumental you play'."

Style Scott became the key figure in the On-U artist portfolio. He not only drummed for Dub Syndicate, but also for Creation Rebel, African Head Charge, Singers & Players and other projects. Sherwood, in turn, mixed everything with everyone, and incorporated his dub aesthetic into the music of crossover acts like Little Axe, Tackhead and Gary Clail. Likewise with the New Age Steppers, the parallel project started in 1981 by the Slits singer Ari Up (1962–2010), who had worked with Dennis Bovell a year earlier.

It was the phase in which the London "punky reggae party" experienced its peak. The Clash collaborated with Lee Perry and Mikey Dread, releasing a 10-inch with dub versions and borrowings from Studio One[46] in 1980. A year earlier, The Members had already come through Virgin with the reggae (maxi) single "Offshore Banking Business", supported by the Cuban-born Jamaican trombonist Rico, with a dubby deejay touch from their singer Nicky Tesco. Favoured by major record company distribution, punk and reggae showed mutual solidarity, so that dub finally lost its status as the exclusive form of resistance by the Windrush generation and their descendants. Neil Fraser, known as "Mad Professor", could not resist this trend, either. In 1982 he worked with The Ruts punk band on an LP for their Bohemian label.[47] A year later, he recorded a punk/reggae/dub crossover album for Ariwa with the trio Anti-Social Workers[48], and had the band sing over the "Declaration Of Rights" riddim.

Neil Fraser was born in the British colony of Guyana in the spring of 1955. Like almost all analogue pioneers across genres from Rupert Neve to King Tubby, he also became involved with radios at a young age. Fraser, however, didn't repair radios but built them, because that enabled him to receive a reggae broadcast from the Virgin Islands on Saturday nights. Every week four hours infected him with reggae, while the rest of the time he listened to his favourite Stax, Motown and Atlantic US soul. His parents emigrated to the UK while still young in the hope of finding work, and when Neil was 13, he followed them. The father, by then a laboratory technician in a London hospital, encouraged his son's interest in electronics, which, combined with his passion for music, led to Fraser beginning to analyze Jamaican records from a studio perspective. He remained untrained, but read and taught himself everything. In the mid-70s, after long since having moved out of his parents' home, he responded to a job advertisement by Soundcraft, a recently established company involved in developing mixing consoles for live operations. He was taken to a room full of broken desks and if he managed to repair them, he would get the job. Two days later, Neil Fraser was given the job at Soundcraft. He stayed for two years, and then decided to build himself a studio. Using discarded Soundcraft components, he assembled a Series 2 console and, in 1979, set up his first studio in his apartment on

Pablo). The naive melodica melodies and the ethereal voice of singer Bim Sherman took the heaviness away from Dub Syndicate's dark material.

43 Quoted from Veal ibid p. 228.

44 See chapter "Lee Perry, Dubstrumentalist", and "30 Jahre On-U Sound" ("30 Years of On-U Sound") in the German reggae print magazine *RIDDIM* 06/2011.

45 Neo dub is not a defined term. It refers to dub-like music produced outside Jamaica. The expression came about in connection with the digital steppers/steppaz dub instrumentals programmed in the UK. Today this includes all dub currents that are designed as a solitary event.

46 *Black Market Clash* Epic UK 1980.

47 At that point, the band was already called Ruts DC. The LP *Ruts DC Present Rhythm Collision Vol. 1* was later licensed by ROIR and Echo Beach, among others.

48 *Anti-Social Workers – Punky Reggae Party. Positive Style* Ariwa 1983.

Bruce Road in the London suburb of Thornton Heath. The studio featured a TEAC 3440 ~~¼~~ quarter-inch 4-track tape machine, a self-made phaser, a spring reverb and a Revox G36 2-track tape recorder for echoes. In 1981 it was here that Aquizim, a Brixton band, created a cover version of the "Kunta Kinte" dubplate for Ariwa, the newly founded label, including the same signature melody, but a different bass line.[49] He repeatedly picked up this instrumental over the next few years, mostly in a tuned form, which was extremely important for the British scene. The Aquizim version was comparatively thin because the technical equipment of his Thornton Heath studio did not yet capture the frequency volume on tape as well as Channel One with Sly & Robbie had done.

His early customers included Laurel Aitken and Desmond Dekker, but also labels such as Jah Thomas' Midnight Rock or the London sound system "Moa Anbessa International", founded in 1977, which brought in tapes from King Tubby. "Yeah, 4-track masters from Tubby's. They wanted them mixed down to two. They are doing all kinds of crazy shit. Some of it they're taking off versions from one tape and putting it on another. They might have one tape and make three albums out of that tape. And I was the guy [who was supposed to do it]."

Fraser quickly expanded from 4 to 8 to 16 tracks. The aforementioned album with Ruts DC was created with an Ampex MM1000 16-track machine. In May 1982, he relocated from the suburbs closer to the action, moving his studio to a basement on Gautrey Road in Peckham, south London. In the same year, he began experimenting with dub. On the *Dub Me Crazy* LP, he explored pushing sound effects and gimmicks to the limits of pleasing consumability. "One of my influences for *Dub Me Crazy* was the *African Dub* series from Errol Thompson." Fraser admitted. "I just loved the mood, the fun and the whole kind of blackness of those records."

Fraser pressed 1,000 LPs and ended up stuck with them! As with Sherwood, John Peel's enthusiasm enabled the record to reach the public. Peel called Fraser and said he liked the record and would play it on his

49 Aquizim – "Kunta Kinte" Ariwa 10", white label 1981 + LP *Mad Professor – Method To The Madness* Trojan UK 2005.

show, after which everything changed. Headquartered in London, the young European dub community reacted enthusiastically to Peel's ennoblement. The innovative mix adventure aired by the legendary BBC DJ was far away from common dub clichés, and wrote a success story in twelve chapters over the next eleven years. For the *Dub Me Crazy! The Second Chapter. Beyond The Realms Of Dub* artwork, released the same year, comic artist Tony McDermott hung Mad Professor upside down Baselitz style, a symbolic allusion to the fact that the crazy engineer liked to turn listening habits on their head.

Mad Professor stormed through the mixes of the *Dub Me Crazy* series like a boundary-breaking system crasher. As no other engineer in the UK, he stuck to the Jamaican version principle in his mixes, but at the same time, with his bizarre sound design, went the furthest away from it. His effects were excessively loud, harsh, and brittle, cutting through with the aesthetics of an egg slicer. Arising from extremely short echo times, with flanging rock'n'roll-like slapping, the bass modulated and disappeared into deep caverns. These new sounds were only possible because, like the Roland SDE-2000, the first digital echo devices had come onto the market, enabling repetitions to be set with millisecond precision.[50] But Fraser could also do it in the traditional way. His counterpart to Lacksley Castell's *Princess Lady* LP was entitled *Dub Rockers Volume 2. Negus Roots Meets The Mad Professor*[51], and was created at the same time as the first *Dub Me Crazy* albums, in the classic Jamaican style, although the crazy gimmicks were in evidence here, too.

From 1984 on, Neil Fraser produced using 24 tracks. In the same year, his long-term collaboration with Lee Perry began, initially with Sid Bucknor at the desk. By 2021, Ariwa had released a total of 18 LPs with Perry. In 1986 the studio was broken into, causing Fraser to move for the third and final time. He ended up on Whitehorse Lane in South Norwood, where, ten years later, he returned to his roots. He established a second studio named "Are We Mad", using the old equipment from 1979, including the desk he had self-built, but modified for its new purpose. The recollection arose from his relationship to analogue. "I don't think you can program dub. Real dub's gotta be spontaneous. There's a vibe that develops when you're working, and there's something deeper than that. You got elements that exist with analogue which doesn't exist in digital. The feedback. With analogue you could use feedback creatively. I personally suspect there is a deeper reason why digital doesn't work. I suspect all the digital/analogue chips." So, is dub an analogue form of music? "Definitely, it's gotta be! There was no digital when it was made, or when the best dubs were created."

After the end of the *Dub Me Crazy* series, Fraser, who has occasionally posted quotations on social media by his compatriot Walter Rodney, had resurrected dub's militant spirit. In the mid-90s, he went on to release a new, five-part series, called *Black Liberation Dub* with the titles and corresponding vocal samples making each track a political statement. Musically, he responded to a trend in British sound systems, where a special beat was becoming increasingly popular. An effective, up-tempo, four-on-the-floor beat with more drive than groove, as every quarter note was emphasized by the bass drum. For the first time two decades earlier dynamically beaten into reggae by drummer Leroy Horsemouth

50 How crucial the Roland SDE-2000 was to his sound became clear when, many years later, he integrated the device into the artwork for the albums *Mad Professor – Riddim and Dub Series 2018 + 2019*.

51 Negus Roots UK 1983, The title *Volume 2* referred to the fact that the Negus Roots LP *Dub Rockers Delight*, mixed with dubs to Lacksley Castell's *Morning Glory*, had been released a year earlier in Jamaica. A third Negus Roots dub LP was later created in the UK: *Sip A Cup meets Negus Roots – Fire House Dub Volume 1*. It was released in 2007 but was probably mixed long before by Gussie P at the Mafia & Fluxy studio.

on Burning Spear's "Red Gold And Green"[52]. This beat is recorded in the annals of reggae as "steppers" and became gospel to sound systems in the UK as "steppaz". Their prophet was Jah Shaka (1950–2023). The Clarendon-born Jamaican came to the UK in 1956, and had been running a sound system since the early 1970s. He also had the "Kunta Kinte" dubplate from Channel One on heavy rotation. Although Shaka was not an engineer, he ordered dub, produced dub[53], and played dub. In doing so, he established himself as one of the most influential people on the British dub scene, without himself even mixing. For the Rastafarian, dub music was "a spiritual resource"[54] where the presence of Jah could be felt in the vibrations of the bass. The bass waves from the sound system's oversized speaker walls meant that music was not only heard, but also physically felt. For Shaka, it was a sacred ritual, fueled by the steppers beat. Marching and vibrating, he played for eight, nine hours or longer, without interruption, without a break, until he and those attending his dances fell into a trance-like state. I have seen Jah Shaka live several times, in the UK, France and Germany; everywhere during prime time he played steppers non-stop. "It was in the 90s that the steppers thing really started to come up, [because] Shaka was always pushing that side of the music hard." confirmed Bredda Neil.

Fraser responded to this development in the *Black Liberation Dub* series with intense steppers arrangements. His mixes had changed. After the drastic excursions of the *Dub Me Crazy* albums, the sphere was now full of echoes. His dubs were now created using ostinato drum'n'bass, and often repeater-supported frameworks, which ran almost untouched, and were only selectively applied with effects. On top of it were piled up orchestral reverb tails, snatches of voice and waves of differently timed echoes, in half, double and triple tempo, in mono, stereo and ping-pong. Fraser took the best of Jamaican dub – the ever-long echoes of King Jammy, the filter operations of King Tubby, the bass shaping of Scientist, the flanger effects and sound cues of Errol Thompson – and using his own ideas, blended it into a consumer-friendly style. This created Mad Professor's unmistakable signature which at the time of writing, has expanded his dub catalog to almost 100 albums. This has made Mad Professor the most productive engineer in the dub arena, and inspired some creative, innovative ideas.

52 A song from the album *Marcus Garvey* Island Records, Mango, Wolf and other labels 1975

53 Jah Shaka produced singles, maxis and more than 20 albums, some of them with biblical allusions. These included *Commandments of Dub Part 1 to 10* and *New Testaments Of Dub* as well as collaborations with Mad Professor such as *Jah Shaka Meets Mad Professor At Ariwa Sounds* 1984 and *New Decade Of Dub* 1996.

54 Christopher Partridge: *DUB in Babylon* ibid p. 126.

In Jamaican folklore, there is a character called Anansi, who has its origins in West African mythology. Anansi is a trickster, half man, half spider, who makes his way through life by playing clever pranks that are told to children as bedtime stories. Every now and then, Fraser slipped into the role of Anansi, for example, when he crawled across the mixing desk like a spider on *Dubbing with Anansi* (2014), but also when using album titles like *The Roots Of Dubstep* (2011) and *Electro Dubclubbing!!*[55] (2018) to promote sales, although, as Mad Anansi openly admitted, these releases had nothing to do with dubstep, club music or electronics. The first two albums were full of tried and tested Jamaican song riddims, like Keith Hudson's "Felt The Strain" or Dennis Brown's "Three Meals A Day" or "Love Me Always", reaching back to Prince Buster's "Swing Low" from *The Message* LP. The third LP was partly based on original tapes, with Studio One edits, made with the Revolutionaries at Channel One around 1980. This included "Ya Ho" by the Viceroys in an interpretation by the

55 There was a sound tour of Mad Professor and Lee Perry in 2017 under the name "Electro Dubclubbing". The LP had nothing to do with it.

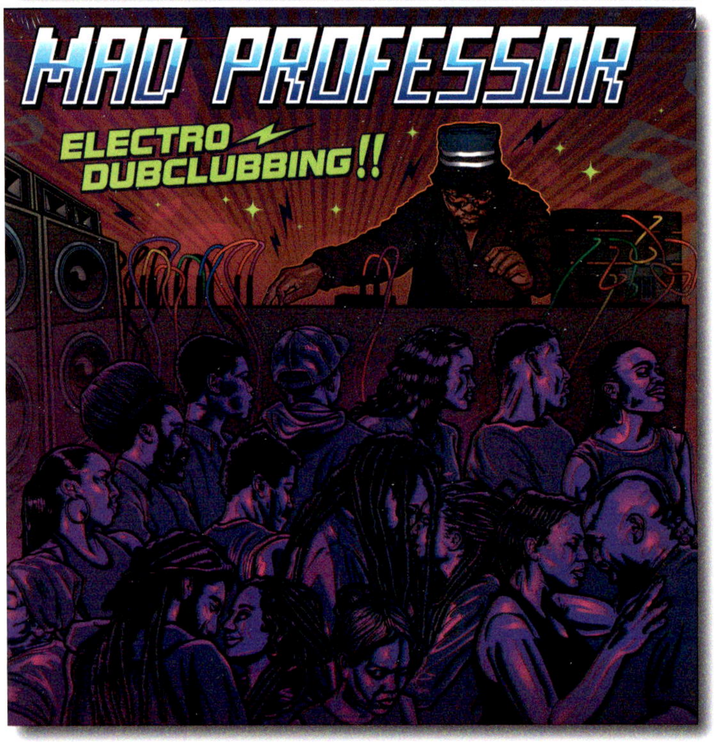

Jays, and the widely covered Heptones riddim "Give Me The Right". All recordings had already been dubbed in Kingston at the time they were made. Fraser's versions, mixed decades later, made *Electro Dubclubbing!!* one of the most appealing dub albums of his entire oeuvre. They showed how different dub from the British pop environment sounded, compared to its rough Jamaican origins.

Mad Professor's most successful coup came in 1995 at the peak of the trip hop hype. He remixed the second Massive Attack album *Protection*[56] and achieved worldwide attention, driving sales into the seven-figure range. *Massive Attack v Mad Professor – No Protection*[57] became by far the best-selling dub album of all time, although the backing tracks were close to ambient and 100% free of reggae. This in turn contributed significantly to dub becoming a cross-genre event. "Over a million people heard dub for the first time, [because] technically it is a dub album with versions." Fraser emphasized the significance of the album. "That's a lot of people. I mean I run a label, and the nearest thing that comes to that is probably about a hundred thousand."

56 Wild Bunch Records UK 1994.
57 Wild Bunch Records UK 1995.

Style Scott: Drumming the Dub

> "The point I'm trying to make here is, the dub can only be dub through real instruments and analogue recording."
>
> (Style Scott 2012)

Lincoln Valentine Scott, nicknamed "Style", (April 29, 1956 – October 9, 2014) was a commuter, travelling between two dub worlds. When he sat at the drums, dub had its beat, both in Jamaica with the Roots Radics, where dub should be nothing other than a dancehall version, and also outside his homeland with Dub Syndicate, as the head of an expedition in search of the psychedelic depth inherent in dub. When we met in Kingston, we wanted to discuss whether this was a contradiction. For several hours we sat under an old mango tree in Chinna Smith's yard, and pondered the nature of dub. Nyabinghi rhythms echoed from the veranda, played by the Inna De Yard drummers. Infused with this vibe, a lively and intense exchange unfolded, with Style Scott frequently weaving his life journey into our conversation. Style spoke of the boy who discovered the fascination of drumming at Junkanoo parades, who learned to play the drums in the jazz clubs of Montego Bay, and who was trained for tightness and groove in the army until he finally became dub's metronome.

Our dialogue took place in the spring of 2012; two years later, Lincoln Valentine Scoot was dead, the victim of violence that remains unsolved to this day. His personal look back provides insights into the atmosphere and circumstances under which dub emerged in Jamaica at the height of the Roots Radics, and how Dub Syndicate came into being in the UK. Style tells the story in his own words, after all, he was the drummer in both bands.[1]

> I grew up with my grandfather, he was a very rough guy. He went to the Royal Air Force in England and came back to Jamaica. I think these are some of the people who gave service to the Queen and when they came back, they get lots of land. So, my grandfather got land in Clarendon and that's where I grew up. I went to a secondary school first, and then I moved up to Clarendon College after the graduation. I didn't spend long there either, about two years. Cause there was a problem with the family that I was growing up with and I wanted to leave to where my father was, he was in St. Ann's. While I was a youth, I usually used my khaki pants and shirt and made drums with clay dirt, when I was a kid, I usually do all of that. There were people back in the area who remembered that. Even when I go back at age 50 one of my friends say "Bwoy, a music you play? You know, when you was a youth you were more inclined to play drums" and I say "I can't believe it, how you know that?". He says "When you was a youth you usually made drums with cheese pans". And I say "True man, I usually used my khakis when it's old, made drums, stayed at the yard and play it".
>
> By then we had a thing in our district, it was more like a carry-over sort of, I don't know if I should use the word ritual or whatever.

Style Scott, 2012 during the interview in Earl Chinna Smith's garden in Kingston.

1 Without the statements that are quoted elsewhere in the book.

They called it merry-go-round and they usually have some people that put on some things, and their head looks like the head of a horse. We called it Junkanoo. In these days every little parish got their little Junkanoo, and they usually have a man playing the drum. The drum was made from goatskin and something else. I saw a lot of those things and I love it. And that is how me start make my own drum with my khaki pants until I grew out of that. But then my grandfather he taught me and my sister to play a Hawaiian guitar. Every evening we come from school it was a lesson that we had to do before we go to bed. He taught us a song called "Boers, Why Do You Mourn?" Let me tell you something. Way down in my life I get to understand, I realize what that man try to say to me. Boers is the South African settlers, it's the story of the South Africans, the argument about the Boer War in South Africa. He was teaching us this thing, on the guitar he was teaching us that. And it never ring a bell to me as a youth, I don't know what the hell was happening then but he was teaching us this song. I remember every time we come from school, me and my sister, it was a lesson we had to learn that. Then I left at 18. I fell out with my grandparents and I wanted to be at my dad's. I graduated out of school at 16, went to Clarendon College two years, and then I leave from Clarendon and my father picked me up and take me from them and took me to St. Ann's with him. So, I lived in my father's house in Brown's Town/St. Ann's, my father was working in the bauxite industry in Discovery Bay. But I still wasn't satisfied, I moved on from there. Cause for a young boy growing up, that place was dead. There wasn't anything happening there. So, I left my father's portfolio and moved on to Montego Bay.

I went there and got involved in the tourist industry. I usually worked in hotels as a waiter, so I got to see lots of bands, lots

of musicians who played in the hotels and meet a lot of people. Back then I was just starting to play drums. There was a club in Montego Bay called Boys' Club, which was down in Barnett Street. When I say Boys' Club, I mean a club where young youths they have instruments, they have all sorts of things, workshops where you could learn something. There was a lot of drums there because they have a marching band as well. All of these drums was to my disposal where I could always pick up a drumstick and learn. So, while I was doing hotel works, I usually go down to Boys' Club and meet up with a man who was training the guys and teaching them how to play drums.

Montego Bay was a hot city then. When I say hot, nice city with lots of things happening down there, lots of clubs, lots of things happening through tourism. I met Scully, who was a Congo drum player, and a wicked guitarist out of Jamaica, we call him Frater, and a drummer called Morgan. These guys were playing in a club right opposite the airport in Montego Bay on a beach, they call it Sunset Beach. The hotel I was working at was called Bay Rock. After me come from my work at Bay Rock Hotel, the first place me gone down to the beach and listen to the band play. These days I was a youth, about 18 years old and I'd do it for years until they left. After the tourism thing got a bit dodgy. There was problems in Jamaica in the 80s and the tourism industry dropped, we got laid off in the hotel. So, I started taking off another opportunity and said "Yes, I have to survive", and I joined the army. I joined the military in Montego Bay because they have a base down there called The Delta, Delta Force or whatever, so I joined down there as a reserve. I could go to the army and when there was a little job to do in the hotel, I could still get some work on the side. I could do both. Until one time I noticed the hotel still looked like it will get down, not better, so I just decided I'm gonna do full time in the army, and joined up full time. By then in the evenings, I still usually go to the clubs where the bands are. There was a club in Montego Bay called the Banana Boat Club, very popular club back then, and I usually go there and met up with a drummer called Wade Hampton, Monkey Man. Wicked drummer, a Jamaican guy, lived in Montego Bay. I mean, baaaad

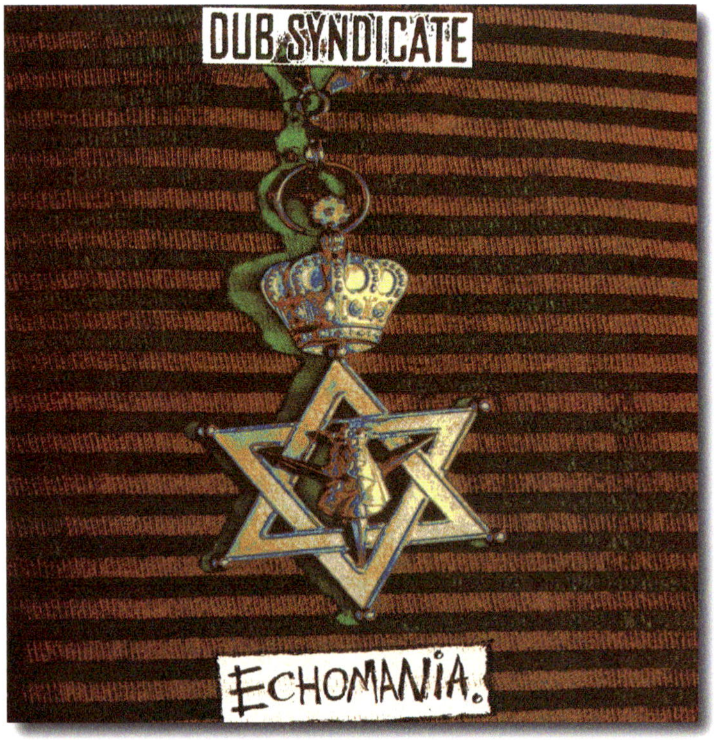

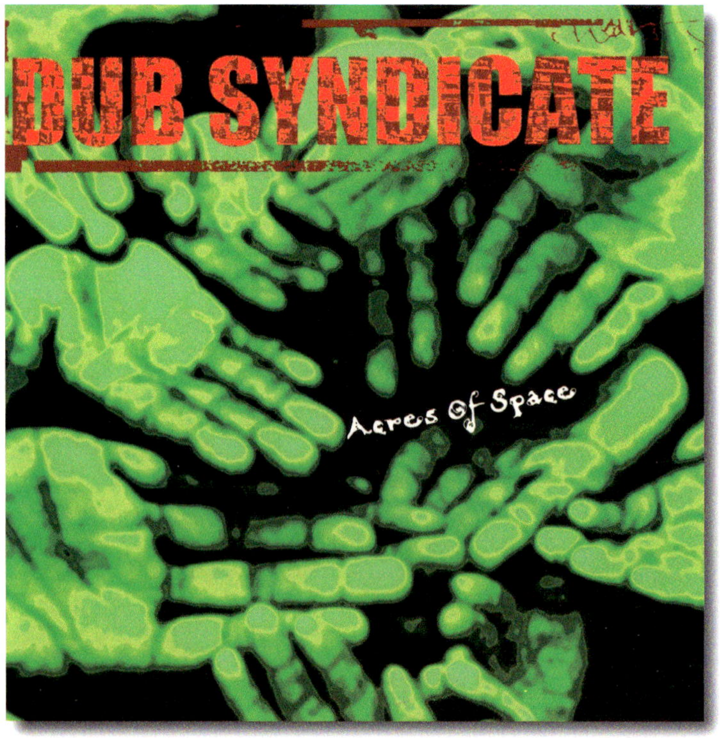

drummer. I can't forget, this guy took me and say "Look, I see you love music and I'll teach you to play the drum. You gonna have to play it." So, I usually go to that guy's yard every evening and take lessons while he rehearsed. And he played by himself. I was there with him for a couple of years and learned a lot from him.

I learned and learned what I could learn till something went on in the army and they transferred me to Kingston. So, I left Monkey Man. In Kingston they saw I was more inclined to music although I was doing infantry work like doing guards and all of them things, they go out with the regular annual camping and all of that. They said they're gonna transfer me to drums in the army, which was like the military band, and I went inside there and started playing a lot of things. They had a little band there as well, with a good drum set, and there was a drummer, his name was Plummer, who controlled the drums in the band. I usually go inside of the band room every evening and play the drum, and Plummer never liked it. The drum major never liked it, but then they know me and say "No man, that youth is bad, I want to hear him play". And I started to play the drum till one day there was a military band down at the police academy. And there was a man called Manners down there with the band. He came to the camp and asked me to come down to his place because he had a little band and he wanted me to play. By then he had a drummer called Kojak, the baldhead. He was a good drummer but for some reason, when I go down there and play, although Kojak was a good drummer, Mr. Manners usually heard something in me. I don't know what he heard but he always wanted me to play. So, I go down there and play. That man was the first man who gave me a chance to record in a studio. With that police academy band. It was a reggae band, and it was a reggae song we recorded. That man who was the band leader wanted us to go down to Studio One to record the song. He hired the studio and that was the first time I got a chance to go to Studio One to record a song. I don't know what that man did with that record, if this was ever released.

Later I go back to Studio One when things start getting good with me, when I started recording professionally now. That is when I start leaving the army and meet Flabba, and we'd build a group called Roots Rock. Me and him play from day one. Me and Flabba, and Bingy Bunny, yeah man. That was way down in the 70s, bout '77. When reggae got popular in Jamaica. Me and Flabba, we recorded and played as Roots Rock band, we usually go up to Pluto Shervington studio in New Kingston. The studio never had a name. We just go up there and record. One of the first tracks I recorded up there was a track with Sugar Minott called "Hard Time Pressure". Up in that studio with Flabba them. It was the first tune that came out and was popular. The second hard, tough track that I recorded was "Just Like A Sea", David Isaacs (1978), we made the number one. That's how we started. These days we never named Roots Radics; Roots Rock was the name.

When we started with Gregory Isaacs, we were named Roots Radics. Gregory had African Museum (his record store) down at Chancery Lane and he listened to us and heard us play and said the band is bad. Gregory love us and said "That's the band I want to have as my band to go on tour". That's how we started hooking up with Gregory. We did the album called "Night Nurse" with Gregory (1982). When we do "Night Nurse", it was one of the biggest albums that came out that year. Chris Blackwell had to say yes, and sign Gregory right there. Then we started touring with Gregory. Those days we had Don Taylor who was the manager for Bob Marley. He was our manager then, working with Gregory Isaacs and Radics.

By then we would also record for other people, 'cause we were a recording session band now. We were recording for many other different producers like Junjo Laws, Volcano label, and for Techniques, which was Winston Riley. We were recording for Jah Thomas, Linval Thompson, Jah Screw. Most of that stuff was recorded at Channel One. Back in the days when Channel One came along as a recording studio in Maxfield Avenue, they came with a totally different sound. We were working from morning till the evening, all night we were in the studio, sometimes 24

hours a day. And the artists, they were good, they were talented youths, no guess and spell, they had lyrics, they had songs. We, Radics, control the whole dancehall recording in Jamaica. Nobody can dispute that. And the whole dub sound, we controlled that. Scientist, the mixer, wow! He came the hard way! When we recorded at Channel One, the little youth is large, you know. He made some sounds with snare drums, bad! Trust me, that run dancehall. The music, everything the Radics did from that era, that is what's running dancehall to this day now. Because every artist that you see out there take one of the Junjo riddims or Linval Thompson. Some were Studio One tunes before, yeah. But if you notice how me and Flabba play them, we play them totally different. The basslines are the same, but Flabba turned it some way, yeah man.

Israel Vibration, I played all of those albums. We were touring and recording with Israel Vibration and what happened, the Israel Vibration had an internal problem with themselves, the three of them. I think it was somewhere in the 80s (1983), we were on tour and the tour got as far as Philadelphia. I can remember we all was in this hotel room and things start fall to bits and it get very ugly. The tour was stopped there. And I say "Well, alright then, what's gonna happen? Are we gonna go back to Jamaica to sit on our ass not doing anything and waiting for another set of artists?" By then I say "Nothing is gonna be happening between now and the next six months, so I'm gonna go to England and hang out with Adrian up there."

I had met Adrian Sherwood in England couple years back through Prince Far I. He took me to England with him as a drummer. Before me there were The Arabs with Fish Clarke and Flabba, but they had fallen apart and that is how Prince Far I called me into the picture and said he want Style to go to England from Jamaica here. Cause he couldn't take the whole band he just took Style. While going up there with Prince Far I, I build a group called Creation Rebel, that comes out of me, we built that. We picked up little youths from a youth center in Harlesden (Northwest London). All these kids where carried-over Jamaicans, everything that came out of Jamaica they'd hear it and they'd love it. And when me as a drummer went there, they said "Whoa, Style Scott from Radics! Stylo yuh hype so!" Every youth came around me, some of them wanted to carry the drums, so that is how I get to build that little unit called Creation Rebel, which we could use to tour with Prince Far I. Creation Rebel was a pure English band. I'm the only Jamaican in it.

I worked with Far I a couple of years, going on tour with him and that is how I met up with Adrian. I didn't even realize that Adrian was an engineer. We were just going around in England, driving from town to town, Birmingham, Manchester, selling Prince Far I records in a little van and other products as well. I was like "Wow, that's all the work?" and all of a sudden Adrian start go to Europe with us because we usually go to Holland. I remember we had a promoter over there. He promoted a lot of shows in Holland, that is why I get to go to Groningen and some of these names. When I came back to Jamaica my friends called me "Rotterdam".

Dub Syndicate started as Creation Rebel from deh so. Because we were just recording back then and sometime we go to the Manor in up London, Richard Branson's studio, and just record tracks. Until I start bringing some wicked tracks from Jamaica. Back in the past in Jamaica, as Radics, when we go to the studios recording for any producers, we usually have our multitrack tape and sometimes we'd ask for an hour to record tracks for ourselves. But we didn't charge them. What I'm trying to say, I had many riddim tracks that I built. So, when I go to England, I took them with me.

Adrian was afraid to release vocal songs from Jamaica because back then in England what was happening, reggae was getting popular. You had record companies like Virgin, Frontline, you had Island Records, Trojan, Greensleeves, you name them, you had a lot of companies. Many singers in Jamaica who record for producers got a chance to go to England. And when they go there, they heard different things, they saw different things and they said "Whoa, wait a minute!" They went into some of these distributors and get rude with the distributors, some of them were like threatening and some were like attacks. Everybody in England started getting afraid and insecure from the artists out of Jamaica, they said "We don't want to be dealing with no artists". And then Adrian who knows the business and who is selling some of these records too, say "Look Style, I don't think I want to release any vocal tracks from Jamaica because I don't want people to be kicking my door in for royalties".

The name Dub Syndicate came out of me and Adrian, both of us came up with it. What really happened, Adrian came up with the name, he wanted to have another name for dub. Because we were just a syndicate of guys in the studio that go around, and there was a band in Jamaica called Soul Syndicate which had Santa and all the men. We were thinking at that time we should be using that name Syndicate, so we could say Dub Syndicate because syndicate is not a long word really, nobody could own it. It's more like a colloquial word, right? And it brings the concept of the group to the point, it was hitting the nail on top of it.

One day we got up, me and Adrian, and we said "Look, let's start record seriously now, I'm gonna be the artist". So, we started *Secret Laboratory*, all of these are my tracks. The whole riddim tracks, every one of those tracks. These were tracks that I brought from Jamaica, that was meant to be Dub Syndicate now, but I recorded with Radics. Some of them, we had Akabu,

Style Scott and the author at the gate to Chinna's yard in Kingston 2012.

the female group, doing vocals and it moved on from there until we had Lee Perry coming in. Lee Perry wanted to do an album and there wasn't any. He heard my tracks and said "Jesus, Style, them tracks me want!". And Adrian gave him the tracks and he got his album, got his deal with Island Records and got his money and bla bla bla. I didn't feel any way because those people are teachers to me, I respect Lee Perry a lot and I was glad a man like him go on top of my riddim. So, it was a joy. There was another album that he did called *Time Boom X De Devil Dead* (1987). All of those tracks was my tracks again.

At that time Dub Syndicate already existed. It was a bass player from England, which was a carry-over from Creation Rebel, and we used Bubbler in England on keyboards and Tony from Ruff Cut on guitar. I can remember we did a tour for Island Records with Don Cherry, the American trumpet player, great musician. He was living in Stockholm, Sweden and he had a daughter called Neneh Cherry. So, the same time on that tour Neneh Cherry came with us and her father was on the same tour, about 1981 or '82.

Maybe I could say the Creation Rebel vibe never washed out as yet, it never finished yet. Because we had those people coming along with us. We had this guy Prince Hammer, Adrian liked him. He was a deejay and I brought him from Jamaica along with Bim Sherman. We toured with Prince Hammer; he was deejaying with us as we were playing Dub Syndicate tracks. What makes Dub Syndicate is the spoken words and the faces we put on our albums without singers. That is what Dub Syndicate is, the real Dub Syndicate now. Without Prince Hammer, without Bim Sherman, without... you understand? With Prince Far I, we do some of his spoken words as well, on top of Dub Syndicate.

Adrian had tapes with lots of spoken words. He got serious then again and say "We're not gonna put out any vocals from Jamaica because I don't want the problems, we use samples and spoken words." By putting out tracks with just delays and white noise and distortion it sounds like an instrumental, so that is when Adrian and I said "alright, we put faces to those tracks". That is how the spoken words come in with Lee Perry and Jim Morrison (from The Doors) and many other people. Our dubs were originals, it's not a version of anything. It was something that we intentionally went in the studio and made it like that, and composed dub music. It's really un-Jamaican and that was Adrian Sherwood then. Up till then everything was just a version or a skeleton of a riddim that King Tubbys emphasize on the drum and bass, which me and Adrian do the same thing but we do it more technical, there was a technical approach to it than the King Tubbys thing. That is where a lot of the interest start grow for this music. Because we go as far as putting people like Talvin Singh from India, (who) plays tablas. And on some of our records we used a sample from Ravi Shankar which was a great sitar player from India as well.

I can't recall the track but there's one track that we do with a sitar sample on it. Even when Bubbler played it back, he captured it exactly like that, programmed it and made sure it came out like that. When we go on stage and reproduce it, people are like "what?", and then we have Alon Adiri, from Israel. Alon becomes the mixer on stage. We mix on stage and give it to the house. Alon is on stage mixing my drums, I can hear it back while I'm playing. Every tour we do, that's how we do it. It makes you react more to the music when you hear those effects coming through your monitor. It's wicked. It's not like when you play and you're hearing raw sound, but a mix is going to the house.

I can say my band was one of the premier dub bands in Europe, every other dub band, they are following what me and Adrian was doing years ago. When we go on stage and play as Dub Syndicate you hear real dub, ca' the drum and bass they a roll and Alon is there with his white noise and his effects. Adrian looked at me the other day and said "Scotty, you gotta go on doing Dub Syndicate, you are the only band in the world that does things like that, there is no other person that is doing it the way you do."

On October 8, 2014, Style Scott met Flabba Holt in Kingston; they were the last living members of the Roots Radics. Three months earlier, guitarist Noel "Sowell" Bailey (1953–2014) had died, rhythm guitarist Eric "Bingy Bunny" Lamont (1955–1993) and keyboardist Wycliffe "Steely" Johnson (1962–2009) had both already passed away. Flabba said goodbye and added "Rotterdam, yuh a go country, tek care a yuhself 'cause only mi an' yuh lef'."[2] The next morning Style "Rotterdam" Scott was found dead at his home in Mandeville. He was only 58 years old.

2 Quoted from the Jamaica Observer obituary of October 16, 2014 "A drummer with style".

Unknown Sound System, Kingston ca. 2000.

Tippy I Grade and the author in front of
Kunterbunt Sound System, Germany 2024.

Dubbin' in America: Roots, Rock & Artificial Intelligence

"The detour of having a song first and then reducing it cannot be avoided by immediately building what would ultimately be the dub."

(Mark Ernestus)

Early on, it was evident that the reception of reggae in the US was incomparable to the Windrush-influenced scenario in the UK. When Bob Marley was performing in Santa Barbara on November 25, 1979 with a 12-piece big band[1] at the open-air bowl, the camera's view into the audience[2] showcased the difference. Attempts had been made to counteract this impression with seven early concerts at the Apollo Theater in Harlem, but it was clear that, in the States, reggae in general and Marley's music in particular, were attracting a predominantly white audience. Reggae in the US was a concert phenomenon. Apart from Jamaican communities and internationally active New York sounds like "Downbeat The Ruler", "King Addies" and "LP International", the sound system landscape, however, remained for decades a largely barren desert. This was not to change until the new millennium, and finally manifested itself in 2024, at a location two and a half hours' drive from New York, with the launch of the three-day Soundscape Fest, "the first US-based outdoor music festival dedicated entirely to sound system culture"[3].

Musician, producer and dub engineer Victor Rice lived in the Big Apple from 1985 to 2002 and confirmed the impression in 2023. "There is no sound system culture in New York, [just because of] the regulations for being able to play, to set up a sound system. You need a place where you won't get arrested for playing reggae in the open air. You may not even get to drop the needle by the time the cops are there."

Years earlier, Lloyd Barnes had also had similar experiences. As Kingston Joe, the Jamaican had sung some tunes for Prince Buster before emigrating to the US at the age of 23. In 1967 he landed in Harlem, settled in the Bronx, built a sound system and "would ride [the subways and] transit to play"[4]. Remembering the posse he hung out with in Kingston, he called the sound "Bull Wackie's Disco". "I used to be a 'Bull Wackie' boy. The name 'Wacky' really comes from 'Cocky'. It was like saying 'Cocky Boys'. The name just stick."[5] Six years later, increasing violence and bullets in the speaker boxes put an end to the sound adventure; instead, a studio with modest means was installed in a damp basement on 211th Street. The first productions used riddims and tunes by Lee Perry, which Barnes edited with overdubs to make them ready for release. The first highlight of this kind was the Heptones with their song

1 Actually, there should have been 13 musicians on stage, including the horn section and two percussionists, but Marcia Griffiths was missing that day

2 *Bob Marley – The Legend Live Santa Barbara County Bowl 1979* Trojan 1980.

3 Newsletter https://www.soundscapefest.com/.

4 Lloyd 'Bullwackie' Barnes interview, Reggae-vibes.com.

5 ibid

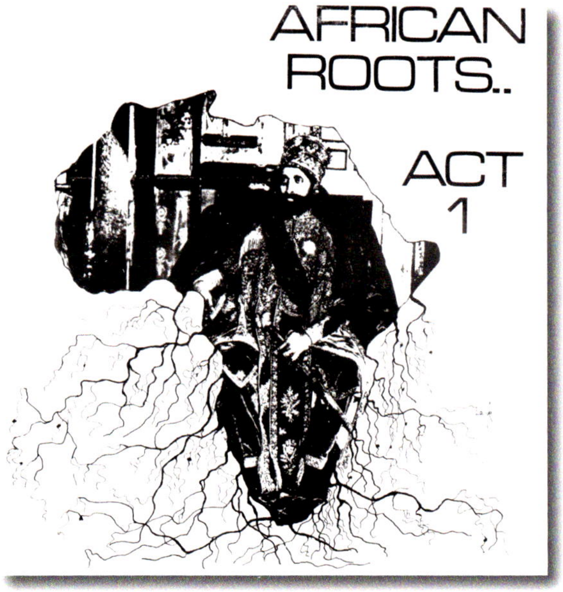

"Revolution" in 1974. In 1976, Barnes moved to 4731 White Plains Road and expanded the studio to eight tracks.[6] In a cramped 40 sqm, including a drum booth, over the following years nearly 80 albums[7], in addition to singles and maxi-singles, were produced. Among them were the brilliant showcase masterpieces *Wayne Jarrett – Bubble Up*[8] and *Horace Andy – Dance Hall Style*, both from 1982, as well as around 15 dub LPs

- **Free for All Aires 1975**
- **Dub Unlimited** Wackie's 1976
- **Reckless Roots Rockers** Rawse 1976
- **Tribesman Assault** Wackie's 1977
- **African Roots Act 1, 2 + 3** Wackie's 1977 – 1983
- **Black World Dub** Hardwax 1979
- **African Roots Act IV + V** Wackie's 198X
- **Prince Douglas – Dub Roots** Wackie's 1980
- **Natures Dub** Wackie's 1980
- **Jamaica Super Dub Session** Wackie's 1983
- **Creation Dub** City Line 1977
- **Creation Dub** Wackie's 1985 (same title but different artwork, different tunes)
- **The Dub Generals** Wackie's (no dub but flute instrumentals by Azul)

6 At the end of the 1980s, the building on White Plains Road was sold. The studio moved to Inglewood, New Jersey, was expanded to 16 tracks and focused primarily on digital productions and services such as mastering.
7 Plus CD editions and compilations.
8 Was entitled *Showcase Vol. 1* in the first pressing.

Multi-instrumentalist Clive Hunt, who lived in New York during those years, became the musical mastermind at Bullwackie's studios, producing his own songs for the label under the pseudonym Azul. Clocktower's Brad Osbourne, Bunny Lee and Lee Perry recorded overdubs here for their US releases. Wackie's became a meeting place for prominent visitors from Jamaica such as Sugar Minott, Johnny Osbourne, Keith Hudson and Ken Boothe, as well as for no-names from the local immigrant community. "We could have been recording a lot of top name artists," said Barnes, "but I don't think it's always the best to ride the wagon. I feel better if it's a talent that was based around us and we keep trying to do it work."[9]

Barnes' productions are often compared to the sound of Lee Perry, but the comparison is flawed. If anything, it is the rhythmic structure and not the sound that evoked similarities to the Black Ark. Perry's sound was created via phasers and space echoes, but the magic of Wackie's sound was low-fi perfection due to the basic level of the technical equipment. In addition, Perry had the better musicians, while Barnes' drums were kept simple, and the brass often sailed on the edges of tonality. His sound was permeated with influences from the urban underground in the neighbourhood of Funkadelic or Parliament, reflected in his use of synthesizers and guitars. But the decisive factor for the Wackie's sound

9 *Bullwackie In New York, White Plains Road* VHS 1984.

was the singing, whose spiritual depth gave the songs their special aura. Since the dubs did not include vocals, the Wackie's dubs oscillated between spartan aesthetics and ingenious minimalism, which 20 years later made them international bestsellers. At the time of their first release, Wackie's singles, maxis and LPs were released in maximum print runs of between 500 and 1,000 copies. Due to the lack of proper distribution, the records were not sold in large margins but rather piece by piece. Reggae shops from Japan or Europe had to order directly from the label and hope for delivery.

Towards the end of the 1990s, Barnes agreed on an exclusive reissue deal with the Berlin-based label Basic Channel, after which maxis and LPs from his back catalogue were re-released on vinyl and CD with the original artwork and remastered in top-notch quality, this time with a professional distribution structure paralleled with promotional support. The new releases achieved previously unimagined sales revenues and received a level of media and hype-driven attention that the first pressings had not experienced. Wackie's became iconic. Because the sound was now coming from a city where "techno had big balls," was how Mark Ernestus explained the sudden interest. Ernestus was a DJ and one of the two label owners who took Wackie's into a different environment. As part of the Berlin scene, he produced minimal techno and dub music himself. "Techno was simply a force, like a revolution." He described the mood in the city at that time. "Because techno works completely differently, and rhythm-based music has been rediscovered. Techno and house prepared people to understand dub and reggae from an understanding of rhythm-based music in a way they hadn't done before. Techno has made us realize that repetitive is not boring, but just the opposite."

Shortly before the minimalistic roots sound from the basements of New York experienced an unexpected revival, thanks to the German initiative, enabling dub to conquer new territory, a collective of American reggae nerds and Jamaican exiles had come together in the US metropolis calling themselves Easy Star Records. Originally, they only wanted to be a label for Jamaican productions, but then they came up with an idea that could only work for the target group described at the beginning, while elsewhere people turned up their noses. The label owners formed an in-house band, called them Easy Star All-Stars, and began to recreate album classics from European rock and pop history in a reggae format. At the beginning it was purely a fun project; commercial profit was not planned. The Easy Star All-Stars just wanted to experience what would happen when they took on Pink Floyd's *Dark Side Of The Moon*. They covered the album one-to-one as reggae and called it *Dub Side Of The Moon*. The reggae copy played with reverb and echo gimmicks that seemed to justify the word "dub" in the title and replaced the famous ringing of the cash register on "Money" with the bubbling draw from a steam pipe. Bassist Victor Rice, who was involved in the project, still remembers it exactly: "Nobody was asking them to do it. It was a pet project that they just wanted to do because they wanted to hear it. They took their time, did it nice, experimented... It was not like: 'Oh, this is going to be a money maker.' They weren't testing a market; they weren't even thinking of a market." When the album was finished in 2003, with no deadline, no pressure, and with Victor "Ticklah" Axelrod as experi-

enced co-producer[10], something had been created that Victor Rice calls a "masterpiece". The originators were also surprised to discover: "Who's listening to it? Fraternity kids?[11] That's crazy." So, they decided "okay, alright, well, let's do another!" Between 2006 and 2023, the Easy Star All-Stars released the albums *Radiodread*, *Lonely Hearts Dub Band, Thrillah* and *Ziggy Stardub*[12]. These albums have nothing in common with dub, even if the titles suggest they do. However, the marketing idea behind them, according to Victor Rice, "turned out to be genius".

Thanks to their success, American bands such as Rebelution and John Brown's Body also found their way to Easy Star Records and helped US reggae gain a steadily growing following. As a matter of course, these bands released dub versions of their albums. The Loving Paupers, produced by Victor Rice, with their mix of indie pop and reggae, have since 2023 also been signed to Easy Star. Beyond that, the US is experiencing a rocksteady revival in the tradition of Studio One and Treasure Isle through retro groups and performers such as keyboardist and dub mixer Roger Rivas (since 2014), Jr. Thomas & The Volcanos (since 2015) and The Frightnrs with their album *Nothing More To Say* (2016). Victor Rice and Victor Axelrod have mixed lounge-style dub LPs by both the Loving Paupers and the Frightnrs, which, due to the dignified charm of their originals, sound as if time had been standing still.

Victor Rice positions dub in an international context. He postulates "it's got to be live, you know" and calls his idea "romantic", saying "there is one thing that's so significant about dub music. It's a Jamaican invention. Somewhere in the 60s, the Jamaicans put the machines to work as musical instruments. Up to that point, the machines had made the musicians play like machines. After years of music being free, we came under the control of the metronome, to be able to synchronize to television, to film and everything else. And then there were effects to simulate reality. Echo and reverb units were being used to simulate real world behaviour of sound. [But] not in creative use. And then the Jamaicans took that back. Not consciously, but suddenly you have forms of music

10 Has worked on Amy Winehouse's *Back To Black* among others.
11 Meaning college students, high school graduates.
12 All Easy Star Records US.

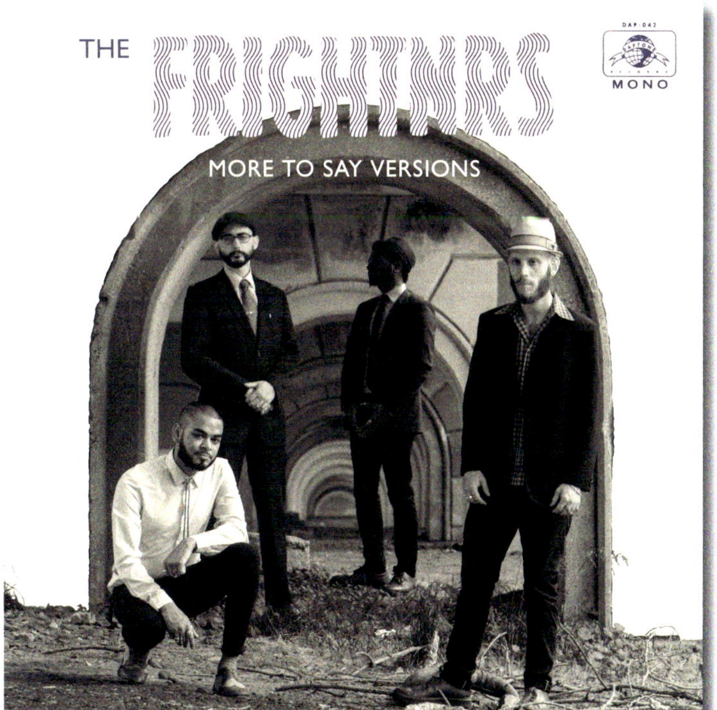

in which the machines are again subjugated by the musicians through effects. In the war against the machines, the Jamaicans created one of the greatest innovations in music history. The reason people don't think like that is because it didn't happen in Salzburg. It didn't happen in Paris; it didn't happen in Europe. So, it's not in the schoolbooks. But from a historical perspective, it's huge!"

Victor Rice and the author, Cologne 2023.

Born in 1967 in Huntington, Long Island, the accomplished bass player, whose father was Irish and his mother of Italian descent, is today a global dub player. Rice has relocated his life from New York to Brazil, releases ska and dub solo records in the US on Easy Star Records, cooperates as a dub mixer with the British band The Soothsayers[13], and until the Covid epidemic started, toured Europe with an 8-track tape machine and mixing console as a one-man live dub act. He had begun his dub

13 *Soothsayers Meets Victor Rice & Friends Vol. 1 + 2* Red Earth Records UK 2022 + 2023

Pachyman live in Germany 2024.

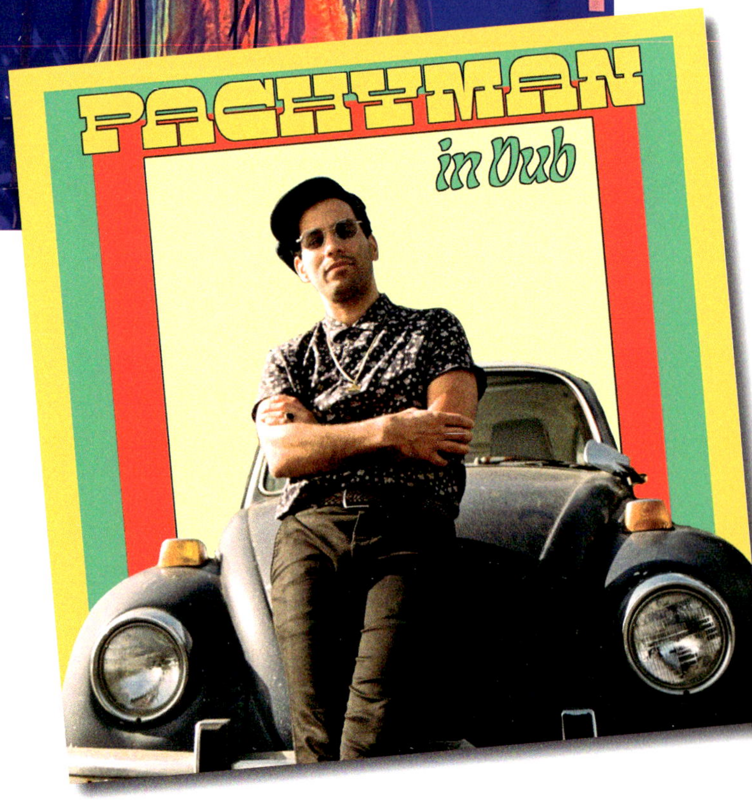

career in 2001 at a studio in Germany with a remix album for Dr. Ring-Ding & The Senior Allstars[14]. Even then, it was clear what his dub formula would sound like, as, without using spectacular reverb effects, Rice puts a song's specifications into permanent swing through feedback from self-modulating echoes.

Like Victor Rice, Puerto Rican dub artist Pachyman also operates as a one-man dub machine. Initially only with appearances on the World Wide Web, now also live in front of an audience. Pachyman is a multi-instrumentalist. In his home studio in Los Angeles, he records reggae riddims on his own and then dubs them on an analogue mixing console. Following the Mad Professor postulate "it's only dub if it's a version", Pachyman mixes instrumental music, because his designer dubs are songs without a preceding vocal version. But the stylish atmosphere brings back memories of the glory days of Jamaican dub. With videos to accompany the action, Pachyman increased his popularity and became an insider's tip.

14 *Dr. Ring-Ding & The Senior Allstars Meet Victor Rice – Pick Up The Pieces* Grover Records Germany 2001

The first LPs *Pachyman In Dub*[15] and *The Return Of Pachyman*[16] sold out quickly, and since then demand has exceeded supply.

While Pachyman, along with the rocksteady traditionalists in the US, cultivate their restorative dub character, the future is already unfolding on a small American group of islands. At the turn of the millennium, the US Virgin Islands in the Caribbean became a hot spot where reggae found its way back to its militant spiritual roots, even before the revival of the Jamaican nu-roots movement. With uncompromising lyrics and an understanding of reggae as a vehicle for protest, both lyrically explosive and rebellious, groups and artists such as Midnite, Bambú Station, Batch, Dezarie and many others[17] have developed enormous appeal on the American roots scene. "The VI had a golden age from, like 1999 to 2005," enthuses Tippy I Grade, "endless music coming out from all directions, and the world was taking notice." Laurent "Tippy I" Alfred, born in 1974 and owner of the I Grade Records label, has always lived on Saint Croix. In 2007, he formed a producer trio with Andrew "Moon" Bain from the Lustre Kings label and David "Jah D" Goldfine from Zion High Productions, who collectively called themselves Zion I Kings. Together they worked on Snoop Dogg's reggae album *Reincarnated*[18] and produced *Still*[19] by Jamaican roots singer Micah Shemaiah, one of the most promising albums of 2021. *Still* was mixed ambitiously dubwise and enriched with four dubs created at the Zion High studio in Florida. In 2023, Jamaican singer Protoje commissioned the collective to give his three-year-old album *In Search Of Lost Time*[20] the roots and reggae touch that his fans had missed. Zion I Kings took only the vocal tracks from the original material, created a tightly woven modern roots garment around them, called the result *In Search Of Zion*[21] and mixed dub versions of the new arrangements. They were included on a second LP of the vinyl edition, and critics spoke of "masterstrokes of the genre"[22]. As with all their productions, the three had recorded the riddims themselves with several different drummers and Moon on guitar, Tippy I on keyboards and Goldfine on bass.

15 Permanent Records US 2019.
16 ATO Records US 2021.
17 Ras Attitude, Abja, Niyorah, Iba, Jacob Seed and many more.
18 RCA 2013.
19 Zion High Productions Florida 2021.
20 In.Digg.Nation Collective / RCA Jamaica / US 2020.
21 In.Digg.Nation Collective / RCA Jamaica / US 2023.
22 https://www.reggaeville.com/artist-details/protoje/releases/mode/review/release/protoje-in-search-of-zion/.

Tippy I Grade describes how the trio works: "It's kind of like collective economics and collective security. For years we have rented studio time, mostly in Miami. Wherever we travelled [we booked] the best studios with the best mixing boards. SSL, Neve, API, we tried to get the best sound for live drums, live bass and riddim we could, going in. We would treat riddim sessions like a factory building. We make 12 in a night, or 13. Then we'd have a draft where we select. I get the first pick, Moon gets the second, Jah D gets the third. So, we select out the riddims exclusively and then each of us put the overdubs in our own style and way. Each of us mix in their own style and way. Find artists, release it on our labels. So, the three of us are always coming with something new. It's a great model, you know. It's what so many of our teachers reminded us. Collective economics work. Cooperation works. Unity works."

At the time of the merger to form Zion I Kings, Tippy I was already the regular producer for Midnite, the band founded in the late 1980s by the brothers Vaughn and Ron Benjamin, whose meditative, purist concerts lasted for hours in the form of word-heavy preaching. "I linked up with Vaughn Benjamin in the year 2000," recalls Tippy I, "that started a steady stream of work. We were releasing three, four albums a year." The collaboration inspired a special feature in his dubs. When it plays without an offbeat, the bass is always accompanied by the bubble organ. In the days of four tracks, where riddim guitar, piano and organ were combined on one track, the organ was automatically muted when the riddim was turned off. When Tippy I removes the offbeat in the mix, the organ continues to run imperceptibly with the bass, bringing a subtle forward drive to the groove. "I learn that from Midnite, from (the bassist) Ron Benjamin." Tippy I describes the unusual technique and says "He used to do that a lot. Just left-hand bubble, no bang (offbeat). It creates a power and a feeling."

The dub from the Virgin Islands does not follow the Jamaican style. When asked about its original purpose in the dancehall, Tippy I responds "That's where it started but now obviously dub is a appreciated genre of itself, a subgenre. It's something that people wanna put on when they work out, when they do their gardening, when they're reading, when they're working, driving. They like dat. So, it has become what it is." A statement like Bunny Lee's "every spoil is a style" fits into the concept just as little as the notion that a dub is finished after one run-through, and doesn't require more time than the song itself. "You tell me the spoil is the style, hahaha" laughs Tippy I. "I can hear Bunny Lee saying that. Big up! I have to embrace that more because I get very hard on myself. I do sometimes seven takes of a studio dub, choose the best take and work on it from there." Tippy I's dubs are based on the simultaneity of version and pure mixing pleasure, with results that couldn't be more different. On the one hand, he sees dub music as a studio production. The source material here is not songs, but riddim frameworks. Following the modular principle, melodies as well as intricate layers of different effects and echo timings are then assembled. "I love synthesizers, I love ping-pong delays," he says, knowing full well that "these things are not in the original dub school, but I like adding new elements." When asked whether such productions even fall into the category "dub", Tippy I answers "(they are) instrumental dub albums". Albums like *Cosmic Farming Dub*[23] or *Future Ocean's Echo*[24] impress the listener with their musical richness and virtuoso use of effects, yet they refrain from aiming for immediate impact for its own sake. They paint gentle backdrops built with many instruments, and show in titles like "Seahorse Bubblin'" or "Whale Song Skank" that the songs condensed into esoteric dreams

do not come from dancehall but play more in the chillout league of Café del Mar.

On the other hand, Tippy I has perfected the concept of live dubbing using mobile digital technology[25] and brings it to the stage in real time, both as a playback supplier for performances by artists such as Samory I or Mortimer[26] as well as for solo dub appearances. "Ableton software allowed me to start dubbing in 2012. And it immediately became a live thing for me. Wasn't so much for studio dubbing. It was for dubbing the fish market, dubbing the rain forest, dub on the beach. It was really crucial for me building my sonic identity. Working with a singer live and mixing delays and reverbs with the live voice and crafting atmospheres, to me that doesn't exist in any other presentation. You don't get that in a

23 Was not yet published in spring 2024.
24 Digital release 2022.
25 Laptop, Ableton software, various digital effects, Faderfox digital mixing console with 12 channels and 10 different sends.
26 Live Dub Europe Tour 2024.

Tippy I Grade dubbing live in Germany 2024.

sound system, you don't get that with a live band. Only with a live mixing with this kind of set up."

The first experiences using artificial intelligence (AI) take dub far into the future. AI algorithms can extract every single element from a fully mastered stereo mix. They identify individual vocals, drums, bass, brass, etc. and separate them with the exact sound, including reverb and compression, originally given to the instrument or voice in the mix at the time. AI not only opens the door to sampling and remixing, but also invites individuals to dub old recordings for which no dubs exist, years or decades later, even if there are no tapes left. First attempts were with a cover version of Gergory Isaacs' song "Night Nurse", sung by Mortimer over the original playback from 1982, disassembled by AI and pulled through the live dub grinder by Tippy I during the Live Dub Europe Tour in 2024. They illustrate the direction and possibilities open to the dub genre from now on. "*Scientist Wins The World Cup*, *Prince Jammy vs. Scientist*, I would listen to those for hours before I started dubbing. Just mesmerized. But I love what we do, which is embracing the now, embracing other technology and mixing it with that foundation", emphasizes Laurent "Tippy I" Alfred at the end of our conversation. "We have to stay at the cutting edge. That's what dub was. Cutting edge!"

King Earthquake and Iration Steppers at Garance Festival, France 2013.

Epilogue: An Echo doesn't make it Dub

> "We improvise without knowing the goal. That sets us free. We are not afraid of situations that we do not know. We have a song, have a rhythm, and start playing with it, turning everything upside down. We are not afraid to let things go."
>
> (Abdullah Ibrahim[1])

These concluding reflections begin with the years before dub emerged. In 1962, Coxson Dodd released the first LP he had ever produced. *I Cover The Water Front*[2] was named after a pop song from the 1933 movie of the same name, which had become a jazz standard. At the time, Dodd didn't have his own studio; the record with the Cecil Lloyd Group was recorded at Federal. In addition to the bandleader on the piano, also involved were Australian drummer Lowell Morris, Lloyd Mason on double bass, trombonist Don Drummond and Rolando Alphonso on tenor saxophone. *I Cover The Water Front* was a pure jazz record, the quartet played modern jazz, influenced by Charly Parker and John Coltrane. On the back cover there was a remarkable accompanying text, unmistakably aimed at how American tourists viewed Jamaican music in those years. "Most foreigners tend to think of Jamaica as the land of calypso" it said, conceding that "there is an approach to rhythm and construction that might be termed 'Afro-Caribbean'. But the main influences are those which are guiding principles in the international world of jazz." Coxson's production debut came at a time when highly trained jazz musicians were playing at the island's hotels, whose considerable skills were often hidden behind the clichés of bar music. Many came from the Alpha Boys' School, a boarding school in Kingston run by Catholic nuns, where difficult-to-educate and homeless boys were rehabilitated, partly through participation in a brass band. The instrumentalists trained here were highly regarded internationally. Trumpeter Dizzy Reece, for example, who has been firmly established on the American jazz scene since 1958, has released four solo albums with Blue Note and played in Dizzy Gillespie's band. Trumpeters Leslie Thompson and Oscar Clarke toured with Louis Armstrong, Roy "Bubbles" Burrows performed with Duke Ellington, Max Roach and Sonny Rollins. In 1969, an LP produced by Burrows with Jamaican musicians in New York was released, which, in addition to standards such as Thelonius Monk's "Round Midnight", contained an interview with the Jamaican station RJR in which Burrows talked about his career.[3] In 1973 Duke Ellington wrote: "A whole strain of West Indian musicians came up who made contributions to the so-called jazz scene, and they were all virtually descended from the true African scene... There are many resemblances to the Marcus Garvey schemes. Bop (bebop), I once said, is the Marcus Garvey extension."[4]

A striking number of Jamaican jazz musicians found jobs in Germany, or produced there. Trumpeter Sonny Gray was a member of the Norddeutscher Rundfunk[5] big band in 1969, and also worked in Paris. Saxophonist Wilton Gaynair played with Kurt Edelhagen and Peter Herbolzheimer. In Bonn, saxophonist Fitz Gore led an international spiritual jazz ensemble called Talismen, and recorded three LPs in Germany. Pianist Monty Alexander, born in 1944, is, after Bob Marley, one of the most enduring musicians ever to emerge from Jamaica, and has released over 100 albums worldwide. Thirteen LPs were released in Germany alone between 1971 and 1983 on MPS[6], the renowned Black Forest jazz label. Also involved in some of them was Jamaican guitarist Ernest Ranglin, who also recorded a solo album on the same famous label.[7]

The beginning of Jamaica's own music, popularized by visionary business people, involved local jazz musicians and jazz lovers. From The Skatalites, Jamaica's first supergroup, to The Mystic Revelation Of Ras-

1 Translated from „Überwinde deine Angst" ("Overcome your Fear"), German national weekly newspaper DIE ZEIT 20/2013.

2 Port-O-Jam.

3 *A Live Interview And Set with The Jamaican Jazz Crusaders* J.M.A. Records New York 1969, with Ernest Ranglin, Roland Alphonso et al.

4 Edward Kennedy Ellington: Music is my Mistress New York 1973 Da Capo Press Paperback 1976 p. 109.

5 Norddeutscher Rundfunk (NDR) is a national public radio and TV broadcaster in Germany.

6 MPS produced 13 LPs with Monty Alexander: *Here Comes the Sun* 1971 USA, *We've Only Just Begun* 1972 USA, *Perception* 1973 USA, *Love and Sunshine* 1975, *Rass* 1974 Jamaica, *Monty Alexander Live At The Montreux Festival* 1976, *Estade* 1977, *Cobilimbo feat. Ernest Ranglin* 1978, *The Way It Is* 1979, *Monty Alexander/Ernest Ranglin* 1981, *Monty Strikes Again. Live in Germany* (with Ernest Ranglin) 1976, *Cool feat. Monty Alexander Trio* 1983, *The Duke Ellington Songbook* 1983. Six of the albums were recorded in Villingen in southern Germany, the others were recorded in New York, Jamaica, and Switzerland, including the legendary recording from the Jazz Festival in Montreux in 1977, which brought Alexander worldwide attention.

7 Ranglypso MPS 1976 (with Monty Alexander).

tafari, jazz musicians provided decisive impulses, and remained jazz musicians even after the establishment of ska and reggae. During my productions with trombonist and Alpha Boys' School student Rico Rodriguez[8], I experienced how, 40 years later, he still thought in jazz categories and did not see himself as a ska musician.

When Skatalites' trumpeter and Alpha Boys' School graduate Johnny "Dizzy" Moore died in 2008, promoter, lecturer and former Peter Tosh manager Herbie Miller in an obituary emphasized Moore's lifelong self-image as a Rastafarian and jazz musician. Miller went on to describe bebop as a "paradigm of a postmodern approach to contemporary Jamaican music".[9]

Of the music scene in the 20th century, among the Jamaican movers and shakers, jazz was ever present. Merely the many brass overdubs by soloists like Cedric Brooks, Reuben Alexander, Karl "Canonball" Bryan and other graduates of the Alpha Boys' School on Studio One dubs and dubplates demonstrate a deep connection to jazz. Coxson Dodd and King Tubby were known for their large jazz collections. In 1991, Lee Perry talked about the music he preferred to listen to privately: "Generally, I play soul and jazz music."[10] The engineer and singer Pat Kelly detected "that sort of atmosphere like jazz"[11] in reggae. He benefited from Tubby's collection, remarking "Tubby had all sorts of jazz – Miles Davis, John Coltrane, Alice Coltrane... I used to tape them and take them off. I don't know if it had any influence on the dub as far as Tubby's concerned."[12] According to Fatman, Tubby began each workday by playing a jazz record. This left its mark on

8 *You Must Be Crazy – The Official Live Album* T'Bwana Sound/Grover Records 1994 + *Get Up Your Foot* Grover Records 2000, both Germany.
9 "The Lion's Last Blow: Johnny 'Dizzy' Moore" by Herbie Miller in the German reggae print magazine *RIDDIM* 06/08.
10 https://www.youtube.com/watch?v=woS40mXN5FE.
11 Liner notes for the reissue of *The Prophets – King Tubby's Prophecies Of Dub* Pressure Sounds 2019.
12 ibid.

his studio work. When Tubby mixed jazzy instrumental records with reggae beats for Bunny Lee, he draped effects as if they were dub mixes:

- **Bunny Lee & King Tubby present Tommy McCook And The Aggravators – Brass Rockers T**otal Sounds Jamaica 1975 (identical to **Tommy McCook and The Agrovators – Cookin'** Horse UK 1975)
- **Jackie Mittoo – The Keyboard King** Third World UK 1976
- **Tommy McCook – Hot Lava** Third World UK 1977 (identical to **Tommy McCook – Disco Rockers** Weed Beat Jamaica 1977)
- **Bobby Ellis & The Professionals meet the Revolutiónaries** Third World UK 1977
- **Agrovators Meets The Revolutionaries Part II** Micron CAN 1979

The artwork of the Bobby Ellis LP made clear how extra-musical influences associated with jazz were also being reflected in Jamaican music, from the 1970s onwards. The cover showed an armed guerrilla scene and listed titles such as "Militant Salute" and "Black Unity". After a delay of ten years, the island's music began to reflect what was happening in the States. This was preceded by a decade of mass mobilization in Black America. It was when jazz was being influenced by Pan-Africanism, the spirit of the civil rights movement and revolutionary thought. Black musicians in the USA were freeing themselves from traditional musical structures and using their pieces to comment on specific incidents. In "Alabama", John Coltrane solemnly lamented the victims of a Ku Klux Klan attack on a church in which four black schoolgirls died; Archie Shepp dedicated a blues to the black activist George Jackson, who was murdered in prison, and recorded a stirring requiem for the civil rights activist Malcolm X two weeks after his assassination. Above all, the spirit of the times was reflected in the titles and atmosphere of instrumental pieces. They were now "Freedom Dance" (Shirley Scott), "Lament Mankind" (Michael White), "Africa/Underground Railroad" (John Coltrane) or "The Rights Of All" (Oliver Nelson). Sometimes an African mask on the cover was enough to make a statement, like on the Dizzy Gillespie Quintet's LP *A Musical Safari*[13] recorded in 1961 or on the 1963 LP *Katanga!*[14] by saxophonist Curtis Amy.

13 Cheri Booman Records US 1974.
14 Pacific Jazz Records US 1963.

With the politicization of music, Ethiopianism, with its orientation towards a specifically African spirituality, found its way into American jazz, which, in addition to clothing style and artwork, was primarily expressed in the titles of albums and songs. Trombonist Grachan Moncur III named a track on his free jazz LP *New Africa*[15] "Ethiopian Market". Donald Byrd's album *Ethiopian Knights*[16] contained pieces like "The Emperor" or "The Little Rasti". On *A New Perspective*[17], Byrd's "The Black Disciple" paid homage to Simeon, a disciple of Jesus nicknamed "Niger", also known as "the Black".[18] And "Garvey's Ghost" was evoked musically by Max Roach fully 15 years before Burning Spear's 1976 dub LP of the same name.[19]

A year earlier, Roach had commented on the recordings of his LP *We Insist! Freedom Now Suite*[20] in Down Beat Magazine with "I will never again play anything that does not have social significance". He had demanded: "We have to employ our skill to tell the dramatic story of our people and what we've been through."[21] Black music in the US has shed its "Niggers don't talk. They just play, dance [and] make people happy"[22] innocence, and Jamaica was not unaffected. Gone were the days of jump up jazz, swing and sweet soul rocksteady. Dub tracks such as "Rise And Fall Of The South African Regime"[23] as well as instrumentals called "Black Power"[24] or "Ethiopia"[25] soon followed. With politically militant statements in their titles, American jazz musicians led the way, and when naming dub mixes Jamaica adopted this. However, they focused less on equality in a white society than on repatriation and the liberation movements in Africa. Dub mixes now carried headlines like "March Back

15 Actuel/BYG Records France 1969.
16 Blue Note 1973.
17 Blue Note 1963.
18 The Jamaican producer Jack Ruby later called his studio band "The Black Disciples". In 1977 Burning Spear sang on his LP *Dry And Heavy* (Mango + Island Records 1977): "Black disciples will never run away".
19 LP *Max Roach – Percussion Bitter Sweet* Impulse! US 1961.
20 Candid US 1960.
21 Quoted from the obituary of Max Roach in the New York Times August 16, 2007.
22 Archie Shepp in „Fire Music. Archie Shepp, die Poesie und der Sound der Freiheit" ("Fire Music. Archie Shepp, the poetry and the sound of freedom"), a feature on the German radio station Südwestrundfunk 2019.
23 The Thing 1977, B-side of the Iron Phoenix single "Natty Dread Christmas". Iron Phoenix were actually the Heptones. When the single was re-pressed in 2010, the situation in South Africa was different, so the dub of the B-side was only called "Part 2".
24 Winston Wright with Tommy McCook Treasure Isle 1968.
25 Im (= Cedric Im Brooks) & The Invaders Studio One/Ironside 7-inch 1972 on the "Java" riddim.

To Africa", "Riot In Soweto", "Dread In Johannesburg"[26] and "Open The Gate Of Rhodesia"[27]. Dub LPs took a stand with titles like *Rebel Dub, Freedom Fighters Dub*, *Liberated Dub*, *Guerilla Dub*, *Rebel Soldier*, *The War Is On* etc.

Most of the time, however, dubs were given imaginary names or modulations of the original title. Ken Boothe's "Ain't No Love" became "Ain't No Dub" at King Tubby, Scientist turned Johnny Clarke's "Every Knee Shall Bow" into "Every Dub Shall Scrub", "Declaration Of Rights" emulated into "Declaration Of Dub" and so on.

Alongside this, the revolutionary theme continued to make itself felt. Also in the UK, where the cover of *Desmond Popsy Benup – Dubbing In The UK*[28] 1981 LP showed a street scene on Railton Road in Herne Hill, taken directly after the Brixton Riots. Or in 1994 when Mad Professor launched a series named *Black Liberation Dub.* But when Sly & Robbie came out with *Militant Dub*[29] in 2018, you wonder whether the Marvel aesthetic on display was really meant seriously.

Legendary dancehall selector Rory "Stone Love" Gilligan, who has been active since the 1980s, tried to reshape what he considered to be "polished" dub music from Europe in a much more serious manner. In 2017, he produced the radical, spiritual modern roots album *Black Gold*[30] with singer Samory I for his Black Dub label, and mixed dark, militant dubs exclusively for the limited vinyl edition. In 2021, Gilligan spread dub experiments of Bob Marley songs across his social media channels. "We need a more spiritual sound", he stated. "The roots today is too clean, really really polished. Me nuh want nothing pretty. It fi sound gritty, dutty, it fi sound

26 All on the LP *Revolutionary Dub* Trenchtown UK 1976, produced by B.B. Seaton, mixed by Errol Brown.

27 *DEB Players – 20th Century Deb-Wise* D.E.B. Music UK 1978, produced by Dennis Brown, mixed by Prince Jammy.

28 Starlight Records UK.

29 Tabou1, Taxi.

30 *Samory I – Black Gold* JA 2017.

dread. An eye opener still. The music supposed to [be] vibrant [and] can play by itself, and you feel the message even without the lyrics."[31]

The dub from Europe, which Gilligan reviled as "polished", was the result of a development that configured dub in the UK for global consumption. The metamorphosis of Jamaican dub into European neo dub simplified the passion for dub into consumer-friendly echo food. By proclaiming dub to be a spiritual experience, Jah Shaka also unintentionally contributed to this. He explicitly welcomed the growing number of white visitors by saying "if someone was to come to our dances, they might see that 50% of the crowd is white, or even 60%. It depends on where I'm playing. We are not only in this for black. It's for those who believe in the truth… to help them in their lives."[32]

During the annual carnival in the UK in 1976, a dub LP called *Contempo* was released on the streets of Brixton. The album, distributed for free, was a private pressing by an enigmatic band called Black Jade, although no one knew who was behind them or whether they were even a band from London. The LP did not attract much interest. Eyewitnesses reported that most of the copies were lying around on the street and had been thrown away by the rubbish collector. The few examples that survived are now highly sought after collector's times.

While *Contempo* with its heavy bass sound met with relative disinterest, every year during the Notting Hill Carnival, dub triggered a more massive vibe. From the 80s onwards, it was no longer just Jah Shaka and long-established UK sounds such as "Iration Steppas", "Abba Shanti I" or "King Earthquake" with steppaz beats that generated huge autonomous energy, but also white acts such as Manasseh[33], Alpha & Ome-

31 "Die fantastische Metamorphose des Rory Stone Love" ibid.
32 Quoted from Partridge ibid p. 125f.

33 Nick Manasseh (real name Nick Raphael) was a member of Sound Iration. In 2022 he produced the album *Soul Revivers – On The Grove* with David Hill with its counterpart *Dub The Grove*, both on Acid

ga, The Disciples, Zion Train and others. Without intending to do so, they filled the gap of Jamaica's post-Sleng Teng withdrawal from the dub orbit with programmed, digital riddims. They composed related pieces of music, integrated musicians into their live performances and used Jamaican voices and samples from singers like Earl 16 to give their style authenticity. UK neo dub developed into a fusion of effects-laden, bass-heavy instrumental music with Jamaican ingredients and European influences à la Kraftwerk. "They (Kraftwerk) influenced the avant-garde" was British music journalist Paul Morley's analysis. "Even in the harder, alien realms of dubstep, the spirit of Kraftwerk can be heard."[34] One consequence of this mélange was the constantly rotating, innovative club variants, with styles such as jungle, drum'n'bass, grime, hyperdub and dubstep. Similar modulations also emerged in the States, such as the Crooklyn Dub Consortium, which included acts such as Unitone Hi-Fi and Dr. Israel. Among them was Bill Laswell, who experimented with deeper sound collages with Sly & Robbie. In the mid-90s, two compilation albums were released[35], on the labels of which was emblazoned a quotation from 1980 by Jamaican singer Pablo Moses, widespread in the neo scene, which was "Dubbing is a must." However, Moses rolled his eyes when his song title[36] was associated with reverb and echo. "To enjoy reggae music, dubbing is a must." Moses sang, but what he had in mind was the Rub-a-Dub. That movement from the dark corners of the dancehall, in which couples locked together in the middle, their bodies seemingly gliding over the basslines together. This was what George Bernard Shaw in another context aptly described as vertical expression of a horizontal desire. Pablo Moses meant exactly that when he sang "Man, hold your daughter close, then she love you the most." He emphasized: "It's the dance! In those days, the rude boys in the corner with a gal, we call that dub." Junior Delgado alluded to this when he sang "I know a girl, she's gonna dub with me"[37] in the dub of his 1979 cover version of the Shades' then ten-year-old hit "She's Gonna Marry Me"[38].

Jazz UK. The album was influenced by the British nu jazz movement, Tommy McCook and the golden years of roots reggae and marked a departure from the steppaz sound.

34 Translated from *Kraftwerk – Pop Art*, TV documentary by Simon Wittler and Hannes Rossacher 2013.

35 *Crooklyn Dub Consortium – Certified Dope Vol. 1 + 2*, USA 1995 + 1996.

36 7-inch on Penetrate, Jamaica or 12-inch Island Records, UK, both 1980.

37 "Mister Dub", on the LP Dance A Dub, Incredible Jux, Jamaica 1979.

38 Mummy 1969, produced by Winston Riley.

Watty Burnett also wanted nothing less with "Put on your dancing shoes pretty baby, I want to dub with you tonight."[39]

Although the days of the Rub-a-Dub are over, the incorrectly understood quotation has survived. Today's dub community is swaying in a trance. Even veteran UK sounds who have played a pivotal role in establishing the Jamaican sound system culture in the UK have followed the development and contributed to Europe's dub becoming different. A chilled (cheap would also be accurate) new age soundtrack emerged from the Jamaican culture of dancehall and version. Based on the same technical processes, neo dub pursued its own goals, i.e., echoes for everyone instead of exclusive mixes and competition. Spirituality and harmony were the new goal. "In dub, there is a strong emphasis on concord." said Paul Zasky, bassist and leader of Dubblestandart, the Viennese band, which has been successfully spreading its understanding of dub around the globe through live concerts. Since the late 90s, Dubblestandart have made more than 20 albums. "For me, dub means painting landscapes with sounds, because it allows for this place and space. And of course, because dub reggae is always about rhythm. For me, reggae was always the rhythm of breathing. For me it's all about harmony. Even if it's just about the harmony, that we as a band harmonize with the listener in the same rhythm."

Seductive play with echo combined with the technical possibilities of producing music mechanically has shaped version culture into another genre that deserves the "euro dub" name. Compared to the dancehall mixes from Jamaica, it's a gentle breeze! Perhaps the most extreme examples are psydub, a genre with its own Wikipedia article that Mad "Anansi" Professor has already caricatured in episode ten of his *Dub Me Crazy* series in 1990, calling it *Psychedelic Dub*. Psydub is a spineless offbeat Goa trip suitable for yoga and meditation classes, and is pretending to be world music. People call it open minded, but they mean Pink Floyd. The neo dub environment is full of non-reggae fans who embrace everything they reject about reggae, i.e., the supposedly alternative, psychedelic and consciousness-expanding, the esotericism and the symbiosis of dub and weed. And this, although it is well known that quite a few of the dub fathers – King Tubby, King Jammy, Pat Kelly, and Mad Professor among them– strictly refused to smoke ganja.

Well aware of the difference, the blue-eyed euro neo dub community speaks of "contemporary" dub, although the term paraphrases the

39 Watty Burnett – "Dancing Shoes", 12-inch Dread At The Controls, UK 1982.

misunderstanding. Dub stands for the processing of existing music, so contemporary can at best be the template. Let's not talk about dub-like remixes of historical pop, punk, folk or classical recordings. When the neo dub makers use the word "contemporary", they include abandoning the reggae genre in favour of musical forms from other cultures. On-U Sound's African Head Charge has shown that sounds and samples from Japan or India can be synthetically copied, serving as a minimalistic playground of effects. "World music" atmosphere becomes the driving factor. When the German pop philosopher Diedrich Diederichsen spoke of the "stoned, caring coziness" of dub[40], it was not merely evidence of a misunderstanding, but also accurate analysis.

Dub in its origin is deafening. A widespeaker experience that penetrates through the ears into bodies shaken by bass. In addition to the physical experience, its impact thrives on the selective silence of particular frequencies, achieved by muting instruments. In these breaks, echoes become nets, capturing memories and allowing melodies to resonate in the mind. The so-called inner hearing of the brain continues to perceive what is missing. Phil Pratt, producer of various dub LPs[41], has described it as "half of it is missing, the rest is in your head."[42]

Dub is based on the three-dimensional play of the elements of riddim, space and reverberation. Neo dub, on the other hand, is two-dimensional instrumental music made of groove and space. Neo dub suffices in itself, it needs no memories. Here the music oscillates with uniform dynamics in often unvaried arrangements. It does not rely on the silence of frequencies, but rather creates a carpet of sound for effects. Although bass frequencies are temporarily turned off in live sets for the sake of switching them on, echoes determine the flow of the music. Surprises are not welcome, as a comment from the dubblog "In Bass We Trust"[43] on the Alborosie *Back-A-Yard Dub*[44] LP shows "I don't know any dub record where the effects are so unexpected… I was genuinely startled… constantly turning down the sound, it confuses me and doesn't bring me

into a meditative state at all… My greatest wish would be for a second dub album to come out, with a more relaxed mix."[45]

In addition to neo dub, there are also intellectual-seeming non-reggae projects from Europe that work with analogue formats and fall into the misconception that the use of echoes justifies the name dub. For example, the German Quasi Dub Development or the electronic/jazz musician Burnt Friedman, who interprets dub as a "production method" or "style"[46]. The Japanese Hiroshi Fujiwara has released records like *Hiroshi Fujiwara in Dub Conference*[47], on which the music was decorated with the word "dub", but the tracks played on grand piano and synthesizers floated between minimal music and downtempo, free of dub. Mark Lusardi

40 Diedrich Diederichsen – „Drones, Dubs und Bässe: Musikalische Räume für postmusikalische Ideen" ("Drones, dubs and bass. Musical spaces for post-musical ideas") in Über Pop-Musik p. 322.
41 See footnote "George Philpott" in the chapter "Clive Chin, The Story of Java Java Java Java".
42 Booklet *Skin Flesh & Bones – Dub In Blood*, Pressure Sounds reissue 2016.
43 www.dubblog.de
44 VP Records 2021
45 https://dubblog.de/alborosie-back-a-yard-dub/#commentsa
46 In various interviews, e.g., https://www.irieites.de/interviews/Burnt_Friedman_Interview.htm or https://www.cyclicdefrost.com/2008/04/burnt-friedman-interview-by-bob-baker-fish/ (both last accessed on March 15, 2022).
47 Victor Japan 1995. Due to the cover artwork with a picture of painter Jean-Michel Basquiat, the LP is a sought-after collector's item outside of the dub scene. Fujiwara also used the term "dub" on other albums such as *Studio66 – In Dub With Luv* (Tune Bakery Record Japan 2010) or *Classic Dub Classics* (Cruel L-Records Japan 2005).

showed some understanding by commenting "it's entertaining fun, but results in a sort of sub-genre that doesn't currently have a name. True dub music would have to be confined to the reggae domain." Effects jugglers like Friedman and his Nu Dub Players, the Quasi Dub Development or Fujiwara appropriate the term, without considering the cultural context discredit it, and under the "dub" heading produce ambient-like music in the tradition of Brian Eno, Robert Fripp and Klaus Schulze. They overlook the fact that the essence of dub is not based on echoes, but rather on the processing of real pieces of music. Dub is not about playing with effects; it's about playing with the elements of a song. Echoes don't show the way into the world of dub; there are countless titles in the dub archives in which not a single echo pops up.

The popular theory that dub is drum & bass is nothing more than a myth. It goes back to the technical limitations in the early days of Jamaican studios, and is fueled by the effective bass speakers (scoops) of the sound systems. Sylvan Morris pointed out that, initially, with only two or three tracks, it wasn't possible to do more than limit yourself to the rhythm section. Apart from a few early single B-sides, there is hardly a dub album that is consistently reduced to bass and drums. On the contrary, the dubwise atmosphere is created through the interplay of off-beat, brass, vocals, and snippets of melody only.

Let's recapitulate the statements of two dub pioneers. Mad Professor has admitted his Massive Attack remix wasn't reggae. Technically, however, it was dub, he says, since they were versions. Style Scott knew Dub Syndicate's music, designed in the UK, would have been characterized as instrumental music in Jamaica.

Ergo: dub is always related to something that already exists. Dub without an original is instrumental music.

In contrast, in the steppaz scene, which is widespread throughout Europe and in which the tradition of the sound system family with self-built, massive sound systems is maintained, a sacred interpretation of the term, as nurtured by Jah Shaka, has taken root. Dub sound systems are often closed communities with their own codes and moral and spiritual standards.[48] They were described by an unnamed insider as "removed from society into a self-created counter-model". The operators have refused to accept the fact that all paths of dub lead back to the Jamaican dancehall. They see their roots in the UK, not in Jamaica. Their music takes a stand against Babylon and stands for righteousness, for which they are paving the way as "dub soldiers in Jah army, as defenders of roots and dub"[49].

In addition to analogue pressure building through dub sound systems, often going hand in hand with the cultivation of hippie customs and a broad, digital new age euro dub sound reinforcement, a growing number of small biotopes have emerged around the world in which engineers have been cultivating the basic idea of "dub = version".

This trend is also being followed by the Sicilian Alborosie aka Puppa Albo, who years ago moved his base to Jamaica and is now a naturalized citizen. Albo sees himself as the keeper of the reggae tradition. "I go for the history. I go for the roots and the foundation of the music" he explains. Puppa Albo hoards historical equipment from the Kingston studios, which he uses intensively in his productions. This includes all makes of reverb devices that were in King Tubby's studio. But although his understanding of dub is based on the culture of versions, he interprets dub in a European way. "Dub now for me is like when you go to the doctor and the doctor give you a good news. Seh yu good, no problem, you're in good health. Dub is my doctor." Alborosie is by no means representative of Jamaica, but when it comes to dub, he now has the largest output on the island. Since 2013, he has been mixing a dub version of each of his vocal albums in his own studio, which, while far from being compatible with sound systems, he is increasingly staging as a spectacle. After the self-published *Dub Clash*[50] in 2010, every two years via Greensleeves/VP Records Alborosie has released the following:

- **Dub The System** 2013
- **Alborosie meets King Jammy – Dub Of Thrones** 2015
- **Freedom In Dub** 2017
- **Alborosie Meets Roots Radics – Dub For The Radicals** 2019
- **Back-A-Yard Dub** 2021
- **Shengen Dub** 2023
- **Embryonic Dub** 2023

Alborosie is well respected in Jamaica's reggae business circle, but his fan base and market are in Europe. From a dub perspective, despite his

48 See "Jamaican Creole in German Reggae Subculture" by Michael Westphal in: *The Language Of Pop Culture*, Routledge, New York and London, 2018.

49 Westphal ibid p. 105.

50 J.D.F./Shengen Clan, Italy.

location in Kingston, the Sicilian is one of the European blue-eyed dub activists with a traditional understanding of the genre.

On the north coast of Spain, producer, musician, and singer Roberto Sánchez works at a high technical level with Jamaican veterans such as Linval Thompson and Willi Williams, as well as Swiss singers & players. He cultivates the version culture by adding dub LPs to his vocal productions and reviving the tradition of showcase albums.[51]

In France, Sébastien Bizeray aka Westfinga develops replicas of old filters, spring reverbs and similar devices, and creates furious dubs with a self-built console, the look of which is reminiscent of Tubby's MCI console.[52] Jericho, in-house engineer of the French Irie Ites label, operates with similar virtuosity at his analogue console.

In north Germany, Nicolai Beverungen runs the "Echo Beach" label, a globally networked trading point for "international dub reggae", at least, according to his own advertising. Always following the version principle, since 1995 more than 200 LPs, CDs, maxis, singles and digital formats have been published here, which exploit and interpret the genre in the gray area of dub and remix. Specialists such as German Dubvisionist, the Austrians Dubblestandart and the Jamaican Lion & Roots label founded by Style Scott have their home here.

In the south of Germany, in Munich and the surrounding area, a hot spot of producers and dub mixers has emerged who work in a global network. Besides aDUBta (Vin Gordon, Earl 16, Marcus I et. al.) and Cpt. Yossarian (*Bob Marley In Dub*[53]), Umberto Echo mixes dubs for acts like Gentleman, Seeed, Steel Pulse and Sizzla, as well as for the production houses Oneness Records and Real People Music. He releases his own dub albums on Echo Beach and Enja Records, and is an accomplished master of live dubbing. He refines the Dub Syndicate tradition at concerts with surround sound together with Dub Spencer & Trance Hill, the Swiss band. Behind the Umberto Echo pseudonym is an audio engineer also highly respected outside the reggae environment, who approaches his dubs in the studio rather cautiously. For him, "dub is actually instrumental music. You don't necessarily have to hear echo for it to be dub."

51 *Shanti Yalah & Sons Of Nansa – Creation In Dub* (2017) / *Benjammin – Sons And Daughters. Vocals & Dubs* (2018) / *Willi Williams – Glory To The King* (2020) / *Irregular Roots – Showcase* (Spain 2020), *Lone Ark Riddim Force – Balance Dub* (2021), *Roberto Sánchez & Chalart58 – Audio Merge In Dub* (2021) all: A-Lone Productions Spain. *Lone Ark meets The 18th Parallel – Showcase Vol. 1* (Fruits Records Switzerland 2021).

52 https://youtu.be/LqDux_IWycQ.

53 Echo Beach Germany 2022.

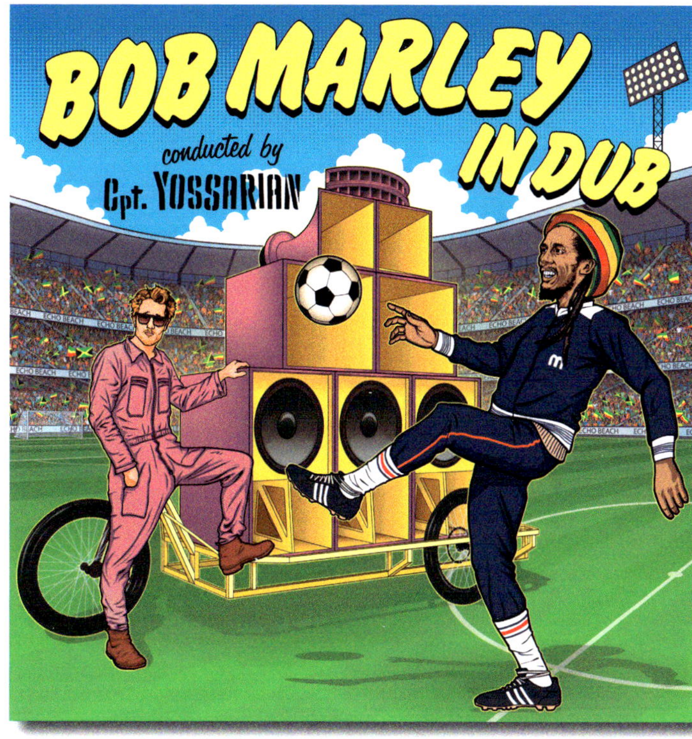

Paolo Baldini is completely different from the previous entry. He is also a specialist in live engineering, having dubbed his way into the pole position of classic dub in front of audiences in Jamaica and in his studio in Italy. Aided by a connection to the British Pressure Sounds label, he enjoys access to multitrack tapes from Bunny Lee's archive, the main supplier to the reissue label. Baldini succeeds in creating a connection between Jamaica and Europe with style and impressive virtuosity. When he dubs live, he delivers for the dancehall, but his albums are complex works that leave little room for performances by deejays, singers or instrumentalists, and thus accommodate the listening habits of white dub consumers.[54]

In the UK, the Tuff Scout label manages to bridge the gap between UK steppaz and traditional Jamaican dub with the help of engineer duo Gil Cang & Demus (aka Dilip Harris & Gilbert Cang) on single B-sides

54 His mixes appear with the name Paolo Baldini DubFiles on Pressure Sounds (UK), Echo Beach (Germany) and La Tempesta Dub (Italy).

and two LPs[55]. In 2021 they dubbed a playback by the Wailers from 1976 found in Larry Lawrence's estate for the *Out On The Floor Dub* album.[56] Whenever the Wailers were in London, Lawrence, owner of the Ethnic Fight label, recorded riddims with the musicians around Barrett brothers Carlton and Family Man for his own purposes. When Lawrence's daughter found tapes in a locked box, four and a half decades after the recordings, one of the rare dubs of the band behind Bob Marley came about.[57]

Al Breadwinner goes back to the time when the Wailers' material was created. Since 2010, the musician and engineer has been pursuing a return to dub's original elements in the country where it underwent its greatest change in action and reception. In his studio in Manchester, he brings the poles of jazz and dub together again using analogue equipment, with Black Ark reminiscences buzzing through Mu-Tron Phasor and Space Echo. "I feel jazz and the evolving styles coming out of Jamaica throughout the 1960s and 70s are inextricably linked" he says. Musically, recording and mixing-wise, Al is technically back in the mid-70s, he creates a sound that Nat Birchall also strives for. Born in 1957, the British saxophonist wrote to me that he "would like to make an album that sounded like 'Tommy McCook meets Yabby You at The Black Ark mixed at King Tubby's studio'. My earliest experience of the instrument was the Jamaican players like Tommy McCook and Cedric Brooks. The *Grounation* triple LP[58] had a very big effect on me especially. When I heard John Coltrane, I could hear it was a similar sound concept as the Jamaican players." Birchall's intention is to "give voice in music to the esoteric renewal of the soul and mind that lent spiritual strength to the black counterculture, and complemented the political radicalism of the late 1960s and 1970s."[59] The saxophonist sees jazz and dub as united, and emphasizes that you should "expect the unexpected. Both jazz and dub are improvised in real time. In both cases things are not planned, they are both very natural, organic ways of making music." In Al Breadwinner, Nat Birchall has found a like-minded soul. Together with Alpha Boys' School trombonist Vin Gordon, who has lived in the UK since the 1980s and who recorded *Musical Bones*, his first solo album,

for Lee Perry, both are working on recordings that are charmingly out of time. According to Breadwinner, they always follow the same blueprint. "Restricting the styles of instruments, recording and mixing techniques to try to put it sonically in the mid-1970s." With this in mind, they have been creating jazzy dub gems since 2010, such as:

- **The Breadwinners – Dubs Unlimited** Kingspinna 2012
- **Nat Birchall Meets Al Breadwinner – Sounds Almighty** 2018*
- **Vin Gordon – African Shores** 2019*
- **Nat Birchall Meets Al Breadwinner (feat. Vin Gordon) – Upright Living** 2020*
- **Nat Birchall Meets Al Breadwinner – Tradition Disc In Dub** 2020*

* all Tradition Disc

55 *Inna London Dub* 2017, *Out On The Floor Dub* 2021.

56 Playback for Junior Hibbert's single "Really For A Reason" on Ethnic Fight.

57 There are almost no dubs of Bob Marley's music. The backs of the Tuff Gong singles are almost exclusively instrumental versions. Apart from an uncredited tune by I-Roy, there are no deejay versions. Albums with Marley dubs like *Captain Yossarian – Bob Marley In Dub on Echo Beach* 2021 or *Delixx – Uprising In Dub on Micron*, Canada 1980 are based on replayed cover versions.

58 *Count Ossi & The Mystic Revelation Of Rastafari – Grounation* New Dimension Jamaica 1972.

59 https://natbirchalljazzman.bandcamp.com/album/invocations (last accessed March 15, 2022).

In Manchester, Birchall and Breadwinner were bringing jazz back into dub at the same time as a young, post-American jazz movement in London was turning towards the future, almost casually integrating a radical version of Jamaican dub into their improvisations. Most of the activists were descendants of the Windrush generation. They experienced their musical socialization at UK sound systems[60] second hour, and were trained at Tomorrow's Warriors, a jazz school founded in 1991, that plays a similar role in London to the Alpha Boys' School in Kingston. The British nu jazz movement took the term "spiritual" back to its original meaning, as a counterpoint to a (white) interpretation that sees the spiritual as a source of improvisation, towards an Afrofuturist vision formulated from a black perspective. Jazz veteran Idris Ackamoor, who in 1973[61] dedicated an album by The Pyramids, his ensemble, to the Ethiopian Rock-hewn churches of Lalibela, described in a 2018 interview where the term originated. "Our music came out alongside the civil rights movement, it was all about black consciousness. Some people called it 'our thing'. Others called it 'spiritual jazz'. There was a revolutionary spirit running through African American music. Musicians were looking for a different kind of spiritual experience. It was about affirming our African heritage."[62]

Key figures in the new British movement are soloists such as Shabaka Hutchings (saxophone), son of Jamaican dub poet Anum Iyapo, who immigrated to the UK in the 1960s, Nubya Garcia (saxophone), Zara McFarlane (vocals), Joe Armon-Jones (keyboards), Theon Cross (tuba) and others, as well as ensembles such as the Ezra Collective or the Sons Of Kemet. They all embrace a militant attitude and spirit, from which music is played with reference to past origins and daily reality. No album of theirs is created without borrowing from offbeats with swinging reggae basslines or pumping dancehall grooves. Dub elements with sometimes harsh effects are naturally mixed in. Joe Armon-Jones released dub mixes of his music and performed a "high-lauded hybrid"[63] jazz'n'dub DJ set at the We Out Here Festival in the UK in 2023. Among other things, he played in Nubya Garcia's band, and contributed to her

60 Such as Saxon, Sir Coxsone, Jah Tubbys, Channel One, Fatman Sound, King Earthquake etc.
61 *Lalibela*, Pyramid Records US 1973.
62 *How Idris Ackamoor's African odyssey helped shape Afrofuturist jazz*, Interview The Vinyl Factory, 2018.
63 We Out Here website.

award-winning debut album *Source*[64] from 2020. Its title track, which extends over an entire LP side, is steppers jazz infused with dub effects. At Garcia's concerts, long stretches of "jazz dubbing" are accompanied by gun finger poses from the dancehall.

A year earlier, Zara McFarlane had provided us with a jazz vocal interpretation of the "East Of The River Nile" melodica leitmotiv, from the 1971 Augustus Pablo classic. The dub version was mixed by Dennis Bovell.[65]

Shabaka Hutchings is considered the scene's "cultural instigator"[66]. "When I step on the stage in Sons Of Kemet, I'm not trying to be Sonny Rollins or John Coltrane. My core vocabulary is jazz, but I'm not trying to have the energy of someone in a suit standing stationary in front of a microphone giving a nice round sound. I'm trying to just spit out fire like

64 Concord UK.
65 12-inch Brownswood Recordings UK 2019.
66 This is how the British writer Emma Warren described him in her biography of the Sons Of Kemet album *Black To The Future*, Impulse! 2021.

Capleton or Anthony B or Sizzla."[67] In their titles "My Queen Is Mamie Phipps Clark" on their *Your Queen Is A Reptile*[68] album and "Think Of Home" on *Black To The Future,* Sons Of Kemet provide prime examples of the innovative combination of jazz, dancehall energy and dub.

The fact that dub as a form of expression has quietly crept into the British nu jazz style cannot disguise the fact that Jamaica's dub has changed in the European diaspora, chiefly because Jamaica has failed to give its dub the same recognition as ska. When it comes to the latter, there is undisputed consensus that it should be viewed as genuinely Jamaican music, a status that dub also deserves. But the functional music that emerged in Jamaica became, apart from British jazz, a ubiquitous style, soaked in echoes. It adopted the name because D, U and B are three overly seductive letters. Short. Concise. Memorable. Inviting. Just like jazz, rock, pop, punk, or blues. Dub became a music of Europe.

Jamaica never seems to have fully grasped what it brought into the world half a century ago; remember Gussie Clarke's dub talk debacle[69]? Today, the dub originators are seeing their radical approach to music recordings not only become fair game for echo nerds, but also the esoteric soundscape of a new age lifestyle. Neo dub, psydub, contemporary dub, and euro dub are derivates of an unstoppable music-cultural misunderstanding. Jamaica has allowed dub to be taken out of its hands and is leaving the counteraction to other countries.

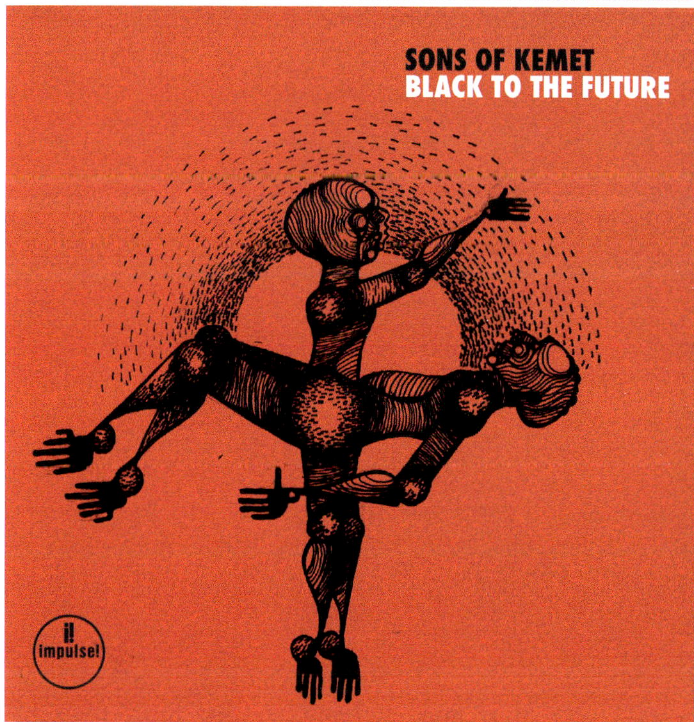

67 Shabaka Hutchings on his website: http://www.shabakahutchings.com/biography/ (last accessed March 15, 2022).
68 Impulse! 2018.
69 See chapter "Prologue, Counteraction".

Acknowledgements

First and foremost, I would like to thank all those who made themselves available for interviews in Jamaica, the UK, Germany, France, Belgium, the Netherlands and elsewhere. Without their stories, this book would not have been possible.

A special thank you goes out to Ursula "Munchy" Münch for her translation, her comments, and her commitment. You have done a great job.

To my German editors Gerd Gummersbach, who was a helpful discussion partner and motivator from the first word to the last period of the book, and Karl-Olaf Kaiser, who contributed valuable advice and details from his veranda in Kingston.

Heartfelt thanks to Arwen Quellmalz and Heike Graw for their familial and mental support.

A fundamental thank you goes to all those who have given me opportunities for interviews, provided materials and information or exchanged ideas with me: Alex Domhöver, Chris Lane, Christoph Kraus, David Katz, David Rodigan, Deniese Sealey, the Embassy of Jamaica in Berlin, Frank Balczynski, Garance Reggae Festival, Götz Alsmann, John Masouri, Julian Schmidt, Katharina Pfaff, Maja Bernard, Martin Campbell, Mint magazine, Nicolai Beverungen / Echo Beach, Olaf Karnik, Pekka Vuorinen, Pete Lilly & Ellen Köhlings, Ralf Frochte, Red Bull London, Reggae Jam, Riddim magazine, Rob Chapman, Ruhr Reggae Summer, Stephanie Wetzold-Schubert, Steve Barrow, Summerjam, Tine Dub & Community Rockers Soundsystem, U-Club Wuppertal, Ulli Güldner, Valentin Gube, VP Records, and all the ones I forgot here. You know who you are.

Finally, big up to all the sound systems that have invited me and will invite me to present the book at the place where the story originated.

Conversations & Interviews

Engineers:

Alborosie – July 27, 2014 Ruhr Reggae Summer Germany
Alan Redfern aka Al Breadwinner – April 07, 2021 UK, by mail
Barnabas – April 06, 2012 Kingston
Dennis Bovell – January 08, 2020 Vienna
Don Corleon – August 05, 2011 Reggae Jam Germany
Ernest Hoo Kim – March 06, 2017 Kingston
Errol Brown – July 03, 2011 Summerjam Germany
Kevin Metcalfe – April 18, 2005 London
King Jammy – April 02, 2012 Kingston
Laurent "Tippi I-Grade" Alfred – March 08, 2024 Germany
Leroy "Fatman" Thompson – February 17, 2017 Kingston
Mad Professor – February 17, 2012 Netherlands
Mark Lusardi – September 11, 2020 London, by phone
Pat Kelly – August 31, 2010 Germany

Philip Winter aka Umberto Echo – April 29, 2010 Germany
Rory Stonelove – December 31, 2013 Germany
Scientist – November 18, 2010 London + December 01, 2010 Germany
Soljie Hamilton – May 22, 2010 Germany + July 04, 2015 Summerjam Germany
Sylvan Morris – April 04, 2012 Kingston
Victor Rice – April 21, 2023 Germany

Musicians, Producers et.al.:

Bredda Neil (King Shiloh Sound System) – March 12, 2011 U-Club Germany
Bunny Lee – July 27, 2012 Garance Festival France + March 06, 2017 Kingston
Clive Chin – August 06, 2011 Reggae Geel Belgium + March 28, 2013 + April 05, 2013 Germany
Clive Hunt – March 06, 2017 Kingston
David Rodigan – July 24, 2010 + July 23, 2011 Germany
Dubblestandart – January 08, 2020 Vienna
Dubtonic Kru/Jallanzo – July 05, 2014 Summerjam Germany
Dubvisionist Felix Wolter – April 14, 2010 Germany
Earl 16 – January 22, 2011 Netherlands
Freddie McGregor – July 24, 2009 Germany
Johnny Clarke – March 03, 2017 Kingston
Linval Thompson – November 14, 2010 + August 27, 2011 Germany
Lloyd Parks – April 08, 2012 Kingston
Mark Ernestus (Rhythm & Sound) – June 21, 2011 Germany
Martin Campbell (Channel One UK) – 2014/15 by mail
Natalie Deseke (Lee Perry / Soon Come Tour) – April 05, 2020 Germany by phone
Nat Birchall – April 26, 2021 UK by mail
Pablo Moses – November 17, 2009 Germany
Roger "Fatman" Lewis (Fatman Riddim Section) – July 30, 2016 Reggae Jam Germany
Roy Francis – March 02, 2017 Kingston
Style Scott – April 03, 2012 Kingston
Tony James (Sizzler Sound System) – March 03, 2017 Kingston
Tyrone Downie (Wailers) – November 16, 2011 Germany

Index

PERSONS (SORTED BY LAST NAME & ARTIST NAME), GROUPS, SOUNDS

ALBUMS (SORTED BY TITLE)

Sources

Books:

Augustyn, Heather & Reeves, Adam
Alpha Boys' School. Cradle Of Jamaican Music. Half Pint Press, USA 2017

Barrow, Steve & Dalton, Peter
Reggae. The Rough Guide. Rough Guides Ltd., London 1997

Bartsch, Alex
Covers. Retracing Reggae Record. Sleeves in London. One Love Books, London 2018

Bradley, Lloyd
Bass Culture – When Reggae Was King. Penguin Books, England 2000

Bradley, Lloyd
Bass Culture – Der Siegeszug des Reggae. German Edition. Hannibal, Germany 2003

Collingwood, Jeremy
Lee ‚Scratch' Perry. Kiss Me Neck – The Scratch Story In Words, Pictures And Records. Cherry Red Books, London 2010

Collingwood, Jeremy
Scratch The Superape. The Jamican Releases. Lick It Back, UK 2023

De Koningh, Michael & Cane-Honeysett, Laurence
Young Gifted And Black. The Story Of Trojan Records. Sanctuary Publishing 2003

De Koningh, Michael & Griffiths, Marc
Tighten Up! The History Of Reggae In The UK. Sanctuary Publishing 2003

Dooley, Jim
Interviews From The Culture Reggae Archive. More Axe 9, I Am The Gorgon, London 2013

Dooley, Jim
The Small Axe Guide To Dub. Muzik Tree & I Am The Gorgon, London 2010

Ehrengardt, Thibault
King Tubby The Dub Master. The Official Biography. Dread Editions, France 2020

Ellington, (Duke) Edward Kennedy
Music is my Mistress. New York 1973. Da Capo Press Paperback 1976

Fingers, Al
Greensleeves The First 100 Covers. Stussy 2010

Foster, Chuck
Roots Rock Reggae. An Oral History of Reggae Music from Ska to Dancehall. Billboard Books, New York 1999

Goodman, Steve
Sonic Warfare – Sound, Affect and the Ecology of Fear. The MIT Press, Cambridge 2010

Hainard, Jacques & Mathez, Philippe
Vodou. Kunst und Kultur aus Haiti. Exhibition catalog, German edition. Berlin 2010

Hawks, Noel & Jah Floyd
Reggae Going International 1967–1976. The Bunny ‚Striker' Lee Story. Jamaican Recordings Publishing 2012

Hendler, Maximilian
Vorgeschichte des Jazz. Vom Aufbruch der Portugiesen zu Jelly Roll Morton (The prehistory of jazz. From the departure of the Portuguese to Jelly Roll Morton)
(Contributions to jazz research) Beiträge zur Jazzforschung 13, Graz Austria 2008

Henriques, Julian
Sonic Bodies. Reggae Soundsystems, Performance Techniques, and Ways Of Knowing. The Continuum International Publishing Group, New York 2011

Jones, Simon
Black Culture, White Youth. The Reggae Tradition From JA to UK. Communication and Culture. Palgrave Macmillan, Houndmills, Basingstoke 1988. Bassline Books 2016

Karnik, Olaf & Philipps, Helmut
Reggae in Deutschland (Reggae in Germany). Kiepenheuer & Wietsch 2007

Kaski, Tero & Vuorinen, Pekka
Reggae inna Dance Hall Style. Black Star, Helsinki 1984

Kaski, Tero & Vuorinen, Pekka
Volcano Revisited. Kingston Dancehall Scene 1983. Eronen 2011

Katz, David
People Funny Boy. The Genius of Lee „Scratch" Perry. 1st edition Payback Press, Edinburgh 2000.
2nd revised edition Omnibus Press 2006

Katz, David
Solid Foundation. An Oral History Of Reggae. Bloomsbury, London 2003

Kelley, Robin D.G.
Africa Speaks, Amerika Answers. Modern Jazz In Revolutionary Times. Harvard University Press 2012

Kemper, Peter
The Sound Of Rebellion. Zur politischen Ästhetik des Jazz. Reclam, Germany 2023

King, Stephen A.
Reggae, Rastafari, And The Rhetoric Of Social Control. University Press of Mississippi 2002

Lesser, Beth
Dancehall. The Rise of Jamaican Dancehall Culture. Soul Jazz Publishing 2008

Lesser, Beth
King Jammy's. ECW Press, Toronto 2002

Lesser, Beth
Rub-a-Dub Style. The Roots of Modern Dancehall. Beth Kingston, Toronto 2012

Lowe, Rich Opre
The Matador. Lloyd Daley – Sonic Pioneer of Jamaican Music. Jamaica Way Publishing, Sonoma Kalifornien 2019

Lowe, Rich Opre
Two Kings. King Edwards „The Giant" Sound System. The Era Of The King, The Duke, & The Sir. Jamaica Way Publishing, Sonoma Kalifornien 2021

Milner, Greg
Perfecting Sound Forever. The Story Of Recorded Music. Granta Books UK 2009, Paperback 2010

Muggs, Joe & Stevens, Brian David
Bass, Mids, Tops: An Oral History Of Soundsystem Culture. Strange Attractor Press UK 2019

Niaah, Sonjah Stanley
DanceHall: From Slave Ship to Ghetto. University of Ottawa Press 2010

Partridge, Christopher
Dub In Babylon. Understanding the Evolution and Significance of DUB REGGAE in Jamaica and Britain from King Tubby to Post-punk. Equinox, London 2010

Potash, Chris
Reggae, Rasta, Revolution. Jamaican Music from ska to dub. Schirmer Books, New York 1997

Rodigan, David
My Life In Reggae. Constable, London 2017

Sherlock, Philip & Bennett, Hazel
The Story of the Jamaican People. Ian Randle Publishers Ltd., Kingston 1998

Small, Geoff
Ruthless. The Global Rise of the Yardies. Warner Books, London 1995

Stolzhoff, Norman C.
Wake The Town And Tell The People. Dancehall Culture in Jamaica. Duke University Press, Durham and London 2000

Sullivan, Paul
Remixology. Tracing The Dub Diaspora. Reaction Books Ltd, London 2014

The Reggae Vibes
Studio One Files. A Collection Of Reviews, Articles, Photos, and more. Reggae Vibes Productions NL 2021

Thomas, Pat
Listen, Whitey! The Sights and Sounds of Black Power 1965–1975. Fantagraphics Books, Washington 2012

Toop, David
Ocean Of Sounds. Aether Talk, Ambient Sound And Imaginary Worlds. Profile Books, London 1995

Turner, Michael & Schoenfeld, Robert
Roots Natty Roots. The Discography of Jamaican Music. Second Edition: 78 & 45 rpm Records 1950–1985. Nighthawk Records 2002

Veal, Michael E.
DUB. Soundscapes & Shattered Songs In Jamaican Music. Wesleyan University Press, Middletown 2007

Essays, newspaper and online articles:

Addis Pablo. Suns Of Dub. Bridging The Gap by Ellen Köhlings & Pete Lilly, in: RIDDIM 03/2014

Adrian Sherwood Boiler Room Collection Youtube 2016 https://youtu.be/g86SI-bljt-E (last accessed January 02, 2022)

Adrian Sherwood on Lee ‚Scratch' Perry interviewed, edited and put into narrative form by Olaf Karnik, January 2022 in: I feel everything you say I feel everything you hear, Ed. Weekend Fest Strzelecki-Books, Cologne 2022

Archie Shepp – Fire Music. Archie Shepp, die Poesie und der Sound der Freiheit Feature of the Südwestrundfunk 2019

Lloyd 'Bulwackie' Barnes Interview https://www.reggae-vibes.com/articles/2021/07/lloyd-bulwackie-barnes-interview/ (last accessed April 01, 2024)

Bunny „Striker" Lee – Reggae Gone International by John Masouri, in: RIDDIM 02/2012

Carter Van Pelt – Linval Thompson: Can't Stop Natty Dread Again 2001 http://www.niceup.com/artists/linval_thompson (last accessed January 01, 2022)

Clive Chin Interview
by Adrian Nowak, Köln April 08, 2013, unreleased

Clive Chin. One Music
by Angus Taylor, in: Reggaeville Festival Guide 2012

David Rodigan: „My name was adopted by a Kingston gangster. He's dead now." by Alexis Petridis, in The Guardian, February 23, 2017

Die Mutter aller Remixe
by Marcel Beyer, in SPEX 10/1993

Drones, Dub und Bässe: Musikalische Räume für postmusikalische Ideen by Diedrich Diederichsen Über Pop-Musik, Kiepenheuer & Witsch, Cologne 2014

Dubtonic Kru – Foundation Medicine by Ellen Köhlings & Pete Lilly, in: RIDDIM 01/2013

Errol Brown – De Treasure Isle à Tuff Gong by Carlos Rapéri, in: Natty Dread No. 58, Dezember2009/Januar 2010, France

Graeme Goodall – Mr. Goody
Interview von Peter I, http://www.reggae-vibes.com/, 2011 (last accessed January 30, 2013)

Idris Ackamoor – How Idris Ackamoor's African odyssey helped shape Afrofuturist jazz. Interview The Vinyl Factory, https://thevinylfactory.com/features/idris-ackamoor-pyramids-interview/, 2018 (last accessed May 17. 2018)

In Search of the First Dub LP
by David Katz, www.redbullmusicacademy.com/magazine/first-dub-lp-in-search-of, 2013 (last accessed May 15, 2014)

Jamaican Creole in German Reggae Subculture by Michael Westphal in: The Language Of Pop Culture, Routledge, New York and London, 2018

Jazz Jamaica, At Home And Abroad by Herbie Miller and Roberto Moore in: Jamaica Jamaica!, Catalog for the exhibition, National Gallery Of Jamaica 2020

Johnny „Dizzy" Moore. The Lion's Last Blow by Herbie Miller in: RIDDIM 06/2008

King Jammy's – The Godfather
by Ulli Güldner, in: RIDDIM 03/2017

King Tubby – Mister Dub
by Dave Hendley, in: Natty Dread No. 19, June/July 2003, France

King Tubby the dubmaster. The Teacher and the apprentices by Beth Lesser, in: Reggae Quarterly Vol.1 No. 3, Canada 1983

„Klang!" Garvey's Ghost meets Heidegger's Geist by Ian Penman, in: Experiencing The Soundtrack, Sidney 2001

Lee Perry Interview 1992
by René Wynands, in »Do The Reggay!« Piper, Munich 1995

Lee Perry Interview
in: Grand Royal. The Magazine Of Champions Issue 2 1995, Ed. The Beastie Boys

Lee 'Scratch' Perry remembered by Neil 'Mad Professor' Fraser
in: The Guardian UK December 12, 2021

Lee „Scratch" Perry – 10 Commandments The eccentric reggae legend shares his golden rules for life, in: Q-Magazine July 2019

„Leroy's Gonna Fight"
by Peter I, in: http://www.reggae-vibes.com/concert/leroysibbles/leroysibbles.htm (last accessed July 07, 2014)

Linval Thompson – Can't Stop A Natty Dread Interview by Peter I 2004
https://www.reggae-vibes.com/articles/2019/01/linval-thompson-interview/ (last accessed December 30, 2021)

Lloyd „Bullwackie" Barnes: North Bronx Roots Interview by Carter Van Pelt, in: Wax Poetics 20 Dec/Jan 2007, New York

Mad Professor – Analogue is...
Interview Analogue Foundation 2019, https://www.analoguefoundation.com/analogue-is/10/ (last accessed December 30, 2021)

Marcus Meets Rockers
by Carl Gayle, in: Black Music 2/1976, London

Paul ‚Groucho' Smykle – Surgeon Of Dub Paul Bradshaw in: New Musical Express February 21, 1983

Pop Culture and the Globalization of Non-standard Varieties of English. Jamaican Creole in German Reggae Subculture by Michael Westphal, in: The Language of Pop Culture
Routledge Studies in Linguistic, New York + Abingdon UK 2018

Reggae Revival Online Movement
http://www.jamaicansmusic.com/news/Culture/Reggae_Revival_Online_Movement (last accessed December 09, 2021)

Roots'n'Future. Wie die Stimme des Reggae verschwand und wieder auftauchte – von Dub über Dancehall bis Garage Rap by Simon Reynolds, in: Futuromania. Elektronische Träume von der Zukunft. Ventil Verlag, Mainz Germany 2023

Rory Stone Love. Die fantastische Metamorphose des... by Ursula „Munchy" Münch in: RIDDIM 06/2014

Scientist at the controls
by Beth Lesser, in: Reggae Quarterly Vol.1 No. 3, Kanada 1983

Scientist, dub reggae's experimental genius. A beginner's guide by David Katz, in: FACT Online Magazine 2015 http://www.factmag.com/2015/07/14/a-beginners-guide-to-scientist/ (last accessed December 30, 2021)

Scientist Interview by Mike Pawka
Nice Up Enterprises, Jammin Reggae Archives 1998
http://www.niceup.com/interviews/scientist (last accessed December 30, 2021)

Scientist Interview by Angus Taylor
United Reggae 2008, http://www.unitedreggae.com/articles/n212/092408/interview-scientist (last accessed December 30, 2021)

Scientist Interview by Seb Carayol
United Reggae 2012, http://unitedreggae.com/articles/n1022/070612/interview-scientist-2012 (last accessed December 30, 2021)

Scientist On Dub
Red Bull Music Academy 2010, https://www.youtube.com/watch?v=-GvhMH-JKJvM (last accessed January 02, 2022)

Studio One – The essential dubs
by Chris Lane, in: Black Music 3/1980, London

Style Scott – Deconstructing The Rythm
An interview with drummer Style Scott from Dub Syndicate by Pavle Djukic, Reggae-News Co.UK 2004 http://www.reggaenews.co.uk/interviews/style_scott.asp (last accessed April 29, 2015)

Sylvan Morris Interview by Shivu Rao und Sean Stewart
Babylon Falling 2008 https://babylon-falling.tumblr.com/sylvan_morris_interview (last accessed December 12, 2021)

Sylvan Morris. Tales Of Brentford Road
by Tero Kaski, in: More Axe 7, Finland 1989

Talking Dub and Vampires with Scientist
Large Up Interview 2012, http://www.largeup.com/2012/09/21/largeup-interview-scientist/ (last accessed January 11, 2016)

Sources

The Ariwa / Mad Professor Story by David Katz
https://www.ariwa.com/ariwa-story (last accessed January 11, 2019)

The Dub Lp Archives
http://dubwise.smokeyroom.net/ (last accessed December 09, 2021)

The law according to Junjo
Howard Campbell in: Jamaica Observer November 02, 2012
http://www.jamaicaobserver.com/entertainment/The-law-according-to-Junjo_12891667(last accessed May 05, 2016)

"The media want to see us hype and nuff" – Zwischen lokaler Praxis und globalem Medienhype: Eine Ethnographie über das Reggae Revival in Jamaika. Thesis for the award of the academic degree M.A. Cultural and Social Anthropology at the University of Bayreuth
by Lisa Katharina Jung 2015

"The Sound Of Surprise"
Richard Williams in: Melody Maker August 21, 1976 page 21

U-Roy. Godfather Of The Deejay School
by David Katz, in: RIDDIM 01/2013

Versions, Dubs and Riddims:Dub and the Transient Dynamics of Jamaican Music
by Thomas Vendryes, in: Dancecult: Journal of Electronic Dance Music Culture 7/2015

VP Records celebrates the life of producer ands businessman Joseph „Jo Jo" Hoo Kim
https://vprecords.com/vp-records-celebrates-the-life-of-producer-and-businessman-joseph-jo-jo-hoo-kim/ 21.09.2018 (last accessed December 30, 2021)

Vuorinnen, Pekka – A conversation with
https://legendaryreggae.com/2013/04/15/reggae-inna-dancehall-style-a-conversation-with-pekka-vuorinen/ (last accessed December 07, 2023)

Waterhouse: Terrorised By Gangsters!
Gary Spaulding in: The Gleaner 25.04.2010 http://jamaica-gleaner.com/gleaner/20100425/lead/lead2.html (last accessed August 21, 2016)

Wayne Smith. Sleng Teng Revisited
by Ulli Güldner, in: RIDDIM 02/2006

What is the reggae revival?
Let's Talk Reggae mit Dutty Bookman, in: Jamaica Observer December 05, 2021

30 Jahre On-U Sound. Psychedelische Löwen aus einstürzenden Häusern
by David Katz, in RIDDIM 06/2011

Documentaries:

Bullwackie In New York, White Plains Road
Brighton Video 1984

Deep Roots Music
6-part TV documentary, Channel 4, England 1982

Dub Echoes
A Film by Bruno Natal. Soul Jazz Records DVD 2009

Dub London: Bassline of a City
Materials for an exhibition in the museum of London Okt. 2020 – Jan. 2021

Dub Not Dub
A radio broadcast by Westdeutscher Rundfunk April 09, 2011
by Olaf Karnik in German radio station WDR 3 „Open Frei Raum"

Duke Vin and the Birth of Ska
Gus Berger, Hackney Film Collective 2011

Dub Talks
in: Gussie Clarke – Dub Anthology (3CDs + 1 DVD). Music Works Records 2018

Gelobte Länder
Interart, Netherlands 2013

King At The Controls
Dokumentation + Jammy's In His Own Words 2006
in: King Jammy's Roots Reality And Sleng Teng. VP Records/17 North Parade DVD (+ 2 CD) 2014

Kraftwerk – Pop Art
TV-Documentary by Simon Wittler and Hannes Rossacher 2013

Lee 'Scratch' Perry in concert: The Ultimate Alien. Secret Films UK 2003 DVD (incl. Interview)

Lee Scratch Perry – The Unlimited Destruction. Jet Star UK VHS 1991, DVD 2002

Lee Scratch Perry's Vision Of Paradise
A movie by Volker Schaner. Fufoofilm, Germany 2015

Musically Mad. A Documentary On UK Reggae Sound Systems
A Folke/Weslien Film. No Label, Sweden 2008

Randy's 50th Anniversary
VP Records/17 North Parade DVD (+ CD) 2008

Return Of The Rub-A-Dub Style
Walking Road Films USA 2009, published 2011

Roots, Rock, Reggae
A Jeremy Marre Documentary. Harcourt Films 1977

Scientist Porträt & Interview
ARTE TV, Sendung „Tracks" am 7.9.2013

Studio One Story
Soul Jazz DVD (+ CD + Buch) 2002

Soundtrack Of King Jammy
A radio broadcast by Westdeutscher Rundfunk August 15, 2015
by Ellen Köhlings & Pete Lilly in German radio station WDR, Funkhaus Europa Soulfood

The Anthology Of Reggae Drumming
A Documentary by Alex Domhoever 2016

Booklets & Linernotes for CDs and vinyls:

African Dub Chapters 1,2,3&4 All-Mighty
4 CD Box, VP Music Group / 17 North Parade 2007

Byron Lee & The Dragonaires – Uptown Top Ranking
VP Music Group / 17 North Parade 2015

Channel One – Maxfield Avenue Breakdown. Dubs & Instrumentals 1974–79. Pressure Sounds 2001

Dennis Bovell presents 4th Street Orchestra: Ah Who Seh? Go Deh! + Leggo! EMI CD Reissue 2006

Dennis Bovell presents 4th Street Orchestra: Higher Ranking Dub + Yu Learn! EMI CD Reissue 2006

Dennis Bovell – Decibell
Pressure Sounds 2003

Dial M For Murder In Dub Style
Pressure Sounds 2011

Drum Sound – The Revolutionaries
More gems from the channel one dub room – 1974 to 1980. Pressure Sounds 2007

Dub Gone Crazy. The Evolution of Dub at King Tubby's 1975–1979. Blood & Fire 1994

Dub I – Jimmy Radway & The Fe Me Time All Stars. Pressure Sounds 2008

Duke Reid International Disco Series
Doctor Bird UK 2021

Evolution Of Dub Volume 1–8
4 LPs each on CD in a box, Greensleeves Records 2009–2013

Hitbound! The Revolutionary Sound Of Channel One. Heartbeat LP/CD 1989

Impact All Stars – Forward The Bass
Dub From Randy's 1972–1975. Blood & Fire 1998

I-Roy – Don't Check Me With No Lightweight Stuff (1972–75). Blood & Fire 1997

Jammy$ From The Roots 1977–1985
Greensleeves Records 2010

Joe Gibbs & The Professionels – No Bones For The Dogs. Dubs From The Mighty Two 1974 to 1979. Pressure Sounds 2002

Johnny Clarke – Dreader Dread 1976–1978
Blood & Fire 1998

King Tubby & Prince Jammy – Dub Gone 2 Crazy: In Fine Style 1975–1979. Blood & Fire 1996

King Tubby meets Jacob Miller – Ina Tenemant Yard. Motion 2006

Linval Thompson – the early sessions 1979–1982. Thompson Sound CD + DVD 2006

Prince Jammy Presents Strictly Dub
Pressure Sounds 2010

Skin Flesh & Bones – Dub In Blood
Pressure Sounds 2016

Sound System International Dub LP – King Tubby & The Clancy Eccles All Stars. Pressure Sounds 2009

The Crowning Of Prince Jammy
Pressure Sounds 1999

The Prophets – King Tubby's Prophecies Of Dub. Pressure Sounds Re-Issue 2019

The Ring Craft Posse – St. Catherine In Dub 1972 – 1984. Moll-Selekta 2004

The War Is On Dub Style
Pressure Sounds 2018 Re-Issue

Yabby You – Dread Prophecy
Shanachie 2015

Photo Legends & Credits

(from left to right, from top to bottom)

Unless otherwise stated, all objects and images are from the author's archive.

Page Item/Photo

Cover Community Rockers Sound System, Germany

005 Brother Sound, France + Blackwood Sound System, Germany, photo: Blackwood Sound

006 LP *Channel One Sound System – Down In The Dub Vaults* Greensleeves UK 2023

007 LP *The Upsetters – Super Ape*, Island Records Germany 1976

LP *The Congoes – Heart Of The Congoes* Black Art Jamaica 1977 Reissue VP Records US 2017

008 LP *Harry Mudie meets King Tubby in Dub Conference Vol. 1* Moodisc Jamaica 1976

LP *Winston Edwards & Blackbeard – Dub Conference At 10 Downing Street* Studio 16 UK 1980

LP *The Simeons – Dub Conference in London* Freedom Sounds UK 1978

009 Kokoteni HiFi, Germany, photo: Gardy Stein

010 Streetdance in Kingston, ca. 2000, photo: Julian Thomann

013 LP *Lone Ranger – On The Other Side Of Dub* Studio One Jamaica 1977

014 LP *Keith Hudson – Pick A Dub* Mamba UK 1974

015 LP *Page One – Rock A Dub* Jamaica Sound UK 1979

016 10-inch Don Corleon – "Luv A Dub" / "Ghetto Life Dub" + "Warning Dub" / "Sweet Treat Dub"

buyreggae.com Germany 2012 provided by Outernational Sounds, Germany

017 LP *Ital Dub Sounds & System* Studio One Jamaica 1974, provided by Rob Chapman

LP *Mellow Dub Sounds & System* Studio One Jamaica 1973, provided by Rob Chapman

020 7-inch Burt Walters – "Honey Love" / "Evil Yenoh" Jamaica 1968 Reissue Trojan 2019

021 7-inch Burt Walters – "Blowing In The Wind" Doctor Bird UK 1969 Reissue Trojan 2019

12-inch back cover of King Stitt – "Herbsman Shuffle" Trojan UK 1980, shows Linford Anderson at the MCI board which is later sold to King Tubby

022 LP *Ital Dub* Studio One Jamaica 1975

LP *Mello Dub* Studio One Jamaica 1970s

LP *Roots Dub* Studio One Jamaica 1977

LP *Zodiac Sounds* Studio One Jamaica 1975

023 LP *Big Youth – Reggae Gi Dem Dub* Nichola Delita Jamaica 1978

024 LP *Sylvan Morris – Reggae Workshop* (front + back) B & M Records Jamaica 1975

025 LP *Bunny Wailer – Dub D'isco Vol. 1* Solomonic Jamaica 1979

Sylvan Morris at Harry J Studio, photo: Pekka Vuorinen

027 LP *Sylvan Morris – Cultural Dub* Harry J US 1978

028 LP *Sylvan Morris – Morris On Dub* Jaywax Jamaica 1975

029 unknown Sound System, Kingston ca. 2000, photo: Julian Thomann

030 Blackwood Sound System, Germany, photo: Blackwood Sound

032 7-inch Augustus Pablo – "Java" Impact! Jamaica 1971

033 7-inch The Victors – "Me A Tell Yuh" / "More Echo" Syndicate Jamaica 1971

034 LP *Java Java Java Java* Impact! Jamaica 1973 Reissue VP Records US 2011

LP *Dub Serial – More Dub* Joe Gibbs Jamaica 1973

035 LP *Aquarius Dub* Aquarius Jamaica 1973

LP *Upsetters – Blackboard Jungle Dub* Clocktower US 197x

LP *Prince Buster – The Message* FAB UK 1973

036 LP *Dub Store Special* Studio One Jamaica 1974

LP *Rupie Edwards All Stars – Dub Basket* Cactus UK 1975, provided by Marvin Böhm

038 LP *Joe Gibbs & The Professionals – African Dub All-Mighty* Joe Gibbs Jamaica 1975

039 LP *Joe Gibbs & The Professionals – State Of Emergency* Joe Gibbs Jamaica 1976

Umojah Sound System Nairobi, photo: Jah Schulz

040 Randy's Studio 2012: mixing board, various tape machines (2, 3, 16-track), organ, dub cutter

041 Randy's Studio 2012: pricelist from 1974

043 LP *This Is Augustius Pablo* (front + back) Kaya Records Jamaica 1974

044 LP *Clive Chin presents Randy's Dub* (front + back) Only Roots Records France 2015 (Reissue of LP *Randy's Dub* Impact! 1976, then without cover, now with Clive Chin at the board)

046 LP *Burning Spear – Garvey's Ghost* (front + back) Island Records UK 1976

047 Super Power Sound System, Germany, photo: Tom Battery

048 LP *King Tubbys Presents Soundclash Dubplate Style* Firehouse Jamaica 1988

LP *Rupie Edwards All Stars – Dub Basket Chapter II (A King Tubby's Mix)* Cactus UK 1976

LP *Yabba Youth (i.e. Yabby You) – Chant Down Babylon Kingdom* Nationwide UK 1977

LP *Yabby You – Beware Dub* Grove Music UK 1978

050 LP *Big Joe At The Controls* Live And Love UK 1978

051 LP *King Tubby The Dub Master Presents Dub From The Roots* Total Sounds Jamaica 1974

052 LP *King Tubby The Dub Master Presents The Roots Of Dub* Total Sounds Jamaica 1975

LP *King Tubby The Dub Master Presents The Roots Of Dub* Grounation UK 1975

053 LP *Natty Locks Dub* Fay Music UK 1974

LP *King Tubby meets The Upsetter At The Grass Roots Of Dub* (front + back) Fay Music UK 1974

054 7-inch Augustus Pablo – "King Tubby meets the Rockers Uptown" (sleeve front + back + promo vinyl) Island Records UK 1975

056 Kingston, 18 Dromilly Avenue, photo from 2017

057 View down the street from 18 Dromilly Avenue. The picture of a 7-inch single on the left wall is a reminder that Tubby's studio was once located here, photo from 2017

058 LP *King Tubby – Majestic Dub* Star UK 198x

059 LP *Bunny Lee & The Aggrovators Presents Super Dub Disco Style* Jamaica Sound UK 1979

060 King Tubby's chair from his workshop on Dromilly Avenue, stored in a room in Bunny Lee's studio in Duhaney Park, Kingston. Found and photographed in 2014 by Ursula "Munchy" Münch

061 King Tubby and David Rodigan 1985

065 Door of Tubby's new studio building at the back of 18 Dromilly Avenue, where productions never took place, photo from 2017

066 LP *Rockers Arena – Rodigan-v-Williams* Exclusive UK 1980

067 LP *The Ethnic Fight Band – Music Explosion* Ethnic Fight UK 197x

LP *The Ethnic Fight Band – Out Of One Man Comes Many Dubs* Ethnic Fight UK 1975

Photo Legends & Credits

068 Ras Craft HiFi Sound System, Germany, photo: Peter Krowiorsch

069 LP *Fat Man Riddim Section – Tough Guys In Dub* Top Ranking International US 1979

LP *Fat Man Riddim Section – Tribulation Dub* Top Ranking International US 1982

LP *Fat Man Riddim Section – Is It War Or Is It Peace?* Top Ranking International US 1980

LP *Fat Man Riddim Section – Killer Dub* Top Ranking International US 1978

070 LP *Fatman presents – Unleashed Dub From King Tubby's Studio* Fat Man UK 1991

072 LP *Two Big Bull In A One Pen Dubwise* Firehouse Jamaica 1986

073 Sightiva Hi-Fi Sound System, Germany, photo: DiNo

074 King Shiloh Circle Of Sound, Netherlands, photo: King Shiloh

075 LP *Mikey Dread – Dub Merchant* Dread At The Controls UK 1982

076 *The Prophets – King Tubby's Prophecies Of Dub* (front + back) Prestige Jamaica 1976, provided by Valentin Gube

079 LP *Harry Mudie meets King Tubby in Dub Conference Vol. 2* Moodisc Records Jamaica 1977

LP *Harry Mudie meets King Tubby in Dub Conference Vol. 3* Moodisc Records Jamaica 1978

photos show CD-Booklet of the US-release 1994

080 LP *Morwells Esq. – Dub Me* (front + back) Morwells Esq. Jamaica 1975

081 I-Livity I-Fi Sound System, Germany, photo: Julian Thomann

082 Bunny Lee's studio and and shelves of master tapes in Duhaney Park. Photos from 2014 by Ursula "Munchy" Münch, taken a year before a fire destroyed the studio. The tapes survived.

085 LP *Rasta Dub '76* Grounation UK 1976

LP *Kaya Dub* Kaya US 1975

LP *Dub War Vol. 1* Vista Sounds UK 1985

LP *Dub War Coxsone vs. Quaker City* Imperial Records Canada 1981

086 LP *King Tubby verses Channel One* Bumb USA 1980

087 LP *Sly & Robbie – Masters Of Ceremony Dub* Imperial Canada 198x

LP *Bunny Lee The Version Master presents Creation of Dub* Total Sounds Jamaica 1975

LP *King Tubby's and The Agrovators – Dubbing In The Back Yard* Black Music UK 1982

LP *King Tubby The Dubmaster With The Waterhouse Posse* Vista Sounds UK 1983

088 LP *Jack Ruby Hi-Power vs. Gemini Discotheque* Tad's US 1980

091 LP *Bunny Lee & King Tubby Present Tommy McCook And The Aggravators – Brass Rockers* Total Sounds Jamaica 1975 (identical to *Tommy McCook – Cookin'* S. 228)

LP *King Tubby And The Aggrovators – Shalom Dub* 1975 Klik UK Reissue Jamaican Recordings UK 2010

Bunny Lee and the author, France 2012

092 Community Rockers Sound System, Germany, photo: T-Jah

093 Back cover of LP *B.B. Seaton – Colour Is Not The Answer* Jama Music UK 1976: Errol Brown (center) at Treasure Isle, left B.B. Seaton, right Willie Lindo

095 LP *Treasure Dub* Treasure Isle Records Jamaica 1975

LP *Treasure Dub Vol. 2* Treasure Isle Records Jamaica 1976

096 LP *Culture In Dub* Sky Note UK 1978 (identical to *Culture Dub*)

LP *Culture Dub* High Note Jamaica 1978 (identical to *Culture In Dub*)

097 LP *Orthodox Dub* Magic Fire Records Jamaica 1978

LP *Dub Expression* High Note Jamaica 1978

LP *Dubb Everlasting* High Note Jamaica 1977

LP *Medley Dub* High Note Jamaica 1976

098 LP *Revolutionary Dub* Trenchtown UK 1976

LP *Gun Court Dub* Love UK 1975

099 LP *Bag-O-Wire* Klik UK 1975

100 LP *Burning Spear – Living Dub Vol. 2* Burning Spear Jamaica 1982

102 LP *Israel Vibration – Unconquered People Dub* Rave Music Jamaica 1980

CD *Chinna Smith presents Dub It!* Nature Sounds US 2004

103 Cpt. Yossarian's Dubtrain One, Germany, photo: Manuel Da Coll

104 Channel One Studio ruin, photo from 2018 by Alex Domhöver

108 LP *Earthquake Dub* Joe Gibbs Jamaica 1978

LP *Skin Flesh & Bones – Dub In Blood* Sun Shot Jamaica 1976

109 LP *Vital Dub – Well Charged* Virgin UK 1976

110 LP *Chemist – Dub Prescription* Kingdom UK 1984

111 LP *Don't Underestimate The Force. The Force Is Within You* (front + back) J&L US 1977

LP *The Revolutionaries – I Came I Saw I Conquered* (front + back) J&L US 1981

112 LP *The Revolutionaries – Jonkanoo Dub* Cha Cha UK 1978

LP *The Revolutionaries – Reaction In Dub* Cha Cha UK 1978

113 LP *The Revolutionaries – Revival Sound* (= *Revival Dub Roots Now*) Well Charge Jamaica 1976

LP *The Revolutionaries – Revolutionaries Sounds Vol. 2* Ballistic Records UK 1979

LP *The Force Of Music – Freedom Fighters Dub* Ballistic Records UK 1978

114 Flabba Holt and the author, Kingston 2012

116 LP *Dawn Of Creation* Sagittarius Records UK 1979 (identical to *Phase 1 Dub Wise Volume 2*)

LP *Roots Radics – Radicfaction* Cha Cha UK 1982

117 LP *Roots Radics Live At Channel One Kingston Jamaica* Live And Love UK 1982

LP *Roots Radics – Radical Dub Session* Solid Groove Records UK 1982

LP *Three Dreads From Zion Dub* GG's Records Jamaica 1978

118 In the ruins of Channel One Studio, photos from 2015 by Jonas Schaul

119 Barnabas and the author, Kingston 2012

120 LP *Kings Dub* Manzie JA 1980

LP *Universal Dub (King Tubby, Scientist, Bunny Tom Tom & Barnabas)* Zola & Zola NL 1995

121 LP *Heavy Metal Dub* Clocktower US 1982

LP *Scientist & Barnabas & Maxie – Three The Hard Way* (front + back) Silver Camel UK 1981

122 7-inch Pat Kelly – „Barnabas" (Dub to „How Long") Prophets Jamaica 1976

LP *Ranking Barnabas – The Cold Crusher* Express US 197x, provided by Frank Balczynski

124 12-inch Gregory Isaacs & Ranking Barnabas – „Tumbling Tears" GG's Records Jamaica 1977

126 LP *Afrikan History* Mandingo UK 1983

CD *Xterminator All Stars – Xterminator in Dub No Gabbon* Charm Records UK 1999

CD *MLK Dub* RAS Records US 1999

127 LP *Sojie – Rebel Soldier* Taxi Jamaica 1982

128 LP *Raiders Of The Lost Dub* Island Records UK 1981

LP *Sly & Robbie – A Dub Experience* Island Records UK 1985

129 LP *Black Uhuru – The Dub Factor* Mango/Island Records 1983

130 LP *Sly & Robbie – Dub Rising* Tabou France 2014

LP *Sly & Robbie – Disco Dub* Gorgon Records Jamaica 1978

LP *Sly & Robbie and Brinsley Forde – One Fine Dub* Tabou France 2016

131 Soljie Hamilton during the 2010 interview, photo: Martina Markwart

132 Reggae Roast Sound System „The Beast", UK photo: Reggae Roast

134 LP *Negrea Love Dub* Trojan UK 1978

135 LP *Guerilla Dub* Burning Sounds UK 1978

LP *Gregory Isaacs – Slum In Dub* Burning Sounds UK 1978

LP *Elroy Bailey – Red Hot Dub* Burning Vibrations UK 1979

LP *Star Wars Dub* Burning Sounds 1978

LP *Black Magic Dub* FORM Ireland 1980

LP *Dread Lion Dub* His Majesty UK 1979

LP *Burning Dub* Burning Vibrations 1979

136 LP *The Revolutionaries – Outlaw Dub* Trojan UK 1979 (identical to *Strong Like Samson Linval Thompson In Dub* Thompson Sound Jamaica 1979)

LP *Train To Zion Dub* (Tuff Gong Jamaica 1981)

137 LP *King Of Dub* Clocktower US 1979

LP *Rockers Almighty Dub* (front + back) Clocktower US 1979

LP *The Sound Of Macka Dub* Clocktower US 1976

139 LP *Ghost Dubs – Damaged* Pressure UK 2024 (artwork shows The Pressure Sound System by The Bug)

140 Sightiva Hi-Fi Sound System, Germany, photo: DiNo

141 7-inch Barrinton Levy – "Collie Weed" + "Domino Dub" Roots From The Yard Jamaica 1979

142 LP *Scientist vs Papa Tad's – Allied Dub Selection* Tad's Records US 1980

LP *Introducing Scientist – The best Dub album in the World* JB Music UK 1980

143 LP *Scientist Meets The Space Invaders* Greensleeves UK 1981

LP *Scientist Heavy Weight Dub Champion* Greensleeves UK 1980

144 LP *Scientist Encounters Pac-Man* Greensleeves UK 1982

145 LP *Scientist High Priest Of Dub* (front + back) Kingdom UK 1982

146 LP *Scientist – Scientific Dub* Clocktower US 1981

LP *International Heroes Dub* Tamoki Wambesi UK 1994

LP *Scientist – World At War* Black Ovation Records US 1981

147 LP *Scientist – The Dub Album They Didn't Want You To Hear* Jah Life US 2014 (Sleeve showing a very young Scientist at the board of Channel One Studio)

LP *Jah Life In Dub* Jah Life US 2014

LP *Revolutionary Sounds Pre-Release Dub* Revolutionary Sounds US 2016 (This is the LP that was sold in the sleeves of *Jah Life In Dub* in the early 1980s)

148 LP *Scientist Meets The Roots Radics* Selena UK 1982, Picture Disc Record Store Day US 2014

149 LP *Scientist Dubs Culture Into A Parallel Universe* RAS Records US 2000

LP *Scientist Meets Hempress Sativa In Dub* Conquering Lion Records Germany 2017

151 Scientist and the author, London 2010, photo: Alice Peperell (courtesy of Red Bull Studios, London)

152 LP *Barrington Levy In Dub (The lost mixes from King Tubby's studio)* Auralux UK 2005 Reissue of the Jamaica-only version of *Scientist v Prince Jammy - Big Showdown* on the Jah Guidance label, with different mixes and seven different tracks than the Greensleeves release under the same title.

153 LP *King Tubby Prince Jammy And Scientist – First, second and third generation of Dub* (front + back) KG Imperial UK 1981

155 LP *Scientist Wins The World Cup* Greensleeves UK 1982

LP *Junjo presents: Wins The Worldcup* Greensleeves/VP Records US 2016

Above: Excerpt of the *Junjo presents Wins The Worldcup* cover, where the referee shoots the goal. The original cover shows Scientist as the scorer.

156 LP *Scientist Rids The World Of The Evil Curse Of The Vampires* Greensleeves UK 1981

LP *Junjo presents The Evil Curse Of The Vampires* Greensleeves/VP Records US 2016

Note: The original artwork shows Scientist sitting in front of a sound system on the right, while the Junjo version covers his face with a spotlight.

LP *Scientist v Prince Jammy – Big Showdown* Greensleeves UK 1980

LP *Junjo presents: Big Showdown 1980* Greensleeves/VP Records US 2016

Note: The original artwork shows Jammy in the right corner, Scientist in the left and a number girl in the middle of the boxing ring. In the *Junjo* version, the number girl has been moved and now holds the "Round 1" sign in front of Scientist's face.

157 LP *Scientist In Dub Volume 1* Jah Guidance US 1981

LP *Dub War Coxsone vs. Quaker City* Reissue Dubmusic Productions 2023

LP *Scientist – Dub Landing* Starlight Records UK 1981

LP *Linval presents Dub Landing Vol. 1* Greensleeves/VP Records US 2017 (same album as *Dub Landing*, different artwork, different title)

158 Painted record labels on the outside wall of Jammy's studio complex in Kingston, photo from 2012

160 LP *Prince Jammy presents Strictly Dub* Jammy's Records Jamaica 1981. The cover shows Jammy at the MCI console in King Tubby's studio.

161 LP *African Anthem (The Mikey Dread Show Dubwise)* Cruise Records UK 1979

LP *King Jammy – Waterhouse Dub* Greensleeves/VP Records US 2017

162 LP *Horace Andy – In The Light In Dub* Hungry Town Jamaica 1977

LP *Escape From Hell* Stars Jamaica 1977

163 LP *Prince Jammy In Lion Dub Style* (front + back) Jammy's Records Jamaica 1978

LP *The Agrovators – Jammy In Lion Dub Style* Live and Love UK 1978 (both albums are identical)

164 LP *Prince Jammy – Kamikazi Dub* Trojan UK 1979

LP *Scientist and Jammy Strike Back!* Trojan UK 1982

LP *Creation Rebel – Close Encounters of the Third World* Hitrun UK 1978

LP *DEB Music Players – 20th. Century DEB-Wise* DEB UK 1970

LP *Inner Circle – Killer Dub* Top Ranking US 1978

LP *Prince Jammy Destroys The Invaders* Greensleeves UK 1982

LP *The Rass-Es Band – Harder Na Ras* Ballistic Records UK 1980

LP *Rockers All Stars – Chanting Dub With The Help Of The Father* Rockers Jamaica 1978

LP *Prince Jammy – Uhuru In Dub* CSA UK 1982

165 LP *The Agrovators – Kaya Dub* (front + back) Third World UK 1978

167 LP *Prince Jammy's – Computerized Dub* Greensleeves UK 1986

168 LP *Alborosie meets King Jammy – Dub Of Thrones* Greensleeves/VP Records US 2015

169 King Jammy dubbing live at Garance Festival, France 2013

171 King Jammy and the author, Kingston 2012

12-inch Jamdown Players – "Levi's Choice Dubwise" (4 tracks on B-Side of Movement – "No Man Is An Island")

12-inch Jamdown Players – 3 tracks on B-Side of Third-I-Band – "Go Find Yourself A Fool"

12-inch Jamdown Players – 3 tracks on B-Side of Wolete Miriam – "Warrior"

All: Ballistic Records UK 1980

172 Basskateers Sound System, Germany, photo: Basskateers

174 7-inch Byron Lee & The Dragonaires – "Squeeze Up (Part 1)" + "(Part 2)" Trojan UK 1970

175 7-inch Byron Lee & The Dragonaires – "Superior" Tiger Jamaica 1970

7-inch Byron Lee & The Dragonaires – "Don't Call Me Nigger Whitey" Tiger Jamaica 1970

Street Sign Cardiff Crescent, Kingston, photo from 2023 by Karl-Olaf Kaiser

176 Cardiff Crescent, view from Perry's Studio, photo from 2023 by Karl-Olaf Kaiser

177 LP *The Mighty Upsetter – Kung Fu Meets The Dragon* Reissue Justice League UK 1995

CD *Lee Perry – Dubstrumentals* Trojan UK 2005

178 LP *Revolution Dub* Cactus UK 1975

The original Roland Space Echo from 1974, provided by Frank Balczynski

180 LP *The Upsetters – Scratch The Super Ape* Upsetter Jamaica 1976

LP *The Upsetters – Return Of The Super Ape* Lion Of Judah Jamaica 1978

182 The ruins of Lee Perry's Black Ark Studio, photos from 2023 by Karl-Olaf Kaiser

183 Excerpt from the cover of the 7-inch "The Invisible Man" by Solid Bronze from Delaware (Schnitzel Records Rough Trade 2019), where it is claimed to be a "Lee 'Scratch' Perry Dub Mix". The truth is written small underneath: Engineer Mad Professor.

184 CD *Lee Scratch Perry vs. Robo Bass HiFi vs. Dubblestandard – Nu School Of Planet Dub* Echo Beach Germany 2014

Photo Legends & Credits

186 LP *Lee Perry – Who Put The Voodoo 'Pon Reggae?* Ariwa UK 1996

LP *Mad Professor & Lee Perry – Dub Take The Voodoo Out Of Reggae* Ariwa UK 1996

187 LP *Lee $cratch Perry – Rainford* On-U Sound UK 2019

LP *Lee $cratch Perry – Heavy Rain* On-U Sound UK 2019

188 Reggae Roast Sound System „The Beast", UK photo: Reggae Roast

190 LP *Augustus Pablo presents Ital Dub* Trojan UK 1975

191 LP *Jah Shaka – Warrior (Commandments Of Dub Chapter 7)* Jah Shaka Music UK 1987

193 Dennis Bovell and the author, Vienna 2020

CD *Dennis Bovell – The 4th Street Orchestra Collection* Doctor Bird UK 2023

194 7-inch (no artist) "Red Gold Green" / "Jah Almighty" Kool Records 1977

7-inch Black Starline Band – "Suffer Height" / "Revolution Must Come A Yard" T Bone Records 1977 (both singles are said to be from Kingston)

195 LP *Blackbeard – Strictly Dub Wize* United Artists Records UK 1978

196 LP *Creation Rebel – Dub From Creation* Hitrun UK 1978

LP *Mawamba Dub* D-Roy Records UK 1978

LP *The Arabs – Crytuff Dub Encounter Chapter 1* Hitrun UK 1978

LP *Blackbeard – I Wah Dub* More Cut UK 1980

LP *LKJ In Dub* Island Records UK 1980

LP *Matumbi – Dub Planet Orbit 1* Extinguish Records UL 1980

197 LP *Revelation – Variation On A Theme* Burning Vibrations UK 1979

198 LP *Tradition – High Risk Dub* Venture Records UK 1980

LP *Creation Rebel – Rebel Vibration* Hitrun UK 1979

199 LP *Tradition – Captain Ganja And The Space Patrol* Venture Records UK 1980

200 LP *Dub Syndicate – The Pounding System (Ambient In Dub)* On-U Sound UK 1982

201 LP *Creation Rebel – Starship Africa* 4D Rhythms UK 1980

Adrian Sherwood, photo: Nicolai Beverungen

203 LP *Mad Professor – Dub Me Crazy* Ariwa UK 1982

LP *Mad Professor – Beyond The Realms Of Dub (Dub Me Crazy The Second Chapter)* Ariwa UK 1982

204 LP *Negus Roots Meets The Mad Professor* Negus Roots UK 1983

205 LP *Mad Professor – Dubbing With Anansi* Ariwa UK 2014

206 CD *Mad Professor – The Roots Of Dubstep* Ariwa UK 2011

LP *Mad Professor – Electro Clubdubbing!!* Ariwa UK 2018

LP *Massive Attack v. Mad Professor – No Protection* Wild Bunch Records UK 1995

207 Style Scott, 2012 during the interview in Earl Chinna Smith's garden in Kingston

208 LP *Prince Far I & The Arabs – Crytuff Dub Encounter Chapter III* (front + back) Daddy Cool UK 1980

209 LP *Dub Syndicate – Murder Tone* On-U Sound UK 2002

LP *Dub Syndicate – Mellow & Gully* Lion And Roots / Echo Beach Germany 1998

210 LP *Dub Syndicate – Echomania* On-U Sound UK 1993

LP *Dub Syndicate – Acres Of Space* Lion And Roots / Echo Beach Germany 2001

211 LP *Dub Syndicate – Hard Foot* Echo Beach Germany 2015

LP *Dub Syndicate – Ital Breakfast* On-U Sound UK 1996

212 LP *Dub Syndicate – Fear Of A Green Planet* Lion And Roots / Echo Beach Germany 1998

10-inch Dub Syndicate – "93 Struggle" On-U Sound UK 1993

213 Style Scott and the author at the gate to Chinna's yard in Kingston 2012

214 LP *Lee "Scratch" Perry & Dub Syndicate – Time Boom X The Devil Dead* On-U Sound UK 1987

LP LP *Lee "Scratch" Perry – From The Secret Labatory* Island Records UK 1990

215 unknown Sound System, Kingston ca. 2000, photo: Julian Thomann

216 Tippy I Grade and the author in front of Kunterbunt Sound System, Germany 2024

217 LP *Wayne Jarrett – Showcase Vol. 1* Wackie's US 1982 (since 1984 released as *Bubble Up*)

LP *Horace Andy – Dance Hall Style* Wackie's US 1982

218 LP *Bullwackie – Free For All* Aires US 1975

LP *African Roots Act 1* Wackie's US 1977

LP *African Roots Act 2* Wackie's US 1982

219 LP *Nature's Dub* Wackie's US 1980

LP *Tribesman Assault* Wackie's US 1977

LP *Creation Dub* Wackie's US 1985

220 LP *Easy Star All-Stars – Dub Side Of The Moon* Easy Star Records US 2003

LP *Easy Star All-Stars – Ziggy Stardub* Easy Star Records US 2023

221 LP *The Loving Paupers & Victor Rice – Lines In Dub* Jump Up! Records US 2019

Victor Rice and the author, Cologne 2023

LP *The Frightnrs – More To Say Version* Daptone Records US 2017

222 LP *Dr. Ring-Ding & The Senior Allstars meet Victor Rice – Pick Up The Pieces* Grover Germany 2001

Pachyman 2024 live in Germany, photo: T-Jah

LP *Pachyman In Dub* Permanent Records US 2019

223 LP *Protoje – In Search Of Zion* In.Digg. Nation Collective / RCA France 2024

224 LP *Zion I Kings – Future Oceans* Echo Galactic (digital release) Soul Music 2022

225 Tippy I Grade dubbing live in Germany 2024

226 King Earthquake and Iration Steppers at Garance Festival, France 2013

228 LP *Tommy McCook & The Agrovators – Cookin'* Horse UK 1975 (identical to *Bunny Lee & King Tubby Present Tommy McCook And The Aggravators – Brass Rockers* Total Sounds S. 91)

LP *Tommy McCook – Hot Lava* Third World UK 1977

LP *Bobby Ellis & The Professionals meet The Revolutionaries* Third World UK 1977

230 LP *Rebel Dub* Third World UK 1976, provided by Valentin Gube

LP *The Force Of Music – Liberated Dub* Ballistic Records UK 1979

LP *The War Is On Dub Style* Phill Pratt UK 198x

LP *The Force Of Music – Freedom Fighters Dub* Ballistic Records UK 1978

231 LP *Dubbing In The UK* Starlight Records UK 1981

LP *Black Jade – Contempo* Jade UK 1975 (private pressing)

LP *Soul Revivers – Grove Dub* Acid Jazz UK 2022

233 LP *Alborosie – Back-A-Yard-Dub* VP Records US 2021

235 LP *Cpt. Yossarian – Bob Marley In Dub* Echo Beach Germany 2022

236 LP *Out On The Floor Dub* Tuff Scout UK 2021

237 LP *The Breadwinners – Dubs Unlimited* Kingspinna UK 2012

LP *Vin Gordon – African Shores* Tradition Disc UK 2019

LP *Nat Birchall Meets Al Breadwinner – Sounds Almighty* Tradition Disc UK 2018

238 LP *Joe Armon-Jones & Mala – A Way Back* Aquarii Records UK 2022

LP *Nubya Garcia – Source* Concord Jazz UK 2020

12-inch Zara McFarlane & Dennis Bovell – "East Of The River Nile" Brownswood Recordings UK 2019

239 LP *Sons Of Kemet – Your Queen Is A Reptile* Impulse! US 2018

LP *Sons Of Kemet – Black To The Future* Impulse! US 2021

240 LP *.357 Magnum Dub* C and W US 197x

LP *Roots Radics – Roots Dub Style* Scorpio Canada 1984

LP *Selassie I Rockers – 30 Pieces Of Dub* Jah Lion UK 1983

241 LP *Greatest Hits Super Dubb Wise* Hatchet Jamaica 197x